Bad Girls

Also by Caitlin Davies

Downstream: A History and Celebration of
Swimming the River Thames
Family Likeness
Camden Lock and the Market
Taking the Waters: A Swim Around Hampstead Heath
The Ghost of Lily Painter
Friends Like Us
Black Mulberries
Place of Reeds
The Return of El Negro
Jamestown Blues

Bad Girls

A History of Rebels and Renegades

CAITLIN DAVIES

JOHN MURRAY

First published in Great Britain in 2018 by John Murray (Publishers)
An Hachette UK company

1

Copyright © Caitlin Davies 2018

The right of Caitlin Davies to be identified as the Author of the Work has been asserted by
her in accordance with the Copyright, Designs and Patents Act 1988.

A CIP catalogue record for this title is available from the British Library

Hardback ISBN 978-1-473-64774-9
Ebook ISBN 978-1-473-64775-6

Typeset in Bembo by Palimpsest Book Production Limited,
Falkirk, Stirlingshire

Printed and bound by Clays Ltd, St Ives plc

John Murray policy is to use papers that are natural, renewable
and recyclable products and made from wood grown in sustainable
forests. The logging and manufacturing processes are expected to conform to
the environmental regulations of the country of origin.

John Murray (Publishers)
Carmelite House
50 Victoria Embankment
London EC4Y 0DZ

www.johnmurray.co.uk

To Mum

Contents

Prologue   1

Introduction   3

Part One: The Victorian Jail

1. The Model Prison   11
2. The Duchess of Holloway Jail   22
3. The Baby Farmers   34
4. Turnkeys and Colonels   44

Part Two: The Battle for Suffrage

5. The Hollowayettes   57
6. Forcible Feeding   74
7. The Fight is Won   81

Part Three: Crimes Against Morality

8. The First World War   99
9. 'The Messalina of Ilford'   107
10. Reform   118
11. Celebrity Prisoners   125

Part Four: Holloway at War

12. Enemy Aliens   137
13. Fascists and Spies   147
14. Pacifists   158

Part Five: A Change in Regime

15. The Lady Governor and the Borstal Girls   165
16. Protest Against Evil   174

Part Six: The New Holloway

17. A Worthwhile Job   191
18. Escape   201
19. Category A Prisoners   210
20. Sex and Love   217

Part Seven: Holloway Hospital

21. A Place of Healing   227
22. Jailed for an Ideal   238
23. The Women of Greenham Common   244
24. C1: The Psychiatric Unit   255
25. Childbirth   266

Part Eight: Holloway in the Twenty-First Century

26. Holloway Rebranded   281
27. The Monsters Ball   287
28. Life After Prison   294
29. The End of an Era   302
30. Hope Dies Last   307
31. The Ghosts of Holloway   317
32. What is the Point of Prison?   324

Conclusion: Reclaim Holloway   334

Acknowledgements   341
Illustration Credits   343
Notes and Sources   345
Select Bibliography   361
Index   363

Prologue

On a winter's night in 1913 two young women knelt unseen in the back garden of a fashionable residential street in north London. They worked quickly and silently, assembling gunpowder-filled canisters sealed with paraffin-soaked rags. Then they placed the canisters beneath the fourteen-foot wall that divided the garden from its nearest neighbour, lit the fuse and ran.

The first explosion was heard at 9.30 p.m., followed by a second a minute later. A servant rushed out of a neighbouring house, scarcely able to hold her lighted candle, believing her master had shot himself. But the truth was far more dramatic: two suffragettes had just bombed Holloway Prison, Western Europe's oldest and most infamous prison for women.

The explosions were heard a mile away at the Caledonian Road police station where sixty officers were immediately dispatched to the scene. They arrived to find broken windows on the west side of the prison and several holes in the wall, large enough to allow a prisoner to escape. The police also found a dozen yards of fuse leading from Number 12 Dalmeny Avenue, which had served as a suffragette headquarters for the past two years. A few days earlier, a group of suffragettes had climbed on to the roof of the house to serenade Emmeline Pankhurst, then imprisoned inside Holloway. After the explosion, rumours circulated that underground wires ran directly from the house into the prison. But on the night of 18 December there was only one suffragette in Holloway: Rachel Peace, an embroideress who had already suffered a breakdown and who had been forcibly fed while on remand. At her Old Bailey trial a few weeks earlier, where she had been sentenced to eighteen months' hard labour, one suffragette had thrown a hammer at the judge, others hurled tomatoes. But whether they would go to the extent of bombing the prison to release one of their colleagues, when until recently there had been hundreds of suffragettes inside, seems unlikely.

The Islington police discovered a foot-long velvet ribbon in the garden of 12 Dalmeny Avenue and a 'handful of fair human hair'. Perhaps whoever had set off the bombs had been injured, though it was also possible that the suffragette responsible deliberately left a piece of hair as her calling card to taunt the police.

The 'perpetrators of the outrage got clear away', explained the press. Such was the force of the explosion that windows of houses half a mile away were shaken, and those of neighbouring buildings were smashed. The bomb was headline news; the following day a press photographer captured a woman peering serenely out of a nearby house, neatly framed by the broken glass. But despite all the media coverage, no arrests were made. The authorities tried to downplay the incident; it had not been a serious attempt to blow up the prison, they said, and the suffragettes were targeting prison wardresses who lived in quarters on the other side of the wall. But the press insisted that the bombs were 'very powerful'; the women were clearly dangerous and determined to use 'this inhuman method of warfare on society'.

That summer three suffragettes had been charged with assaulting the prison's medical officer. The magistrate had advised them to 'run away like good girls'. But the suffragettes were anything but good girls. Whatever their intentions that night, the two anonymous women had successfully bombed a building that symbolized everything the suffragettes were fighting against: a place where women were humiliated, assaulted and degraded, a prison that always had – and always would – punish women who fought for freedom.

Introduction

I first visited Holloway Prison in the summer of 1990. The officer on reception was efficient but disinterested; I was not a prisoner or a member of staff but a twenty-six-year-old trainee teacher about to start my work placement.

Obediently I followed another officer, a set of keys hanging from a chain attached to her waist, and every few steps we stopped; each door had to be unlocked and locked before the next one could be opened. I wanted to ask her questions about life inside the jail and if she liked her job, but she didn't once look me in the face.

My supervisor, a man named Richard, asked why I wanted to work at Holloway and I told him it was because prison frightened me. He said that was exactly his reason for being there too. As he led me down a shiny-floored corridor, where the air smelled of disinfectant and the walls were painted custard yellow, I felt I could have been walking through a hospital, had it not been for the constant sound of rattling keys and clanging doors.

Richard said we would take the scenic route to the education department and so we headed outside and down a path bordered with flowerbeds of purple pansies. He pointed out the chapel, told me about the prison swimming pool, and then up ahead, on the crest of a small hill, I saw what looked like a cage. This was the segregation block, he explained, its exercise yard tightly covered with wire netting like the aviary at London Zoo. He gestured in another direction to where two strange stone creatures sat on a patch of concrete, their heads chipped and splattered with pigeon droppings, pieces of food lodged in their claws.

We walked across a small garden and entered a classroom, large and bright with rows of Formica-topped tables. Richard showed me the panic button in the far corner of the room, told me to press it if I needed help, and then he left me alone. I don't remember being given any security advice, but I know I stood by the window with an increasing sense of dread, watching a group of women walking towards me across the garden from where I'd just come, some swaggering, others shuffling with their eyes held down. Was I safe? And what if someone made a mistake and locked me up here as well? I'd only been in prison for half an hour but already I had the queasy sensation that I might be found out for having done something wrong.

I had always known of Holloway Prison, the largest and most famous prison for women in Western Europe. I'd grown up just a mile away and it was a landmark that couldn't be missed. As a six-year-old I would stop to stare at the magical castle jail, with its high turrets and gothic battlements. To my childish eyes all that was missing were a moat and drawbridge, Rapunzel at a window letting down her hair. There it was, right on the main road, a looming building of dark brick with windows designed for bows and arrows. But something about the height of the central tower, the stained wall around the perimeter, the blank mouth of the gate in the entranceway, told me it wasn't a real castle at all. And who was the man in black walking up the driveway, was he in charge of all the women? Holloway wasn't the only local prison: Pentonville was half a mile away to the south. But that was for men, while Holloway was for women. I couldn't understand it: who were the women and what bad things had they done?

By the time I started my teacher training I knew much more about Holloway. This was where the suffragettes had been held and forcibly fed for demanding the right to vote, and not long ago women from Greenham Common had been incarcerated for protesting against nuclear weapons. Prisons were in the news: there had been a riot at Strangeways in Manchester where male prisoners were filmed on the rooftop wearing balaclavas and holding weapons. In South Africa Nelson Mandela had just been released from Victor Verster Prison after nearly three decades. But what was life like inside a prison such as Holloway? I'd asked to do my teaching placement here because I had the curiosity that came with privilege.

The Victorian castle that I'd seen as a child had been knocked down by then, and the prison completely rebuilt. The new building was designed to resemble a hospital, with modern facilities that included a brand-new education unit. On my first day at Holloway I gave the prisoners a creative writing exercise taken from a handout I'd been given at university. It asked them to take a 'mental journey' and describe what they saw. But throughout the class there were constant interruptions. The women wanted to ask me personal questions: did I have a boyfriend and children, and if I didn't then why not? Two women at the back were holding hands and whispering to each other, lovers who had come to the education unit so they could be together. One prisoner seemed anxious and unable to settle and the others told her mockingly to go back to the Muppet House, the prison's psychiatric unit. But I left the class feeling relieved: the women seemed to have enjoyed the session and the atmosphere had been as friendly as any adult education lesson; those who had warned me that going into prison would be dangerous were wrong.

During my placement I learned more about the women of Holloway. On one occasion I spent the day alone in a cell with a woman writing an exam, acting as her invigilator. When she lifted her arm to consult a dictionary I saw a long fresh scar on her wrist. I later heard she was in the process of having a tattoo removed, and that the prison doctor had sliced off a layer of skin with a scalpel. The woman would need to go back to have two more layers removed. Another day I was persuaded to have my hair cut by an inmate studying a beauty course. She was West African, like the majority of the women in the education unit, and had been sentenced for drug offences. She told me she'd been forced to swallow a condom of heroin; otherwise her son would have been shot. Her family back home in Nigeria had no idea where she was, that she'd come to England and was imprisoned.

At the end of my six-week placement Richard offered me a job at Holloway Prison, but after qualifying as a teacher I moved abroad and spent the next twelve years working as a journalist and editor in Botswana.

In 1997 I was arrested and charged with 'causing fear and alarm', under a law left over from colonial times that carried a two-year sentence, after publishing a newspaper report that covered the activities of a street gang in the delta village of Maun. I appeared in court seven times, always expecting to be jailed because if I could be arrested for something I hadn't done, then who was to say I wouldn't end up in prison? I might have briefly taught inside Holloway, but the idea of being locked up without any control over my life still terrified me. The following summer the Attorney General withdrew the charges; I wasn't given the chance to put my side of the story or to find out the evidence against me.

A year later I was arrested again and this time put on trial for contempt of court. I had written a news report about a woman who was on death row for killing her husband, and for the first time in Botswana's history her lawyers were arguing Battered Woman Syndrome. I appeared before Justice Aboagye, popularly known as the 'hanging judge'. At the end of the day I was acquitted, but my source was jailed. The woman on death row was reprieved but the following year the judge sentenced another woman to death, after she allegedly killed her husband's mistress, and she was eventually executed.

I returned to England in 2003 and ended up near where I had begun, living just a fifteen-minute walk from Holloway Prison. Every now and again I saw news coverage on TV of striking prison officers or human rights demonstrators. I read that officers were cutting down five women a day who had tried to hang themselves, heard vigils outside on New Year's Eve, saw photographs of inmates dressed as devils for the Monsters Ball at Halloween. I started researching Holloway's early years, surprised that no one had written its full history, and I wrote a novel based on the arrest and execution of the first two women to be hanged at the prison.

But I never came that close to the place, always passing it on a bus and taking in a quick uncomfortable glance, until in November 2015 the Chancellor of the Exchequer George Osborne announced it was closing down. He argued that Victorian prisons were no longer suitable in the modern age, that women needed to be treated more humanely. But Holloway was not Victorian; it had been completely rebuilt forty years ago. So why was it really closing?

First built as a House of Correction in 1852 for both men and women, Holloway's express purpose was to be 'a terror to evil-doers'. In 1903, such was the rise in the female prison population that it became a women-only jail. In the coming decades it would be home to inmates from all walks of life – royalty and socialites, spies and prostitutes, sporting stars and nightclub queens, Nazis and enemy aliens, terrorists and freedom fighters. Women were sentenced for treason and murder, for begging, performing abortions and stealing clothing coupons, for masquerading as men, running brothels and attempting suicide. Holloway's inmates included the most in-famous women in the UK's criminal history, such as Myra Hindley and Rose West, while five women suffered the ultimate punishment, hanged on the gallows and buried behind the prison walls.

The day after the closure news I went to look around, walking down Parkhurst Road, a one-way stream of lorries and cars, towards the prison driveway. It looked less like a hospital and more like a gym, with pink geraniums in hanging baskets placed at intervals along the red brick wall. The building was discreet, as if it didn't want to announce itself, block after block of windowless brick with no doors, no visible way to get in or out. On the other side of the driveway was a prison sign where someone had written 'SHIT HOLE' and 'R.I.P.' in black pen.

I couldn't help but be transfixed by the place. Perhaps it was because a prison had been on this site for over 150 years, or because Holloway was solely for women when we aren't supposed to be bad, criminal or violent.

I left the prison driveway that November afternoon and continued down Parkhurst Road, turning right into Dalmeny Avenue. I was looking for the Copenhagen Pub where I used to go for a half-pint at lunchtime with prison officers, but the pub had closed; instead there was a banner, 'Join the Kindness Offensive', and a brightly painted Routemaster bus parked on the forecourt. Council flats have replaced the old nineteenth-century houses on Dalmeny Avenue and it was hard to picture how the street once looked.

Then I saw an elderly woman crossing the road, heading towards the flats, and stopped to ask her if it was still possible to see the prison from the back. 'What are you writing?' She looked at my notebook and pen. 'A history?' She told me to come with her; she would let me in.

When the door opened I found myself in a quiet deserted courtyard laid out with benches and grass and there on my right, only a stone's throw away, was Holloway Prison. 'I hear the prisoners sometimes, speaking in the yard,' said the woman, glancing at the rows of white barred windows, all blank but for one with a pink curtain, 'it must be when they're exercising.' I asked if she'd heard that the government was going to close down the prison, that they want to keep women more humanely. 'Never believe what the government says,' she muttered, 'never believe them.'

Still I stared at the prison. It seemed so strange that in the streets just outside people were off to buy a newspaper or take their child out on a bike, when nearly 500 women were locked up inside Holloway. I walked across the wet grass, wanting to reach the prison wall, to hear what the women in the exercise yard were saying. Who were they, what crimes had they committed and what had happened in their lives that they'd ended up in Holloway Prison?

Writing this book was a way to try to hear the voices of all the women of Holloway – from across the centuries, right back to 1852 when the prison was built. Who were the 'bad girls' locked up in here? How did it feel to be a warder, with the keys to freedom hanging from your waist, or a governor visiting the condemned cell the day before an execution? What happened when a woman arrived at the Holloway House of Correction, when she passed through the bolted outer gate and into the courtyard, when the solid oak doors closed behind her, when she was stripped of her clothing and identity and woke up the next morning in prison? I wanted to know what it was like here in Victorian times and how it had changed. What could Holloway's history tell us about the nature of women, crime and punishment in our past, present and in our future?

PART ONE
The Victorian Jail

I

The Model Prison

I'm standing in the heart of a Victorian prison, my feet in the exact centre of a blue six-pointed star. This is the prison's central hub and from here I can see directly through locked gates and along five wings. This is where the orderly officer for the day would have stood in the 1850s, ringing a bell and sending guards to their posts, observing the inmates on the rare occasions they were let out of their cells, walking single file with their hands behind their backs, forbidden to speak, their faces covered in masks.

Architecturally the building is impressive, even beautiful, the way the hub is circled by galleries stacked on top of each other, the winding staircases that connect each tier of cells, the high glass dome in the ceiling that lets in the April sunshine. But I also feel exposed, with the impulse to turn around to see who is behind me, to constantly glance up and find out who might be looking down. I tell my guide, Stewart McLaughlin, that the building makes me feel as if I'm being watched. 'You've broken the law,' he says, 'now you're going to jail; it's meant to be imposing.' I hear the clang of metal, a long deep moan from somewhere above, and an insistent beeping noise. This is Wandsworth Prison in south-west London, opened as the Surrey House of Correction for both male and female prisoners in 1851, just a year before Holloway, and built along very similar lines.

It was based on the radial design, which had grown out of the panopticon model invented by philosopher Jeremy Bentham some sixty years earlier. The aim was to keep inmates separate and easily observed at all times. Today Wandsworth is one of only a handful of Victorian radial prisons still in operation, and with around 1,800 inmates it is the largest jail in the UK.

Stewart unlocks a gate to one of the wings and shows me into a holding cell, the exact dimensions of a Victorian prison cell. It takes me two steps to cross the width of the room and I have visions of being pushed from behind, of being locked in with nothing to look at but four white walls. Stewart lets me out and I glance down a set of stairs, see men milling about at the bottom, a glimpse of a shoulder, a back, a pair of legs. They seem to be both moving and immobile at the same time. Every sound echoes in here, and everything is metal: grilles and mesh, handrails and barred gates, wire netting suspended under a gallery like an iron trampoline.

Stewart has worked in the prison service for twenty-seven years; he is also the curator of the Wandsworth Prison Museum and has arranged this tour for historical purposes. I follow him to E wing where the prison's final set of gallows was housed; 135 executions were carried out here including one woman, Kate Webster, whose ghost is said to appear as a grey lady in the prison grounds. We come to a series of cells with low doorways and thick whitewashed walls and Stewart shows me it's eight paces from what was the condemned cell to the trapdoor. Today the lobby area, where the condemned person started their journey, is the substance misuse room, while the condemned cell is the staff restroom.

As we set off walking down another wing Stewart stops to respond to a cell bell, the high-pitched noise I'd heard earlier. He's not on duty today, but he puts his entire face up to the slit in the door and asks, 'What is it, mate?'

'When am I getting out?' comes the reply, the voice of a young man, both plaintive and annoyed.

We continue through to an exercise yard, a bare patch of concrete surrounded by wire walls. At one end there are two palm trees, one dead, the other thriving. I look up: the building is towering over us like a Dickensian monstrosity, built to intimidate and contain.

Wandsworth was one of several new jails established in the mid-1800s, when prison became the main form of punishment in the UK. Traditionally punishment had meant removing people from society, whether through banishment, execution or transportation, and while prisons had been around for centuries they had generally held people awaiting trial or sentencing. By the late eighteenth century, transportation had come to an end after the independence of British colonies and new places were needed to hold prisoners. This was also a time of penal reform, led by campaigners such as John Howard who gathered evidence on prisons both at home and abroad, finding filth, overcrowding and disease. In 1777 he published *The State of the Prisons*, with recommendations covering every part of prison life, from the building to the treatment of inmates.

Two years later Parliament agreed to build two new penitentiaries. But while dozens of prisons were rebuilt, no new jail appeared until Millbank in 1816. It was to be secure, clean and well ventilated, and prisoners would be separated and silent so that they would see the error of their ways through hard work and religious reflection. But the penal regime soon grew harsher, with an emphasis on control and deterrence. There were debates about the cost of imprisonment, and which forms of discipline worked best. And then there was the question of women: should females be sent to prison, and once inside how should the weaker sex be treated and punished?

Historically some prisons had held women and men in separate wings, others held them together, and then in 1853 a female convict prison opened at Brixton, south London. Females made up around 20 per cent of the total prison population, often sentenced for drunkenness or lodging in the open, with the vast majority receiving short sentences of under a month. From the start the emphasis was on correcting their 'impulsive and excitable' nature and replacing it with a 'truer life in respectable pursuits'. Manual labour, used in male prisons, was felt to be inappropriate so female prisoners would spend their time sewing, cooking, cleaning and washing clothes, occasionally whitewashing walls and growing flowers.

When journalists Henry Mayhew and John Binny visited Brixton they were struck by the fact that females were in charge, from the lady governor to the warders and chaplain's clerks, and 'how admirably the ladies really manage such affairs.' The prisoners fell into two categories: 'the many who are good, and the few who are bad'. Some conducted themselves outrageously, 'insensible to shame, to kindness, to punishment'; others behaved well but would then 'suddenly break out, give way to uncontrollable passion, and in utter desperation commit a succession of offences, as if it were her object to revenge herself upon herself'. Henry Mayhew was intrigued by this distinctly unfeminine behaviour and tried to investigate further. The worst inmates were those who had been sentenced to transportation and now found themselves incarcerated in a London jail: 'disappointment rendered them thoroughly reckless . . . they constantly destroyed their clothes, tore up their bedding, and smashed their windows.'

It was becoming clear that men and women reacted to imprisonment in very different ways. 'Female prisoners, *as a body*, do not bear imprisonment so well as the male prisoners,' concluded Brixton's medical officer; 'they get anxious, restless, more irritable in temper, and are more readily excited, and they look forward to the future with much less hope of regaining their former position in life.' Men could work outside building dockyards or sea defences, while the nature of a woman's imprisonment was 'more sedentary'; she was 'continually dwelling on "her time"' and a prison sentence therefore seemed 'more severe to the woman than . . . to the man'.

Despite this, Henry found the Brixton women 'simple and picturesque', in their brown robes with a blue check apron and neckerchief, and a muslin cap 'made after the fashion of a French *bonnes*'. But it didn't take long for inmates to adapt this uniform. One had taken the ropes off her hammock and put them round the bottom of her dress to make the skirt seem fuller, while another had filled her gown with coals. Some used the wire from round the dinner cans as stiffeners for their stays, fashioned tinfoil into jewellery, and scraped the walls of their cells to whiten their complexion. This was an annoyance to the authorities, but if the women worried about what they looked like, perhaps Henry Mayhew thought that they were getting ready to re-enter the world.

Most of the inmates were in for thieving, having 'led the most abandoned lives'. The vast majority traced their ruin to drunkenness or bad company, and many had run away from home or service. The lady governor Emma Martin, who lived with her eleven children in the prison grounds, also believed that women suffered mentally in prison far more than men. 'There are many of them subject to fits of the most ungovernable fury,' she explained; 'very often there is no cause at all for their passion except their own morbid spirits; perhaps their friends haven't written, so they'll sit and work themselves up into a state of almost frenzy, and when the officer comes they will give way.' The year after the Brixton female convict prison opened there were 1,290 recorded punishments: women were handcuffed, put in a canvas dress that resembled a straitjacket, and many were thrown in the refractory cell on a diet of bread and water. But they then became 'terribly violent indeed, they tear up and break everything they can lay their hands on.' One prisoner broke all the windows in her cell, tore all her bedclothes into ribbons, and pulled open her bed. It was after she had wrenched off the gas-jet and pulled an iron shelf from the wall that male officers were called in to restrain her. But the governor also found the women 'very sensitive to family ties, and I'm often touched myself to think such wicked creatures should have such tender feelings'. This then was the contradiction: how could women be both violent and maternal, and why did they get in such a state? Henry Mayhew was impressed by Brixton, yet the issues he'd found, the resistance to discipline and the smashing of prison property, would soon be seen at Holloway, only on a much larger scale.

In 1842 the City of London had decided that a new jail was needed in the capital, and appointed a committee to find the best spot. It chose a ten-acre site in north London that the City already owned, bought shortly after a previous cholera epidemic and initially intended as a burial ground. An Act of Parliament converted the use of the land to a prison and James Bunning, who had designed the Corn Exchange and the Metropolitan Cattle Market, was appointed architect. On 26 September 1849 the Lord Mayor, Sir James Duke, laid the foundation stone. And if there was any doubt about the purpose of the new prison, the inscription on the stone made it perfectly clear: 'May God preserve the City of London and make this place a terror to evil-doers'. But the builders went bankrupt, and it was only after new contractors were brought in that the City House of Correction opened, on 6 October 1852.

The prison was intended for men, boys over the age of eight and a small number of women. It was apparently modelled on the medieval Warwick Castle, with splendid battlements and turrets, surrounded by an eighteen-foot-high brick wall. The governor's and chaplain's houses stood on either side of the outer gate, which was made of solid oak four inches thick, riveted with strong bolts of iron and with a narrow wicket gate to allow visitors in and out. This led into a courtyard and then a massive inner gate where new arrivals were greeted by two winged griffins mounted on pillars. One held a key and a leg-iron in its talons; the other had a claw extended as if about to seize hold of a prey.

As with Wandsworth, the plan was radial, although of a slightly different design. There were four wings for adult males, one for juveniles and one for females. The total capacity was 400, with the majority reserved for adult men, and its first inmates were 120 males and 27 females. One of Holloway's earliest female prisoners was Emma Mary Bird, a 'stout' thirty-year-old from the East End with a 'sallow complexion', jailed for six months for assault and unable to provide a surety – a person who would take responsibility for her during bail and pay a fine if she misbehaved. Others included fifty-six-year-old Mary Pullen, of no fixed residence and no trade, who had received six months for 'using threats', a woman sentenced to seven days for disrupting a church service while drunk, and a wretchedly clad girl jailed for three weeks for begging.

In these early years of Holloway the female population never numbered more than around twenty, although it had enough cells to hold sixty. While its role was to inspire terror and punish evil-doers, there were also hopes of rehabilitation. The day after it admitted its first prisoners, Alderman Wire expressed his earnest hope that the new House of Correction would produce 'permanent reforma-tion' so that 'very many would leave its walls to become honourable and useful members of society'. However, punish it certainly did and London's Lord Mayor Sir Robert Carden was said to very much enjoy sentencing people 'down that pantomimic trap which leads to Holloway Prison', all the while a sardonic grin on his face.

Ten years after Holloway opened, journalists Henry Mayhew and John Binny found much to admire at the new prison. It was a self-sufficient institution with all the latest in Victorian engineering and gadgetry. A mill ground the prisoners' cocoa, men and boys worked the treadwheel that pumped water from a seventy-foot well, while a lifting machine in the central hall allowed trays of provisions to be hoisted up from the kitchen. Dinner was apparently served to several hundred prisoners in just ten minutes. The cells were 'very healthy' and ventilators provided 'pure air', there were fires in the winter, and prisoners had a bath once a fortnight in the summer. If an inmate needed to call a warder then they turned an iron handle on the cell door which set off a gong in the corridor 'giving notice to the warder in charge that his attendance is required'.

Everywhere the prisoners were working. Men made mats, clothes and all the shoes for inmates and officers, while women picked oakum, stripping old rope down to fibres, as well as needlework, laundry work (where they were allowed a pint of beer a day), general cleaning, nursing and knitting. The prisoners had five exercise grounds, access to education and a teacher visited each cell on a weekly basis to distribute books such as *Life in New Zealand* and *Summer Days in the Antarctic*. Even the prison's infirmary was like a druggist's shop, with the phials carefully labelled and arranged.

But all this came at a cost. Henry Mayhew drew up an exhaustive list of expenditure, well aware of complaints about new prisons such as Holloway and objections from the press that they were 'all but a costly experiment' built out of good intentions but unlikely to do any good. Prisoners were said to be enjoying a better lifestyle than those on the outside and taxpayers were paying the price for the 'whimsical indulgences of philanthropists' with 'places of punishment converted into palaces'.

But despite these 'indulgences', Henry found Holloway a place of strict discipline, and he noted 'a number of good-looking felons' among the sixty-six female prisoners. There was no mention as yet of any of the sort of scenes he had heard about at Brixton, no furious females shredding clothing or displaying uncontrolled temper. But then Henry Mayhew hadn't met Selina Salter.

In the summer of 1864 a 'miserable looking girl' was charged with assaulting a police constable in her hometown of Bath. The sixteen-year-old had annoyed and irritated him by knocking violently at the police station door at night. She was ordered to keep the peace for a month and agreed to go to the workhouse.

Selina was the daughter of a poor gardener from Ireland, whose mother had died when she was young. She was sent to school and then put in service, but hated both. One day Selina stole her stepmother's money and ran away to London to look for a young man who had 'paid his addresses to her in Bath'. But when he refused to take her in she took to a wandering life, from street to street and from workhouse to workhouse until, 'becoming troublesome', she was sent to Holloway Prison. Not long after her release, she was in court again, charged with creating a disturbance at the vagrant ward of the West London Union workhouse, and by the time she was eighteen she had already been in court nineteen times for disorderly conduct. Her great failing, according to the press, was 'a violent and uncontrollable temper, that amounts almost to madness', but apart from her vagrant life she was 'strictly honest, sober, and virtuous'.

Selina refused to reform. Five times she had been sent back to Bath, but each time she soon turned up in a London workhouse 'screaming, fighting, and blaspheming'. Each time she was sent home, her father and the parish clergyman 'endeavoured to reclaim her'. But every time they put her in domestic service 'her vagrant propensities' overcame her good resolutions and Selina was back in London. Eventually she agreed to be sent to America, and an officer accompanied her to Liverpool and saw her safely on board a vessel. But Selina hid, and then escaped to shore. Three days later she appeared, almost destitute, at the gates of Holloway Prison. She was again dispatched to New York, and 'this time reached her destination, and hopes were entertained that in another country she would become a better girl. Such hopes were futile.' Selina determinedly worked her way back across the Atlantic to London.

It was a lamentable case, agreed the City magistrates, and while gentlemen in the medical profession had pronounced her sane, her violent temper would 'ultimately derange her mind'. So in May 1866 Selina was sent to Holloway again, 'not in the expectation that the punishment would do her any good, but in the hope that some of the kind friends who visited the prison might devise some means of reclaiming her'.

Arriving at Holloway, Selina was weighed and measured in the basement reception ward, and her now familiar details checked in the description book. She was then told to wash, given prison clothes and a number, which she wore on her arm, as well as a brass ticket attached to her chest to show her corridor and cell number. Her own clothes were put in a steam fumigating pot, to kill any vermin. Her prison costume consisted of a blue gown with a red stripe, petticoats made of linsey-woolsey, shifts of red-striped calico, a checked apron, a blue checked neckerchief, a small printed pocket-handkerchief and a white linen cap. She was also given a pair of blue worsted stockings and a shawl, both knitted by female prisoners. Then she was sent to F wing on the eastern side of the prison, where three floors were reserved for women and girls.

Her cell was seven feet wide, thirteen feet deep, and nine feet high, with an asphalt-covered floor. It was furnished with a small folding table, a gas burner behind glass, a copper basin with soap, a nailbrush and a small flannel, and a tub for washing her feet. There was also a water-closet pan for a toilet; 'slopping out' would only be introduced a few years later after water closets got clogged and pipes burst. Beside the door were three small shelves. The upper one held her bedding: a pair of blankets, a rug, two sheets, a horse-hair mattress and a pillow. On the second shelf were a plate, a tin jug for gruel, a wooden saltcellar and a wooden spoon. The last shelf held a Bible, prayer book and hymn book, two combs and a brush, and a coconut-fibre rubber for polishing the floor. Selina slept in a hammock, suspended from hooks on either side of the room and hanging low just above the floor. On the wall was a card with her name and a copy of the prison rules listing everything she must do between 5.30 a.m. and 8.55 p.m. This included chapel and schooling, the ten hours she was expected to work each weekday, and the two half-hour exercise breaks when she joined the other females in the yard, their heads covered with hooded shawls, keeping the regulation three and a half yards away from each other. Just before 9 p.m. the gaslight was extinguished, and prisoners were to 'sling hammock, go to bed'.

Selina's life – like those of the other prisoners at Holloway – was now controlled entirely from outside the cell. Warders could watch without her knowing by looking through a small florin-sized opening in the door, glazed on the outside and covered with wire on the inside. After six o'clock in the evening warders wore felt overshoes so prisoners wouldn't hear them approaching. In the centre of the door was a small trap, through which Selina received food – her cocoa, gruel, soup and bread.

Did Selina Salter find Holloway a place of safety where she was warmer, cleaner and better fed than in the union workhouse or out on the streets? After all, she had been here over a dozen times and had deliberately committed minor crimes in order to get sent back. The authorities had already discovered that prison discipline had 'wrought no favourable alteration in her character; instead diametrically opposite results ensued', and during Selina's numerous times inside Holloway no kind visitors found a way to reclaim her. She didn't obey the rules and she took out her fury and distress on her surroundings, destroying the furniture in thirteen cells, tearing up six prison gowns and all her clothing. She was reported 400 times for refusing to work, 200 times for violent and outrageous conduct, and 130 times for shouting and singing. While there was 'great doubt' about Selina's sanity, explained the press, and prison rules required all insane prisoners to be removed as 'speedily as the law will allow', the medical gentlemen still declared her sane.

In the spring of 1867, having been released from Holloway again, she deliberately broke a police station window. Selina was put in a court cell, where an officer found her doubled up on the ground with her garters tied around her throat. She was then arrested for attempted suicide. Selina was a headstrong, ungovernable woman and had been a 'pest' to the civic authorities for years. She had been offered every opportunity and wasted it. Now she was sent to the City Lunatic Asylum in Kent where she was placed in the kitchen to help the cook and everything was done to 'make her feel herself a servant, instead of a patient'. But she rejected her role as servant, and having been declared sane enough to take care of herself she 'demanded and obtained her discharge'. A few days later, she was back at Holloway Prison. 'What is to be done with Selina

Salter?' asked the press. She was incorrigible; she had rung bells, kicked doors and reportedly attempted to throttle officers. She had bitten policemen, scratched jailers and thrown shoes at magistrates. She had 'shrieked herself into hysterics' and tried to strangle herself twice. She had now been to Holloway 'fifty or sixty times' and needed to be sent back to the asylum 'for her own sake, as well as for that of society'.

Then, in March 1868, the police discovered a woman 'wandering about'. She was about twenty years old, and gave the name of Harriet Coles. Once at the police station she confessed to having escaped from the City Lunatic Asylum by tearing the sheets and blankets, fastening the pieces together and letting herself down from an upper window and then climbing over the walls. The police discovered this was none other than Selina Salter, and so they sent her back to the asylum.

There were no further reports in the press after this; the woman whose second home had been Holloway Prison apparently disappeared. For four years she had gone out of her way to seek punishment, yet it was clear to everyone that prison hadn't reformed her; instead it had made her increasingly destructive, suicidal and insane.

A new model prison required model prisoners. The House of Correction was designed for those who broke the law and the systems of silence and segregation would assure they were controlled and subdued. Yet Selina Salter had steadfastly refused to obey the rules. Her time in Holloway had served to remove her from society, but on release she was more destructive than ever. If one of the purposes of prison was rehabilitation, if female inmates would see the error of their ways and turn to a truer life in respectable pursuits, then it had already failed.

But Selina Salter was from a poor family, her experience was far different from those who were wealthy, and it wasn't long before Holloway admitted someone at the other end of the social scale.

2

The Duchess of Holloway Jail

At the end of Pall Mall in the West End of London is a three-floored mansion built of thick slabs of Bath stone. Lancaster House was once the most valuable home in the city, it has entertained more heads of state than any other house in the capital, and while it's normally closed to the public, I've been given permission to look around. I want to get a sense of what it was like to live here in the 1890s, when the actions of a wealthy duchess sparked the era's most scandalous case of contempt of court.

I pass groups of tourists on guided tours blocking the pavements outside St James's Palace, and then as I get closer to Lancaster House I'm stopped by two armed police. I'm about to enter a high-security area; next door is Clarence House, the official residence of the Prince of Wales and Duchess of Cornwall, while Buckingham Palace is just a few minutes' walk away. I show my ID and head across Stable Yard towards a sturdy and rather serious-looking building. Today Lancaster House is managed by the Foreign and Commonwealth Office and used as a centre for government hospitality, but from 1829 to 1913 it was home to the Dukes of Sutherland, one of the richest landowning families in the UK.

It was first known as York House, commissioned by the 'grand old' Duke of York and then bought by the Marquis of Stafford, who became the 1st Duke of Sutherland. For nearly 100 years it was known as Stafford House, host to an array of distinguished guests where the 'elite in high life' were wined and dined at grand receptions and waited on by the largest staff of servants in London. In April 1893, during a family battle over a will, documents were removed from here and taken to a solicitor's office. It was then that the behaviour of May Caroline, the Dowager Duchess of

Sutherland, was deemed so shocking that she was sent to Holloway Prison.

I enter a foyer and walk between two marble pillars the colour of butterscotch, then through a doorway draped with red velvet and into the grand hall. I'm surrounded by gold, in the stairways leading up from a central flight of steps, on the huge paintings hanging on the wall, and most of all on the high ornate ceiling decorated in vivid gold leaf.

Jacky Devis, who organizes conferences and events, arrives to take me on a tour. We sit at a table by a bust of the Duke of York while I explain the house's link with Holloway Prison and ask where the documents in question might once have been kept. She takes me first to the library, a bright room with yellow walls, the chairs and mirrors all edged in gold. There are a couple of small glass cabinets lined with old books and it seems like a suitable place to keep important papers. Then Jacky takes me through one of the secret doors, disguised as part of the wall, and into a corridor where we almost bump into the head butler. I tell him the tale of Duchess May Caroline; he's never heard this story before. We enter another of the duke's workrooms, where the documents could also have been kept, and by the time we get to the drawing room the gold leaf is beginning to feel oppressive, ceilings gleaming like the foil inside a lavish box of chocolates.

In the spring of 1883 May Caroline reportedly dined here at Stafford House with her husband's employer and the man who would become her lover, the 3rd Duke of Sutherland, George Granville William Sutherland Leveson-Gower. May was born in 1848 in Oxford, where her father was a reverend and professor of logic. At the age of twenty-four she had married a cousin, Arthur Blair, with whom she had a daughter, Irene. When Arthur was mysteriously killed during a pheasant shoot in Scotland in the autumn of 1883 there were rumours he had shot himself, or had been deliberately shot.

The Duke of Sutherland was a former Liberal MP and the tenth richest man in the western world. He owned 1.4 million acres of land in Britain, palatial homes, a private train and station, as well as several yachts. His wife Anne, Countess of Cromartie, was a friend of Queen Victoria and the couple's London residence was Stafford House, a place so grand that when the Queen came to visit she once remarked, 'I come from my house to your palace.'

The duke was known for his affairs, and well before May Caroline became his mistress he and his wife were leading largely separate lives. Anne died while the couple were in the United States, but rather than respecting the conventional mourning period and waiting a year to re-marry, and despite a commanding telegram from the Queen, three weeks later the duke announced his engagement to May Caroline. The couple married in March 1889 and when they returned to England they were snubbed by high society. There were frequent clashes over property with the duke's children, who accused May of taking their mother's possessions and even of wearing Duchess Anne's old underwear.

In 1892, with family relations still fraught, the duke died and his eldest son Cromartie became the 4th Duke of Sutherland. Cromartie hoped he would inherit the entire family fortune and was furious to find that his father had written dozens of wills to ensure that May and her daughter Irene were left financially secure, including a legacy of £100,000 and the use of the Staffordshire diamond jewellery collection for life. The 3rd Duke had also appointed May as executor of the will, and all the furniture at Stafford House, from china to pictures to objets d'art, would go to the dowager.

The new duke objected to May keeping the family jewels, took her to court and won. Then he contested the will. When the case came to court the duchess's lawyer argued that there were papers of an 'exceptionally private character' among her late husband's documents at Stafford House. The duchess had been denied access to the palatial home, and she wanted the papers destroyed. The judge, Sir Francis Jeune, refused the request, but agreed that May Caroline could look through the papers and if there was anything too sensitive – and if the 4th Duke agreed – then they would be kept sealed and not made public in court.

And so boxes of papers and tables containing letters were removed from Stafford House, taken to the administrator's offices in Whitehall and handed to the duchess in the presence of solicitors. She examined the letters carefully, and as she put some to one side she was reminded that nothing could be removed or destroyed. But to the astonishment of the assembled men, May Caroline ignored the warning. Instead she took out one of the letters, hid it in her hand, turned round and threw it in the fire. When the officials objected, she allegedly replied, 'I shall do as I please. You are here only on sufferance.'

Just what was in the letter wasn't clear, but it had apparently been sent during a yachting excursion and concerned 'an unpleasant occurrence between a steward and a maid'. The duchess insisted it was up to her what happened to the letter and 'without the smallest intention of doing anything contrary to the order of the Court . . . put it into the fire'. The press responded to this with outraged disbelief. The 'wilful destruction of documents is one of the gravest offences known to the law,' declared the *Spectator*. Now the letter had been destroyed, no one would know whether its contents would have affected the probate case. The paper hoped 'no misplaced compassion' would interfere with the law taking its course.

When questioned, the duchess initially said she had written the letter, but then later claimed the duke had written it, and that a few hours before his death he'd told her to take papers from Stafford House and destroy them. What was in the mystery letter isn't known, although historian Gilbert Bell has speculated that it may have related to the duke's alleged involvement in the death of the duchess's first husband.

On 18 April 1893 May Caroline, the Duchess of Sutherland, was found guilty of contempt of court, fined £250 and sentenced to six weeks in Holloway Prison. She was informed of this while waiting in the barristers' room, whereupon there was 'a great scene' and she and her friends 'all shed tears and exhibited great indignation'. While the punishment seemed severe to the duchess's supporters, the press was largely in favour. 'She seems in need of a reminder that an impetuous and imperious woman with a past, even when promoted to the rank of Duchess, is not allowed to run the universe on her own lines,' warned one paper. The duchess was condemned as a social climber, a woman who had progressed from mistress to wife in a matter of months and who now stood to inherit a fortune. She needed to be taught a lesson and what better than to send her to Holloway? Now that May Caroline had been convicted, the press began to speculate on her treatment inside, clearly not believing the assertion that 'her Grace will be treated in the same fashion as ordinary prisoners committed for contempt of court', and relishing the idea she would be forced to mingle with the lower classes.

Under the Prisons Bill of 1840, convicts in England and Wales had been divided into two categories, first and second division, and it was up to the courts to decide who should go into each. Those in the first division were generally convicted of 'non-criminal' offences, such as libel, sedition and contempt of court. They could buy their own food and wine from outside, were not required to work, a prison officer cleaned their quarters and they could wear their own clothes and see friends, write and receive letters. The system was later refined, with the creation of three divisions for those who had not been sentenced to hard labour. But as Victorian journalist George Sims explained, first-class prisoners remained the 'aristocrats of the gaol', and their punishment was 'separation from the rest of the world . . . with no serious discomfort or lasting disgrace'. So while poor prisoners had a hammock for a bed, a wooden stool for furniture and a tin plate to eat their gruel, prisoners in the first division were accommodated in 'private apartments' and given the sort of privileges only the rich could afford.

The press assured its readers that Duchess May Caroline would occupy an ordinary cell, and that she had ridden straight from court to Holloway Prison. But this turned out not to be true. The judge had in fact allowed May Caroline to go to her residence in Windsor, on the condition that she surrendered herself to jail the next day. However, the duchess was taken suddenly ill, suffering from 'nervous shock', and her doctors said she couldn't be moved. In the end, on 22 April, four days after her sentencing, she was arrested at Windsor and sent to Holloway.

The duchess was driven to Slough station with her maid, her doctor and a pile of luggage. A horse-drawn carriage was waiting in London and, along with her brother and 'travelling companions',

May Caroline was driven to Holloway Prison by liveried coachmen. Received by the chief warder and two prison physicians, she was taken to the female wing and according to the Press Association was shown to 'a specially appointed apartment in front of the prison', which lay 'between the two main towers forming the entrance, and immediately overlooking Camden-road'. Her cell was furnished with a handsome brass bedstead, draped with curtains, two easy chairs and couch, a writing desk, a wardrobe with plate-glass panel, and 'other articles of furniture specially selected'. The carpet was underlaid with felt; there were mirrors, ferns and flowers, and plenty of books. Such was the interest in the duchess's cell its contents were reported as far away as Australia, where one paper asserted 'it bore as much resemblance to an ordinary prison cell as a cotter's kitchen does to a ducal drawing-room'.

During the duchess's stay at Holloway, British readers were treated to day-by-day reports. Local tradesmen tendered for the duchess's catering contract, which was awarded to a confectioner who had 'supplied a good many distinguished visitors', and on Sunday she 'partook of all her meals with a healthy appetite'. According to Gilbert Bell, the duchess ordered in delicacies 'from the likes of Harrods'. A 'buxom young matron' who had set up shop on a low stool opposite the prison gates and who for nine years had done a roaring trade, told the press that the duchess had 'wanted all kinds of dainty things', but that her meals had come from the nearby Holloway Castle Tavern, which was 'rather a swell place'.

Aside from her own food and well-furnished room, the duchess was allowed plenty of lengthy visits, held outside normal visiting hours. The press soon concluded that her punishment 'seems more nominal than real', and that her incarceration was 'nothing but a sham'. It was only a matter of days before questions were raised in Parliament. On 27 April three MPs fired off a series of questions to the Secretary of State Herbert Asquith. They wanted to know the conditions in which the duchess was held, whether the rules had been relaxed and if so, who had authorized them and on what grounds. Would these special indulgences now be allowed to all first-division prisoners? The Secretary of State responded that first-class inmates were allowed private furniture and utensils 'suitable to their ordinary habits' paid for out of their own pockets. 'In the present case,' he concluded, 'the ordinary Rules have been followed.'

On 29 May the duchess's sentence was over and at eight o'clock in the morning a horse-drawn carriage arrived outside Holloway Prison. Once back at Windsor, her friends presented her with a silver casket containing £250, to cover the cost of the fine, not because she was unable to pay it but as a protest against 'the severe order by a Judge for having unflinchingly carried out a dying request of her husband'. Eventually a settlement was reached in the duke's will: May Caroline was awarded a lump sum of £500,000, bought a house in Belgrave Square in London, and the 4th Duke built her a home in Scotland, Carbisdale Castle. But by the time the castle was finished the duchess had died.

May Caroline is generally portrayed – both then and now – as a greedy, scheming woman; a social upstart who had been 'promoted' to the rank of duchess. 'The press seemed to have been particularly harsh and gleefully vindictive,' says her great-grandson Dr Bruno Bubna-Kasteliz, a retired consultant geriatrician in Bath. 'I do find it hard to imagine she played the role ascribed to her, especially when she was challenged by the officials at the solicitors' office. It sounds uncharacteristically high-handed and snobbish for May.' Bruno sends me extracts from May Caroline's diary from 1887 in which she describes her happiness with the duke who was tender and kind. 'He was quite well known as having had other affairs,' says Bruno, 'but this one seemed to be more intense and longer lasting, and possibly more public.' The fact that the duke then married May Caroline, 'doubled the family's hatred'. I tell Bruno that his great-grandmother apparently wore her predecessor's underwear. He laughs. 'Did she really? It would have been very fancy underwear, much fancier than what she would have been used to.'

Bruno agrees that his great-grandmother 'had transgressed in a very obvious way' by burning the letter, but her treatment was 'most likely to have been as a result of a very powerful family, together with the close relationship of Anne with the Queen, and their sustained view of May as the interloper'. Bruno has no idea what was in the letter that was burned, though another of May Caroline's relatives, Dr Catherine Layton, a retired academic who lives in Australia, has a theory that casts a whole new light on the predicament of the duchess. 'I first came across May when researching my own family history,' she explains, 'and when I found that my relative, Sir Albert Rollit, had married the much criticized Dowager Duchess of Sutherland in 1896, I could not help but look further.' May Caroline had been left a widow and a single parent after the duke's death, at a time when women had no legal rights over their children and if deemed immoral they could lose guardianship and even access. Catherine suspects that the document the duchess burned contained proof of her affair with the married duke. If this had come to light then she could have lost everything and never seen her daughter again. Under the circumstances, contempt of court may have seemed like the lesser evil.

The Duchess of Sutherland had fallen foul of expected behaviour for women. She had risen too far above her social status, and Holloway was used to remind her of her true place. Like Selina Salter, she had refused to obey the law, and both had broken moral and social codes that governed women. However, her class afforded the duchess a different experience of Holloway than Selina; poor women might be condemned to hard labour in freezing cold cells, but when it came to a dowager duchess then the purpose was public humiliation. Rich women who transgressed would be held up to ridicule, and prison would force them to live among the working classes.

The Duchess of Sutherland wasn't the first high-society woman to be sent to Holloway; other cases involving wealth and scandal occurred both before and after and they too were treated differently from 'ordinary' inmates. In 1880 Georgina Weldon, the most famous litigator in England, was sentenced to four months in prison for libelling Jules Rivière, a theatrical musical director. Some five years later she was back in Holloway, again for libelling Jules, and this time she would stay for six months. But she made the most of her prison sentence and her room was 'a veritable workshop of literary and legal projects', reported the press. Georgina kept goldfish in her cell and a newt that she 'fed on minced beef'; Holloway's governor gave her a musk plant on her birthday and on release she left him a signed photograph 'in grateful memory of my six months'. She successfully sued the French composer Charles Gounod for libel while still in prison, and sent the *Pall Mall Gazette* a 'poem of many stanzas' about her time in Holloway: 'For six long months, through cunning deep as hell, / I've been the Inmate of a prison cell.' Georgina appeared to revel in her time in Holloway, and was keen to prove to her detractors that she had not suffered as a result.

Three years later another socialite arrived, Mary Ann Sutherland, described by the press as one of 'the most amazing women swindlers of all time'. Born in Peterhead, Scotland, she had started out as a Bible woman addressing religious meetings. After a spell in Perth Jail, Mary Ann had moved to London where she took a 'lavishly furnished house' in St James Terrace using the name Miss Ogilvy Bruce; one of several aliases. A few years later she was charged with fraud under the name Kate Miller, having tricked 'a number of merchants of their wares'. She evaded arrest and sailed to America; then presented herself in Australia as a Scottish aristocrat. In London once more she appeared as a Greek maiden at a ball at the Prince's Hall; and then returned to Scotland using the name Mrs Gordon Baillie, 'the Crofters' Friend', collecting subscriptions and offering sanctuary on a vast estate she apparently owned in Australia. In 1887 Mary settled back in England with a man named Robert Frost, and the following year both were charged, along with their butler James, with conspiring to obtain money by false pretences. Unable to pay bail, 'the heroine of so many adventures' was now in Holloway Prison.

The number of charges against Mary Ann Sutherland soon rose to forty-five, and she had changed her identity so many times the press had difficulty separating fact from fiction. The police had identified forty different aliases over a fifteen-year career, and there had been complaints 'from all parts of the Continent' as well as Australia and New Zealand. She was sentenced to five years, but her time in Holloway didn't seem to change her ways, and in 1894 Mary Ann Sutherland was arrested once again, this time for stealing paintings, for which she received seven years.

The 'amazing' woman swindler wasn't the only prisoner using an alias at Holloway, and the jail served as a training ground for City detectives who made thrice-weekly inspections to identify known criminals going under assumed identities. During one visit the prisoners on parade included a man who had been travelling the world as a Russian prince, but who was in fact an American with a 'first rate education', and two brothers who called themselves Honourable Frank and Honourable Reggy Plantagenet, titles that the detectives dismissed as bogus.

Despite the scandals surrounding the convictions of Georgina Weldon and the Duchess of Sutherland, Holloway was still overwhelmingly a male prison and it was home to several well-known men in the late Victorian period. In 1895 the playwright Oscar Wilde was taken to Holloway to await trial for gross indecency, spending a month in a 'special cell' for remand prisoners where he was said to be low-spirited and despondent, unable to sleep and pacing his cell. His lover Alfred Douglas later described a visit: 'Poor Oscar was rather deaf. He could hardly hear what I said in the babel. He looked at me with tears running down his cheeks.'

In contrast, two noted male journalists thoroughly enjoyed their time at Holloway. In January 1885 Edmund Yates settled in very comfortably to serve a four-month sentence for libel. The founder of the weekly newspaper the *World*, he had been sued by the Earl of Lonsdale over an article concerning 'his lordship's elopement'. Edmund denied writing the article, but refused to say who had, and after an unsuccessful appeal he was sent to Holloway as a first-division prisoner. The day before sentencing, he paid a visit to the prison where he met the governor and was shown 'the rooms in which first class misdemeanants were confined', after which he ordered in the necessary furniture. His cell wasn't nearly as large as the Duchess of Sutherland's, but it was over twice the width of second-class cells, with a fireplace 'always well supplied'. It was furnished with Persian rugs, a bed, writing table, chest of drawers, and a 'huge screen to exclude the draught'. After serving just under two months, Edmund was released on grounds of ill health and his friends celebrated with a champagne party.

Not long afterwards, William Thomas Stead, editor of the *Pall Mall Gazette* – the paper that had published Georgina Weldon's prison poems – enjoyed a 'first class' stay at Holloway. He was sentenced to three months for 'buying' a thirteen-year-old girl as part of an exposé into child prostitution, in a case that would lead to a change in the law and inspire the play *Pygmalion*. 'Never had I a pleasanter holiday, a more charming season of repose,' wrote William, who paid 6 shillings for a private cell in the 'enchanted castle' on the ground floor of E wing where he was 'jealously guarded by liveried retainers'. His staff visited him every other day and his wife came twice a week, food and wine were sent over from Holloway Castle Tavern, and his children joined him for 'high jinks' on Boxing Day. Such was the 'rare luxury of journalistic leisure' that William suggested a 'small voluntary gaol' run on the first-division principles be provided for the 'over-driven, much-worried writers of London'.

But the majority of Holloway's prisoners were still poor, home-less and often ill. Conditions in the once model prison had become increasingly grim and some inmates arrived in a state of total destitution. While those in the first division could plead poor health and receive hospital treatment, round-the-clock care or early release, others' pleas were ignored, even if they were yet to be convicted of any crime. A servant girl charged with attempted suicide after eating rat poison complained of being unwell but was not moved to the prison hospital, and later died in her cell. 'Do you mean to say it was necessary to ask permission to lie in bed?' asked one jury member during the inquest. 'But she was not a prisoner; she was merely on remand.' To which Holloway's medical officer replied, 'It is no concern of ours what she is.' Gone were the days of clean, well-ventilated cells and the prison was now overrun with vermin. A prisoner waiting trial for murder had half his chest eaten by rats and his solicitor was afraid that 'there will not be much left of him by the time he comes out'.

The nature of the inmates' crimes had changed as well. Holloway was no longer home to just petty criminals sentenced for drunk-enness, vagrancy or theft; aside from the ten inmates awaiting trial for murder there were eleven cases of manslaughter and four of attempted murder. This, it was noted, was a 'record list'. Holloway had lost its reputation as a successful penal experiment, but its purpose was clearer than ever: it was there to punish. Before long the model jail would be the site of the ultimate sentence – execution.

3

The Baby Farmers

In the summer of 1902, after half a century of housing men and boys, the former House of Correction became an all-female jail. London's prison population was on the rise; Newgate had just closed and it was difficult keeping women in separate blocks at predominantly male prisons. The prison commissioners had a solution that would provide more prison accommodation in the capital and ensure the absolute separation of the sexes. Holloway's male population would go to Pentonville, Wormwood Scrubs or Brixton and from 16 August 1902 north London's 'terror to evil-doers' would house only women and girls. Public hangings had ended in 1868, the nation's gallows had been moved inside prisons and now Holloway would partially supplant Newgate as a place of execution. Work had already begun on a new scaffold, and local residents were said to be very indignant.

Virtually nothing remains of the original Holloway Prison but for a selection of objects in the Museum of London's Social and Working History collections store, on the banks of the Regent's Canal in east London. It's cold and brightly lit in reception, where curator Vyki Sparkes is waiting to take me down to the ground floor. She shows me into a big warehouse room smelling faintly of sawdust, lined with metal shelves. I scan the orderly jumble of objects, a massive wooden barrel big enough for two people, a sign for Bank Tube station. 'These are the first Holloway Prison objects we have,' says Vyki, pointing at the floor. I'm puzzled and a bit disappointed. There are just a few pieces of metal lying on a pallet. One is a roundel from the old catwalk railings, painted inside the colour of wet clay; another is a cast-iron bracket from a gas lamp.

We enter another room with more Holloway objects, including a fitting from a 1890s gas lamp used in corridors and cells. I stop to look at a carved wooden head of Jack Sheppard, a highwayman hanged at Tyburn, and a shelf of leg-irons, handcuffs and shackles. Then I see a huge noticeboard leaning against the far wall, green with white lettering. It's the prison sign that was attached to the outside of the gatehouse and probably dates from 1902, the year that the House of Correction became a female jail. 'H.M. Prison Holloway Notices' is a list of rules and punishments, beginning with the warning that anyone who aids a prisoner to escape faces five years in jail. Those who try to bring in 'any spirituous or fermented liquor or tobacco' could receive a six-month sentence, a £50 fine, or both, and the numerals have been re-painted as the size of the fine increased over the years. The final rule concerns prohibited items thrown over the wall or smuggled inside, such as money, clothing, food, drink, letters, paper, books, tools, all of which 'may be confiscated by THE Governor'. We both laugh at the capitalized 'THE', the stern emphasis on who exactly is in charge.

Next to the sign, and also leaning against the wall, is a heavily studded iron-clad wooden door. There's an oval indentation in the top half, with a spy hole in the middle and I step closer to peer through. I know there is nothing to see except a brick wall, but there is something about a hole that makes you want to put your eye up to it. How many warders peered through this in the early 1900s, and what did they see when they did? It is both direct and at my eye level, but also intimate and voyeuristic. Then Vyki points out that this is the prisoner's side of the door, this is where a woman locked up would have looked out. What would she have seen? Nothing. Except a warder's eye looking back at her. A woman imprisoned behind this door couldn't have just looked out when she wanted to; the warder on the other side would have had to open the flap on the spy hole first.

There are faint letters written vertically down the door, spelling out 'porridge'. 'Can I touch it?' I ask, wondering if someone scratched the letters. Vyki puts a small torch up to the paint; we can see it's been written in pen. Who wrote it and when? It could have been as recent as the late 1970s and a reference to the TV

35

sitcom *Porridge*, although the slang term for a prison sentence had been in use since at least the 1950s. This might be a museum store but it's also real life, this cell door that dates back to the year when Western Europe's largest prison for women was born.

When Holloway first opened it had accommodation for just sixty female prisoners. But in 1902, following wing extensions, new reception blocks and additional cells in the 1880s, it could hold 949, and a new wing was later added that could house a further 101. Two-thirds of its new inmates were serving sentences for prostitution or drunkenness, and the vast majority had been inside before. They were locked up in their cells for sixteen out of every twenty-four hours. Holloway 'takes both kinds of women', wrote journalist George Sims, the 'tried' and the 'untried', and the contrast among those who were on remand was to him 'very marked' due to the 'endless variety in female costume; in bonnets alone, every style, every fashion almost, may be seen in the exercising yard'. When he visited Holloway, its prisoners included a 'notorious dipsomaniac', splendid in a crimson silk shirt and white opera cloak; a 'virago' who had blackened her husband's eyes 'excusably perhaps'; and 'a poor starving soul with a baby nestling in her arms, whose offence was no worse than a theft of food'. All would suffer the 'pains and penalties of wrongdoing' and there was 'hard work and plenty of it' at Holloway, whether in the laundry or the kitchen, stitching, sewing, knitting or making mats.

But the authorities were soon overwhelmed by the inmates' behaviour, as they had been at Brixton in Victorian times, and it was now considered common knowledge that women were far more difficult to manage than men. 'Certainly it is so in Holloway,' wrote George Sims; 'misconduct, chronic and persistent, is intensified by hysteria, and these unsexed creatures respect no authority. At times the place is like a pandemonium.' Female prisoners were seen as a particular problem because they weren't behaving as women should. Men were expected to be rebellious and violent, but women were meant to return to their 'true nature' in prison and so their behaviour was even more disturbing. Yet George Sims felt pity too: 'Before we condemn these degraded specimens of the softer sex we should remember what they have suffered,' for there they were on the morning of their arrest 'torn and bedraggled, sodden with drink, their faces bruised, and with other marks of ill-usage'.

Holloway also now held all the women who were sentenced to death in London, and between 1902 and 1910 eleven women were kept in the condemned cell. Their sentences followed sensational trials and avid press coverage, with close attention paid to what the accused looked like, the way they spoke, their hair and clothes. The press speculated about what could have driven these women to commit such violent acts: had their emotions got the better of them, or were they insane?

The first woman to be sentenced to death and held at Holloway was Mary Spillane, found guilty of killing her baby. She had given birth a few days after her husband had returned from military service in South Africa, where he'd been for three years. He 'promised to overlook his wife's unfaithfulness on condition that she sent the child away', reported one newspaper, while another said he'd insisted the baby be 'put in an institution'. The dead child was found in a dust heap and initially both parents were charged with murder, but only Mary stood trial. The defence argued she had acted in an ungovernable fit of passion and was suffering from puerperal mania, although the judge said it looked like a case of cool premeditation to him. Mary was sentenced to death. But the jury recommended mercy on the grounds that she was a woman, and a week later she was reprieved.

That same year Kitty Byron, a milliner's assistant from London, killed her lover Arthur Reginald Baker, a stockjobber. Arthur was a violent alcoholic and Kitty stabbed him in public, using a knife concealed in her muff, saying, 'I killed him willingly, and he deserved it.' She was described as stepping 'briskly into the dock' where she appeared calm and collected. But in general the press had sympathy for this 'slender, dark-eyed girl . . . decidedly prepossessing in appearance', and condemned Arthur as 'a brute'. Kitty had been in such a state of mental distress on learning that Arthur intended to 'discard her' that she was 'for the time being almost incapable of knowing what she did'.

There were 'pathetic scenes' at the Old Bailey when she pleaded not guilty and turned from the dock to seize the prison matron's hands. The jury took eight minutes to find her guilty of murder, with the 'strongest possible recommendation to mercy'. A petition was launched and a stream of people called at her solicitor's offices, including 'a gentleman from Trinidad' and a man who promised to supply 300 signatures. Soon 15,000 people had demanded a reprieve, and the sentence was commuted to life imprisonment.

Both Mary Spillane and Kitty Byron were transferred to Aylesbury Prison in Buckinghamshire, and Kitty was released after six years. But for the next two women sentenced to death and held at Holloway, there would be no sympathy or public petitions.

In August 1902 domestic servant Ada Galley came across an advertisement in her local newspaper: 'Accouchement, before and during. Skilled nursing. Home comforts. Baby can remain. Hertford Road, East Finchley'. The advert was for a lying-in home called Claymore House in north London, where women could stay before giving birth, and sounded perfectly respectable. But it was the term 'baby can remain' that alerted Ada, who was then heavily pregnant. She knew it meant she could give birth and then have the child informally adopted.

Ada moved into the lying-in home and on the evening of her son's birth the father of the child, a clerk, came to pay the adoption fee of £25. The proprietor of the lying-in home, twenty-nine-year-old Amelia Sach, then sent a telegram to Annie Walters, a fifty-four-year-old midwife, telling her to fetch the baby. Annie would take Ada's son to a 'titled lady' and he would grow up in luxury. But three days later Annie Walters was discovered in a toilet at South Kensington station with a dead boy in her arms. She admitted having given the child chlorodyne, a lethal but legal mixture of laudanum, cannabis and chloroform. It was originally used to treat cholera, but was now sold for a variety of ailments, including coughs and colds, and like other opiates often given to 'sooth' hungry, crying children. Annie may well have been addicted to chlorodyne, a drug that led to many a fatal overdose, as she told the arresting officer: 'I never killed the baby, I only gave it two little drops in its bottle, the same as I take myself.'

The two women were charged with murder and in January 1903 Amelia Sach and Annie Walters stood trial at the Old Bailey in one of the last major cases of baby farming. Baby farmers were women who worked as child minders. Most were honest and legitimate, and the children usually belonged to unmarried women forced to 'farm' out their 'illegitimate' child to keep their job. Mothers paid a few shillings a week, or a one-off 'premium' to have their baby adopted. But a handful of criminal baby farmers took the money and then starved or murdered the babies, abandoning the bodies on the streets. Between 1871 and 1908 eight baby farmers were convicted of murder and seven were executed, including Margaret Waters at Horsemonger Lane Gaol in Surrey and Amelia Dyer at Newgate.

Amelia Sach didn't fit the common stereotype of the baby farmer: she wasn't a drunken working-class foster mother. Instead she was 'a remarkably handsome woman, with dark eyes and hair' who dressed for her court appearance in 'a blue cloak, trimmed with white fur'. Whether she knew what would happen to Ada's child when she handed him to Annie Walters isn't known, and neither woman spoke during the trial at the Old Bailey. The father of Ada's child, the man who had paid the adoption fee, was allowed to appear as an anonymous witness, while Amelia's husband Jeffrey, who lived near the lying-in home with their four-year-old daughter, was kept out of the proceedings.

Amelia Sach and Annie Walters were found guilty. Judge Justice Darling accused them of systematically setting out to kill babies, while the press decried their 'unwomanly callousness'. The *Islington Gazette* questioned their right even to be called women, although it was happy enough to continue receiving money for suspiciously worded classified advertisements offering 'good homes', fully qualified midwives and the possibility of adoption. 'If ever a woman forfeits her claim to consideration on account of her sex,' agreed the *Morning Advertiser*, 'it is when, in defiance of all her natural instincts, she ill-treats and slaughters helpless infants for the sake of greed.'

Midwifery was in the process of being professionalized – scientific medical men were seen as far more qualified than working-class midwives whose hands-on knowledge was increasingly being devalued – and under the Midwives Act of 1902 midwives could no longer certify a death or a stillbirth. The case of these two baby farmers was used to illustrate just how murderous such women could be.

Letters were written to the Home Secretary on behalf of Amelia, but there was little chance of a reprieve. The execution was to be private, with the new scaffold situated a few yards from the condemned cell, in a shed at the end of B wing, in the north-west of the prison.

Annie was held in the cell formerly occupied by Kitty Byron and was said to have borne up remarkably well after her sentence. Amelia was put in a separate cell where she was 'at-times very depressed, and gave way to her feelings under the strain of her terrible position'. When assistant executioner Henry Pierrepoint looked through the peephole into Amelia's cell he found 'a poorer wreck of humanity as I have ever seen'.

On 3 February 1903 Amelia Sach and Annie Walters were roused at 6 a.m., and visited by the governor, matron and chaplain. Unable to eat their last breakfast of bread and butter, the women became increasingly agitated as time passed, and Amelia repeatedly expressed a desire to 'meet her fate as soon as possible, and so put an end to her misery'. The hangmen were in position outside the condemned cells just before 8 a.m. and as they waited for the signal from the governor, Henry Pierrepoint again looked through the peephole into Amelia's cell. She appeared to him 'broken up', with her hair tied in a peculiar fashion to prevent it getting caught in the noose. At quarter to nine the under-sheriff arrived, the final witness needed before the execution was carried out.

Henry pinioned Amelia by the arms, a warder whispered 'words of comfort' as she was led into the corridor and towards the gallows, sobbing and barely conscious. William Billington then placed the noose and caps over the women's heads and as he moved to pull the lever, Annie cried out, 'Goodbye, Sach.' A moment later the drop fell, and death was said to be instantaneous. The women's bodies were taken down an hour later and buried in unmarked graves in the eastern corner of the prison adjoining Parkhurst Road. Holloway had now become the site of the first execution of women in England in the reign of Edward VII, and the only double execution of women since the end of public hangings.

'These two women were baby farmers of the worst kind,' Henry Pierrepoint noted in his diary, 'and they were both repulsive in type.' He paid tribute to the prison wardresses: 'How bravely they went through the great ordeal! Everyone was quite firm and calm, but after they left the death chamber one could detect stray tears trickling down their cheeks.' But there was little outcry over the baby farmers' deaths; they were 'repulsive' midwives who had committed the worst crime a woman could commit: to kill a stranger's child.

The social and economic conditions that led women to turn to baby farmers – young servant girls faced with an illegitimate child that not even an orphanage would take, unable to get financial help from the child's father and faced with shame, stigma and the loss of their jobs – were largely ignored. Edwardian courts and press reports were full of cases of child cruelty and neglect, usually committed by 'persons of inferior social status', with infants found in filthy rooms without food or clothing. While men were often charged alongside their partners, many absconded before the trial or were let off because of lack of evidence. Women, on the other hand, were supposed to be maternal, and they bore the brunt of the blame for the impoverishment that led to neglect.

However, it was those who worked as baby farmers who received the most severe punishment and, if they weren't executed, they faced significantly longer sentences. To look after children for money was unnatural, and it was just as unnatural to want to 'get rid' of a child to another woman. The largely working-class women who hired baby farmers were, said one MP, mothers who had 'lost the best instincts of human nature'. Women like Amelia Sach and Annie Walters, as well as their clients, had fallen foul of assumptions about both femininity and motherhood.

A few weeks after the execution at Holloway a deputation representing ratepayers and the borough council, and headed by four MPs, went to see the Home Secretary. They described the hangings as demoralizing to residents, but they also wanted to stress the effect on property values. 'Strangers of the worst type' had flocked to Islington 'to discuss the details with the executioner and warders' and servant girls in houses backing on to the prison had apparently witnessed the burial of the two women 'with all its gruesome details'. The Home Secretary promised that in future burials 'shall be absolutely private, and that these scandals shall not occur again'.

Over a century later and the sense of scandal surrounding the case of the Edwardian baby farmers remains. Penninah Asher only discovered she was related to Amelia Sach after she posted a family tree online and realized that Amelia's youngest sister Eunice was her own great-grandmother. Eunice never told a soul about what happened to her sister at Holloway, even changing her first name and her father's name and occupation when she married three years after the execution. 'It was a huge story at the time,' says Penninah, 'it was even reported in Australia, and my great-grandmother obviously felt a great deal of shame. Eunice didn't revert to her real name until 1930, fourteen years after her husband died. I don't think he ever knew about her sister.' Amelia's husband Jeffrey took his mother's maiden name after the execution, and sent their daughter to be brought up in Southend-on-Sea in Essex.

When Penninah first found out about Amelia Sach she was hoping she was innocent. Then she went to view her forebear's criminal file at the National Archives in Kew, including the photographs taken on arrest. 'I couldn't even look at Annie Walters, she frightened me. She looks like a Hans Christian Andersen witch. I wouldn't want to meet her in a dark alley, let alone hand her a baby, and yet that's what Amelia did. She was calculating and manipulative and greedy.' While Penninah believes the trial was unfairly heard, 'if these women murdered babies for profit, they deserved to swing for it.' Although it happened over 100 years ago, the nature of the crime means that Penninah's discovery is still taboo. One of her relatives, who is in his seventies, advised her to keep the discovery to herself. 'I can see his point of view, but you come to so many dead-ends when you research your family and if they're poor like mine then there's no information. Even if you find something awful, at least you've found something.'

Ever since Penninah discovered her infamous relative she's been trying to tie up loose ends. Amelia had nine siblings and Eunice is the only one without a birth certificate, which suggests she may have been illegitimate. Amelia was sixteen when Eunice was born; perhaps she was her mother rather than her older sister. And if Amelia found herself an unmarried mother at the age of sixteen, perhaps this was why she went into baby farming.

In the seven years that followed the execution of Amelia Sach and Annie Walters, seven more women were sentenced to death and held in the condemned cell at Holloway Prison. One had killed her boyfriend's wife, another was found guilty of murdering her husband after both had taken poison and only she survived. Five were domestic servants, like Ada Galley, who had been unable or unwilling to hire the services of a baby farmer and had instead killed their own illegitimate child, often shortly after birth. The courts frequently viewed infanticide with some sympathy, acknowledging that a 'fallen' woman with a child could be driven to kill through circumstances, but the same sympathy was not extended to baby farmers: only a monster could kill another woman's child. And yet all seven condemned prisoners were reprieved because, despite their crimes, they were still regarded as women.

Control of female prisoners meanwhile was an increasing problem. 'In the ranks of the really great criminals there have been very few women,' explained Captain Vernon Harris, a former inspector of prisons, shortly after the baby farmers' execution. But 'bad' women were 'the worst of all creatures' and their 'charge far from an easy one to those to whom the duty is confined'. The secret of keeping hysterical women calm and orderly lay in the training of the officers, and 'in the amount of intelligence and force of character that they bring to bear in their work'. It was a heavy responsibility for the men and women now in charge of the country's largest female jail.

4

Turnkeys and Colonels

By the time Holloway became a women's prison the role and character of prison officers had changed dramatically. Traditionally an officer's job was that of a turnkey, making sure a prison was secure and the prisoners locked up. Many were known for their corruption. 'It is impossible for the mind to conceive a spectacle more gross and revolting than the internal economy of this polluted spot,' wrote the governor of London's Coldbath Fields Prison in 1829. The officers were a 'cunning and extortionate crew, practising every species of duplicity and chicanery'. Anything, it seemed, could be bought if there was money to pay for it, and so 'the first question asked of a prisoner was – "Had he any money, or anything that could be turned into money? Or would any friend, if written to, advance him some?"'

But by the middle of the nineteenth century the turnkeys had evolved into a new breed of jailers. Male warders were often ex-police officers, while women came from a background of domestic service, and both were subjected to a life nearly as regimented as the prisoners themselves. In 1860 the City of London issued a list of forty-one fines for those found negligent in their duties, providing a snapshot of not only how strict the prison regime was but what jailers had been getting up to in the past. Timekeeping was of utmost importance, starting with a 6d fine for arriving late (under five minutes), which rose to 1 shilling (between five and ten minutes) and so on until the fine amounted to 2s 6d. This was a significant amount of money when male warders started on a salary of 24 shillings a week – far less than the prison schoolmaster, clerk or storekeeper – and women received only 15 shillings. As would be expected, many of the fines concerned leaving a door unlocked – whether in a cell, passage, yard or ward. Smaller fines were issued for letting prisoners walk around the yard 'without due regularity and out of order', allowing window sills to get dusty, forgetting to sweep wards, falling asleep at chapel and doing night patrol with 'loud talking, laughing, rattling of keys'. Officers found wrangling with each other while on duty faced a 1 shilling fine, as did those who took money or valuables from a prisoner without signing the property book, or entered the goods against another inmate's name. Over half of the forty-one warders who left Holloway in the 1860s were dismissed for 'trafficking with prisoners or their friends' or resigned after 'a short period of service because of dislike of the work'.

While some warders were known for their corruption, others were praised for their compassion, especially when it came to smuggling out letters. One accepted half a crown from an inmate, 'a delicate boy who could not thrive on the prison fare', to take a letter to his parents, bringing back plum pudding and meat. For this the warder lost his job, and was fined 50 shillings or a month's imprisonment. 'It is somewhat to be regretted,' noted the press, 'that a kind act has led to such a serious result.'

To begin with, the vast majority of staff at Holloway were men and while women were needed to oversee female inmates, the prison ran for five years with only one female officer. But female warders had another role as well: unlike male officers they were encouraged to befriend their charges and to exert a good moral influence. They would, explained penal reformer Elizabeth Fry, provide 'a consistent example of feminine propriety and virtue', and their role was likened to that of a nurse.

Female prisoners had broken two kinds of law: criminal law that convicted them for theft or assault, and unwritten societal laws that governed feminine behaviour. They were thus 'doubly deviant', explains historian Helen Johnston, but given the right individual attention in prison 'the hearts of female offenders could be turned away from a life of criminality and their appropriate womanhood restored'. The task of reformation was often left to upper middle-class 'lady visitors' who offered sympathy to prisoners and educated them on the danger of vice and the advantages of an honest and virtuous life. Prison visiting had been an informal affair until in 1817 Elizabeth Fry formed the Ladies Association for the Improvement of Female Prisoners in Newgate, which became a nationwide organization in 1901. But although it was lady visitors who were meant to reclaim 'fallen sisters' like Selina Salter, the female warders still had the closest contact with female inmates, and prison regulations required them to be 'of good moral principles and unblemished character'. Yet how could they exert a proper feminine influence when their job was to maintain order, their every hour was accounted for and they weren't allowed to speak to prisoners except to issue instructions or reprimands?

In 1872 Louisa Henson began work at Holloway and three years later she decided to start a diary recording her frustrations with the job. 'Sunday is such a long dreary day here,' she writes. 'I shall be so glad when it is six o'clock, to get out of this dreadful place.' The hours were long – often fifteen hours a day and only one Sunday off every two months – there was infighting and a high turnover of staff, while the weather was miserable. One morning the prison ground was so slippery that seven warders fell down and one broke her leg. In the summer the prisoners were 'so affected by the heat', that thirty were put on report and the punishment cells were filled to capacity. Then of course there were the fines. One female officer was fined for wrangling, a 'crying shame' and a 'most unjust fine'. Two others left the same day and 'there will be a few more, if things continue as they are at present'. Not long after, Louisa herself was fined for arriving five minutes late in the morning, the second time she had received such a penalty.

But worst of all was night duty: 'I am always glad when the first night is over, but I was fearfully nervous all the week.' Day shifts ran from 6 a.m. to 6 p.m., while those on evening duty finished at 4 p.m. then returned at 5.45 p.m. until 10 p.m. They slept in the prison, where they were on call overnight, and were back on official duty at 6 a.m. One day Louisa came to work to be told a poor woman had been found dead in her cell the evening before 'so that made me dreadfully nervous . . . I fancied I saw her before me all the night.' She describes another woman who kept up an incessant ringing of her bell and 'telling me to bring a policeman to her cell for there was a man there. Poor night officer, your nerves are well tried indeed.'

One of her more enjoyable tasks was to take 'grand visitors' round the prison, such as the sister to Lord Hastings, a 'very nice lady who takes a little piece of oakum away with her so that when she had any little trials or vexations she would look at that and bear them with patience and resignation'. In between shifts Louisa visited her mother and her ailing granny, joined friends for walks in the park or window-shopped in the Brompton Road, and even managed a few days away in Margate. But facing another night duty made her 'forget the pleasures quick enough'. The life of a prison officer was one of pressure and anxiety. Louisa was fearful of the environment, the inmates and other officers, and each day seemed to bring a new disaster. Then a particularly difficult inmate, Maria, arrived, 'one of the worst kind of women that ever came into the prison'. The first night 'she tore up everything in the way of clothing that she had about her' and her screams could be heard by the prison's neighbours. Maria was certified insane and Louisa was given the job of taking her to the asylum, a task that left her 'sick and weary of Prison and my life. I know it is wicked but I can't help it.' She decided to apply to the Post Office 'for I must get out of this soon'.

When fourteen convicted women were transferred from Holloway to Millbank the reason for Louisa's misery became even clearer: 'poor unhappy women, who knows how temptation has been thrown in their way. The majority have seen and heard nothing but vice and wickedness from their birth. It is a most distressing sight to witness the poor creatures cursing (but alas too late) the drunk and bad company that has brought them to it.' If Louisa Henson's job as a female warder was to reform the women, then she felt she had failed and she expresses pity for the prisoners, tinged with moral superiority and a sense of abject helplessness. As the women left Holloway she notes:

a fine prison officer I make for I cannot myself stay the tears as I wished good bye and urging them for the sake of their religion and themselves to keep out of trouble for it is very strange that some going away for a long time do not seem to care how they 'carry on' to use their own words but tear up and smash everything before them, poor deluded women. It has made me feel depressed all day. I am in for duty tonight. I shall be glad to get out of this frightful place.

Whether Louisa Henson did join the Post Office isn't known, but in 1877 the government took control of the nation's jails, which became 'Her Majesty's prisons', and soon afterwards new pay scales were introduced for officers. Female staff received a uniform allowance, quarters in the prison with fuel, light, water and washing, medical attendance and medicine – though male officers were paid more and were more likely to be promoted. Training for prison officers was also introduced, and the training school for female officers was eventually moved to Holloway.

But life for female warders was still heavily restricted. Their quarters could be randomly checked; those who lived in the prison needed written permission if they wanted visitors, to stay out until midnight, or to spend a night away from the jail. They could also be victims of violence. One December day the chief wardress was attacked while making her final round of the cells when a prisoner 'rushed into the corridor, seized the pail, and struck her three heavy blows'. The wardress fell unconscious and had to be taken to the infirmary where her condition was described as serious.

Women warders had 'a life full of . . . dangers,' commented George Sims, 'for assaults are not uncommon; yet are they mild mannered, forbearing to their troublesome sisterhood, and have strong claims to the respect and esteem of the public at large.' Holloway was their home, as well as the prisoners', and the authorities had not forgotten 'there should be play as well as hard work' so now they had 'comfortable quarters and a large well furnished recreation room'. Here the wardresses in their severe black uniforms and hats sat around the piano having a singsong, chatting, reading and sewing.

Matrons also lived in the prison, and were in charge of female wings, with their duties similar to those of a governor. They too were forbidden to be absent overnight, and could not be away from the prison for more than three hours without permission. In 1869 when Holloway's matron Justinia Francess retired she was presented with a silver teapot, to which every officer had contributed, as a reward for her integrity and uprightness. But again the job could be dangerous. The press reported an 'exciting scene' at Holloway when matron Mary Jane Bell visited inmate Eleanor Kennedy in her cell. 'Why do you tell the magistrates every morning that I misbehave myself?' asked Eleanor, who then struck the matron several blows with a sharp instrument, which turned out to be a large pair of scissors bound with a handkerchief. A male warder seized her, but Eleanor stabbed him in the arm as well and was sentenced to a further two months.

While women officers oversaw female prisoners it was always a man, the governor, who was in charge at Holloway Prison. Governors tended to come from the ranks of the military, favoured military uniforms and parades, and ran the prison under their own rules. Holloway's first governor was Captain George Wright, a former naval officer and ex-deputy governor of Newgate who had been in the prison service for eight years. He lived in the grand house on the left of the entrance to the jail, and was provided with free fuel and light, and his kitchen was well stocked with chicken, ham and champagne. George Wright lasted nearly five years at Holloway, and for the first two years refused to take a single day's leave. But then in 1858 the Court of Aldermen noticed a 'palpable discrepancy' in the prison accounts. They sent for the governor, who confessed he'd been embezzling money over a four-year period, and he was dismissed as quietly as possible. His clerk had apparently been aware of the fraud, but had kept quiet 'through loyalty', perhaps knowing the circumstances of the governor's domestic life. Three of his children as well as his father had died in just six months, his wife was ill and needed medical treatment, and he couldn't afford the upkeep of such a grand house.

When it came to electing a new governor of Holloway there were angry scenes at the Court of Aldermen. The three candidates were two captains and John Weatherhead, then governor of Newgate. One alderman refused to vote – 'Suppose I consider none of the candidates to be properly qualified for the situation' – until the Lord Mayor threatened him with contempt of court. In the end John Weatherhead was elected and became the next governor of 'city prison Holloway'. An official portrait shows a self-important man seated at a writing desk, a slight frown on his face as he stares off into the distance, his sideburns growing up his cheeks to meet the hair on his head. He looks well fed and well dressed, and every bit the Victorian prison governor.

John Weatherhead stayed in the post for the next twenty years, appointing his son as clerk, and was extremely diligent when it came to the prison's financial affairs. He was regarded as energetic and determined to succeed, and developed the prison's industries until Holloway became known as 'one of the most self-supporting prisons of the era'. He was also very media-friendly, judging by the number of journalists who were allowed, or invited, in for a tour and it was during his period in office that Henry Mayhew visited, as well as local reporters. Holloway under John Weatherhead was a place of strict discipline; men were not even allowed to grow their moustaches, and he designed his own form of straitjacket for those who refused to work. This was used on one returned felon who had turned sulky, would not speak, and had broken the small windows of his cell. A journalist from the *North London News* described the scene: 'The door is open, and the wretched, hangdog looking fellow stands before us, having more the appearance of an Egyptian mummy than anything else. Stripped of his boots and all outer clothing, he is swaddled in canvas from the shoulders down to the knees, and buckled round with three leather straps.' The man was now 'unable to hurt himself or anybody else', and promised the governor he would behave himself and do his work, upon which the jacket was removed.

John Weatherhead also had his own way of dealing with those who tried to avoid work by 'feigning' illness or madness. When he took up his post there were nine men in the prison infirmary who were 'said to have fits'. The governor didn't believe them and put the men in separate cells, with three buckets of water placed at each door. The warders were instructed to watch the prisoners closely, and 'whenever the fits came on, to supply them plenteously with the cooling stream'. This had a wondrous effect: in less than six weeks, eight were sufficiently recovered to be able to work on the treadwheel. The ninth proved to be a 'real case', and he was 'taken care of', with the result that it was now a 'by-word among the old gaolbirds, that "it's no use to have fits in Holloway"'.

The governor was also subject to numerous rules himself, with an emphasis on good order and security. He was not allowed to be absent at night, he could have no other trade, was not to hire out any of the rooms, had to make sure no officer received any money, fee or gratuity from any visitor, and could not employ any officer or prisoner to work for him privately. The governor made sure all prisoners were strictly searched for weapons or sharp instruments on arrival, oversaw the daily examination of the cells, bars, bolts and locks, made sure the prison was locked for the night, and toured the jail at least once a week at 'an uncertain hour of the night', letting himself in through a private door of his house, to check that all was in order. He also ensured there were no dogs in the prison, except for security purposes, nor any poultry, pigeons, pigs or rabbits.

John Weatherhead was succeeded by another former military man, Lieutenant-Colonel E.S. Milman, and his reign at Holloway would last twenty-three years. But this governor was twice hauled up in court himself. One inmate, Sarah Miller, sued him for false imprisonment after she had been mistakenly arrested instead of her daughter who was wanted for non-payment of rates. The governor argued that Sarah hadn't given her actual name for several days, and hadn't sent for him, and so the case was withdrawn. In a later case, however, a solicitor's clerk successfully claimed damages after he was treated as a convicted criminal rather than a first-class inmate.

While Holloway's governor was in charge of disciplining prisoners, it was the chaplain who took care of their souls and minds. The two positions had the same status, which was why the chaplain's equally grand house was on the right-hand side of the gatehouse. The chaplain played a crucial role in the Victorian penal system, as did religion in general. His job was to raise the moral tone among inmates, while compulsory services and Bible reading would set them on the road to reform. Prisoners would reflect on their crimes in the solitude of the cell, and everyone – prisoners and staff – was expected to attend chapel every day, one of the few times inmates were allowed out of their cells. To Victorian observers, there was something very appealing about watching prisoners at chapel, especially if they were female, and when Henry Mayhew visited Brixton he was entranced by the sight of inmates at prayer in their clean white caps. As women were of a 'more religious and ardent temperament' than men, it was particularly moving to hear their 'confessions of sin and supplications for mercy'.

Holloway's chaplain saw all prisoners the day after they arrived and recorded if they were married and had children, their parish and trade, and whether they had attended divine worship during the last six months. He then gave them something to learn such as scripture texts, 'suitable to their position and state of mind', which they had to memorize and repeat back to him a few weeks later. He also kept a 'character-book' in which he noted prisoners' names and 'such information as he may receive, in his communication with them or otherwise'. His job therefore was to find out more about the inmates, to establish their 'connexions', character, habits and state of mind, and report on their 'moral and religious conduct'. But some of Holloway's chaplains took on another role and were very outspoken about prison conditions. Reverend William Morrison, a prison chaplain for fifteen years, was 'relieved of his post' after writing numerous angry letters to *The Times* and went on to write two books on crime: *Crime and Its Causes* and *Juvenile Offenders*. He was concerned about the rise in serious crime, and the increase in the cost of imprisoning people, and warned that the closer women and men came in social status, the more likely their criminal impulses would be similar. He also questioned how prison could prepare anyone to re-enter the world when it was so far removed from everyday life. The English prison system had a 'machine-like' way of dealing with prisoners; it was a disastrous failure that debased people mentally and morally.

If the chaplain was responsible for an inmate's morality and state of mind, then responsibility for the health of the body lay with the prison medical officer. He examined new arrivals, noting 'any disease of importance' and deciding if they could withstand hard labour. He visited sick prisoners daily, increased or decreased food as he saw fit, kept an eye on those in the punishment cells, and treated sick staff as well. He made 'a searching and minute inquiry into every prisoner's health' once a month, ensured there was daily exercise in the open air, checked that bedding and clothing were sufficient, and regularly examined the state of the thermometers. When an inmate died in Holloway, it was the medical officer who was called on to attend the inquest and Charles Lawrence Bradley, the prison doctor in the 1860s, appeared at several inquiries into deaths in custody. His evidence normally took the form of explaining that the death had been due to natural causes, and that every care and attention had been given in the infirmary.

Victorian Holloway had begun as a model prison to be run along lines of order and discipline and the staff, from the wardresses up to the governor, operated within a strict hierarchy. Yet right from the beginning some had subverted the rules and those like Reverend Morrison were already questioning the wisdom of the penal system.

In the first fifty years of Holloway's existence, it had seen a wide variety of women walk through its doors, from vagrants like Selina Salter to members of the upper class such as the Duchess of Sutherland. Some had been shown sympathy and offered preferential treatment; others had been subjected to further punishment. Prison officers like Louisa Henson had been expected to exert a moral influence; her Edwardian colleagues had been required to accompany women to the death chamber. But it was the role of the prison medical officer that was about to undergo the most radical change.

In 1896 the 'lucrative appointment' of medical officer at Holloway was accepted by Dr James Scott. A former hospital doctor, he had been in the prison service for fifteen years and had become a familiar figure at the Central Criminal Court where he was 'recognised as an authority on criminal responsibility'. But with the arrival of the suffragettes his job would be less about visiting sick prisoners and more a case of inflicting state-sanctioned torture.

PART TWO

The Battle for Suffrage

5

The Hollowayettes

On 21 June 1906 a twenty-nine-year-old woman from Lancashire became the first suffragette to be sent to Holloway Prison. Teresa Billington had been arrested outside the Chancellor of the Exchequer Herbert Asquith's house and charged with assaulting a police officer 'by striking him in the face with her fist and kicking him in the leg'. Three other women were also arrested, and charged with behaviour likely to cause a breach of the peace after ringing Herbert Asquith's doorbell. When the four suffragettes appeared in court, Teresa refused to give her name or address and was fined £10 or two months in prison. The next day the *Sheffield Evening Telegraph* published a drawing of a stern-looking Teresa, explaining she had declined 'to recognise laws in the making of which woman had no voice', refused to pay the fine and had therefore been removed to jail.

Teresa Billington was a schoolteacher, born in Preston and bought up in Blackburn, and known for her powerful public speaking. Women, she said, were 'tired of being walked upon and being made doormats of'.

A member of the Women's Social and Political Union (WSPU), which had been formed three years earlier by Emmeline Pankhurst and her eldest daughter Christabel, Teresa was described as 'the leader of a more aggressive section of the women suffragists'. The WSPU was a more militant organization than its Victorian predecessor, the National Union of Women's Suffrage Societies, its motto was 'deeds not words' and its focus was on getting women the vote. The WSPU used direct action rather than the peaceful lobbying of Parliament and its members, and those of other radical suffragist groups, became known as the suffragettes, a term apparently first used in a derogatory way by the *Daily Mail*.

The month before Teresa's arrest for kicking a policeman she had been charged with causing an obstruction in Ludgate Hill in London by displaying a 'Votes for Women' banner. When she failed to appear at court the alderman in charge expressed the opinion that perhaps she was only seeking an advertisement. 'Why give it to her?' he said, and ordered the summons to be withdrawn.

Teresa had only been in Holloway Prison for a week when the Home Secretary William Gladstone reduced her fine to £5 or a month behind bars, and to her fury the fine was paid. Teresa demanded to see the governor, who 'pointed out that, the fine having been paid, he had no option but to accept, and insisted upon my discharge'. 'Annoyed is not the word,' she told the *Lancashire Evening Post*. 'I am indignant beyond measure at the manner of my release. I am fully convinced that it was a journalistic plot on the part of a certain yellow journal.' According to some reports, it was a reader of the *Daily Mail* who had paid the fine.

Holloway's governor at the time was Richard Frith Quinton, who had replaced Colonel Milman in 1902. He had worked in the prison service for twenty-five years as a medical officer and later published a book, *Crime and Criminals*, in which he portrayed himself as never unduly harsh, and the suffragettes as a thorn in his side. They didn't like prison conditions and were only too ready to protest, whereas the majority of inmates 'had no complaints'. But prison, he explained, wasn't designed for women like the suffragettes, 'educated convicts, who write books and magazine articles after their release, depicting the horrors of penal servitude and the hardships and grievances they experienced in prison, and denouncing the wrong-headedness and barbarity of the penal system'. Such women had 'a standpoint of their own which always seems to imply that the system has been designed for people of their class. This is far from being the case.' The suffragettes did not in fact belong to one social class, although those like Emmeline Pankhurst and Lady Constance Lytton were certainly educated and had highly influential family and friends. As far as Holloway's governor was concerned, such women revelled in being jailed, and the press was only too happy to minister 'freely to the public appetite for the lurid details'.

The day after Teresa Billington was released she attended the trial of the other three women who had been arrested for breach of the peace, but not yet convicted, Annie Kenney, Adelaide Knight and Jane Scarborough. Annie was a cotton mill worker from Lancashire and already a leading figure in WSPU. She had been the first suffragette to be imprisoned, along with Christabel Pankhurst, after they refused to pay a fine for interrupting a Liberal Party meeting in Manchester in 1905. Both had been sent to Strangeways Prison, Christabel for seven days and Annie for three.

In this case, Annie's lawyer argued that she had the perfect right to ring Mr Asquith's doorbell, and when asked 'Will you undertake not to do this again?' she replied, 'I cannot say what I intend until I see the result of these proceedings. I decline to give any undertaking.' The three women were given bail 'on the distinct understanding that during the following week they would not repeat their conduct'. But on 24 October there were 'wild scenes' at court when this time ten women, including Teresa and Annie, were charged with using threatening language during a protest at the opening of Parliament. 'Ladies prefer to go to prison,' announced one newspaper, which reported on 'the agitation which was causing so much trouble to the authorities of London'.

Again the women refused to acknowledge the power of the court. The magistrate appeared exasperated, saying it was nothing to do with whether ladies ought to have the vote or not, he had to keep order: 'This is not the place for politics.' The women were each bound over to good behaviour for six months and taken down to the cells. At this point the doors to the court were thrown open and in rushed a group of suffragettes, including Sylvia Pankhurst, Emmeline's second daughter, waving banners and shouting 'Votes for Women!' Sylvia was arrested and immediately convicted of disorderly conduct.

The original ten prisoners were then brought back into the court one by one and told to pay the fine or face two months in jail, to which only one agreed. Then the 'well-dressed little crowd took their seats' in the prison van and 'nobody would have detected the least sign of mental depression'. Far from being depressed, the women were jubilant. If their aim was to raise publicity for the cause then they couldn't have succeeded better. This was the largest single group of suffragettes to be sent to prison; their sentence was seen by many as shockingly harsh and the WSPU gained more support.

Millicent Garrett Fawcett, president of the more moderate National Union of Women's Suffrage Societies, noted that the cause had 'received a great impetus from the courage and self-sacrifice of the group of women now serving a term of two months' imprisonment in Holloway Gaol'. While she was convinced that the best way forward was 'quiet persuasion and argument', it was clear to her that 'the action of the prisoners has touched the imagination of the country in a manner which quiet methods did not succeed in doing'.

The WSPU held a meeting in Caxton Hall, calling for the release of the suffragettes. One of the speakers, journalist William Stead who had been jailed in Holloway in 1885 for abduction, observed that it was only by making themselves a nuisance that women were likely to get their demands met. What had happened that day had 'lit a flame in Westminster' which would spread throughout the country.

On arrival at Holloway the suffragettes were treated as second-division inmates and their battle to be recognized as political prisoners and first-division inmates would become a defining part of their time in prison. English law didn't make a distinction between political prisoners and other convicts, although both the Chartists and the Fenians had previously argued for separate treatment and attempted to claim political status. The Chartists, a mass movement demanding voting reform in the 1830s and 1840s, had wanted to wear their own clothes and have their own bedding, to be able to write letters and see friends, and not to work at menial tasks. Their demands were refused, but it was their complaints that led to the new prison divisions. The Fenians, who fought for the end of British rule in Ireland in the 1860s, had also rejected the idea that they were ordinary felons, but the definition of a political prisoner remained unclear.

Most of the suffragettes at Holloway were kept in the eastern wings of the prison, in D and DX blocks. They were given wooden plank beds (although some reports said they slept on straw), assigned a number and wore prison uniform, which included black wool stockings with red rings round the legs, while opportunities for letters and visits were restricted. Sylvia Pankhurst was sentenced to fourteen days in the third division, and she later described how the suffragettes were constantly marched about and rebuked. 'All of you unfasten your chests,' boomed one wardress as they waited to see the doctor; another screamed, 'You have not put on your stays!'; and a third ordered the women to tie up their cap strings: 'You look like a cinder picker; you must learn to dress decently here!' But for now the suffragettes would do as they were told. 'I obeyed with meekness,' wrote Sylvia, 'for we had agreed to submit ourselves to the prison discipline.' After eight days the suffragettes were transferred to the first division, but refused to wear their own clothes so a new uniform was introduced, a grey serge dress.

Sylvia found Holloway a place of fear and misery, from the 'shrunken forms of frail old grannies' to the 'tense, white looks and burning eyes' of the younger women. While it was WSPU policy to ignore the prison conditions in order to focus attention on the vote, she rejected this as a result of her time in Holloway: 'I thought it good propaganda for our movement to reveal our prison experiences. Moreover, I was far too anxious to secure prison reforms, not for ourselves, but for the ordinary prisoners.' This marked the moment when privileged women – aside from lady visitors – began to work for improved conditions in prison. They were articulate, they knew how to get their message to the public, and the very fact that they had been imprisoned created press interest. But what is less clear is the extent to which they changed the situation of all women in Holloway.

Sylvia Pankhurst and her colleagues were once again sent home early by order of the Home Office, after serving half of their sentence. 'The woman suffragists who have been rusticating in Holloway for the past month are once more free,' reported the *Dundee Courier*, and now it remained to be seen 'what use Miss Teresa Billington and her companions will make of their freedom . . . These outbursts of lawlessness have undoubtedly brought votes for women nearer . . . the probability is the battle will be resumed, for the women who have emerged from the gloom of Holloway are not the kind to sit down and fold their hands.'

The government made a serious miscalculation when it ordered the early release of the suffragettes, for they went straight to Huddersfield where a by-election was about to be held and 4,000 people were ready to welcome them. Electors were urged to oppose a government that imprisoned women and to vote against the Liberal candidate, and although the Liberals held on to the seat, the suffrage campaign was now becoming national.

In the coming months the suffragettes used their prison experience to urge others to follow suit. 'You will never win a strike by paying fines,' Adela Pankhurst, Emmeline's youngest daughter, told a meeting of striking Yorkshire weavers. 'Go to prison, and every paper in the country will know about it, and back you up.' This, as historian Jill Liddington writes in *Rebel Girls*, was 'incendiary fill-the-goals oratory', but it was one thing for a member of the Pankhurst family to be sent to jail and quite another for a low-paid Yorkshire weaver.

Yet the experience of suffragettes in Holloway would change the way the British public viewed the incarceration of women for ever. As the Fabian Society noted at the time: 'No female prisoner recorded her experiences until suffragists in large numbers were sent to Holloway.' Around 1,300 suffragettes were arrested in the UK between 1905 and 1914, of whom 100 were men, and those who ended up at Holloway included upper-class Londoners and working-class northern textile workers. Some were teenagers, others were approaching their eighties. Up to 200 were admitted on a single day, writing letters that were smuggled out and published in the press, and giving interviews on their release. Inside, women wrote poems and diaries, drew sketches of their cells and compiled autograph albums, which they fully intended to be published. The WSPU compiled a book of 'Holloway Jingles' – ''Tis the prison, cold and grey / Of noted Holloway' – which included a poem that mocked the governor who would never 'doff his hat to ladies fair / is it because he has no hair?' The chaplain was satirized for his sanctimonious drone, while the medical officer 'with stealthy tread, / Comes round each day to count his dead'.

The suffragettes made the most of their prison experience, both to garner support and to honour those who had been inside. Sylvia Pankhurst designed a Holloway brooch, featuring the House of Commons portcullis with a broad prison arrow, to be given to women on release and which became the Victoria Cross of the suffragette movement. A Holloway flag was waved on marches, while Christmas cards were produced which read 'Votes and a Happy Year' with an illustration of Holloway Prison. There were demonstrations when women were sentenced, supporters sang carols and 'war songs' outside the prison at Christmas, they organized night-time vigils, processions, reception breakfasts and welcome dinners where ex-prisoners were feted as heroines. Former inmates dressed up in prison clothes to parade through the streets on open-top buses, and during an exhibition in Kensington they built reproduction prison cells.

Holloway was central to the suffragettes' story, and when the authorities later began taking undercover surveillance photographs, a Mr Barrett hid in a van in the yard of Holloway Prison with a camera. His job was to capture a good likeness of the suffragettes – many of whom had refused to cooperate when it came to having their mugshots taken – as they walked unaware around the exercise yard. They were referred to by the code words 'wild cats', and their photos were used to identify future potential troublemakers. Composer Ethel Smyth held a toothbrush out of her cell window to conduct women in the exercise yard striding along to 'The March of the Women', the anthem she wrote for the suffrage movement after she was imprisoned for throwing stones. But most of all, Holloway Prison symbolized the idea of personal sacrifice to the cause, and 'Remember our sisters at Holloway' was a frequent rallying call.

For Adela Pankhurst, her time in Holloway in October 1906 made her feel that 'for the first time in my life I was doing something which would help.' And far from being 'reformed', imprisonment generally served to strengthen their beliefs. 'Oh, Holloway, grim Holloway,' wrote Kathleen Emerson, 'With grey, forbidding towers! / Stern are the walls, but sterner still / Is woman's free, unconquered will.'

But there were also moments of fun in prison, with games held in the shadow of the great perimeter wall, dancing when no outside exercise was allowed because of rain, or playing rounders in the prison garden. The suffragettes held football matches and a sports day, enjoyed singing, storytelling and plays. They organized a fancy dress ball and a mock general election, with canvassing, speeches and addresses. They also formed strong friendships with each other, 'ordinary' prisoners and with staff.

The suffragettes were well aware of the historical significance of their prison experience, hoarding memorabilia relating to their arrest and imprisonment, whether police charge sheets, telegrams, or notes written on prison toilet paper. And it's thanks to this that so many documents remain, such as the world's largest militant suffragette campaign collection held by the Museum of London. Director Sarah Gavron made use of this while researching the feature film *Suffragette*, as did actress Carey Mulligan, and museum curator Beverley Cook was invited to visit the set, where she had a walk-on part.

Yet despite the wealth of suffragette documents there has been surprisingly little written about the details of their life in prison, aside from the later introduction of forcible feeding, and so the image of imprisoned suffragettes remains one of victimhood or martyrdom rather than organized resistance. Modern reports are conflicting as to who was sentenced, when, where and why, and while present-day descendants might know their relatives were in Holloway, they often know very little else. One woman whose grandmother was jailed for taking a petition to 10 Downing Street explains, 'She didn't talk about Holloway Prison, she didn't hide it but . . . It's like the men who came back from war, they didn't feel the need to talk about it.'

In February 1907, during a march from Caxton Hall to Parliament organized by the WSPU, dozens of women were arrested, again including many young women from the north. The next morning fifty-three were put in a prison van and sent to Holloway, singing

'Glory, glory, hallelujah / And the cause goes marching on'. The press reported that the 'suffragists took their sentences with good humour' with many saying to the magistrate, 'Thank you. I will go to Holloway Prison.' They were cheered by hundreds waiting outside the courthouse, put their arms out of the prison van windows to wave handkerchiefs, and sang the 'Battle Song'.

One of those arrested was Alice Hawkins, a forty-three-year-old shoe machinist at the Equity Shoe factory, a workers' cooperative in Leicester. She was an active trade unionist, a member of the Independent Labour Party, and a campaigner for equal pay. A keen cyclist, she had joined the Clarion Cycling Club, launched by the socialist *Clarion* newspaper, and first appeared in the press for 'outraging public decency' by wearing bloomers.

By the early 1900s Alice had grown disillusioned with the male-dominated trade union movement; equal pay was paramount and this couldn't be achieved without the vote. One day she attended a public meeting in Leicester, where Annie Kenney and Teresa Billington spoke about their recent imprisonment in Holloway. Alice was not a member of the WSPU, but this meeting proved the catalyst for her to go to London. She joined the march to Parliament and found herself in the middle of a pitched battle against mounted police, where women were mowed down, had their clothes ripped and were sexually assaulted. Alice was arrested for disorderly conduct and sentenced to fourteen days at Holloway. It was the first of five prison terms, both in Leicester and London, and her experiences in Holloway would be life-changing.

She arrived at the prison at 4 p.m. along with the other suffragettes, and immediately 'felt rather sorry for the female officers when about 60 were handed to them at once'. The women were put eight in a cell and it wasn't until 10 p.m. that separate cells were ready. The prison days were long and lonely: up at 6 a.m., an hour's exercise at 10 a.m., 'which consists of walking around a few paths of gravel', then back to the cell where Alice would sew or write until dinnertime. After that, she wrote, 'we see no one until teatime between 4 and 5, unless a warder lets us out to empty any dirty water we may have. After tea we are locked in again until morning and so on day after day.'

But this, she noted, was the daily routine for the first-class prisoners: 'I don't think the others are allowed anything as well as this . . . many's the time my heart ached for the poor women that are in hard labour, for it is one long grind from early morning until late at night.' Alice found the regulations strict; the suffragettes were not allowed to speak to each other, although 'we manage a word now and again.' But the prison was 'beautifully clean', they were allowed a book twice a week and the food was enough to keep a person alive 'providing they can eat it': a pint of tea and a small loaf of brown bread for breakfast, haricot beans and potatoes for dinner, a pint of cocoa and another loaf of bread for tea.

It was the sense of isolation that was hardest to bear, locked alone for hour upon hour, away from her colleagues, her husband and six children. 'Oh the long, long nights from 8 o'clock when the electric light is put out until 6 in the morning when it's turned on again. Lying on a hard mattress until every bone in your body aches and you are only too pleased to see the light again so that you may get on your feet again.' While each cell had a bell, 'you might ring it 20 times a day and not get it answered, unless it happens that the matron, governor or chaplain were in the corridor.'

Although the suffragettes were generally kept apart from other prisoners, Alice Hawkins keenly observed her fellow inmates at Holloway: 'one in particular that I saw in church set me thinking, "what ever could have brought her to prison?" She was a girl not more than 16 with, oh, such a sweet face and pathetic eyes. I could not keep my eyes off her every time we went to church. Some had such lovely faces. It was impossible to think they could have committed any crime.'

On the day of Alice's release 200 women were waiting outside, with a welcoming band, ready to march into London for a 'reformed breakfast'. On the night of her arrest Alice had written to Ramsay MacDonald, her local MP and secretary of the Labour Party, asking him to object to the Home Secretary for ordering mounted police to ride down women. Holloway's governor had given her special permission to receive a reply, and now she read it out to the crowd, providing the 'sensation of the day'. Ramsay MacDonald was sorry to hear that Alice Hawkins had been 'run in', but 'I really do not think you are doing any good to the cause.' This, she noted, came from an MP who had promised to vote for a Women's Suffrage Bill. If the Leicester shoe machinist had not been a suffragette when she went into Holloway, then she certainly was when she came out. Two months later Alice held a meeting to form a local branch of the WSPU, and invited the Pankhursts to meet the workers at Equity Shoes.

But other suffragettes at Holloway were more distressed by their prison experience, such as Dora Thewlis, a sixteen-year-old mill worker. During her court hearing the magistrate had objected that 'you are only a child. You don't know what you're doing.' It was disgraceful that she had been 'enticed' from her home in Yorkshire and 'let loose in the streets of London'; he would contact her parents at once and in the meantime she was sent to Holloway on remand. But when Dora's mother Eliza wrote to her daughter in prison it was to say: 'Dear Child, I am very proud of the way you have acted, so keep your spirits up and be cheerful . . . do your duty by the WSPU.' Dora was held separately from the other suffragettes because of her age, and told a reporter from the *Evening News* that she felt isolated: 'I want to go back home. I have had enough of prison . . . everyone has forgotten me.' All her clothing had been removed, down to the locket around her neck which was pulled so hard the chain broke. She was put in prison clothes and given a number, even though she had yet to be convicted, and when she objected she was told, 'Perhaps you won't come here again if you wear those.' It was inconceivable that a member of the Pankhurst family would have been treated this way, and if she had then she would have immediately protested and complained.

When Dora appeared in court for the second time the press noted 'a sad change in her' and she agreed to go back to Huddersfield, accompanied by an elderly wardress from Holloway. The press accused the women's movement of exploiting the young mill worker and said her case should serve as a lesson to others; this was what happened when a young mind was filled 'with ridiculous ideas about the "emancipation of women"'. In an interview with a London reporter, Dora said the prison authorities had 'tried to break my spirit, and they succeeded. They held me up to ridicule as a "baby".' She was glad to be home again, 'from horrid London, and still more from Holloway Gaol'.

For other suffragettes, their time in prison only made them more militant. Edith Whitworth, imprisoned while Dora was on remand, said she was not sorry to have been jailed for the cause and was 'quite ready to do the same again'. Edith was the secretary of the Sheffield branch of the WSPU and when asked what she thought of prison life, she responded: 'If you are not a rebel before going into Holloway, there is no reason to wonder at your being one when you come out.'

Towards the end of 1907, seventy members of the WSPU left to form the Women's Freedom League (WFL), including Teresa Billington. This followed objections over the running of the WSPU, accusations of a lack of consultation, and concerns that the organization was dominated by a small group of wealthy women. When Emmeline Pankhurst challenged those who wouldn't accept her leadership to resign, they did. The WFL believed in non-violent methods of protest, but its members were soon locked up in Holloway too. The league designed a banner representing the prison, with the quotation: 'Stone walls do not a prison make'.

And so the protests continued. In January the following year Flora Drummond was sent to Holloway for three weeks after leading a group into Downing Street and then chaining herself to the railings. The following month over fifty suffragettes were arrested while taking a petition to Parliament. On release they were welcomed with a hired band ('mere men' reported the press), and the women were 'hugged and kissed for some minutes'. Vera Wentworth, a trade unionist from the East End who was jailed in March 1908, was given an extra day for writing 'Votes for Women' on her cell wall. 'It was worth the punishment,' she 'gleefully' told a journalist. 'I cut the letters deep into the wall that they will not be able to get them out, unless they pull the wall down.' As the demonstrations increased in size, so did the number of suffragettes inside Holloway and the authorities were feeling the strain, from the governor down to the wardresses.

On 21 June the WSPU held a demonstration in Hyde Park with

seven processions, twenty platforms and eighty speakers – many of whom had been in Holloway. When Prime Minister Herbert Asquith ignored the suffragettes' demands, stones were thrown at Number 10 Downing Street, in one of the first examples of violence against property. If obstructing traffic with banners, interrupting public meetings or insulting policemen didn't work, then perhaps it was time for criminal damage.

In October that year Christabel Pankhurst organized a rush on the House of Commons. She was imprisoned along with her mother, and the suffragettes were now dubbed 'the Hollowayettes'. On arrival Emmeline demanded that the governor be sent for and told him 'that the Suffragettes had resolved that they would no longer submit to being treated as ordinary law-breakers'. They would refuse to be searched, which the governor agreed to, but when she claimed the right to speak to her friends, the Home Secretary refused. Of all the hardships inside Holloway, Emmeline found 'the ceaseless silence of our lives was worst'. After two weeks she decided she would no longer endure it, and began talking to her daughter Christabel in the exercise yard. She was seized by a group of wardresses, declared a dangerous criminal, and put in solitary confinement for two weeks. On release she told the WSPU that 'henceforth we should all insist on refusing to abide by ordinary prison rules.' It was a matter of principle; the suffragettes wanted the treatment given to 'men political offenders in all civilized countries' and would never again submit to being classed with ordinary criminals, not because they didn't identify with the other inmates at Holloway, but to make a political point.

However, not all the suffragettes were given the same treatment, as Constance Lytton, the daughter of a viceroy and sister to a member of the House of Lords, discovered when she was jailed at Holloway in early 1909. As a member of the WSPU, she had heard plenty about the prison and was eager to experience it herself, whether the 'bath of evil fame' on reception, or the clothing marked with broad arrows which 'for propaganda purposes' was 'an absolutely priceless garment and I determined that, if possible, it should accompany me out of prison'.

Her description of life inside, as recounted in her book *Prisons and Prisoners*, begins as if she were on a research trip and like some of her colleagues the idea of scrubbing a floor or making a bed was a novelty. But while Constance was nicknamed 'your ladyship' her one desire was to be treated the same as everyone else, for she believed the 'weakest link in the chain of womanhood is the woman of the leisured class'. She did, however, ask to be allowed flannel underclothing and vegetarian food.

Constance was given special letter and visiting privileges not afforded to the other suffragettes, and soon realized that her ex-perience of prison life was different to those 'without influential friends'. When the matron handed her a letter, Constance asked, 'Is it not against prison rules that I should have the letter?' and the matron replied, 'We make the rules as the occasion calls for.' Constance refused to take the letter, though she did see her sister, and was then indignant when she realized no ordinary prisoner would get such a visit.

Like Alice Hawkins, she was intrigued by women in the third division, wondering what crimes they had committed: 'Why are they there? What has driven these poor wrecks into this harbour?' One was a servant 'seduced by her master' who killed her baby; another had been sentenced to three years for stealing her mother's skirt; while a third was on remand for attempted suicide. But some suffragettes showed less solidarity: Mary Nesbitt asked to be moved out of her cell because its former occupant had left a message on the wall: 'Thank God I am going out in two days – had a month for soliciting in Hyde Park.' The authorities agreed Mary couldn't be expected to sleep where a prostitute had slept, and she was moved. It would seem that some suffragettes were not petitioning for first-class status purely as a political statement, but as a way to distance themselves from the majority of women who had been imprisoned for drunkenness, vagrancy and prosti-tution.

Constance Lytton was put in a hospital ward because of a heart condition, along with Emmeline Pethick-Lawrence, the treasurer of the WSPU. The authorities feared that Emmeline had too much control over the other suffragettes and that this 'would far outweigh the authority of prison rules and rulers should she choose to exert it'. Emmeline would later say that 'as a graduating university for Suffragists Holloway Prison was the best thing in the world' and advised 'those who had not been to go and get their degrees'.

Constance Lytton was surprised by the attitude of some of the staff in Holloway. On one occasion when she broke down and sobbed, instead of the wardress scolding her, Constance was given sympathy: 'On looking up at her face I saw that the customary mask-like expression had vanished. She was kind, she inquired tenderly why I was crying, sat down on my bed and held my hands.' Constance then rubbed the wardress's chest to ease her hacking cough, although both were afraid that as a result of this gesture she would lose her job. But when Constance urged her jailer to 'come down to us in the country', she couldn't understand why her offer wasn't taken up.

This caring relationship between prisoner and jailer was radically different from the public view of prison wardresses. The press preferred to portray them in opposition to the suffragettes, for if prison officers shared the same views as their militant sisters then who was going to punish them? A prison full of inmates and wardresses who wanted the vote was a frightening prospect. One commercially produced board game directly pitted the two together. The 'Suffragettes in and out of prison game and puzzle', with the exhortation to 'Find the way out of Gaol', was produced by a private company and sold for a penny. It was designed like a bull's-eye with Holloway Gaol in the middle and was played along the lines of Snakes and Ladders, with card discs in the centre representing suffragettes. If a disc landed on a square marked 'wardress', then it was straight back to prison.

Governor Richard Quinton also portrayed the female warders as having nothing in common with the suffragettes, being 'somewhat lukewarm in the matter of the vote', an idea that was eagerly promoted by the press. 'The other day some suffragists boasted that all the wardresses at Holloway Prison desired the vote,' reported one paper in April 1909. 'Out of curiosity, a responsible person was sent from the Anti-Suffrage League' – formed the year before to oppose the vote and which now had eighty-two countrywide branches – 'to make inquiry at Holloway, and out of 72 wardresses there 68 signed the League's petition.' But other suffragettes also found support from staff at Holloway and Kathleen Emerson described the matron as 'one we'll ne'er forget, / She says she's not – and yet and yet/ We feel she *is* a Suffragette.'

In Constance Lytton's continuing efforts to be treated like her colleagues she began to strike, refusing to eat 'all diet extras', sleeping on a mattress on the floor to prove she could withstand the hardships of a plank bed, and then deciding to carve 'Votes for Women' on her chest. Her plan was to scratch the words with a needle, 'beginning over the heart and ending it on my face', so that on the day of release 'the last letter and a full stop would come upon my cheek, and be still quite fresh and visible.' But her sewing needle wouldn't do the job, and nor would the needle she used for darning her stockings, so she was delighted to find a hairpin in the exercise yard, which she cleaned with a stone under her cloak. 'The next morning before breakfast I set to work in real earnest and, using each of these implements in turn, I succeeded in producing a very fine V just over my heart. This was the work of fully twenty minutes, and in my zeal I made a deeper impression than I had intended.' Not wanting 'a blood-poisoning sequel' she asked a wardress for lint and plaster and when this was applied, it 'gave the scratch a quite imposing look, as if half my chest had been hacked open'.

Constance was summoned to see the governor, but given a scolding rather than punished, and then the senior medical officer played a trump card: if she carried on like this they would dismiss her from the prison altogether. Finally she was moved to an ordinary cell, although she was not allowed to scrub the floor or do any of the routine labour, and was taken to DX wing and put in cell number 10 on the third floor. From here Constance managed to pass messages to two other suffragettes, who had been 'active in maintaining the rights and decencies won by their predecessors' which 'affected the welfare of all prisoners besides ourselves'. Apart from the prior relaxation of the silence rule, these included drinking out of an earthenware mug instead of tin, permission to empty slops more frequently, a better standard of food, and the right to appeal directly to the governor. Until that point applications to see the governor had been 'frequently not delivered', especially if it was a complaint about an officer.

But again it's unclear to what extent these changes were granted to all of Holloway's prisoners. While the suffragettes succeeded in altering the lavatory doors, for example, this appeared to apply only to them. The 'cowsheds' had a foot space below the door and no lock or bolt, which was justified on the grounds of cleanliness and because of 'the tendency amongst prisoners to commit suicide'. But, wrote Constance, 'obviously neither of these precautions were necessary in the case of Suffragettes' and so they asked that when there were more than sixteen of them, one toilet would be set apart for their use, with a bolt and a curtain.

Overall Constance found the prison system petty and cruel. The fact that cells were provided with an instructive book on domestic hygiene, *A Perfect Home and How to Keep It*, struck her as a 'rather ludicrous form of sarcasm'. But it was an exercise area in the inner yard that symbolized all that was wrong with Holloway: 'The prison from here looks like a great hive of human creeping things impelled to their joyless labours and unwilling seclusion by some hidden force . . . The high central tower seemed to me a jam pot, indicative of the foul preserve that seethed within this factory for potting human souls.'

In July 1909 the suffragettes in Holloway started to carry out their threat to resist prison discipline unless they were moved to the first division. First they had refused to wear prison clothes or to work, and now they stopped eating.

6

Forcible Feeding

Marion Wallace-Dunlop, an artist from Inverness and a member of the WSPU, was the first suffragette to go on hunger strike. She had been sentenced to a month at Holloway for stencilling a phrase from the Bill of Rights on the walls of the House of Commons: 'It is the right of the subjects to petition the King, and all commitments and prosecutions for such petitionings are illegal.'

She took the decision to go on hunger strike alone, having written to Holloway's governor to explain that 'a person imprisoned for a political offence should have first-division treatment; and as a matter of principle, not only for my own sake but for the sake of others who may come after me, I am now refusing all food until this matter is settled to my satisfaction.'

On 5 July 1909 she began a fast that lasted nearly four days. The ordinary prison diet was replaced by the 'most tempting food', which was kept in her cell day and night, while the doctor, governor and wardresses attempted to alternately coax and threaten her. But Marion would not 'surrender', the doctor reported she might die at any time, and she was released on the grounds of ill health. Others immediately followed suit, and on the day Marion left Holloway fourteen women convicted of window breaking held a discussion in the prison van and 'agreed to follow her example'. The hunger strike, an act of extreme self-sacrifice, now became a central part of the suffragettes' political protest. The newly sentenced women refused to wear prison clothes or to be medically examined. They broke prison windows after their appeals for fresh air had been repeatedly ignored, and 'declined to express regret', and all refused to take food for 'several days'. Six were then discharged on medical grounds. The Home Secretary refuted reports that they were being 'held underground' and noted that the only difference between their cells and ordinary cells was that their windows were unbreakable – which resulted in laughter in the House of Commons. Two were also found 'guilty of kicking and biting female warders', an allegation that they vigorously denied, and their sentences were extended. The prison officials were 'panic stricken' by the hunger strikers, according to Emmeline Pankhurst, and Holloway became a den of 'violence and brutality' where one suffragette, Lucy Burns, described being dragged along the ground by her hair before having her clothes ripped from her back.

But the hunger strikers presented a new dilemma for the government, which didn't want a suffragette to die in prison and become an overnight martyr. Women could either be allowed to starve to death, or they could be released early, as had happened several times before. Three months later, however, it was decided the best response was to introduce a policy of forcible feeding, and so began a form of torture that would last nearly five years. The method involved the use of stomach pumps, as well as feeding tubes which had traditionally been used on asylum patients. This was described as safe and humane, and the official term was 'artificial feeding' or 'hospital treatment'.

One of the first suffragettes to endure forcible feeding was Mary Leigh, a teacher from Manchester. She was drum major of the WSPU drum and fife band, and in the summer of 1908 she and Edith New had become the first suffragette window smashers, having broken windows at 10 Downing Street. In September 1909 Mary was arrested in Birmingham, along with three others, after holding a rooftop protest at Bingley Hall where Herbert Asquith was addressing a meeting. The women were held in Winson Green Prison, they all went on hunger strike and after four days were forcibly fed. When Mary's description was published in the press, it caused outrage. It was not just the physical pain of having a tube forced down the mouth or through the nose, but the deliberate degradation involved, as a woman was held down by wardresses while a man violently inserted food into her body. One imprisoned suffragette heard the doctor exclaim, 'This is like stuffing a turkey for Christmas.'

While the policy came from government, it was the prison medical officers who were required to carry it out and it was they who decided if a prisoner was fit enough to be forcibly fed in the first place. If a hunger striker died, it was the prison doctor who would be held responsible. But forcible feeding, wrote physician Frank Moxon, was 'a prostitution of the profession' and couldn't be excused on the grounds that it was saving life.

Then in 1910 there was a change in treatment when the suffragettes became, in theory, first-division prisoners under Rule 243A. This gave 'certain classes of prisoners, such as Passive Resisters and Suffragettes . . . a special prison treatment', explained Holloway's former governor Richard Quinton. They could supply their own food, wear their own clothes, exercise and talk together, and enjoy 'various privileges which are at present attached to the First Division'. And now there was, at last, a definition of a political prisoner. The Home Secretary Winston Churchill explained this was 'a person who has committed an offence, involving no moral turpitude, with a distinct political object'. The aim of prison therefore was purely to restrain liberty, without conditions 'calculated to degrade or humiliate'. Prisoners could lose privileges granted under Rule 243A, but forcible feeding temporarily stopped.

'One wishes these very willing martyrs to be treated without any harshness or severity,' wrote Richard Quinton, but he hoped the courts would decide who went into this new class, rather than prison officials, or it would be 'apt to give rise to suspicions of favoritism, or abuse, which it is very essential to avoid'.

But as had always been the case at Holloway, the first-division privileges could only be taken advantage of by those who could afford them, just as in Victorian times when the Duchess of Sutherland had been jailed for contempt of court. Only wealthier suffragettes could wear fur coats or kid gloves in the exercise yard or have friends send in food from outside, and not all suffragettes were being sentenced as first-class prisoners, as Constance Lytton discovered when in 1910 she travelled to Liverpool using the pseudonym Jane Warton and posing as a working-class London seamstress. She was arrested during a protest against forcible feeding outside Walton Prison, and this time sentenced to two weeks' hard labour as a third-division prisoner. She was forcibly fed eight times and her 'serious heart disease' that had been identified at Holloway was not examined until the third time. The prison doctor inserted a four-foot-long tube into her mouth and poured in the food, then he gave her a slap on the cheek on his way out 'to express his contemptuous disapproval'. Constance now knew only too well how non-aristocratic suffragettes were treated inside prison.

That year she had a heart attack, and became partly paralysed after a series of strokes, but in November 1911 she was back in Holloway again, after smashing a Post Office window. Unlike her previous sentence, however, 'all was civility, it was unrecognisable from the first time I had been there.' Medical officer Dr James Scott had now been appointed governor and Constance found him 'amiability itself'. Exercise time was 'a changed world. All of us assembled were walking about arm in arm, as we liked . . . all talking to one another, and all, of course, wearing our own clothes. One or two wardresses were there, but they were smiling all the time and chatted with us.'

By now Christabel Pankhurst had taken over leadership of the WSPU, and tactics had switched from passive resistance to militant action, which resulted in longer sentences, the loss of first-division privileges and often hard labour. On 1 March 1912, 148 suffragettes were arrested in London after a sustained window-smashing campaign. 'I dare say you are horrified at the wanton destruction of property, especially private,' wrote Constance Craig in a letter to a relative sent from Holloway Prison. She was on remand after breaking 'one or two' Post Office windows, because the destruction of property was the 'only thing that makes this government bestir itself . . . as long as we only hurt <u>ourselves</u> nothing will be done.'

The suffragettes' details were recorded in the prison's Nominal Register in red pen; page after page of women charged or convicted of malicious damage, breaking glass, damage to windows, insulting behaviour and throwing missiles. While some refused to give their trade and occupation, others were recorded as nurse, artist, clerk, teacher, student, singer, sculptor, typist, musician, journalist, poet and actress. The details of 'ordinary' prisoners meanwhile were recorded in black pen, sometimes interspersed among the suffragettes, whether a servant convicted of loitering or a laundry worker charged with stealing coal. As the days went by more suffragettes arrived at Holloway, until the Nominal Register became a who's who of the militant suffrage movement: Emmeline Pankhurst, Kitty Marion, Vera Wentworth, Ethel Smyth, Emmeline Pethick-Lawrence and Louisa Garrett Anderson. Betty Archdale, then four years old, remembered visiting her mother Helen at Holloway, having gathered the stones used to smash Whitehall windows. On release, Helen became the WSPU prisoners' secretary, finding accommodation for those from outside London, attending trials and providing food.

Another imprisoned suffragette was Myra Sadd Brown, and soon the issue of forcible feeding was in the news again. 'I was surprised to learn through the Press on Saturday last that my wife was forcibly fed by nasal tube,' her husband Ernest wrote to the governor. 'I ask for an explanation.' Myra had been sentenced to two months for window smashing and had been forcibly fed despite having a broken nose, but the Secretary of State explained the pain was her own fault for resisting. Myra asked her husband to let their children 'know a little where I am so that they can send their loving thoughts to me. They need not think because I am shut up I have done wrong.'

Some of the prisoners kept detailed accounts of being forcibly fed. 'Saturday: Put in remand Hosp. and fed after leaving Court. Nasal tube twice through throat,' wrote Elsie Duval in her 1913 prison diary written on sheets of brown toilet paper. 'Sunday: After big struggle fed me through throat – pain at heart after – Monday: Fed throat – smashed up cell and cut fingers – sent to convicted Hospital. Afternoon fed through nose. Felt very sick.' On Friday she was visited by the governor who 'commenced jabber about still refusing food and myself charged with smashing 16 panes of glass and crockery of cell and what had I to say to it'. A week later the nasal tube was used: 'Beastly wardress left in cell with me until quite late, and when I was sick told me I wasn't to and said I did it for purpose and told me to keep still on my back.'

Female prison officers were supposed to care for their charges, to form relationships and assert a moral influence, so what did the

Holloway wardresses think about being required to hold a woman down while she was forcibly fed? No prison officer had been told to do such a thing before, and while some argued they were following orders, others were clearly distressed. 'I know I must have looked as if I was being hurt,' wrote Laura Ainsworth, 'because of the wardresses' faces,' while Mary Leigh reported that three of the wardresses had 'burst into tears', as had the matron. But whatever their views or possible resistance, from now on prison officers at Holloway would be widely viewed as sadists.

The public was increasingly repulsed by the methods used on hunger-striking prisoners at Holloway, including May Billinghurst, who had been paralysed as a child and used a mobility tricycle, and who would later be released after ten days, 'a physical wreck'. 'Holloway and Hell are synonymous terms,' wrote Gertrude Ansell. 'What have we done to merit such treatment? Is it justice or is it vengeance?'

In February 1914 the Bishop of London would pay a 'surprise' visit under the urging of the WSPU. He found the suffragettes 'well and kindly and considerately treated' and declared that the only effects of forcible feeding were sickness and indigestion. The women in prison told another story and Mary Richardson, imprisoned for slashing the Rokeby Venus in the National Gallery, described wardresses kneeling on her ribs and the doctor removing the tube with two vigorous jerks that 'seem as if they were splitting the face in half'. Some suffragettes were also 'fed' through the vagina or rectum; Fanny Parker reported being assaulted in both ways while imprisoned in Perth.

But for many of the suffragettes who arrived in March 1912, a term in Holloway was still seen as a reason to rejoice. 'How triumphant Mrs Pankhurst must feel today that there are hundreds of us here,' wrote artist Katie Gliddon. 'It is so splendid to be living in the storm centre of the earth which is at present Holloway gaol.' No wonder that a few months later governor Dr James Scott retired on medical grounds. The press explained that 'owing to the suffragettes' behaviour in prison' which had 'caused him much worry' he 'has just had a physical breakdown'. Katie managed to be in frequent contact with the other suffragettes, exchanging shouted messages through the cell windows until the 'Governor yelled from garden to shut up'. The WSPU also kept in contact with those inside, setting up base at a house on Dalmeny Avenue, near enough to the prison that suffragettes could shout out messages from their broken cell windows, wave handkerchiefs and Votes for Women badges. Katie sent a postcard to her mother asking for an eiderdown, handkerchiefs and a copy of *Middlemarch*, with the comment: 'Fancy spending 2 months with 300 or 400 of the best women in the world.' But she was aware of the worry for those at home, reassuring her mother that she had 'resolved not to do the hunger strike even if all the others in Holloway do it'. There is little documentation as to whether suffragettes felt under pressure to go on hunger strike, although one woman feared that others would 'scorn' her if she 'chose' to be forcibly fed by a cup rather than a tube.

Like her colleagues, Katie Gliddon kept a prison diary, pencilling notes in the margins of *The Poetical Works of Percy Bysshe Shelley* and setting down her reasons for supporting the WSPU: 'I am a sane adult human being and therefore responsible to myself and to society for all my actions . . . So I broke a window – glass a thing of no real value in itself – to call attention to the evils which have always and which will always result from the subjection of women.' But while Katie – and many other suffragettes – took pains to assert their sanity, in the eyes of the government and the prison authorities there was only one useful explanation for a woman who committed criminal damage and then 'sought her own torture': she must be mad.

7

The Fight is Won

In the early hours of 8 February 1913 a night stoker at the Royal Botanic Gardens at Kew was carrying out his rounds when he came across several smashed windows at the Orchid House. The vandals had disappeared, leaving 'feminine fingerprints' and an envelope with the words 'Votes for Women'.

Kew's director, Sir David Prain, informed the police that 'the damage done is trifling compared with what it might have been' but he wanted the extent of the destruction to be 'carefully concealed from the public and especially from the newspapers lest its publications provoke another attempt'. He need not have worried; the press was happy to report widespread destruction at the famous royal gardens in south-west London. 'Mad women raid Kew Gardens!' ran one headline. Dozens of panes of glass had been broken, up to 100 orchid plants had been ripped from their pots, thrown on the floor and trampled underfoot, causing hundreds – even thousands – of pounds' worth of damage. Twelve days later, at 3.15 a.m., a flame of fire shot up from the centre of Kew's tea pavilion and police constable George Hill, then on duty a mile away in Richmond, rushed to the scene and arrested two women running from the direction of the gardens. He found a lump of tow smelling of tar and oil inside their bags, as well as a saw, a hammer and some paper smelling of paraffin, while around the fence of the gardens were the 'marks of small feet, I should say ladies' footprints'.

The ladies in question were two suffragettes, twenty-three-year-old Olive Wharry and twenty-two-year-old Lilian Lenton, who were arrested for maliciously setting fire to the tea pavilion. 'We understand the charge,' said Olive, 'what happens next?' When they appeared at Richmond police court, both refused to give an address. They asked for bail, warning that if they were sent to prison they would be obliged to go on hunger strike. The court chairman said he was not 'going to be frightened by an intimidation', at which Olive swept up a handful of papers and a book and hurled them across the room. The book just missed the chairman's head and as Olive lunged for more missiles the police grabbed her and removed her from court. The two women were sent to Holloway Prison on remand.

By now Holloway's medical officer was filing daily reports on the suffragettes, noting if they were eating and what the effect of forcible feeding might be. On the day Lilian Lenton arrived, he couldn't say if she was 'taking food voluntarily . . . as she has only just come in'. However, her general conduct was 'bad, very defiant'. Another report, made by phone the next day, explained that Lilian had smashed up everything in her cell and had been removed to 'a special strong cell'. She was being kept apart from all other prisoners, not allowed to communicate, and all privileges had been suspended. The report for Olive Wharry was identical, except her conduct was 'bad, destructive & insolent'.

A few days later Lilian was released and the Home Office wrote to the authorities at Richmond to explain: 'On her reception in H.M. Prison, Holloway, this woman refused to take food and by Sunday morning her condition was such that it became necessary to administer food artificially.' Her condition then became 'so serious that in the opinion of the experienced Medical Officer of the Prison her life would have been in immediate danger if forcible feeding had been continued or if she had been allowed to remain longer without food.' What had actually happened was that on the first attempt to forcibly feed Lilian, she had been tied to a chair by half a dozen wardresses and the two doctors had accidentally pushed the feeding tube into her windpipe. 'Food' was then poured into her left lung, and she collapsed. Olive had also been on hunger strike, but it had been possible 'to feed her artificially without injury to her health'.

Lilian went into hiding after her release and on 4 March Olive appeared alone at the Old Bailey, charged with 'feloniously setting fire to a certain building belonging to His Majesty the King'. But what the suffragettes apparently hadn't realized was that although the gardens in Kew were royal property, the refreshment pavilion had been leased to 'Mrs Strange and another lady' and its contents were worth up to £1,000.

Olive was found guilty, but told the judge, 'It is no use imposing any fine upon me because I shall not pay it.' She then made a lengthy statement, some of which was recorded by the court, saying she was sorry that Mrs Strange and her partner had 'sustained loss, as she had no grudge against them'. But she wanted to 'make the two ladies understand that they were at war, and in war even non-combatants had to suffer'. Olive insisted that morally she was not guilty, and would 'not submit to punishment' but would go on hunger strike. She was sentenced to eighteen months in the second division.

Olive Wharry was a London-born art student, while Lilian Lenton was a dancer from Leicester. Both were members of the WSPU, and this was not the first time they had been to prison. The Old Bailey recorded two previous convictions for Olive, although her conduct in Holloway had then been described as 'good'. That year had already been a dramatic one for the suffrage cause: arson attacks had been stepped up in January and now the suffragettes were targeting not just public buildings but golf courses, cricket pavilions and racecourses. In February Leonora Cohen, a suffragette from Leeds, had gone to the Tower of London – 'I thought, that's the place. They've never had a woman there before causing trouble' – taken an iron bar from under her coat and smashed a cabinet in the Jewel House. Royal palaces were now closed to the public and on the day that Olive and Lilian appeared at Richmond police court, suffragettes in Edinburgh had set fire to twenty pillar boxes.

A full three weeks into her sentence and Holloway's medical officer still wasn't sure if Olive was eating: 'She may be taking a little, but how much is impossible to say.' Her general conduct was now 'indifferent'. She had been weighed that morning and was ninety-seven pounds, but it was then discovered she had a full hot-water bottle under her clothes, so her actual weight was four-teen pounds less than it had been on arrival. 'She is decidedly thin,' noted the medical officer, '& probably a little weaker.'

Another report was made the same day, by Maurice Craig MD, Physician for Psychological Medicine at Guy's Hospital in London, whose speciality was mental health. He explained that although Olive had given her word that she would not go on hunger strike if she were 'allowed to remain in a certain part of the prison, there is little doubt that she is surreptitiously getting rid of her food'. But he did not regard her 'to be a good subject, at the moment, for feeding'. She refused to let the doctor examine her, or to be weighed and 'she would not even let me feel her pulse'. But it was clear that Olive had seriously 'reduced her bodily health': her hands were cold and very blue, her pupils widely dilated. On 8 April the Kew 'incendiary' was released, having been on hunger strike for four weeks and four days, ever since arriving at Holloway.

Lilian was re-arrested for the Kew arson attack in October and the magistrate decided she should be examined to 'ascertain if she was really and truly responsible for her actions'. She was sent to Holloway, where she went on both hunger and thirst strike and was forcibly fed. On release, she failed to appear at her trial and went on the run once more. She was jailed in Leeds the following year, for another arson attack.

By now the government had introduced a new way of dealing with hunger-striking suffragettes. The Prisoners (Temporary Discharge for Ill-Health) Act, which the suffragettes renamed the Cat and Mouse Act, meant that those who were ill from hunger striking and/or forcible feeding could be released, then re-arrested once they were deemed to have recovered. But to the humiliation of the government, many went underground and evaded re-arrest, while others committed criminal damage while out on licence.

In the summer of 1914 two suffragettes were arrested for breaking windows at Criccieth in Wales during a Liberal Party meeting. When the case came to trial, Phyllis North was carried into court with her boots removed so she couldn't kick anyone, where she denounced the proceedings as a farce: 'You ought to have women on your juries. I see one of the torturers on the jury, the prison doctor.' Phyllis turned out to be none other than Olive Wharry. She was sentenced to three months' hard labour and on 6 July was transferred from Carnarvon Prison back to Holloway.

Two days later Francis E. Forward, Holloway's deputy medical officer, wrote to the prison commissioners: 'It is apparent she has altered considerably and deteriorated both in mind and body.' She was very thin, 'one may almost say emaciated', and he wanted this noted 'in case it might be attributed later to malnutrition due to artificial feeding'. But the medical officer wasn't sure if the wasting was due to disease, the result of previous hunger striking, or whether 'previous to her incarceration she had purposely reduced her weight with a view to embarrassing the Prison authorities'.

Olive's mental state had also become 'more unsatisfactory'. Although her conduct during her prison term in 1911 had been good, the medical officer now asserted: 'It was always realised from the first time she came to Prison, that she was mentally unstable and showed evidence of mental disability partaking more of the moral than the intellectual type of disorder.' She might have declared herself 'morally innocent' at the Old Bailey trial, but Dr Forward concluded that it was her lack of morals that had driven her mad. 'Her irrational views on social things in general – her lack of moral fibre, diminished will power combined with obstinacy and her habits of cunning and deceit, all point to the fact that she cannot be credited with a full measure of responsibility for her actions.' She was 'fast approaching the border line of insanity', although Dr Forward wasn't certain if it would be possible or desirable to certify her.

Olive wasn't the only suffragette suspected of being insane. Annie Bell, a Braille worker, had been arrested the year before while carrying a loaded five-chamber revolver during 'picket duty' outside Holloway Prison. The court was informed that she had threatened the crowd by announcing: 'If any man interferes with me I have a revolver in my pocket and will shoot him.' Annie was remanded for a medical report because the magistrate suspected 'there was a certain amount of craziness about the thing'. She was presumably found sane as she was then fined £5 or twenty-one days in the second division. The magistrate also gave her some advice: 'Keep the needle, and drop revolvers.'

Olive Wharry was released from Holloway Prison along with three other suffragettes, all on the grounds of serious ill health. She had again been secretly hunger striking, this time for thirty-one days. There was now 'a more or less general' hunger strike going on at Holloway, reported the WSPU, and 'indignation and passionate protest are the order of the day inside prison as well as out.' Emmeline Pankhurst described 'sickening scenes of violence . . . as the doctors went from cell to cell performing their hideous office'. According to Dr Forward, Olive Wharry was at breaking point, she had been mentally unstable for years and now her judgement was truly warped. Yet at the same time that Holloway's medical officer was on the verge of getting her certified, Olive was busy keeping a scrapbook that recorded her time in prison in lucid detail.

In the manuscripts reading room on the third floor of the British Library I'm waiting to be handed a small grey box. Olive's scrapbook was presented to the library in 1958, and while it's usually on display behind glass in the Treasures Gallery I've been allowed to take a look.

I open up the box's flaps to find a beautifully covered book, just a bit bigger than my A5 notepad. On the front is a drawing of a prison cell, above which is a sticker 'Votes for Women' and on either side a hand-drawn scroll that begins with the words, 'Holloway 1911 & 1912. 2 months'. This scroll includes Olive's other prison sentences, in Aberdeen and Birmingham in 1912 and Holloway again in 1913.

I stare at the cover, thinking of the love and care that went into this, the way it's bordered with two meticulously coloured lines, one purple and one green, set against a white background, the campaign colours of the WSPU. Inside the scrapbook is a list of twenty-one suffragettes held in 'the castle of grim Holloway' in December 1911. Each woman has written down her sentence and crime, starting with Vera Wentworth, who carved 'Votes for Women' on her cell wall, and ending with Emily Wilding Davison, who 'came in December 14. Setting fire to post offices on remand. Deeds not words.'

Emily Wilding Davison would become one of the country's most famous suffragettes. She had first been arrested in 1909, when she fasted for five days and carved 'Rebellion against tyrants is obedience to God' on her cell wall. In 1912 she was back in Holloway and forcibly fed, an event that would 'haunt me with its horror all my life'. In protest she barricaded herself into her cell, until officers hosed water into the room and she was carried off to be forcibly fed again. Emily returned to Holloway once more, sentenced to six months for arson, and was forcibly fed even though she was not on hunger strike. At one point she broke out of her cell and threw herself down the stairs. She landed on the wire netting, then threw herself twice more, ending up on the iron staircase with severe injuries. Her aim, she later said, was to distract attention from her colleagues being forcibly fed, as 'one big tragedy may save others'. She died in June 1913, trampled by one of the King's horses while protesting at the Epsom Derby, and her funeral attracted tens of thousands of people.

Aside from the roll-call of suffragettes, Olive Wharry's scrapbook contains sketches, poetry, newspaper clippings, memorabilia, political cartoons, photographs and an appeal for prison limericks:

> Oh convicts dear!
> I really fear
> In lines so few
> I cannot do
> You justice true!
> Say now, can you?

Some write about 'the footer' played in the 'muddy yard, where green and purple fought so hard'; another declares, 'for tho in prison we must rot because of our convictions / We simply do not care a jot for Government restrictions.' The limericks are rousing, a case of keeping the spirits up and anticipating the day of release: 'No more bells in the middle of the night, applications and "are you all right?"' There are poems that mock prison food: 'when is a cheese not a cheese? when it's a poison'; one is dedicated 'to my plank'; and another is called simply 'Prison', written on a Sunday afternoon:

> Tramp, tramp of prison feet
> Ring, rang of bells
> Clash, smash of prison glass
> Suffragettes in cells

Olive includes a pencil drawing of her cell, 'No 19 O. Wharry', with her mattress rolled on the plank bed, metal buckets on the floor, and a dozen hefty books just about balancing on a corner shelf. She also added adverts and jokes from the *Hammerer's*, a magazine produced by suffragettes in Winson Green, with a cover showing a line of women entering a castle-like prison, with two hammers in the foreground.

Holloway's staff make several appearances in the scrapbook. One officer named Fatima, a wardress said to be eighteen stone, is cruelly mocked: 'There once was a wardress named "Fatty" / Who made all the suffragettes ratty.' She was known to stand at one end of the exercise yard to make sure prisoners were walking in single file, telling them off if they tried to speak to each other with 'Keep back there, 19. No disorder.' But Olive has added a note, 'with apologies as she was afterwards very kind to us', while another drawing shows an officer, a Miss Finan, bringing hot whisky and water on a tray to the suffragettes.

Overall the tone of the scrapbook is satirical, poking fun at the world of prison. An 'illustration of Eve bathing', shows a woman in a tin tub, water shooting everywhere, with the caption 'Or how to empty your bath and clean your cell in 2 seconds'. Olive also offers 'cell songs for sleepy suffragettes':

> Hush-a-by Asquith, at the tree top
> When the suffragette comes, the party will rock
> When the suffragette strikes, the Government will fall
> Down will come Asquith, parliament and all

But there are also poems of 'prison pain', references to distant screams and infants' wails during the 'weary dreary silent days' of 'far famed Holloway'. When it comes to her conviction for arson, Olive provides only a matter-of-fact few lines on her sentence, the number of days she was on hunger strike, her usual weight (seven stone eleven) and her weight on release (five stone nine). Then she includes a newspaper photograph of a 'policeman with our hand bags', and dedicates a full page to the damage done at Kew, under which she's written two triumphant words: 'Before & after!' Olive Wharry's scrapbook rejoices in the suffragettes' defiance of prison rules and the destruction of property, whether cell windows or the arson at Kew, but this hardly makes her insane. Instead, with insight and humour, she records the experiences and views of her comrades. There is little evidence of a woman who was mentally unstable, lacking moral fibre or willpower; rather the medical officer's diagnosis was simply a way to pathologize the actions of a rebellious suffragette.

Olive was released from Holloway under a temporary discharge for ill health notice, which she immediately stuck into her scrapbook. But she records nothing of the years that followed, no mention of her life or the war. Then, as I turn the pages, I come to a hand-drawn box explaining that in 1918 the vote was given to women householders and wives of householders over thirty, and in 1928 it was finally given on the same terms as men. How long it was coming, she must have thought, fourteen years since her last time in Holloway Prison. Was she waiting all those years so she could finish her scrapbook, so she could write 'The End' as a banner linking the Union Jack and the flag of the WSPU?

Olive Wharry did her best to document the struggle; she would have been happy to know her scrapbook is safely here in the British Library. She died twenty years after women got the vote, in January 1948, and perhaps as a result of all her time inside, she asked that her ashes be scattered 'on the high open spaces of the moor between Exeter and Whitstone'.

Holloway's medical officer Dr Forward was a hated figure among the suffragettes and became a target for their justifiable fury. In July 1913 a 'suffragist party' of around 300 women and men, carrying sticks and stones, marched from the East End to Holloway where Mary Richardson threw missiles at his quarters. A couple of months later, as Dr Forward was leaving his home one Saturday morning, a suffragette rushed up, took him by the collar, slashed him with a sjambok and 'belaboured the doctor unmercifully', while two others 'barred his progress'. Dr Forward protested, 'You know perfectly well I cannot help forcible feeding,' but the women told him he ought to resign. A plain-clothes officer who appeared to be acting as Dr Forward's bodyguard failed to intervene, and the suffragettes escaped before they were arrested. Three women were eventually charged with assault, refused to give their names, struggled in the dock, and called the doctor 'beast, torturer, devil, and similar names'. They then refused to be bound over, to which the magistrate replied, 'You are bound over whether you like it or not, now run away like good girls.'

A few weeks later the medical officer was attacked again. This time two suffragettes thrashed him with horse whips outside Holloway Prison. On arrest they made 'a rambling and rather incoherent statement . . . that this beast is responsible for the torture'. The doctor refused to charge his assailants, a gesture the press regarded as generous, but they were taken into custody for disorderly conduct.

The suffragettes also attacked the prison building itself, when on the night of 18 December 1913 two bombs were set off from a garden on Dalmeny Avenue. While it caused a 'great sensation' in London, the attack has rarely been written about since then. Instead the enduring image of suffragettes in Holloway – and the image I grew up with as a child – is of near prostrate women being forcibly fed, not of sjambok-wielding, bomb-making militants, which would have been far more inspiring to my teenage mind.

The summer after the bomb attack, seven years of incarcerating suffragettes at Holloway Prison came to an end when on 4 August 1914 Great Britain declared war on Germany. Six days later the government ordered the release of all those serving prison sentences for suffrage agitation and Emmeline Pankhurst announced that the militant campaign was over. The ex-Holloway prisoners then went on with their lives. Some joined the war effort; others emigrated to Australia or the United States. Many wrote books, some were eventually awarded honours. Their political careers were varied, whether standing for election to Parliament, becoming a trade union organizer, emigrating to Russia and joining the Communist Party, or signing up with the British Union of Fascists. But many suffered permanent health problems as a result of their time inside, leading to premature deaths sometimes described as due to 'exhaustion'. In 1926 the Suffragette Fellowship was formed, to keep alive the suffragette spirit and to acknowledge 'the defining act of imprisonment'.

The links between the fight for suffrage and Holloway Prison were not over with the release of the suffragettes. In 1918 Irish nationalist Constance Gore-Booth became the first woman to be elected MP, from her north London prison cell.

Constance, also known as Countess Markievicz, was the daughter of a wealthy Irish landowner, and a member of Sinn Féin and Inghinidhe na hÉireann, the Daughters of Ireland, a radical Irish nationalist women's organization founded by Maud Gonne. During the Easter Rising of 1916, a rebellion against British rule, Constance was second-in-command of the Irish Citizen Army at St Stephen's Green in Dublin. Her garrison held out for six days, but when the Irish republicans surrendered she was put in solitary confinement in Kilmainham Prison. The male leaders of the uprising were executed, while Constance was sentenced to hard labour in Aylesbury. She was released under an amnesty and returned to a mass welcome in Dublin, but less than a year later an alleged 'Hun plot' in Ireland sparked the sudden arrest of around 100 Sinn Féin leaders and she was imprisoned in Holloway, along with Maud Gonne and activist and actress Kathleen Clarke.

'Our arrests carry so much further than speeches,' Constance wrote to her sister Eva Gore-Booth. She promised to use 'this jail as a rest-cure!', explaining she had put on one pound 'and am *not* going to hunger-strike, but get fit and strong'. She also used her time inside to paint dozens of watercolours, building on her experience as a landscape artist. But her companion Kathleen Clarke was 'in a fair way to break down', desperate for news of her children and unable to eat or sleep.

Constance's main adversary was the 'wretched censor', and letters to her sister were 'kidnapped en route'; one was stopped because it was deemed political when she was only allowed to write about domestic and business affairs. But she tried to stay 'chirpy': 'For a jail-bird I'm not so badly off! Health splendid.'

In February 1918 the Representation of the People Act was passed, enabling women over thirty to vote if they met certain qualifications such as owning property, and nine months later women over the age of twenty-one could stand for election to government. 'By the way, shall you stand for Parliament?' Constance wrote to her sister: 'One does not have to go to Parliament if one wins, but oh! To have to sit there and listen to all that blither.' She was elected Sinn Féin MP for Dublin St Patrick's from her cell in Holloway Prison, but refused to take her seat in Parliament: 'I would never take an oath of allegiance to the power I meant to overthrow.' Even if she had, she would have been barred on the grounds of her previous conviction for treason.

After Constance was released from Holloway she took her seat as a member of the Dáil Éireann, Irish nationalists who had been elected to the House of Commons but chose to sit in Dublin as a self-proclaimed Irish parliament, and in 1919 she became one of the first women cabinet ministers in Europe. Kathleen Clarke was later appointed the first female Lord Mayor of Dublin.

Some of the suffrage fighters have since been immortalized in books, film and TV; others have disappeared from public view. The personal pressures of imprisonment made the lives of those like young Dora Thewlis, the mill worker from Huddersfield, almost unbearable once they returned to their own communities. They were, writes Jill Liddington, 'pushed to the margins, even in local histories'. And when this happened, it was often up to modern-day relatives to rediscover them.

'Holloway Prison had a very big impact on my great-grand-mother,' says Peter Barratt, the great-grandson of Alice Hawkins, the shoe machinist from Leicester who travelled to London in 1907 and was jailed for disorderly conduct. 'Those two weeks at Holloway, and whoever she was with then, formed Alice's views on becoming a suffragette. It was not exactly radicalization, but it was the tipping point.' The year after her first jail sentence Alice Hawkins was a keynote speaker during a mass rally in Hyde Park, attended by over 250,000 people, and she then helped to form the Women's Independent Boot and Shoe Trade Union. She was sent to Holloway again, for breaking windows at the Home Office, and in 1913 joined a suffragette delegation that met Lloyd George at the Treasury. Alice continued to support the local trade union and labour movement up to her death in 1946, at the age of eighty-three.

'Our family is very lucky,' says Peter Barratt, as we sit in his kitchen in Northamptonshire, rain hammering down on the conservatory windows while he makes tea and pauses to take a phone call from BBC Radio. 'We have perhaps one of the most complete collections in the UK today of suffragette memorabilia. It was luck that everything survived, they were just kept in an old box and Mum would let local kids play with the suffragette sash.'

He first heard about his great-grandmother when he was around seven years old: 'My grandfather Alfred would tell me escapades about his mother and her fight for the vote. To be honest I wish I remembered more. But he told me how she was such a strong, determined woman.' What did Peter think about the fact his great-grandmother was sent to prison? 'To be honest, I was more interested in playing football. In the early 1960s there were still a few suffragettes around, it didn't have the same attraction as now. But my grandmother told me that when Alice first went to London she knew there was a fair chance she'd be arrested so she'd get the kitchen sorted and bake bread, and one of her daughters was told to be mum.' Alice's relationship with the Pankhursts didn't go unnoticed in the area, and when they sent the family chauffeur to fetch her, 'All the children came out and it was quite a spectacle. It's interesting that as a shoe machinist from Leicester, she came into contact with the leading political figures of the day.' Peter shows me Alice's scrapbook: newspaper clippings and postcards, all carefully preserved. One was sent from a fellow suffragette at Christmas: 'Dear Mrs Hawkins I hope you are quite well after your Holiday at Holloway Castle.'

While Peter never met Alice, she lived with his grandfather and mother for ten years after her husband died. 'She was not an easy woman to live with' – he laughs – 'she never backed down in a family argument.' His second cousin inherited Alice's suffragette sash and hunger strike medal, awarded in 1909 while in Leicester Prison. 'For a woman of her age a hunger strike was quite an extreme thing to do,' says Peter, 'but I don't think she was ever force-fed.' He also has a replica Holloway Prison badge, made by the original manufacturers Toye & Co., which he keeps in a little blue jewellery box, and sometimes wears as a brooch.

For the past eleven years Peter has been a magistrate, and recently he's launched a new career, performing Punch and Judy shows. 'Not the domestic violence, it's more the crocodile and sausages.' But it's the rediscovery of his great-grandmother's life that now takes up much of his time. In 2003, after he was asked to give a talk at a local women's guild, he began researching Alice's life and got in touch with distant cousins. 'My mum had seen two relatives on the *Antiques Road Show* with their suffragette memorabilia that belonged to Alice. It was the 1990s and they were told it was interesting, but not really of any value. Imagine! That's when I realized what they had and appreciated what we had as a family.' Since Peter began giving talks to history groups and schools, and attending suffragette commemoration events, he has twice walked in his great-grandmother's footsteps.

In 2015 he was an extra in the film *Suffragette*, along with his daughter Kate. He found himself, dressed in Edwardian clothes with an impressive handlebar moustache, inside the Houses of Parliament when a delegation of working-class women arrive to appeal to Lloyd George. Peter couldn't help himself: 'I stood up and said my great-grandmother was one of these women, she addressed the Prime Minister. The filmmakers couldn't believe it.'

Two years earlier Peter had been involved in events to mark the hundredth anniversary of Emily Wilding Davison's death, where he shared a platform with Helen Pankhurst, Emmeline's great-grand-daughter. He was then invited to give a talk at Holloway, and when he caught a taxi from the station, 'the driver turned and said to me, "Got a relative there, mate?"' The original prison building had long gone by then, but how did it feel to be on the site where his great-grandmother had been locked up? 'I felt slightly . . . I wouldn't say emotional but I felt I'd spoken about Alice for years but *this* was the place where she was. They showed me the griffins that she would have seen when she arrived, and it was almost a reflective time for me. It brings it home to you, that this is not just history.'

In 1992 Leicester City Council erected a blue plaque on the wall of the Equity Shoe factory in memory of Alice Hawkins, and a statue in her honour is to be unveiled in the new market place in 2018. But as Alice was never one to speak publicly of her achievements, what would she have made of this? 'I'm not sure she'd be that happy actually.' Peter smiles. 'It was something she never spoke about, but I think it should not be forgotten. I am keen that the public becomes aware of the likes of working-class women such as Alice. It's an inspirational story and Holloway was a big part of it.'

Holloway Prison had been home to one of the first suffragettes imprisoned for demanding the right to vote and to the first woman elected an MP. While some argue that the vote was only won as a result of the role women played during the war, Holloway was where women met, planned and plotted the suffrage campaign; the Victorian castle jail had become a graduating university for militants.

PART THREE

Crimes Against Morality

8

The First World War

The outbreak of the First World War saw a new type of inmate at Holloway: women imprisoned for alleged crimes against the state. Some were the alien enemy believed to be engaged in deadly acts of 'sexspionage', while others were condemned as the enemy within.

Wartime Britain was a paranoid place, a time of censorship and anti-foreigner violence. National security was paramount and the Defence of the Realm Act (DORA) introduced numerous ways in which the average citizen could fall foul of the law. DORA placed restrictions on movement for those of 'hostile origin' and for British subjects, while discussion of naval or military matters in public places was forbidden. All references to the war were censored, whether official reports from the front or letters from soldiers to their families, and books that were deemed seditious were banned. DORA also gave the British government the power to detain and imprison without trial.

Now Holloway Prison would be used to remove any perceived threat to the war effort, whether citizens who opposed the ongoing slaughter on the battlefields or foreign nationals whose trials were kept largely secret. Propaganda and censorship created suspicion and the public were warned to be on the lookout for spies, especially women pretending to be innocuous travellers. 'One of them may sit next to you in an omnibus to-morrow or be opposite to you in the train,' warned journalist Frank Dilnot. 'You will not know it, be sure of that, for it is part of their work to look quite English and harmless.'

The most dangerous – and 'one of the most beautiful' – German spy operating in Britain during the First World War was Eva de

Bournonville. A naturalized Swedish citizen who had been born in Denmark, she was well educated, 'a mistress of several European languages', and had worked as a secretary at foreign diplomatic missions in Stockholm. In the autumn of 1915 Eva was approached by a German agent and set off for England, where as 'a lady by birth' and with perfect manners, she had no difficulty getting in to the country. She arrived in London and settled at a hotel in the West End, where army officers often spent their leave. Her method, according to the press, was to 'insinuate herself into the company of officers' whom she would 'artlessly question' on military matters. She was also sending letters to a German intelligence officer in Stockholm.

Eva was arrested on 15 November and protested her innocence until a letter was produced, written in secret ink – an offence in itself under the DORA regulations. She then asked to see Basil Thomson, assistant commissioner at Scotland Yard. A former prison governor, Basil had become known as the 'man who countered the spy peril', spending sixteen hours a day interrogating suspected spies in a private room at Scotland Yard. At the time of Eva's arrest, nine men had already been shot as spies at the Tower of London, and two more would follow in the next few months.

Basil agreed to see Eva de Bournonville alone, whereupon she told him, 'You may think it curious, but I always wanted to work for you and not for the Germans.' A few weeks later, however, Eva was sentenced to death. The judge was Justice Darling, the man who had sent baby farmers Amelia Sach and Annie Walters to the Holloway scaffold thirteen years earlier. The news of Eva's sentence only became public in February 1916, after questions were raised in the House of Commons. The Home Secretary confirmed that an unnamed woman spy had received the death penalty, but this had been commuted, out of 'mercy towards her sex', to penal servitude for life. No further details were given, except that she was not a British subject.

Eva was sent to Holloway, where she wrote 'to the people holding her wardrobe' asking them to 'please hang up my evening dresses and cover them well'. She also requested a manicure set, which suggests she was being treated as a first-division prisoner. She was then transferred to Walton Prison in Liverpool, released in early 1922 and deported.

Although Eva had been dangerous enough to receive the death sentence, her interrogator Basil Thomson later described her as 'probably the most incompetent woman spy ever recruited by the Germans'. The letters she sent contained 'information that would not have been of much use to the enemy had he received it'. Eva was 'remarkably stupid at the business of espionage', but then women did 'not make good spies'; lacking in technical knowledge they were apt to send misleading reports 'through misunderstanding what they hear'. Three years after Eva's arrest, Basil appeared to have indulged in his own version of 'sexspionage', after being found in the 'company of a woman' in Hyde Park. He told the police his name was Hugh, and initially failed to appear in court, but then explained he'd been researching soliciting and when a woman accosted him, he gave her a few shillings for her 'assistance'. Basil was found guilty and fined £5 for violating public decency.

Another 'very dangerous' enemy agent, according to the Secretary of State, was Madame Marie Edvige de Popowitch, 'a Serbian lady of a well-known wealthy family'. She was arrested under Defence of the Realm Regulation 14b, which imposed 'restrictions on or internment of persons of hostile origin or associations'. Once detained, such women were sent to Holloway and then Aylesbury, where they were held without trial. A leading player in Marie's internment was, once again, the unreliable Basil Thomson of Scotland Yard. He recalled 'some very remarkable telegrams' written in secret code detailing the passage of steamships from Malta. But Marie became so violent during interrogation that the police sent for 'the proper people to get her into a taxi'. She was medically examined 'as to the state of her mind' and Scotland Yard was advised that 'it would not be wise to try her on the capital charge'. So she was sent to Holloway where she made several complaints to the prison commissioners about the air in her cell and insufficient food. These were dismissed as unreasonable, and Marie was transferred to Aylesbury where she was allowed to keep two pet canaries as they had 'a calming effect upon their mistress'. After two years in prison she was declared insane, although she had still not been charged with any crime.

But the most dramatic and public wartime trial came in 1917 when a fifty-year-old English woman, Alice Wheeldon, along with two of her daughters and a son-in-law, was accused of conspiring to kill Prime Minister Lloyd George. Born Alice Marshall in 1866 in Derby, she had left school at the age of twelve and at the outbreak of the war she was running a second-hand clothes shop from her home in Pear Tree Road. A pacifist and suffragette, she had disagreed with the WSPU's support for the war and together with her four children she had joined the No-Conscription Fellowship. In 1916 the Military Service Act had introduced compulsory military service for men, and those who wanted to be exempted on the grounds of conscientious objection had to be assessed by a tribunal. But few exemptions were granted, and most were sent into the Non-Combatant Corps. Thousands of conscientious objectors were court-martialled and jailed, and it wasn't long before many were on the run, including Alice's son William.

At the end of December 1916, a man named Alex Gordon arrived at the Wheeldon Derby home. He told Alice he was a conscientious objector (CO) seeking shelter, that he had helped COs escape from Home Office work camps and now he wanted to poison the camp's guard dogs. Alice agreed to obtain the poison from her son-in-law Alfred Mason, a pharmacist, and in return Alex would help get COs to safety in the United States. He then came back with another man, Herbert Booth, introducing him as Comrade Bert. What Alice didn't know, but what her daughter Hettie suspected, was that both Alex Gordon and Herbert Booth were working as undercover agents for PMS2, the intelligence unit of the Ministry of Munitions. The unit had been set up in early 1916 with the aim of protecting munitions factories, but was now busy spying on the labour movement and using agitators like Alex to incite violence.

According to Basil Thomson at Scotland Yard, the 'three militant suffragettes' in Derby had intended to shoot the Prime Minister with a poisoned dart as he was playing golf. The alleged plot had been discovered by an anonymous informant and Basil decided to intercept letters between Alice Wheeldon and her son-in-law.

Scotland Yard also intercepted a parcel of four phials, two of which contained curare, a South American arrow poison. Basil then insisted that the anonymous informant came to London. 'There walked into the room a thin, cunning-looking man of about thirty; with long, greasy black hair.' Two other men present, a CID superintendent and a fingerprint expert, both immediately recognized 'Alex Gordon' as known criminal William Rickard who had a previous conviction for blackmail. But this didn't deter Scotland Yard. 'We had to use the man,' wrote Basil, 'there was no alternative.'

On 31 January 1917 Alice, her daughters Hettie and Winnie and her son-in-law Alfred were charged with plotting to murder the Prime Minister, as well as Arthur Henderson, the leader of the Labour Party. The trial began in Derby but was moved to the Old Bailey in London, where the prosecutor was the Attorney General Sir Frederick Smith. He had previously run the War Office Press Bureau, and the Wheeldon trial became a centrepiece of pro-war propaganda. The newspapers were immediately full of the 'poison plot' and *The Times* outlined the 'grave conspiracy charge' in which the family were accused of 'unlawfully and wickedly' conspiring to 'kill and murder' Britain's Prime Minister.

Alice, Winnie and Hettie were sent on remand to Holloway and the trial began on 6 March. The Attorney General went on the attack at once, describing 'the persons in this case [as] a very desperate and dangerous body of people', while the Wheeldon women were 'in the habit of employing, habitually, language which would be disgusting and obscene' even coming from 'the lowest class of criminal'. The working-class Derby women were denounced as unwomanly, and their language taken as proof of murderous intentions.

The state's case relied on the intercepted phials of poison and the evidence of the two undercover agents, while the Wheeldons were defended by an inexperienced legal team. The fact that the phials had been accompanied by detailed instructions that made it clear they were intended to kill guard dogs was dismissed, and the fact that no guard dogs – or even guards – existed at the work camps was used to discredit the Wheeldons' defence. 'Alex Gordon' was never called to give evidence, and the court was not told that he had twice been declared criminally insane and had been released from Broadmoor asylum just two years before being hired by PMS2.

He had also been in Holloway Prison himself, as a ten-year-old child on remand, under his real name William Rickard. In October 1898 'a little fellow, with a peculiar look and hideous grin' had been arrested for maliciously wounding a six-year-old boy on the banks of the New River in Islington, hitting him 'on the head with a chopper'. He was, reported the press, 'possibly the youngest prisoner ever committed for trial'. Holloway's medical officer testified that William was subject to hysteria and incapable of understanding the nature of his offence. He was too young to be sent to a criminal lunatic asylum, so William was ordered to be detained at His Majesty's pleasure 'in such a place as was most suitable'. Less than twenty years later he was working for the Ministry of Munitions and on his way to Derby posing as a conscientious objector.

The intelligence agent who did go into the witness box, Herbert Booth, had plenty of lurid tales to tell against Alice Wheeldon. She had allegedly confessed to bombing a church as part of a WSPU arson campaign, and had accused David Lloyd George and Arthur Henderson of being 'traitors to the labouring classes', saying she hoped 'the buggers will soon be dead'. These wild, unsubstantiated stories of arson and assassination attempts were vehemently denied by Alice Wheeldon. But her supposed 'threats' were taken literally, the evidence of Herbert Booth was enough and it took the jury less than thirty minutes to find Alice, Winnie and Alfred guilty of conspiracy to murder. Alice was sentenced to ten years, Alfred to seven and Winnie to five. Hettie was found not guilty. It was a chilling example of the lengths the government would go to in order to discredit the anti-war movement and portray conscientious objection as a danger to the state.

Alfred was sent to Brixton Prison, while Winnie and her mother were taken to Aylesbury. Alice went on hunger strike, in protest at being repeatedly stripped, 'in the presence of a number of wardresses in a manner which, to her mind, was humiliating', and like the suffragettes before her she was forcibly fed. In December 1917 she was moved back to Holloway, seriously ill after having refused food for eight days. She was examined by three doctors who 'detected vascular disease of the heart' and declared it 'impossible to have her forcibly fed'. Alice again went on hunger strike, and Holloway's medical officer Dr Wilfred Sass reported her condition was rapidly deteriorating. Her daughter Winnie wrote to her mother from Aylesbury: 'Oh Mam, please don't die – that's all that matters. You were always a fighter but this fight isn't worth your death.' Alice's lawyer urged the Home Secretary 'to release her in the interests of justice and humanity', while her friends said they were 'in hourly expectation of news of her death'.

On 29 December the Prime Minister advised the Home Office that 'on no account should she be allowed to die in prison'. As with the suffragettes, the last thing the government wanted was a martyr, this time to the anti-war movement, and shortly afterwards Alice was released. But she never recovered from her false arrest, imprisonment and forcible feeding and died of influenza just over a year later in February 1919. Winnie and Alfred Mason, who had now been released, were too ill to travel to Derby for the funeral, at which Alice's friend the socialist John S. Clarke declared, 'We are giving to the eternal keeping of Mother Earth, the mortal dust of a poor and innocent victim of a judicial murder.' Alice was buried in an unmarked grave, as there were fears it would be defaced, while William Rickard, the man responsible for her imprisonment, was sent to South Africa where he became a stage performer called 'Vivid – the Magnetic Man'.

And this is where Alice Wheeldon's tragic story might have ended, had it not been for the independent work of two historians, Sheila Rowbotham and Dr Nicholas Hiley in the 1980s, as well as a modern campaign to clear her name launched by the Derby People's History Group and her great-granddaughters Chloe and Deirdre Mason. For the past five years Chloe Mason, a lawyer in Australia, has been collecting evidence to present to the Criminal Cases Review Commission. Her aim is to clear the Wheeldons' names so that history will record their trial and imprisonment as a miscarriage of justice. In 2013 a blue plaque was unveiled at Alice's home on Pear Tree Road where speakers, including Derby's mayor, celebrated her as 'a fearless woman' with 'ideas ahead of her time' who should never have been sent to Holloway Prison. In March

2017, 100 years to the day since Alice and her family were convicted, Chloe and Deirdre Mason travelled from Australia to hold a vigil outside the Royal Courts of Justice in London and declared that 'our quest for justice will not falter'.

At the end of the First World War, Holloway Prison was about to go through another transition. Soldiers were returning from the trenches, and women who had discovered a new independence were forced out of 'men's work' and back into the domestic sphere. Those who refused to adopt their pre-war roles were frowned upon, and men like Basil Thomson of Scotland Yard feared 'a marked deterioration of public morals'. Women were not just threatening men's jobs, they were sexually a threat as well, according to Basil. A whole generation of women had lost 'mates' of their own age and 'their subconscious instinct impels them to attract'. The 'Roaring Twenties' might be on their way, with talk of sexual liberation and thrill-seeking flappers, but it wasn't long before a British 'court of morals' would sentence another woman to death at Holloway Prison, and this time she would hang.

9

'The Messalina of Ilford'

It's 7 a.m. on a cold January morning and the streets of Upper Holloway are empty but for a cat slinking home after a night out. There are few passengers on the train heading east, and when I arrive at Woodgrange Park no one else seems to be out. I walk past boarded-up pubs and shuttered newsagents, across a railway line and down terraced roads. It's that odd hour before the street-lights go out, when the sky is just turning blue and even the birds are silent. But inside St Barnabas Church the vicar is waiting for us; the memorial service begins at 8.30 a.m. Today I'm part of a little-known ceremony held to commemorate a woman whose death at Holloway Prison was one of the biggest travesties of justice in British history.

St Barnabas is a pretty red brick building in Manor Park, an Anglican parish church built in the early 1900s, with three arched stained-glass windows overlooking a double wooden door. To the right of the entrance is a thin tree, its branches bare but for a hanging length of rope. When I open the door the space inside seems vast, and I hesitate on the threshold until a man appears from the darkness to welcome me in. Reverend James Ramsay has been the vicar here for ten years but it wasn't until he got a phone call one winter's evening asking about the possibility of a memorial service the next day that he first heard of Edith Thompson.

The vicar points to the side chapel where a couple of people are waiting, and invites me to sit. But I've just seen a figure near the entrance, with long red hair and a full-length black coat. I recognize her from the photo on her website, 'Molly Cutpurse – transgender author'. Molly is the pseudonym of Jean Winchester, the author of fifty-six historical novels, two of which are about Edith Thompson.

Her parents used to come to this church in the early 1950s and they were friends with Edith's family. 'As a small child I knew there was a local family whose daughter was executed,' she says. 'I knew that from a very young age. It made me want to find out more.'

On 9 January 1923 Edith Thompson was executed at Holloway Prison, having been found guilty of inciting her lover Freddy Bywaters to murder her husband Percy Thompson. It was the first hanging at Holloway for twenty years, and Freddy was executed on the same day at the same time at nearby Pentonville Prison.

We head to the side chapel where I'm handed a sheet, 'Requiem Eucharist for Edith Thompson', and sit down on a wooden pew. Reverend James Ramsay appears, wearing a white hooded gown, and stands in front of a cloth-covered table, a candle flickering at either end. He gives an opening prayer and the audience responds, their words echoing off the stone walls: 'Lord, have mercy. Amen. Lord, have mercy.'

The vicar tells us this is a particularly important time to commemorate Edith Thompson. The death penalty is 'back on our agenda as a country' for the first time since the 1980s, and there has been a huge increase in capital punishment among the UK's economic and political allies. 'Capital punishment is an abuse of humanity,' he says. 'Let us remember not just Edith and Freddy, but Percy, the police officers, and those whose job it was to commit judicial murder. We pray for Edith, and for all those around the world sitting in prison knowing at any time they will be killed in the name of justice.' The vicar speaks softly, his words slow and considered, as morning light begins to seep in through the stained-glass window behind him, burgundy panels turning mauve.

Just before 9 a.m., the time that Edith was hanged, Professor René Weis gets up to speak. A solid-looking man with furrowed eyebrows, he is a vice-dean at University College London, an expert on Shakespeare, and the author of a book on Edith's life. 'Edith had an affair,' he tells us, 'that's all it was. She was innocent of murder. Her sentence was unjust and her name must be cleared.'

Edith Jessie Graydon was born in Dalston, east London, on Christmas Day 1893. She met Percy Thompson when she was fifteen and this was the church where they married, after a six-year engagement. Just before she left her home – a short walk away – for her wedding at St Barnabas, Edith told her father, 'I can't go through with it,' but she did.

The couple ended up buying a house, 41 Kensington Gardens, in the then fashionable district of Ilford in north-east London. Edith worked as a bookkeeper and buyer at Carlton & Prior, a wholesale milliner in the city. The firm sent her twice to Paris and she was soon earning more than her father and husband. In 1920, while on holiday in the Isle of Wight, she started an affair with eighteen-year-old Freddy Bywaters. He was an old school friend of her younger brother, and now travelling the world as a ship's laundry steward. Edith saw Freddy as her soulmate; they were 'two halves' not yet united. She told him how unhappy she was in her marriage, and her letters were full of passionate declarations: 'Shall we say we'll always be lovers – even tho' secret ones, or is it (this great big love) a thing we can't control – dare we say that – I think I will dare.'

Freddy moved into 41 Kensington Gardens as the Thompsons' paying guest, and the atmosphere was fraught. After one confrontation, Percy hit Edith and threw her across the room, and a witness described her arm as covered with bruises. Percy discovered the affair but refused to agree to a divorce, and when Freddy returned to sea Edith wrote letters of longing for her 'pal'. Both voracious readers, they discussed their views on the latest novels and plays. She also wrote about pregnancies and abortions, explaining she had added an 'abortifacient powder' to her porridge and her husband had eaten it by mistake.

When Freddy decided to end the affair, Edith was distraught, but after meeting in London the relationship continued. 'You are my magnet,' wrote Freddy, 'I cannot resist darling – you draw me to you now and always.' On 3 October 1922, the day before he was due back at sea, the lovers met up again. Then Edith joined her husband and friends for dinner and a play in the West End, before catching the eleven thirty train back to Ilford. Freddy was waiting, walking unnoticed behind them and then taking a short cut and hiding in a front garden. As the couple passed he grabbed

Edith and pushed her to one side, the two men fought and Freddy stabbed Percy with a knife. He later told the police, 'The reason I fought with Thompson was because he never acted like a man to his wife.'

Edith screamed for assistance, hysterically telling a neighbour, 'Oh, my God, help me, my husband is ill, he is bleeding on the pavement.' She didn't at this stage tell the police about Freddy, instead she said her husband had suffered a seizure, although an officer heard her saying, 'They will blame me for this.'

Later that morning, after the police established Percy had been murdered, Edith was taken to Ilford police station, and by evening Freddy had been arrested. When Edith caught sight of him at the police station, a meeting deliberately engineered by the police, she exclaimed, 'Oh God; oh God, what can I do? Why did he do it; I did not want him to do it.' Inspector Francis Hall told her, falsely, that Freddy had confessed, and so she signed a statement saying he had killed her husband. But when the police searched Freddy's ship and found over sixty of Edith's love letters, documenting their passionate affair, she was arrested as well. She was charged with poisoning her husband, and soliciting and inciting Freddy to kill him. After the two appeared in court, Edith was taken to Holloway, while Freddy was sent to Brixton and later moved to Pentonville. The lovers tried to keep in touch, unaware that their letters were not always being delivered. 'You asked me what I do all day – I suppose practically the same as you,' wrote Edith from Holloway. 'Sit on a chair – think or read, eat at specified times & then sleep.'

The average population at Holloway Prison in the early 1920s was around 400, and the general behaviour of inmates was said to be 'more quiet and orderly'. Conditions inside the prison had changed for the better since the war. Dr Mary Gordon, appointed the first lady inspector of prisons in 1908, 'brought a much-needed feminine view to the matter of women in prison', writes Holloway historian John Camp. She introduced the Swedish drill, a popular form of physical exercise that was used in schools and hospitals, lighting and ventilation in the cells were improved, and prisoners no longer wore clothing marked with the traditional arrow. In 1922, the year that Edith Thompson arrived at Holloway, Dr Mary Gordon published a book on penal discipline, calling the prison system demoralizing and cruel and 'a gigantic irrelevance – a social curiosity'.

Edith appears to have had little contact with other inmates, but she would have heard their shouts and cries as she sat in her cell waiting for her day in court. She looked forward to the trial, believing that once she took the stand, against her lawyer's advice, she could tell the full story and would be found innocent. On 6 December Edith and Freddy appeared at the Old Bailey and the crowds began queuing at 1 a.m. in order to be in the public gallery for the following day. Edith was described as the 'dominant partner', and the evidence of the lovers' murderous plot lay in the letters that proved she had won Freddy's love and then 'preyed on his mind'.

Some were withheld, the references to abortion and sex, orgasm and menstruation deemed too explicit. But many of the letters were quoted at length, and printed in the press, and as her intimate words were read out for everyone to hear – as the atmosphere inside the court 'vibrated with whispered exclamations' – Edith collapsed.

The newspapers were fascinated by the case from the beginning; it was squalid and indecent, a tale of lust and adultery. There were weekly 'sensational developments', and Edith was dubbed the 'Messalina of Ilford', after the 'promiscuous' wife of Emperor Claudius. Like many of her predecessors at Holloway, she defied expectations of femininity and class. She was a sexual creature, she had no children, she worked even though she was married, and her lover was only nineteen years old. Edith contradicted herself during her testimony, and had lied about what happened on the night of the murder. The press portrayed her as a vain woman, dressed in a 'black fur coat and black velvet hat with long feathers', who supposedly enjoyed her time in the spotlight. By day three of the trial, people were queuing for a place from 9.30 p.m. the night before.

Freddy insisted that he had acted without Edith's knowledge, but Justice Shearman warned the jury – eleven men and one woman – that they were 'trying a vulgar and common crime'. He scribbled notes to himself for his summing-up address: 'great love . . . nonsense. Great and wholesome disgust.' He told the jury there was just one question they needed to consider: 'was it an arranged thing between the woman and the man?' He then gave an example: if an assassin was hired to kill a man, then wasn't it plain common sense that the person who hired the assassin was also guilty of murder?

When the verdict was announced on 11 December, Edith had to be held upright by two Holloway wardresses, crying out, 'I am not guilty; oh, God! I am not guilty.' The wardresses then wrenched her fingers from the rail of the dock, lifted her up and carried her out of court.

Edith was sedated repeatedly over the coming days and put in the prison hospital where she was visited by Holloway's new governor, Dr John Hall Morton, who was known to have a 'remarkably extensive' knowledge of psychology and the 'habits of female criminals'. The officers were kind to Edith. She was given breakfast in bed at 7.30 a.m., then got dressed and could 'do what I like', writing, reading and knitting mufflers which were sent to the boys of the Borstal Institute. Then she walked in a yard alone for an hour. 'I see no other prisoners. I do not enjoy that.' At four she had tea and at 8.30 p.m. she went to bed.

When Edith's mother Ethel and her sister Avis came to visit, she told them she was sleeping well, but the food was poor, she was not allowed to have a knife or fork at dinner and it was hard to eat with a wooden spoon. 'The time here, on the whole, seems not as long as in remand – so many things are different,' Edith wrote to her friend Bessie Aitken. 'I can't tell you because it is against the rules.' It was her family she worried about most: 'It must be painful for them – the publicity alone must be more than they can cope with. You see I am shut away here and know nothing of all that.'

Now that Edith and Freddy were to be hanged, public opinion suddenly shifted and the *Daily Sketch* launched a petition to save Freddy, which would reportedly be signed by a million people. But on 21 December it took three judges only five minutes to dismiss

Edith's appeal. One was Justice Darling, who had sentenced the Edwardian baby farmers and First World War spy Eva de Bournonville to death.

Two other women were sentenced to death in the same month as Edith Thompson and held in the condemned cell at Holloway. Daisy Wright, an impoverished charwoman, was found guilty of killing her two-year-old child by throwing her off Tower Bridge into the Thames. The case was described as 'most poignant and tragic' and Justice Shearman told the jury, 'No doubt you deplore these terrible cases as much as I, but we have to do our duty.' Daisy's death sentence was reprieved and she was released the following year. Ellen Jones, convicted of killing her husband's mistress in a fit of jealousy, was also reprieved and now Edith Thompson was the only woman in Holloway's condemned cell.

Edith wrote of her shock to Bessie when her appeal was rejected: 'I had such hopes of it – not only hopes for mercy, but hopes for justice; but I realise how very difficult it is to fight prejudice . . . We all imagine we can mould our own lives – we seldom can, they are moulded for us – just by the laws and rules and conventions of this world.' On the afternoon of Christmas Day, Edith's twenty-ninth birthday, she reportedly became hysterical and Holloway's assistant medical officer Dr Dora Walker injected her with a sedative. 'Why – oh, *why*, am I here?' Edith asked the wardresses who had been assigned to look after her. 'Why did he do it, why?' Again she was injected with drugs. A new date was set for the execution, 9 January 1923, and Britain's chief executioner John Ellis, a former barber, was appointed hangman. Holloway's governor was asked to provide Edith's weight and height; a wooden screen was built so her walk from the condemned cell to the execution shed wouldn't be seen by anyone outside the prison. Preparations had begun, and soon the 'Messalina of Ilford' would be 'duly executed by law'.

Edith noted that she had put on a stone in weight while in Holloway, and that she was being weighed up to three times a day, but didn't seem aware of the reason for this. Her mother wrote to the Queen begging for a reprieve, her sister appealed to the Prime Minister, referring to 'the foolish letters of an over wrought, unhappy woman'. Edith's brother Newenham sent a letter to the governor: 'Might I be allowed to ask one more favour of you before the curtain comes down upon this terrible drama?' He wanted to know if all four family members could visit Edith together on Saturday and Monday, and would later write to Dr Morton to thank him and his staff for 'your kindness and consideration'.

The day before the execution the Bishop of Stepney brought Edith a final message from Freddy, saying they would soon be reunited. Then her family came for the last time, and as her father entered the prison a friend, Mr Warren, passed him a telegram that had arrived at their home after they had left that morning. Edith's father handed it to the governor and as the family sat in the condemned cell, a messenger appeared to read it out.

The relief was overwhelming: 'I have sent telegram to the Home Secretary and the king for pardon for your daughter. Good news coming.' The message was signed 'Bethell' in Lewisham, and the family assumed this was Lord Bethell, a local MP. At the very last moment, Edith had been reprieved.

But the telegram was a brutal hoax, and possibly linked to an anonymous gift the governor had received two days earlier, a box of 'suspicious cigars' that appeared to have been 'tampered with' and which were sent to Scotland Yard for investigation.

Edith was removed to the death cell and the governor read her a final message from the Home Secretary: the execution was going ahead.

People had been gathering outside Holloway since 7.30 a.m. One woman carried a placard with the words 'Murder cannot be abolished by murder'. As the time for the execution approached, more police arrived. The crowd had grown to several hundred, 'men greatly predominated', and they were allowed to stand on the road opposite the prison. Several thousand people had also gathered outside Pentonville, awaiting Freddy's execution, where mounted police had to clear the roadway.

Inside Holloway, the chaplain began to read the burial service as Edith was carried to the shed containing the scaffold, where there were nine men and one woman, deputy governor Elizabeth Cronin, waiting to witness the execution. Less than a minute later

Edith was dead, and so was Freddy. John Ellis reportedly emerged from the execution shed screaming, 'Oh Christ, Oh Christ', while chaplain Granville Murray recalled that 'the impulse to rush in and save her by force was almost too strong for me.'

The crowd outside the prison began to surge around the gates, and the police had difficulty keeping them back. As each minute after the official hour passed, and no notice of the execution was posted, the press reported 'a curious feeling passed over the crowd. "Has anything gone wrong?" was the question that occurred to everyone, but when the chaplain came out at ten minutes past nine suspicion was allayed. He looked very upset.' An hour later Edith's body was taken down from the scaffold, but when her family came to identify her Avis was only allowed to kiss her sister on the forehead. The inquest was then held 'on the body of Edith Jessie Thompson now here lying dead at His Majesty's Prison Holloway'. Yet while the official report noted the cause of death, the part of the form requiring the results of an internal examination had been left blank. Edith was then buried in an unmarked grave within the prison grounds, joining Amelia Sach and Annie Walters in the graveyard for condemned prisoners.

The impact of the execution, however, had only just begun. Rumours about the precise nature of Edith's death started at once, and details were leaked to the press. She was said to have 'disintegrated' on the way to the execution shed, alternatively her insides 'fell out'. Edith appeared to have suffered an internal haemorrhage, and the governor had ordered that her underclothes be cleaned of blood and her dress burned before her family saw her. These details, along with the weight she had gained in prison, led to one conclusion: the British justice system had sentenced a pregnant woman to death.

Holloway's governor reportedly went that night to the *Daily Mail*, urging the paper to launch a campaign to abolish the death penalty. The press described the 'condemned woman's night of agony', lying prostrate and continually 'in the doctor's care'. But the official line was that Edith Thompson had been hanged in the most humane manner possible, she had not been unconscious, and she had only been carried to the scaffold 'to spare her the necessity of walking from her cell'. Two weeks after the hanging, the executioner John Ellis tried to kill himself.

The rumours would continue for decades, resurfacing again in the 1950s during debates on capital punishment. Penal reformer Margery Fry who had visited Edith in Holloway while she was living on Dalmeny Avenue with her brother, the artist Roger Fry, gave evidence on the impact of the execution on prison staff. 'I was greatly impressed by its effect upon all of them . . . I have never seen a person look so changed . . . by mental suffering as the Governor . . . Miss Cronin was very greatly troubled by the whole affair . . . I was struck by this as Miss Cronin was not . . . a sensitive or easily moved person.' Reverend Granville Murray went on to become a campaigner against the death penalty, while John Ellis carried out his final execution in December that year, having hanged 203 people. Some eight years later, after trying to murder his wife and daughter, he killed himself.

Edith and Freddy's story has featured in numerous films, books and plays, inspiring director Alfred Hitchcock and writers James Joyce, Agatha Christie, Dorothy L. Sayers and P.D. James, and more recently Jill Dawson and Sarah Waters. But there are only twelve mourners here at St Barnabas Church this morning as René Weis reads from a letter written by Edith's mother, after she visited Holloway to identify her daughter's body. Edith looked peaceful, she hadn't suffered, and according to her sister Avis she had been dead before she was hanged. When Avis died in 1977 she asked that mass be held for the Graydon family every year on 9 January, which is why we're here today in Manor Park.

We leave the church and I stop to point at the tree outside with the hanging rope. The vicar frowns, this is the first time he's noticed it. He thinks it might be a washing line. Next door in the vicarage, a table in the front room is laid out with cakes and tea. Our tea over, novelist Jean Winchester offers to drive me to Ilford. 'On the night of 3 October 1922, Edith and Percy came out of that station there' – she stops and points to the right – 'they'd been to the Criterion Theatre in Piccadilly Circus and were returning home. And they walked down here, Belgrave Road, probably on this side of the street.' Jean drives slowly on until we reach the corner of Kensington Gardens, and taps me on the arm. 'Then, hiding in bushes over there, was Freddy. So the murder occurred right there.'

We turn into Kensington Gardens and park opposite Number 41, Edith's old house. This was the eight-roomed residence that the Thompsons named the Retreat, where they planted fruit trees in the garden and Freddy briefly became their paying guest. Jean tells me she has nearly 500 items relating to Holloway Prison, and while her interest was initially because of Edith Thompson, she likes the Victorian architecture so much she's designed a 3D model and has filmed it for several YouTube videos. Her dream is to build a huge physical model of Holloway Castle as it was during Edith Thompson's time.

There had been two decades since the execution of the Edwardian baby farmers; other condemned women had been reprieved yet Edith's 'crime' – a love affair – was deemed so transgressive that she had not been allowed to live. In the thirty years following Edith Thompson's death, twenty-five more women were held in Holloway's condemned cell. The majority of them were reprieved; one was declared insane and not therefore given the death penalty, while another had her conviction quashed. It would be another thirty-one years before Holloway would once more become the site of an execution, and as the prison entered the 1930s reform was firmly back on the agenda.

IO

Reform

In the spring of 1927 a new deputy governor took up her post at Holloway, the great reformer Mary Size. Often described as the prison's first female deputy governor, she had in fact taken over from Elizabeth Cronin. But Elizabeth's had been an internal promotion, a step up from her role as assistant matron, whereas Mary Size was one of 130 people who applied for the job of deputy governor at Holloway Prison.

It was still rare to find a woman in a position of authority in the prison service, although the suffragettes, and particularly the Women's Freedom League, had repeatedly petitioned for the appointment of female governors and medical officers in women's jails. While Emma Martin had run Brixton's female convict prison back in the 1850s, and 'lady superintendents' had long been in charge of the women's sections of national prisons, it wasn't until 1916 that Dr Selina Fox became the first female governor, at Aylesbury. Nearly two decades later and there was still only one female governor, three deputy governors and one housemistress in the entire prison service.

Mary Size was born in County Galway in 1883, and became a wardress in her early twenties after moving to England. When she arrived at Holloway she had a wealth of experience to draw on, including her recent role as lady superintendent at Liverpool Prison, and as deputy governor she now had far more freedom to put her ideas into practice. Her focus was educational and 'redemptive work': prisoners needed self-respect and kindness was encouraged, both between staff and inmates and between prisoners themselves. Holloway had a staff of around 100, divided into two sections: Mary was in charge of discipline, while governor Dr John Morton looked after nursing.

The 1920s was a time of penal reform in general. The Victorian prison system, where jails were places of punishment, was getting an overhaul. Young offenders were now treated separately from adults, and were housed in institutions that would become known as Borstals. The training for female officers included lectures on humane treatment and employment as a contributor to reformation, there was a new vision of the purpose of imprisonment and a different attitude towards prisoners. 'The principle of treating the wrong-doer as a human being has everything to commend it,' commented one newspaper. In fact, prisons might not even be needed any more: 'while it may, perhaps, be too much to hope for [their] total abolition . . . within the next decade or so, one is justified in anticipating their substantial reduction.' Several factors contributed to this mood for reform. The suffragettes and imprisoned conscientious objectors had pressed for change, and now there was support within government. Alexander Paterson, appointed commissioner of prisons in 1922, wanted to humanize the nation's jails, to 'bring about change' and offer 'training in habit and character'. Family visits were encouraged; prisoners received wages for prison work. It was the new commissioner of prisons who declared that people came to prison 'as punishment, not for punishment'.

Other factors included the campaigning work of the Howard League for Penal Reform, formed in 1921, as well as the fact that recorded crime was down. Some offences such as housebreaking, which would have resulted in the death penalty a century earlier, were now punished by a fine or probation, with the latter offering a real alternative to prison. Prisons themselves were no longer 'the hideous places they once were'; instead their purpose was corrective rather than punitive and according to the press all prisoners were to be given the opportunity of 'making good' again.

In 1935 Lilian Barker became the first female assistant prison commissioner. 'For the first time in penal history,' writes John Camp, 'a woman in charge of women prisoners could discuss their problems with a woman commissioner and be free of male influence. There was much to be done.'

Lilian Barker had been born in Kentish Town, not far from Holloway Prison, and had worked as a teacher and then principal of a women's 'correctional facility'. She had served as governor of Aylesbury, where her focus had been education, guidance and rehabilitation, and now her mission was to reform women's prisons throughout England, Wales and Scotland. When Lilian was told there was 'room for the advice of a woman on matters not only dealing with staff but also cooking and domestic economy generally', she replied, 'I am quite willing to visit the kitchens, but I have no intention of staying there.' She was said to inspect every corner of a prison, tasting the food, rubbing her face against the bed-linen to make sure it was well aired, and examining each item of prisoners' clothes. She was, explained her niece Elizabeth Gore, known by at least one prisoner as 'dear old Lil'.

Mary Size, meanwhile, set off to Holloway 'with a certain amount of trepidation'. It was a 'unique' prison and 'had within its walls every type and classification of woman prisoner. Here was a fresh challenge, would I be equal to it?' Her aim, as she explained in her memoirs *Prisons I Have Known*, was 'to make it the best women's prison in the country'. Mary's living quarters were above the governor's office, and by the end of the first week she had learned all the names of the officers, marking 'the beginning of a friendship which lasted while we worked together, and in many cases for long afterwards'. Soon she knew 'every hole and corner of Holloway', and such was the falling prison population that up to a third of the cells were empty. The hospital was clean and orderly, the workrooms large, well-lit and warm, but the work done in the prisoners' laundry was 'deplorable', with piles of dirty sheets and underwear that had been left to accumulate for weeks.

The inmates ranged from a terrified sixteen-year-old who cried 'Mother! Mother! Oh, Mother!' when locked up in a reception cubicle, to women who 'could get no peace of mind' worrying about their young children. Prisoners came from 'practically every grade of society' and each one carried 'a load of shame, heart-break, unhappiness and frustration'.

Mary set about introducing new education classes and a wider variety of work. Younger prisoners were given six hours of educational classes a week, and two hours of evening instruction in cookery and 'table service'. After a three-month course they could sit an exam and get a certificate which 'bore no mark of prison', explained the press, and 'proved a great asset to them when they applied for jobs as domestic servants'. According to Mary Size, soon the number of young women who returned to prison was 'negligible'; they had successfully become 'decently established citizens'. Voluntary teachers ran dressmaking, needlework and handicraft classes, while women with longer sentences could attend courses in home nursing, hygiene and the management of children. 'Since the introduction of these classes the whole atmosphere of the prison has changed,' rejoiced Mary; 'the very rigid atmosphere of discipline has died out.'

A new earnings scheme was introduced, and 'an exceptionally good worker' could earn up to 4 shillings a week. A disused cell was turned into a pay office and another converted into 'the Shop', which sold goods from local shops on a sale or return basis. The favourite items were cigarettes, sweets and cosmetics, followed by biscuits, buns, jam and marmalade. Mary attributed the success of the scheme to the satisfaction of collecting wages, however small, and it was also a way to maintain discipline and increase output from the workshops. Holloway was becoming efficient again, as it had under governor John Weatherhead in Victorian times. Older women made the prisoners' clothes, produced items for the air force and mailbags for the Post Office, while younger inmates learned shoe repairing; power sewing machines were installed, and there were more factory-like jobs such as packaging, sorting and putting tops on bottles and jars.

The opportunity to buy make-up was particularly popular, for women had traditionally used any substitute they could find. In Brixton in the 1860s they had rubbed whitewash off the walls, while Holloway's inmates had been using flour, chalk and red ink. Hair had been glossed with margarine rations; grate polish was used for eyebrows and shoe polish for mascara, and some soaked the red covers of exercise books for lipstick.

Mary Size also allowed mirrors to be installed in cells, although some attributed this to governor John Morton. 'It took us some time to realise how important a mirror is to a woman,' he told the press; 'it is extraordinary the pains women prisoners will take to devise some kind of thing to reflect their faces.' Inmates also received a new prison uniform, introduced by prison commissioner Lilian Barker, a dark blue coat frock with a white apron and a blue cape for outdoors, replacing the heavy grey cloak. Lilian inspected women's feet to see that their shoes fitted, and checked that prisoners were getting the personal toilet articles they were entitled to. Women no longer had to keep their caps on at all times, and she suggested female officers also be allowed to take them off 'at certain times in certain situations' to form a more natural relationship with the prisoners.

The grim castle building was also redecorated. Lilian suggested the prisoners repaint the walls cream and green, replacing the old orange and brown colour scheme, while the cells were painted in pastel shades. Flowerbeds were planted in the prison grounds, along with a bowling green for older inmates. An iron staircase was removed from the basement floor and the area used for physical exercise, country dancing, concerts, educational classes and lectures. Gracie Fields, the actress and singer then at the height of her fame, came to give a concert and 'everyone was agog'. After the show she was presented with a bead evening bag made in one of the handicraft classes.

Handicrafts were well established at Holloway by the mid-1930s, with lace-making, beadwork, pottery, cane work, rug-making, weaving, leatherwork, pewter, toy-making, smocking, quilting and patchwork. The work was exhibited annually at the Imperial Institute in London; an afternoon tea cloth with twelve matching napkins was bought and presented to Queen Mary, while 'a peer' ordered a hand-woven white silk scarf.

Mary Size believed that handicrafts were 'the greatest blessing bestowed on women's prisons' in modern times; they brought skilled women in from outside, opened up a new field of knowledge, supplemented scanty incomes and improved self-confidence. But the greatest benefit was that they created a healthier atmosphere: 'the old fashioned harsh discipline that bred hatred and distrust' gradually died out and was replaced by 'a friendly cooperation'.

The punishments cells were converted into a dining and recreation room, which became a modernized wing for juveniles. The condemned cell where Edith Thompson had spent her last days, and which was believed to be haunted, was demolished and turned into a store. The chapel was renovated and in 1937 a separate Roman Catholic church was established in a converted outbuilding, described by one prisoner as 'that little bit of paradise in the middle of a house of many tribulations'. Mary Size also introduced reform to the main Church of England chapel, seating officials and guests alongside the congregation of women so they no longer felt 'that the visitors had come to gaze on them, as they would animals at the Zoo'.

Her description of life inside Holloway was certainly homely. A cell was now 'a neat little bedroom containing an iron bedstead . . . a complete set of toilet ware, a table, chair, shelves for books, a looking glass, a bell and a window and ventilators'. The windows were 'controlled by the prisoner', and efforts had been made to 'make the place as pleasant as possible'.

Inmates could put posters and pictures on the walls of their cell, although for some unstated reason not photographs of animals. The old wooden plank beds were replaced with iron bedsteads with springs and a mattress, electricity had replaced gas lighting and lights out came at a much later time of 10 p.m., which meant women could read or write in their cells after work. The 'detestable' tin toilet ware was also replaced with enamel utensils.

But all these changes met with resistance from some of the older members of staff who felt prisoners were being spoilt, much as the public had feared during the early days of the new Victorian prisons. 'Holloway Prison is not as uncomfortable,' commented one judge, 'as it ought to be.' The press also seemed uncertain what to make of things, with headlines like 'Women dance in prison', and 'How women are helped rather than punished'. But Mary Size was keen to educate the public on the potential for rehabilitation and addressed numerous meetings on 'the care and after-care of women prisoners'. Trade unionist Margaret Bondfield, who in 1929 had become the first woman cabinet minister as Minister of Labour, was so moved by one of Mary's talks that she 'wondered how soon the time would come when they could blow up Holloway Prison and have it rebuilt on modern lines'.

By 1936 the average population inside Holloway had dropped to 350, with the vast majority serving a sentence of under a month.

The chief causes of imprisonment were still alcohol, vagrancy and homelessness, as well as 'a wretched home environment' and most were repeat offenders. By the end of the following year, Holloway's population had fallen still further: there were now just 290 women. A new governor was also in charge. John Morton died in 1935 'in his quarters at the prison' and was buried in nearby Highgate cemetery with a wreath made of flowers from the prison gardens. His successor was Dr John Matheson, formerly of Wormwood Scrubs.

Mary Size recalled little press coverage on Holloway during her time: there were no headlines about forcible feeding or executions, and the prison only made the news 'when a woman was received whose case created widespread interest or shocked the public conscience'. And when that happened, as it did several times, then hundreds of people congregated outside, hoping to get a glimpse of Holloway's latest celebrity inmate.

II

Celebrity Prisoners

One afternoon in the spring of 1929 the governor of Brixton Prison rang Mary Size to say that 'a prisoner received there was found to be a woman' and he was sending her to Holloway without delay. Mary went to the reception ward where she saw two men, one 'an extremely handsome, well-groomed gentleman in a dress suit, the other, a plain looking man in ordinary clothes'. Looking from one to the other she asked, 'Which of you two is the prisoner?' The prison officer, in his ordinary clothes, stepped forward and pointed to the man in the dress suit. 'Madam, this is the prisoner.'

The arrival of Colonel Victor Barker at Holloway Prison would cause a sensation. Born Lillias Irma Valerie Barker in Jersey in 1895, as a child Victor was known to her family and friends as Valerie. During the First World War she had worked as a volunteer nurse, and in 1918 had married Harold Arkell Smith, an Australian lieutenant. But instead of 'tenderness and love' on the honeymoon she found 'only violence', and returned to her parents. Valerie then joined the Women's Royal Air Force as a driver and later moved in with an Australian corporal, Ernest Pearce-Crouch, with whom she had two children. After leaving Ernest, Valerie adopted the name Victor and began living as a man.

In 1922 Victor met Elfrida Haward; the couple moved to Brighton and took up residence at the Grand Hotel, and Elfrida described her lover as 'the kind of companion every girl dreams about'. They married in 1923 and opened an antiques shop in Hampshire. Victor next became an actor and went on tour, and at one stage they ran dog boarding kennels. Then Elfrida left her husband, and he moved to London where he worked as a secretary to a leader of the

National Fascisti, a small fascist organization. Victor – now living as Colonel Barker, a decorated war veteran – leased a café near Leicester Square but the business went bankrupt and the owner took him to court. When he failed to respond to a bankruptcy notice, Victor was arrested and taken to Brixton Prison.

Placed in a room with several men, Victor was told to undress in a cubicle and get ready to see the doctor. When his turn came he went into the doctor's office wearing his singlet. The doctor told him sharply to take it off, and Victor asked to speak to him privately. He pleaded to be 'passed through', recorded Mary Size, to avoid 'the shame' that 'the revelation of [his] secret would bring'. The doctor said this was impossible; Victor was given his clothes back and removed at once to the women's prison.

This was not the first time someone of the 'wrong sex' had been at Holloway. In November 1908 'an extraordinary case of a man masquerading as a woman' had been discovered by the prison authorities. Clara Myer, of German nationality, had been arrested on account of some undisclosed conduct and 'tearfully begged the Magistrate to let her go, on promise to leave the district'. She was sentenced to a month in jail and taken to Holloway, where 'it was found that the prisoner had been sent to the wrong prison. Clara Myer was a man.' Three hours later the governor had moved Clara to Pentonville where 'the masquerader was at once recognised as an old offender' who four years earlier had served a twelve-month term and twelve strokes as 'an incorrigible rogue'.

Colonel Victor Barker, meanwhile, was 'in a state of nervous tension' on arrival at Holloway, and according to Mary Size, 'appeared to be very concerned' about his nine-year-old son and an unnamed woman, both of whom he had been living with in Park Lane at the time of his arrest. Victor was put in the prison hospital to 'recover from the shock' and a few days later, after the necessary bankruptcy documents had been produced, the colonel was ready to be released. But he was 'very indignant' when Holloway's deputy governor said he could not leave prison clothed as a man and 'spurned the suggestion' that a friend could send in female clothing. Victor was 'a powerfully built woman, whose measurements far exceeded any outsize garment' in stock, but by coincidence the next morning a friend of Mary's sent in some clothes, a very large, grey tweed costume with a large blouse to match. After some persuasion Victor put them on. Mary then 're-shaped' his trilby to make 'it look more feminine', and added a pair of grey silk stockings. 'So long was it since I had worn feminine garments that I had forgotten how to put them on,' Victor later recalled, and the 'woman officer giggled as she watched me'.

The press lost no time in circulating news of the release of the 'Man–Woman' and soon men, women and children and prams were outside the prison. The crowd grew so dense that mounted police were sent to keep order, while passing motorists parked their cars near the prison gates, all 'waiting feverishly for a glimpse of the great impersonator'. Victor's wife Elfrida had recently told her story to the *Evening Standard*, explaining that she had 'never for a moment imagined that my husband was anything but the person he always appeared to be'. Now spectators wanted a glimpse of the famous Colonel Barker who had so successfully 'masqueraded' as a man that his wife had been unaware, even on their honeymoon. Elfrida later told police that she thought 'artificial means' had been employed.

On the afternoon of 9 March 1929 there were 1,000 people at the Holloway gates, but to Mary Size's credit she decided to smuggle Victor through a small gate at the back of the prison, normally used only by staff. They hurried west around the perimeter to the back of the houses on Dalmeny Avenue and then climbed into a garden. The colonel vaulted over the wall, Mary climbed up and he grabbed her and lifted her down to the ground, whereupon hidden press photographers started flashing their cameras. The 'secret exit' was certainly dramatic, according to the press: not only had Colonel Barker left by an unknown back door, he had 'walked along a moat, climbed a steep embankment and a 6ft wall'. Victor had already sold his story to a Sunday paper, and the first of four instalments was published the day after he left Holloway.

Soon after his release, however, Victor was arrested for perjury, having sworn to a fake name in the bankruptcy case, and then charged with making a false declaration at his marriage in 1923. He was brought before a criminal court where 'there was a rush for the public gallery . . . women predominating.' There were repeated references to the 'bogus marriage' and 'this travesty of marriage', and the judge declared that the amount of press and public interest was 'part of the punishment for her perverted conduct'.

Colonel Victor Barker had so threatened gender roles, marrying a man and becoming a mother, then living as a man and marrying a woman, that, in the eyes of the court, he might as well have been the devil himself. 'You are an unprincipled, mendacious and unscrupulous adventuress,' declared the judge, 'you have profaned the House of God, outraged the decencies of nature, and broken the laws of man. You have falsified the Marriage Register, and set an evil example which, were you to go unpunished, others might follow.' Victor was sentenced to nine months at Holloway and was reported to be 'quite unmoved' as he was escorted to the cells below.

But the publicity around the case must have been traumatic and Mary Size described Victor as 'quiet and subdued' during his months in Holloway. He worked hard and 'behaved very well', was kind and considerate to the other inmates and helped teachers in the evening handicraft classes. But Victor later described the food as so terrible that it was 'calculated to break the strongest spirit, to impart an intense hatred of mankind and of the forces of law and order'. His nerves 'began to get ragged and it only needed the least thing for me to fly off the handle. One day I became so upset over some trifling incident that I threw a mug of cocoa over a wardress. Then I dashed into my cell in hysterics.' According to Victor, Mary Size put him in solitary confinement for two days.

Once his sentence was up, and having earned a month's remission for good conduct, Victor's second exit from Holloway was far more low-key. 'I shall always remember how, on the morning of her discharge, she stood between the entrance gates of the prison to brace herself before she faced life in the outside world again,' wrote Mary, 'but when I passed her through the outer gate there was no one there to stare at her.'

Victor left London, worked as an assistant to a fortune teller on the Isle of Wight and appeared as Colonel Barker in a Blackpool seafront sideshow, 'making a peepshow of myself', displayed in a bed in a cellar. He also returned briefly to Holloway Prison. In March 1937, while working as a manservant in Mayfair, he was arrested for stealing £5 from his employer's bedroom. When the police asked why he was wearing men's clothes Victor replied, 'Do you know who I am?' He was remanded for a week and kept in the prison hospital, and then fined, with the magistrate advising him to 'get honest work as a woman'.

Victor died impoverished in 1960, under the name Geoffrey Norton. But in recent years Colonel Barker's story has been given a more dignified ending, and in 2006 the Brighton Museum and History Centre celebrated his life as a transgender man during LGBT month. Victor may have posed as a decorated military officer and appeared to seek fame through the pages of the press, but he was brave enough to refuse to live under socially imposed gender roles, despite repeated persecution and imprisonment.

Shortly before Victor's second release from Holloway in December 1929, another new arrival also attracted widespread interest. London nightclub queen Kate Meyrick was born in Dublin in 1875, and after moving to England she became part-owner and manager of Dalton's Club in Leicester Square. Soho in the 1920s was renowned for its nightlife, with clubs and 'bottle parties' that openly flouted licensing laws, and although Kate was fined for 'keeping disorderly premises' she went on to open her own club, the 43 Club at 43 Gerrard Street. This would appear in Evelyn Waugh's novel *A Handful of Dust* as a ramshackle building called the Old Hundredth which stayed open from nine in the evening until four in the morning, selling 'an unimpeded flow of dubious, alcoholic preparations'. The club also appeared in *Brideshead Revisited*, along with its proprietor Ma Mayfield, who was based on Kate Meyrick, 'a stout woman in evening dress' who demanded ten bob before letting customers in.

Kate Meyrick described the regulars of the 43 as 'officers of distinguished regiments, members of the peerage, experienced Men about Town or rich young City magnates'. It was a favourite spot for American actress Tallulah Bankhead, and it was also said to be the centre of the area's drug scene. In November 1924 Sergeant George Goddard led a raid on the club and Kate was sentenced to six months at Holloway for selling intoxicating liquor without a licence. The magistrate described her as 'a lady of good appearance and charming manners' who 'conducted her various clubs with more decorum than many, but with also a fine contempt for the law'.

More raids followed and Kate Meyrick became known as 'the most inveterate breaker of club licensing laws in London'. Arrested again in 1928 she was sentenced to another six months in Holloway and permission was given for her two daughters, the Countess of Kinnoull and Lady Clifford, both peeresses through marriage, to see her before she began her sentence. But if her daughters hoped this was the last time they would visit their mother in prison they were wrong. Sergeant Goddard was soon under investigation for corruption, and one of his clients was a well-known proprietress of London West End nightclubs who had been paying him £100 a week to avoid further raids. The police issued a warrant: 'Wanted, Kate Meyrick, aged 53, height 5ft, 3½ in., complexion pale, sunburnt face, grey bobbed hair, blue eyes.' This time she was sentenced to fifteen months of hard labour for bribing a police officer.

Kate became seriously ill in Holloway and was transferred to the prison hospital with heart trouble. After serving six months she was freed, having earned three months' remission for good conduct, but appeared at a party held in her honour looking haggard. A year or so later she was in Monte Carlo and about to buy a 'well known cabaret', but soon she was back in Holloway for another six months after the police found intoxicating liquor was being 'sold freely at 43 Gerrard Street on most nights'. By the spring of 1932 Kate had had enough, she'd lost much of her fortune and had returned to her house in Regent's Park, where 'all enquirers were told that she was resting.' 'One thing is certain,' revealed an unnamed source, 'London's night life will see her no more. She has finished with all that for ever.'

Shortly afterwards, another famous inmate arrived at Holloway, 27-year-old socialite Elvira Barney who, unlike Colonel Victor

Barker and Kate Meyrick, had links to both wealth and power. In May 1932 the police arrived at her Knightsbridge home to find she had shot her lover Michael Stephen. When an Inspector Campion suggested she bring her fur coat as she might find it a little cold at the police station, she reportedly 'flew into a temper' and struck him in the face, saying, 'I will teach you to tell me you will put me in a cell, you vile swine.'

Elvira was allowed to go to her parents, Sir John and Lady Mullens, before being sent to Holloway. The governor reported that she was of sound mind, aside from 'one or two occasions' of 'hysterical manifestations', and had 'shown no symptoms of drug taking'. The idea of assessing a prisoner for drug use was relatively new, as was drug use inside, although Mary Size recalled a woman on remand whose visitor managed to bring 'a quantity of heroin' inside her baby's clothing.

On the first day of Elvira Barney's trial the crowd were so eager to get in that there were 'cries from women being crushed' at the doorway. She arrived in a private saloon car from Holloway, with the blinds drawn, and accompanied by three women officers. Elvira walked to the dock 'like a woman in a trance', where she soon collapsed. Again the issue of drugs was raised, with Holloway's governor telling the court there was no indication that 'she had ever been addicted'. Elvira was defended by the former Attorney General Sir Patrick Hastings, and the jury found her not guilty of murder. The shooting had been an accident, the couple had been wrestling together after Elvira had threatened to shoot herself, and the gun went off. The evidence of a neighbour who reported hearing Elvira shout that she would shoot Michael was dismissed. The London socialite was described as a tragic figure, and her court appearance as an ordeal. The defence argued that she had 'adored the dead man' and there was not 'sufficient evidence to hang a cat'. Elvira was acquitted – why she wasn't also charged with manslaughter remains unclear – although she was later fined £50 for having an illegal firearm.

While the verdict in the murder trial didn't go down well with the crowds outside the court, some press reports appeared to find the outcome fair, and unrelated to her social status. 'The familiar whispering that prosecution is tempered for prisoners of rich or important connections was once more put to shame,' reported the *Daily Telegraph*. Yet few people on trial for murder could have afforded to hire Sir Patrick Hastings, whose final speech was applauded by the judge as one of the finest he had ever heard. The following summer Elvira was back in court, fined for dangerous driving in the south of France, and some three years later she was found dead in a Paris hotel room. The official cause was a brain haemorrhage, but the press was quick to add that she had been out 'merry making' the night before, and modern reports attribute her death to a combination of cocaine and alcohol.

Two world-famous sporting stars also ended up, briefly, at Holloway in the 1930s. Irish racing driver Fay Taylour was jailed for seven days in June 1935 after refusing to pay a £1 speeding fine. The year before she had won the Leinster Trophy road race in Ireland, for which she was the only woman competitor. However, when the fine was settled anonymously she was released the next day.

Two years later Lady Mary Heath, the Irish athlete and aviator, was jailed for being drunk and disorderly. In 1928 she had become the first person to fly solo from Cape Town to London, a journey that took her three months, emerging in 'a chic brown sports ensemble', fur coat and high-heeled shoes. That same year she broke the solo altitude record, reaching nearly five miles, and saying 'it was the nearest to Heaven I have ever been'. But in 1929 she was seriously injured when her plane crashed into a factory roof in Ohio, fracturing her skull. Eight years later she was arrested at Piccadilly Tube station, although her solicitor said that 'she was being followed by a man and approached a detective for protection'. Unable to raise a surety of £10, she was sentenced to a month at Holloway. After two days she was released and 'disappeared' while on probation. She died in 1939 after falling down the stairs in a tram in east London, and was admitted to hospital as 'identity unknown'.

By the end of the 1930s, and despite all the changes introduced at Holloway under deputy governor Mary Size and prison commissioner

Lilian Barker, the building itself remained a problem. Lilian 'looked at Holloway with horror,' recalled her niece, 'and felt defeated by the vastness and inhumanity of the place'. So she started campaigning to have the old Victorian castle demolished; the only way to modernize Holloway was to begin again, and a new women's prison was needed outside London.

The government was initially loath to invest in such a scheme, especially as Holloway was functioning so well, but the appointment of Samuel Hoare as Home Secretary, a man known to be in favour of penal reform and a great-nephew of Elizabeth Fry, led to the Criminal Justice Bill of 1938. This sparked an extensive programme of prison rebuilding, and when it came to the future Holloway had top priority. Lilian was overjoyed, for it was 'here, she felt, must the battles be fought for all the women's prisons'.

In July that year the Home Secretary announced that the Home Office was to acquire a rural site for women prisoners, to which the word 'prison' would scarcely apply for it was to be a 'camp' where 'a good deal of open-air work will be possible'. Lilian and her colleagues began drawing up plans for the new model jail. 'Instead of parking women in prison,' she explained, 'I should like to imprison them in a park. It should be possible for them to live not in the atmosphere of huge stone buildings, but of trees and grass.' The prison commissioners sent the plans to the Treasury and Home Office, and a site was identified on land that is now part of Heathrow airport, where there would also be a Borstal Institution. Pentonville would be demolished and after the women from Holloway and Aylesbury had been transferred to the new rural prison, the men could move into the castle jail. For once women were getting new facilities, and men were inheriting the old.

The Press Association was invited into Holloway at the beginning of 1939 to see the 'delightful' prison gardens and Mary Size led the way amid the shrubberies and rockeries towards their 'greatest triumph', a flourishing rose garden on what had once been a coal dump. But there was one thing worrying the deputy governor, explained the Press Association: 'In a year or two's time the women's prison will be removed from Holloway to the new building . . . Holloway will then become a men's prison, and Miss Size is wondering if the men will appreciate the gardens and care for them as the women did.' But sadly for Mary Size, she needn't have worried. On 3 September Britain declared war on Germany, plans for the new women's prison were shelved and national defence took priority again. From a prison that had been leading the way in terms of reform, life inside Holloway was about to turn violent once again.

PART FOUR

Holloway at War

12

Enemy Aliens

Katherine Hallgarten is making me tea in her large, bright Hampstead kitchen. Outside the window is a view of Hampstead Heath and a path leading up to Parliament Hill, one of the highest spots in London and below which, just two miles away, is Holloway Prison. In 1940 Katherine's mother Ruth Borchard was held at Holloway before being sent to an internment camp on the Isle of Man. She, along with her husband and one-year-old daughter, was now an enemy alien.

Ruth Borchard was born to Jewish parents in Hamburg in 1910. She studied economics and sociology at university and in 1937 married Kurt Borchard, from a German-Jewish shipping family. The following year they moved to England along with Kurt's mother Lucy, joining around 74,000 German and Austrian refugees who had settled in Britain. A few weeks after war was declared, the Home Office set up Aliens Tribunals to examine every registered German and Austrian refugee over the age of sixteen. There was no need to raise 'the turnip-headed scare of anti-Semitism in Britain', declared one journalist, for while the vast majority were above suspicion, some were 'masquerading here as persecuted Gentiles or Jews but who have been in contact with or working for the enemy'. The tribunals decided who could 'properly be exempted from internment', and legal representatives were not allowed. One hundred and twenty tribunals were set up to classify 'aliens': Category A refugees were deemed a high security risk and interned; Category B were 'doubtful' and subject to restrictions; while Category C were 'loyal to the British cause' and therefore allowed to remain free.

The British government didn't initially intend to intern large numbers of enemy aliens, especially those already officially recognized as racial and/or political refugees. To begin with, 500 people deemed high risk were arrested, but such was the confusion over classification that Category A men and women may have included as many anti-Nazis and Jews as actual Nazis.

The government was also reluctant to intern women en masse, with the Home Secretary John Anderson fearing 'there would soon be a public outcry' when the great majority were 'individually known to British subjects who are convinced of their friendliness'. But, queried one Conservative MP, 'is not the female of any species generally more dangerous than the male?' The public appeared to be largely behind internment, and one town council in Lancashire voted that all enemy aliens should be locked up without exception because, explained the local alderman, 'no one could tell how many were of the Nazi advance guard'. But critics like George Bell, the Bishop of Chichester, were vehemently opposed: 'The refugees are not Hitlerism; they are the enemies of Hitlerism,' and their internment was 'demanded neither by national security nor by justice'.

Between May and June 1940, when the invasion of Britain seemed imminent, around 25,000 men and 4,000 women were interned, including Ruth Borchard. But it was only recently that her daughter Katherine Hallgarten discovered further details of her time in Holloway. 'Mother died in 2000,' she explains as she leads the way into her living room. 'I was looking for something else, among all the family stuff flung in the room, and I came across a typed manuscript dated 1943. I asked my brother and sister if they knew anything about it and they didn't. My first thought was, Oh goodness this is really interesting, and my second thought was, Why didn't she tell us?'

The manuscript turned out to be an unfinished novel, now entitled *We Are Strangers Here*, telling the story of a young German refugee, Anna Silver, imprisoned as an enemy alien in 1940. The semi-autobiographical book, which Katherine and her siblings published in 2008, is one of very few accounts of those interned in Holloway as suspect aliens during the Second World War – and one of only two written in English. Charmian Brinson, professor of

German at Imperial College London, who wrote the foreword to Ruth's novel, explains that even within academic studies on internment, 'the Holloway interlude has been swiftly passed over as representing little more than a preliminary to "internment proper".' Some of those interned were unwilling to talk about the experience afterwards, while 'most people took it in their stride. It was wartime, a time of general panic, they understood.' After the war was over, the refugee population was 'seeking to assimilate into the host community' and so there was 'little appetite for such subjects'.

Ruth Borchard had never mentioned her novel to her children, but she had told them about being imprisoned. 'Mum told stories all the time, she was a storyteller. A story often told to us was that she was in Holloway. She said the worst thing was not knowing if I could go with her or not.' Katherine pauses and sips her tea. 'But it wasn't bad. She liked the women together bit. But she didn't like the waiting, waiting, waiting. It was a holding place.'

Katherine stayed with her grandmother Lucy, and was brought to the train station and handed over when her mother was transferred to the Rushen Women's Internment Camp on the Isle of Man. Ruth had no idea if she would be allowed to take her daughter until the very last moment when she boarded the train. The loss and anxiety of being separated from a child pervades the novel, and includes scenes Ruth must have witnessed first-hand or heard about at Holloway Prison.

We Are Strangers opens in May 1940 with Anna Silver and her husband Bert, a scientist, appearing before an Aliens Tribunal. This marked the beginning of mass internment when all those in Category B were arrested, followed in June by all Category C men. As a result, 3,600 women, over half of whom were officially classified as refugees from Nazi oppression, were sent to Holloway en route to the Isle of Man.

Anna Silver is jailed at Holloway along with Nele, her thirteen-month-old daughter. They arrive at the prison — fictionalized as Holmdale Prison, but instantly recognizable as Holloway — to find a grey and dirty yard encased by greyish black walls with rows of 'hollow-eyed little windows', piles of coal and smoky steam floating across from the prison laundry. Inside the central part of the prison, green iron railings seem 'to lead in all directions into a lower sort of infinity'.

Anna looks through the open doors of cells, and while she sees a few English convicts the majority were internees, 'calm ones, knowing ones, furious ones, frightened ones, desperate ones, bewildered ones, there they sat, in cell upon cell'. Like many newcomers to prison, she was struck by the noise, the 'crying, sobbing, long-drawn-out whining, chattering, nervous laughter'.

Anna is immediately told that her daughter can't stay, contrary to what she was promised by the tribunal judge and the police. 'This is no place for a child,' an officer tells her, 'you will get her back when you go to the Isle of Man.' Her first priority is to get Nele some milk, marking the beginning of 'a war of nerves' when it comes to dealing with the bureaucracy of the prison system.

She also needs to reach her mother-in law Ida to ask her to take Nele, who will otherwise go to an institution. In the meantime they are put in the prison hospital. When Nele refuses bread and milk, and 'kept scratching at the locked room and cried to be taken out', Anna knows it's better that her daughter leaves. Other women who have had their children taken are now constantly in tears; some 'shrieked whenever the door opened'; in other cases 'the nurses had to hold the mother while they tore it away'.

Anna tries repeatedly to get word to her mother-in-law, but it's only when another prisoner, Hilde Gottschalk, bribes 'an old gaol-bird' with a box of cigarettes that a telegram is sent and Nele is taken away. Anna then finds peace in her 'austere nun's cell', although being looked at through the spy hole is 'indecent, how humiliating this defenceless exposure to anonymous observation was'.

Holmdale is a place of petty rules. Women in the prison hospital are not allowed to lie down during the day unless the doctor says so; a letter Anna writes to her husband is sent back a week later by the censor because she's written it in pencil. But Anna rediscovers her independence in jail, and along with other internees sets to work improving the English prison system.

Holloway had its own problems, and its inmates and staff had been evacuated eight months earlier, except for those on remand and hospital patients. On 2 September 1939, the day before Britain declared war on Germany, all prisoners serving a sentence of three months or less were released. 'There was neither commotion nor hysteria,' recalled deputy governor Mary Size, 'everything was done in an orderly manner.' Within forty-eight hours, 200 women – two-thirds of Holloway's population – had been set free. Two days later most of the remaining inmates went to Aylesbury, accompanied by Mary Size, along with thirty officers and other principal staff. Lilian Barker, the prison commissioner, went to Aylesbury to welcome them, aware that the war meant 'the postponement of all her rosy plans for the women's prisons'. Mary Size provides no details on the women who were moved from Holloway, stating only that 'several were aliens'. Some were 'excellent craftswomen' who apparently wouldn't give any assistance to the war effort, but who eventually decided it was best to cooperate and save themselves from 'snubs and sometimes from open hostility'. Holloway historian John Camp also skirts over this period in the prison's history, devoting just a few sentences to 'those of alien origin' who displayed 'a sullen defiance of authority in prison and a refusal to cooperate', having had their 'illusions regarding freedom and tolerance' in Britain shattered.

There is little evidence of a refusal to cooperate in Ruth Borchard's novel, or in oral testimony from other interned refugees. Instead the opposite happened: it was the enemy aliens who imposed order on chaos. After the evacuation of most of Holloway's prisoners around twenty women were left in the jail yet within two years it had one of its largest ever populations, with 863 inmates, many of whom were enemy aliens. The authorities were confused about the new arrivals. Prior to the outbreak of war the prison's Convict Register included around a dozen 'aliens' who had given false statements, failed to register or landed without permission, and who were then deported. By September 1939, however, up to twenty-three 'Alien Suspects' were being admitted a day. On more than one occasion their 'offence' was then crossed out and replaced with '18B', the Defence Regulation under which Nazi supporters were arrested.

'In a funny way,' Ruth Borchard later wrote to her husband, 'I liked being in Holloway very much.' She held English classes for other refugees and felt that she was 'useful and needed once more. We did a good bit of work there.' She told her sister that she wanted to 'make this a fruitful time of my life. I often feel if I had the choice between freedom and having time as now – I would not know what to choose.'

Holmdale's staff are generally portrayed as uncaring, motivated by 'the gloating enjoyment of power' and using 'a shoving gesture peculiar to all officers' in a prison now overflowing with difficult 'bloody foreigners'. The prison is chaotic, with hundreds of newcomers every week and women are now put two in a cell, 'something unheard of in Holmdale Prison before'. Anna has arrived at the height of the internment crisis. 'Why do they keep sending them down here?' asks one officer. 'There's no room for them.' When another officer comments, 'There is no end of you people arriving,' Hilde Gottschalk asks why they don't get more staff. 'They won't come,' is the reply. 'Nobody wants to work with you foreigners now.' There were kindly staff members, however, and Ruth Borchard later wrote to her husband: 'What made even Holloway no prison: the decent tone of the officials.'

Everyone is eager for news from outside: will they be moved or released, has the invasion of Britain begun? Rumours are rife; the tea is said to contain bromide, just as during the suffragettes' time. And then there is the racism. One day, outside by the vegetable plot, a woman walks around 'with her eyes averted from their group in demonstrative loathing'. She asks Anna, 'Are you a Jewess?' And when Anna says her husband is a Jew the woman remarks, 'Oh. Then you are polluted, too.'

Holloway's enemy aliens were kept in C wing, in the north-east part of the prison, where they had their own exercise time. In theory they were separated from members of the British Union of Fascists, but in one scene of Ruth's novel the fascists are installed in the internees' wing and they march into a refugee's cell on the sunny side of the corridor and throw all her belongings out on to the corridor floor. While Anna doesn't 'feel quite up to a group of English Fascists' she goes to investigate. A group have gathered, looking 'only too ready for a fight', with one blocking the door to the cell. Hilde makes as if to poke a cigarette in her face, the woman shrinks back with a scream and Hilde gets into the cell. The passageway is now packed with 'thrilled listeners' and when an officer arrives, not understanding the circumstances, Hilde is removed. 'Don't you know your people?' Hilde asks. 'They are Fascists – they believe in telling lies.' 'Well,' responds the officer, 'to us you are all suspects, or else you wouldn't be here.' And that is what the enemy aliens in Holloway were – not convicted of treason or spying, but foreigners suspected of some as yet uncommitted crime that might happen in the future.

After six weeks Anna is finally told they are to be moved to the Isle of Man, and is terrified to find that her daughter's name isn't on the list. Holloway's governor, a man with 'a gruff appearance and keen eyes', tells her there is nothing he can do. But when they arrive at Euston station Anna is finally reunited with her daughter, and together they journey to Liverpool and from there to their next home, a seaside resort surrounded by barbed wire. Ruth Borchard stayed on the Isle of Man for around eighteen months and 'she had a wonderful time,' says Katherine, 'there was so much time to write.' But there was such a shortage of babies to cuddle that she put a label around her daughter's neck saying 'Don't feed me and don't hug me'.

While some enemy aliens were initially sent to Holloway with their children, others were separated from their sons and daughters while inside. Suzanne Schwarzenberger, a German lawyer, immigrated to Britain five years before the war, after her brother had been condemned to death for being a leader of a student anti-Nazi organization. Suzanne and her husband rented a house in Golders Green, north London, where their son Rolf was born. Then they were told to attend an Aliens Tribunal, where both were classified as Category B and sent to be interned. Suzanne was taken to Holloway with her four-year-old son. 'Rolf was just completely, from one day to the other, taken away from me and put somewhere in a hospital.' For four weeks she had no idea where he was, and was given no news. 'There was quite a bit of administrative chaos. There was good will but . . . he was just lost in the works.' The effect of the separation on Rolf would last for years, and triggered both eczema and asthma. 'He had never been away from me. And he came back to me, when we were taken to the Isle of Man, completely disturbed.'

Eight-year-old Eva Holmes was also removed from her mother, Susanna Maria Friedmann, while in Holloway Prison. Susanna was born in Vienna, and her husband Ludwig Liebermann, a chemist and teacher, was from Berlin. He studied chemistry at university and his work took him around Europe and the States, but in 1937 when his employers sent him to England on a business trip they advised him not to return to Germany as both Ludwig and Susanna's families were of Jewish descent. He was offered a job as technical adviser and export manager of an aluminium foil factory in Wembley. But by September 1939 the attitude towards refugees had changed, and two months later they both appeared at an Aliens Tribunal, where they were classified as Category B aliens. Susanna, like many others, had never thought women with children would be interned, but on 11 June Susanna and her two young children Eva and Albert were taken to Holloway Prison and put 'in a small cell'. 'I feel the atmosphere of prison very much,' she wrote in her diary, 'nervousness, bitter words against being shut in.'

Susanna's children were then removed and taken to the Ladywell Institute in Lewisham. Each day more women were brought to Holloway, 'nearly 1,000 arrived in the last three weeks. They treat us as if we were convicts. I always think they really do not understand . . . Now the doors are shut but I seem to hear crying women all over the place. What a quantity of unhappiness is behind these thick walls.' One night Susanna and the other women were woken at 1 a.m., told to pack and dress and move to B wing. Susanna was nearly at breaking point; the Home Office had not yet decided if she would be reunited with her children. Finally on 30 June the women lined up to leave and one by one they passed the governor's secretary. 'When my turn came, she said first door left; there are your children. I nearly did not understand and there was Eva weeping and Albert laughing. What happiness.' Susanna and Ludwig were held at different camps on the Isle of Man, and the family was released in early 1941, after being reclassified as Category C aliens. Six years later the couple became British citizens and changed their names by deed poll, to Susan and Louis Linton.

Today their daughter Eva Holmes lives in a quiet residential road in Muswell Hill, north London, and we sit in her lounge where she offers freshly brewed coffee and hands me an account she has written of her parents' move to England. Eva can remember little of her week in Holloway, but she clearly recalls the children's home in Kent where she and Albert were later transferred to from Lewisham. They were assigned to different houses because of their age, and taught to sing 'There'll always be an England'.

Eva's mother didn't talk about her time in prison:

> People don't want to burden their children with their stresses. My father had fought in the First War and his brother had died, they didn't talk about things that were traumatic, and they made an enormous effort to establish a new identity. They lost friends; their standard of living went down after they were interned. I was angry that they changed their names, but they did it for us, so it would be easier for us, and it was, it was a further commitment to the country. I have passed Holloway on the bus sometimes and very occasionally I might say in a social situation that 'Yes, I've been in Holloway Prison,' but life's too short to dwell on it.

But Eva says she gets 'very distressed when I see children in England put in refugee centres today, it seems to me we've learned nothing. My parents were aliens' – she leans forward in her chair – '*enemy* aliens. It's the same as now, when you're at war you assume everyone is the enemy; it's like the Middle East today and discrimination against Muslims. When there is such a degree of ignorance, then there is paranoia and people end up in prison.'

For the second time in twenty-five years Holloway had served as a place to imprison women regarded as a threat to national security. They were convicted without trial and guilty of no crime other than, as the sign on their cell door explained, being an 'enemy alien'. The imprisonment of Jewish refugees has rarely been written about; it is a shameful period of Holloway's past. Thousands of women who had escaped persecution in Germany were labelled the enemy and separated from their children, not because of what they had done but because of who they were. And while the British press provided few details on the detainment of enemy aliens at Holloway, it did devote a lot of space to the arrest and imprisonment of those held under Defence Regulation 18B.

13

Fascists and Spies

The incarceration of Nazi sympathizers and members of the British Union of Fascists (BUF) at Holloway Prison was particularly newsworthy because many of those convicted were British aristocrats and well-known military figures. This posed the sort of problem rarely seen at Holloway since late Victorian times: could the upper class really be expected to live in prison and if so how would they be treated?

At the outbreak of war around a dozen 18Bs had been interned; by the end of 1940 there were over 1,000 in custody. Some of the women at Holloway belonged to the BUF, although one insisted she was 'an inactive member' who had 'never done anything to hurt my country'. Others were members of the Right Club, a small and vehemently anti-Semitic fascist group formed by MP Archibald Ramsay. In total nearly 2,000 people were detained under regulation 18B, and as with the enemy aliens they were not charged with any crime nor were they put on trial. Their numbers in Holloway were far smaller – twenty-five women were detained under 18B in the autumn of 1942 – but the incarceration of fascist women lasted years instead of weeks. Conditions for these prisoners were to be 'as in-oppressive as possible', explained the Press Association and the fascists were treated as first-division inmates. Meals could be supplemented, they could have half a bottle of wine every twenty-four hours, smoking was allowed at exercise and recreation, labour was voluntary and they could wear their own clothes, although letters and parcels were subject to censorship and inspection. It was made clear that the point of the detention was for 'custodial purposes only', but Diana Mosley, the most famous 18B prisoner, certainly saw her incarceration as punishment.

★

Born in 1910, Diana Mitford was a member of a family with strong establishment ties: her father was a baron and her cousin was the Prime Minister's wife Clementine Churchill. At the age of eighteen Diana had married Bryan Guinness, heir to the brewing fortune and son of the Minister of Agriculture, and coverage of their wedding filled the society pages. Then in 1932 she met Oswald Mosley and was entranced. 'He was completely sure of himself and of his ideas,' she later wrote. 'He knew what to do to solve the economic disaster we were living through.' A former Conservative MP, and ex-Labour Party member, he 'was about to launch his Fascist movement', the BUF, and 'if I have a regret, it is that I could not have done more to help him and further his aims'. Diana divorced Bryan, and in the summer of 1933 she and her sister Unity set off for Germany. The sisters were mesmerized by Nazi meetings and parades, and over the course of four years Diana saw Hitler 'fairly often', to 'lunch and dine and talk'. They also discussed setting up a pro-Nazi radio station in Britain.

In 1936, after Oswald's wife died, he and Diana married in Berlin in the drawing room of propaganda minister Joseph Goebbels. The couple then returned to England where the BUF held numerous meetings and demonstrations 'campaigning for peace'. On 22 May 1940 Oswald, along with everyone else at the BUF headquarters, was arrested, as was Archibald Ramsay, leader of the Right Club. Oswald was taken to Brixton Prison and around five weeks later Diana was arrested as well. MI5 regarded her as a serious threat, she was 'a public danger', 'far cleverer and more dangerous than her husband', and would 'stick at nothing to achieve her ambitions'.

Diana had four sons (two with her first husband) and her youngest child was eleven weeks old at the time. When the police told her she was going to Holloway for 'a week-end' she decided to leave him with his nanny. On the way to prison Diana was allowed to stop to buy a breast pump, intending to 'continue nursing the baby when it was over, and then wean him in the usual way'. But 'I should have been wiser to have got the salts and bandages which women use who do not intend to nurse their babies; I should have had far less pain.'

On arrival at Holloway Diana was 'locked into a wooden box

like a broom cupboard' where she stayed for four hours. She believed she was being made an example of: 'This was in the nature of a practical joke on the part of the prison authorities, for there was no reason why I should not have been taken straight to my cell,' although it was in fact routine procedure. She was also certain that it was spite that meant parcels sent from outside took a long time to arrive, and letters were delayed by the censor, including one from the composer Lord Berners, asking, 'What can I send you? Would you like a little file concealed in a peach?'

Diana was taken to F wing, Holloway's original female wing to the east of the prison, and thought the wardresses' insistence that she walk first was 'an act of courtesy', unaware that prisoners always had to stay in front of their jailers. As the door to the wing was unlocked 'a sort of gasp went up' and the other fascist women crowded round her with 'kind expressions of sympathy', furious that she had been separated from her baby whom she missed 'in an almost unbelievable way'. Others had lost their children as well – one 18B had her son taken from her arms and handed to the police to be put in an institution.

F wing was now home to English women arrested under wartime regulations, and the vast majority were members of the BUF. They ranged in age from eighteen to sixty-five, came 'from all classes, from every part of England', and had one thing in common, 'love of country'. They welcomed Diana in with biscuits and cocoa, but she was then taken to a dirty cell in the basement, with a tiny barred window covered by rotting sandbags, and a mattress on the floor. 'There is a frightening look about the metal door of a prison cell,' she wrote, 'because it has no handle on the inside,' and she longed for 'my four post bed . . . air scented with honeysuckle coming through the open window'. She was then moved to E wing, to the west of the prison, which was 'fairly empty' but for 18B Germans and Italians with English passports, most married to British men. She was given a cell upstairs and when a wardress gave her a filthy rag and told her to clean the landing she again took this as an act of spite and refused: 'She knew who I was and probably hoped to annoy.' Diana was given food in a greasy metal container and when she looked inside 'the gorge rose; oily greyish water in which swam a few bits of darker grey gristle and meat.' The other 18Bs at Holloway ate together at trestle tables, but Diana got her own china plate and ate alone, living on bread and Stilton sent in by Oswald. She soon realized, however, that far from spending a weekend, 'I was in Holloway to stay.'

The treatment of both Diana and Oswald was of great interest to their political opponents, the press and the public, with coverage reminiscent of the incarceration of the Duchess of Sutherland in the 1890s. Not only was she an aristocrat, she was a self-confessed Nazi supporter, and suspicions that she was getting preferential treatment appeared to be confirmed when Holloway hosted a spring fashion show. A 'hall was provided as showroom', reported the press, and 'mannequins were allowed to parade for the benefit of Lady Mosley' and the other 18B women. The Home Secretary flatly denied there had been any such show. Instead because of the 'clerical and other work occasioned to the staff at Holloway Prison by the ordering of goods by post' a local firm had sent in items that the women could buy with cash, an arrangement that 'proved to be much less troublesome to the prison authorities'.

The press portrayed the 18Bs as regarding themselves a cut above the other prisoners. When a group was transferred to Aylesbury, they staged a 'sit down' strike and four 'took the view that their bags should be packed for them'. In the process of removing them, 'one or two officers' suffered 'slight injury'. The detainees quickly issued a statement: after two years in prison they had been given just two and a half hours' notice that they were to be transferred. They did not ask the wardresses to pack for them, there had been no sitting in a ring and there was no fight and 'no reason for any injuries'.

A few months after Diana's arrival, dozens of BUF women were transferred to the Isle of Man, but after appearing before the Advisory Committee in Ascot, where she was asked 'silly questions' about Hitler, Goering and Goebbels, Diana was returned to Holloway. She was convinced that the Prime Minister knew 'nothing could ever have induced any of us to harm our own country', while the 'gutter press' continued to write that they were living in idle luxury, with the 'prison dustbins choked with empty champagne bottles after our orgies'. Diana was moved again, back to F wing, where she kept herself busy reading Thomas Carlyle's *The French Revolution*. She also attended Beethoven concerts organized by a German inmate who brought in a gramophone, and joined another woman who warmed her cell by burning paper containers in the chamber pot, to which Diana added eau de cologne 'of the cheapest variety'.

The prison staff appeared to single her out at first, and were as hostile to the 18Bs as they were to enemy aliens: 'They had thought we must be traitors, or near-traitors, because otherwise how was it that we had been locked up by the good and noble men who were leading the nation?' But as the months went by the attitude of the wardresses 'changed completely' and they 'came to know us fairly well and most of them were very kind and friendly . . . they told delightful prison stories.' Diana became friends with three wardresses in particular, one of whom later told a prison visitor, 'We've never had such laughs since Lady Mosley left.' Diana was endlessly amused by the language of prison, a place where 'reception' was not a rather dull and formal party but a broom cupboard; court was a police court not Buckingham Palace; a garden party was a group of bedraggled prisoners in the yard; and going to Ascot meant a trip to the Advisory Committee. In the exercise yard one day she mistakenly used an outdoor toilet with a red 'V' painted on the door, assuming this stood for Victory rather than venereal disease. She also noted, as had the suffragettes before her, that within prison the word 'woman' was used as a derogatory term. It was reserved for convicted prisoners, and one wardress was very insulted when a police officer offered her tea and called her a woman.

But despite the friendly officers and the novelty of her surroundings, Diana Mosley couldn't forget there was a war going on outside. One night a bomb fell by the prison and broke the water mains, and the floors were awash with urine. Another night a bomb tore away a landing and when an inmate stepped out of her cell in the dark she fell down and broke her leg. At least ten high-explosive bombs fell in the vicinity of Holloway Prison during the war, with six on or near Dalmeny Avenue.

When Diana reported on conditions to her lawyer he asked,

rather oddly, 'Don't you know anyone in the government I could appeal to for you?'

'*Know* anyone in the government?' she replied. 'I know *all* the Tories beginning with Churchill . . . the whole lot deserve to be shot.'

But Holloway's governor Dr Matheson, 'a sandy haired Scotchman who had lost an eye and a leg in the first war', was clearly receiving instructions about her treatment from the Home Office. One day he sent for her, accompanied by a 'grim-looking hatchet-faced wardress', and said Lady Mosley was to have a bath every day, which 'he knew, and I knew . . . was not possible'.

She was also allowed to see two of her children and would 'never forget their dear anxious faces as they stared at me'. Later her youngest son was brought in to visit: 'He was completely changed from the little baby I had left ten months before. He sat up and gazed about him with solemn expression.' But when one of her sons had an emergency operation for appendicitis, the Home Office refused her permission to see him.

Then in the spring of 1941 Oswald Mosley was allowed to make fortnightly visits from his own prison cell to Holloway. Admiral Sir Barry Domvile, a former Director of Naval Intelligence, a member of the BUF and 'a delightful and very clever man', was also allowed to see his wife Alexandrina. A few months later Diana's brother Tom came to visit; he was dining at Downing Street that evening and was there anything she wanted him to ask? Diana replied, 'If we have to stay in prison couldn't we at least be together?' Both the governor and the prison commissioners had already refused a request for the Mosleys to be united as an 'administrative impossibility'. But 'Cousin Winston was a noted cutter of red tape,' explained Diana, and he 'ordered the prison to find a way'.

In November 1941 the Prime Minister wrote to Home Secretary Herbert Morrison that 'internment rather than imprisonment is what was contemplated'. He explained that Diana had been in prison for eighteen months without the slightest vestige of any charge against her, separated from her husband. No mention was made of the enemy aliens at Holloway, similarly not charged with any crime, who had gone months without even knowing where their husbands or children were. It was then announced that the Mosleys, as well as three other couples, would stay in Holloway together. The Home Secretary explained that as detention under 18B was not for punitive purposes 'he had always had in mind that married couples . . . should be allowed to live together if suitable arrangements could be made'.

Once again the prison authorities were confused: how would they enter male prisoners into a convict register for women? On 20 December 1941 Oswald Mosley was given the register number '1', his name written in red capital letters and his occupation recorded as 'Independent'. The word 'Male' was then scrawled right across two columns, again in red pen. Three days later, three more men were added: Peter McCarthy, Major Harold de Laessoe and Thomas Swan. After a year and a half in prison, Diana and Oswald Mosley were together again. They were 'lodged' in the 'preventive detention block', where the three other couples became their 'stable companions'. The four men became the first – and last – male prisoners in Holloway since it had become a women's prison in 1902.

The Home Secretary described their accommodation, which 'consisted of cells, but also a kitchen where detainees could cook rations supplied to them and two other rooms which could be used as sitting-room and dining-room.' Their rooms were cleaned by two convicts, to whom they weren't supposed to talk, 'but naturally,' wrote Diana, 'I always did.' One told her that 'prison is not the same punishment for everyone. There are women here who are glad to have something to eat and a bed to sleep in.'

While two of the couples were soon released, the Mosleys and the de Laessoes remained at Holloway for another two years. The men took it in turns to stoke the boiler, and transformed a cabbage patch into a kitchen garden with peas, beans and fraises des bois. But the 'yellow press' continued to make it sound 'as if we were living in unimaginable luxury'. One day Diana's mother, coming to visit by bus, heard the conductor calling, 'Holloway Jail! Lady Mosley's suite! All change here.'

The visiting rules were also relaxed and the Mosleys' two children, aged five and three, spent 'occasional week-ends with their parents' in the prison. A Home Office official told a reporter 'this does not establish a new principle. Children's visits from time to time have been authorized,' as had been the case with newspaper editor William Stead in 1886. Yet no enemy alien had been allowed to have their child visit and stay overnight; instead, as with the children of other 18B prisoners, many had been removed and put into institutions.

On the second visit, the Mosley boys didn't want to leave, with the elder clinging to Diana and pressing his face against her skirt, and she decided not to allow any more overnight stays as they 'do more harm than good'. Then, towards the end of 1943, with Oswald's health 'visibly failing', Diana asked her mother to plead his case with Clementine Churchill. Soon afterwards, a doctor warned that Oswald should be released on health grounds and in December that year they left Holloway Prison, to be placed under house arrest until the end of the war.

A number of other well-known fascists were also interned at Holloway during the war, including racing driver Fay Taylour, who had been briefly jailed in 1935 for refusing to pay a speeding fine, and Norah Dacre Fox, who had been in Holloway three times during her suffragette days. As with the other 18Bs, they were not actually charged with any crime, unlike some of those who were sent to Holloway as German spies.

In October 1940 Danish spy Vera Schalburg was imprisoned in Holloway, under the name Vera Erickson. She had been arrested in Scotland, having rowed ashore from a seaplane with two male colleagues, intending to travel to London to gather intelligence before a planned German invasion. The two men were executed the following year, yet Vera did not stand trial. Various theories have been offered as to why she escaped the gallows, including an affair with a high-ranking British man or her subsequent cooperation with MI5. During her time at Holloway Vera provided the British authorities with descriptions of some of the 18B prisoners. One was 'almost mental . . . suffering from persecution mania and is extremely touchy', while another was 'a drug addict and as she was getting no supplies was nearly crazy as a result'. The government concluded that Holloway Prison was 'a hot bed of gossip . . . the inmates get hold of a grain of truth about a prospective guest, very often overheard by a casual remark dropped by one of the officers, and this is so magnified that by the time the inmate arrived there was a terrific story in circulation.' When Vera was transferred briefly to Aylesbury, 'there was considerable speculation as to whether she was leaving to be hanged'. Speculation as to her eventual fate remains today, and it's not known whether she was deported to Germany or remained in England using another assumed name.

While the British public knew very little of Vera Erickson's movements, actions or motives, they knew far more about Dorothy O'Grady, the first British woman found guilty of treason in the Second World War. Born in 1897 in Clapham, south London, Dorothy was adopted soon after birth and by the age of seventeen she was working as a domestic servant. In January 1918 she was arrested under the name Pamela Arland, accused of forging a 10 shilling note and sent to Holloway where the governor reported she was intelligent and bright but not industrious or of good character, had bad associates and 'needs to be detained for her own reformation'. She was sent to Aylesbury, transferred to Maidstone as she was 'incorrigible', then sent to another reformatory institution where she was 'exceedingly insolent and insubordinate'. As with Selina Salter in the 1860s, the authorities couldn't think what to do with her. In 1920 she was sentenced to two years' hard labour for stealing clothes, and then arrested four times for prostitution.

After her fourth conviction for soliciting she married a London firefighter, Vincent O'Grady, and they moved to the Isle of Wight where she ran a boarding house and started to arouse suspicion by walking her dog in restricted areas. In August 1940 she was charged with being in a prohibited area, but instead of appearing at court she went on the run for two weeks, apparently afraid that her husband would discover her convictions for prostitution. She was eventually found at another boarding house, having reverted to the name she had first used in prison, Pamela Arland. By now the police had searched her home and after finding drawings and maps of the coast, she faced nine charges under the Treachery Act, the Official Secrets Act and the Defence Regulations.

After a two-day trial that was held in camera and at which she didn't take the stand, Dorothy was found guilty. The press explained she had made a plan 'likely to be of assistance to the military operations of the enemy, and, to help Hitler, cut a military telephone wire'. The 'short, dark, bespectacled housewife' was sentenced to death as a Nazi saboteur, and was reported to be 'entirely unmoved' by her fate. Her conviction came within hours of the execution of Dutch spy Charles Albert van den Kieboom at Pentonville Prison. A week earlier two other men had also been executed at Pentonville under the Treachery Act, having landed 'surreptitiously in the country, to . . . send military secrets back to Germany by a portable radio transmitting set'. In Dorothy's case, it wasn't clear how she planned to pass her information on to the Germans, and thus she was a saboteur rather than spy. 'Mrs O'Grady has been sentenced to death,' wrote MI5's director of counter-espionage, Guy Liddell, in his diary. 'Personally I doubt whether she is guilty of anything more than collecting information.'

Dorothy kept herself occupied in Holloway Prison trying to signal to German bombers from her cell during air raids, befriended a Russian suspected of being a spy, and embroidered swastikas which she handed out to other inmates. Then in February 1941 her sentence was reduced to fourteen years in prison, after her lawyer successfully argued that the judge had misdirected the jury.

Dorothy O'Grady was transferred to Aylesbury, where she was pronounced intelligent but mentally disturbed. She was clearly a traumatized woman, for the medical officer removed a series of lethal objects from Dorothy's vagina including a medicinal pot and fifty pieces of broken glass. She was taken back to Holloway for further evaluation where a psychotherapist reported that she had deep feelings of resentment and strong masochistic tendencies: 'all her life she has enjoyed punishment, and has often sought it unnecessarily'. She was then returned to Aylesbury, diagnosed as a hysterical psychopath.

Dorothy O'Grady was released after nine years, and like many Holloway inmates before her she sold her story to the press, telling the *Sunday Express* that it had all been 'a huge joke' and that 'the excitement of being tried for my life was intense . . . It made me feel somebody instead of being an ordinary seaside landlady.' She returned to the Isle of Wight and was still giving interviews in her eighties, insisting, 'I never was a traitor. I had a fair trial but I got myself into trouble through being an exhibitionist. I wanted to be noticed.'

Ten years after Dorothy's death in 1985, however, Isle of Wight MP Barry Field, who had set out to clear her name, got a nasty shock when the National Archives released papers relating to her case. The maps she had drawn turned out to be detailed and accurate after all, and would have helped a German attack. 'I am staggered by the treachery she sunk to,' said the MP. 'She could have altered the direction of the war.'

In 1942, with three years of war still remaining, Holloway's prisoners and staff who had been evacuated to Aylesbury were moved back to London. Mary Size had by now been promoted to governor of the Buckinghamshire prison, but she reluctantly agreed to retire on the grounds of ill health. The imprisonment of women for wartime crimes – real or imagined – wasn't over, however, for now Holloway was also home to pacifists and conscientious objectors.

14

Pacifists

In December 1941, with London ravaged from the effects of the Blitz and with all basic food supplies rationed, as well as civilian clothing and furniture, conscription was introduced for women for the first time. Widows and unmarried women, aged between twenty and thirty and without young children, became liable to join the noncombatant women's military forces, or work for civilian defence or industry. Again tribunals were set up to decide whether an applicant could be registered as a conscientious objector (CO) and therefore be exempted from military service. But there was no provision to exempt COs from civil defence or industrial work, and some were absolutists and refused to take up a job if it meant releasing someone else for military service.

Around 61,000 people registered as COs during the Second World War, including 1,000 women. According to the Peace Pledge Union (PPU), they were treated more humanely in this war compared to the previous one and the tribunals were fairer. But by 1945 about 5,000 men and half of all women registered as COs had been charged with offences related to conscientious objection, and 3,000 people had been sent to prison.

The first woman to be jailed as a conscientious objector was Connie Bolam, a parlour maid who was instructed to take up land, canteen or hospital work. As an absolutist she refused, and was jailed in Durham in January 1942. The following year several women were sent to Holloway for refusing to register with their local air-raid precautions warden for fire-watching duties. 'Going to prison was the way that was open to me to make a protest against the war,' explained Barbara Roads, who was jailed for a month. 'If I had been called up to join the army and go into the trenches, I would have refused to do that – but you can only refuse to do what you are asked to do.' Nora Page, a member of the PPU, was also sent to Holloway having refused to register for fire-watching duties, although like many pacifists she was an active member of her neighbourhood fire-watching team.

While no comprehensive records exist on the number of pacifists and conscientious objectors jailed at Holloway, PPU archivist Bill Hetherington estimates there may have been up to 100 women who passed through the prison during the war, many serving short sentences. They included three sisters who ran a café in Camberley, Surrey – Cicely, Lilian and Rachel Dungey. They refused to attend fire-watcher training, or to pay a £5 fine, and at their court hearing in March 1943 Lilian explained that 'as children of God' they 'could not take part in anything to assist the war machine'. They were given seven days to think things over, but insisted they would not pay. After twelve days in Holloway an anonymous letter was delivered to the police, containing the money for the fine. Nine months later the sisters were again sentenced to a month, and again the fine was paid. In March the following year, however, they were sentenced for the third time, but without the option of a fine.

In January 1943 scientist Kathleen Lonsdale became the first Quaker woman to be jailed as a conscientious objector, having refused to register for fire-watching duties until there was a clause for conscientious objectors. She was a noted crystallographer and a pioneer in the use of X-rays, and was then working at the Royal Institution of Great Britain. Her experience in prison led her to write a fierce indictment of conditions in Holloway. Medical examinations were worthless, hygiene was shocking, and she was one of the first prisoners to publicly raise the particular needs of imprisoned women in terms of menstruation and sanitary towels.

On arrival at Holloway, Kathleen was seen by a nurse who examined her hair for nits, and asked if she had fits, varicose veins and if her periods were regular. Next the doctor came and put a stethoscope to her throat for a second, before enquiring again about varicose veins. She was then passed as fit for any work, despite explaining she had had a hysterectomy, and sent to B4 landing where she was told to carry gallons of cocoa and fill coal scuttles.

Kathleen's prison-issue cloak was greasy with dirt round the neck, her shoes were 'like hedgehogs inside after a couple of days' with nails that made her feet bleed, and her underwear and nightgown were stained with menstrual blood from the previous wearer. Mary Size and prisoner commissioner Lilian Barker had ensured that women had new prison clothing that was regularly cleaned and inspected, but the impact of wartime rationing on an understaffed and overcrowded prison was severe. Kathleen's cell was filthy: on the shelf was a dried piece of bread and some crusts; on the floor were dried faeces.

Supplies were running out, especially disinfectant, and the stench from the toilets in the morning, with women emptying sixteen and a half hours' worth of slops and sanitary towels was 'often almost unbearable'. Sanitary towels were supplied one at a time, on application to the landing officer, and many inmates were given a change of underwear just once a month. Toilet paper was in such short supply that prisoners used pages from the Bible provided in every cell: 'Use Moses,' a neighbour advised. Ivy Watson, jailed as a CO in 1944, found this particularly distressing: 'When I say that I am a Christian and believe the Bible to be the inspired Word of God, perhaps you can understand how I felt at having to do such a thing.' After serving four weeks of a four-month sentence, Ivy, believed to be Nora Page's sister, asked her family to pay the balance of the fine 'as I felt further imprisonment might have a permanent effect on my mind'.

Kathleen Lonsdale found many of the staff 'exceedingly kind . . . going beyond their duty to supply the deficiency of the system'. One advised her to skim the grease off the top of the cocoa, which proved an excellent remedy for chapped hands. The main source of conflict between staff and inmates was the ringing of cell bells, and several times she heard an officer on duty call out, 'Oh, *stop* ringing that bell.'

While Kathleen had anticipated that Holloway, like all other institutions during the war, would have a shortage of supplies she had not been prepared for the 'general insanity of an administrative system' that paid lip service to the idea of reform and where 're-education for responsible citizenship was practically nil'. What happened to the women in Holloway 'morally, physically, spiritually' was of 'little concern of the authorities'.

Kathleen was, however, allowed books and papers and, according to the Royal Society of Chemistry, managed to get seven hours' scientific work done each day. Two years after her imprisonment she became one of the first women to be elected a Fellow of the Royal Society, and later the first woman president of the British Association for the Advancement of Science.

Her time in Holloway also marked the beginning of a lifelong interest in prison reform, and she wrote about her experience in a booklet published by the Prison Medical Reform Council. The booklet included testimony from Sybil Morrison, secretary of the PPU's Women's Peace Campaign, who was jailed at Holloway very early in the war, sentenced to one month in July 1940 after addressing a meeting at Speakers' Corner where she delivered a message from Mahatma Gandhi. She was charged with insulting words and behaviour likely to cause a breach of the peace. 'You are extremely dangerous,' the magistrate told her, 'this type of thing must be stamped out.'

When Sybil arrived at Holloway the doctor, who 'thought I looked a bit different from the ordinary round of abortionists and petty thieves', asked what she was in for. When Sybil told her, the doctor 'was simply furious' and said, 'If you'd been a German you'd have been shot.' When Sybil agreed that this was very likely, the doctor replied, 'And that's what I'd do to you.' But like other women jailed for pacifism, Sybil found her fellow prisoners 'extraordinarily sympathetic'. Christian pacifist and veterinarian Stella St John, jailed for six weeks in March 1943, described Holloway's inmates as 'very tolerant' about her alleged crime, 'some even being sympathetic to the point of saying, "Good luck to you, I don't hold with this war, but I wouldn't get put in here for it."'

It wasn't just Holloway's inmates who suffered during the war years. Officers had to sleep in the prison during air raids and take the prisoners down to the basement cells, and when they returned to their own unlocked rooms they sometimes found their belongings had been stolen. But now, at last, the officers had a trade union. The Prison Officers' Association (POA) had been founded in 1939, after a lengthy battle for recognition with the Home Office, and a series of meetings had drawn the governor's attention to staff shortages, extended working hours, poor accommodation, lack of equipment and unsupervised, noisy prisoners. Prison officers had become increasingly militant in the decades before the war and while prisoners had gained more freedom, and the hated term 'warder' had been officially abolished in 1921, conditions for staff were slow to improve. By 1941 the POA reported a 'state of unrest' at many prisons. At Holloway, officers were being denied permission to live in outside quarters, and wing administration was chaotic; there was 'no adequate supervision' on the landings and, as the prisoners knew only too well, a severe shortage of soap, toilet paper and disinfectant. Prisoners could only obtain these items by asking at mealtimes and there was 'a continual interruption' when officers were trying to deliver meals.

Relations between staff and prison management then deteriorated further. Inmates were being exercised inside because of fog, an 'unpleasant duty especially as the prisoners are performing their natural functions inside'. Officers sleeping inside the prison on air-raid duty weren't being allowed to leave on time in the morning; staff now had to buy their own supplies of firewood.

On 8 May 1945 the war in Europe came to an end and two days later many of the defence regulations were revoked. The internment camps on the Isle of Man were closed in September, and the remaining enemy aliens released. The Mosleys were no longer under house arrest; those still detained under 18B had been set free. But it wasn't until 1947 that the last of the conscientious objectors were released, either from their wartime duties or from prison.

Two months after VE Day, meanwhile, Holloway officers were in for a surprise when the press announced that their new governor was to be 'Dr M.D.C. Taylor, who at the age of thirty, will be the prison's first woman Governor'. Some papers even reported that she was 'the first woman to be appointed prison governor', an error that's still repeated today.

Charity Taylor couldn't have taken over the running of Holloway at a more difficult time. The war in Europe had only recently ended; the prison was understaffed, overcrowded and filthy. Officer morale was low, supervision was minimal, and supplies were running out. No wonder the behaviour of both prisoners and officers was about to turn vicious.

PART FIVE

A Change in Regime

15

The Lady Governor and the Borstal Girls

Charity Taylor, like several of her predecessors at Holloway Prison, was a medical doctor. Born in 1914 in Woking, Surrey, she had studied medicine in London and at the age of twenty-eight had been appointed Holloway's assistant medical officer. Promotion for women was notoriously slow in the prison service but two years later, in July 1945, she became Holloway's governor.

Charity Taylor's age and gender were both seen as significant, as was the fact she was married and had children. The *Daily Mirror* accompanied its report on her appointment with a large photograph of a beaming 'Dr May D.C. Taylor, brunette wife of Dr Stephen Taylor . . . and mother of two children'. Charity told the *Mirror* that she would 'move into the official gaol residence' with her family and 'now, maybe I'll have more time' with the children. She added that as a married woman she was bound to have a better insight into the problems of women prisoners because 'the huge majority of them are married'.

Holloway's new governor believed that while prison discipline was necessary, 'self discipline is the side which I shall want to stress'. She instituted several reforms, introducing classes in practical skills and academic subjects, such as typing, first aid, art and current affairs. Prisoners could buy home perms at the canteen, and prison-issue clothing became more 'feminine' with the introduction of 'coloured frocks and cardigans'. She also established a jam factory, in the north-east of the prison, which would become known nationwide. 'It was a popular job,' explains one former assistant governor, 'because it was a full day's work and made a lengthier sentence seem to go quicker.' It also provided access to extra sugar, which could then be bartered for tobacco, although the work was 'hot, hard, and heavy'.

Governor Charity Taylor was generally seen as a reformer with a firm touch who believed that 'in many cases where women have gone wrong and got as far as prison, the psychological approach may do a great deal of good. The thing is to give some of these people the hope that they will become decent citizens again. Severe punishment is not always the way to prevent an individual doing something wrong.' She was also media-friendly, addressing meetings and giving interviews, including speaking on the Home Service. In 1946 she was on the platform of the Conference of Women's Organizations, demanding 'a new world for wives', and sitting side by side with 'grey-haired Mrs Teresa Billington-Greig', the first suffragette jailed at Holloway. 'We are both concerned about improving the lot of woman prisoners,' said Teresa. 'Dr Taylor would like to see the prison system humanized so that prisoners can retain their dignity.'

Charity served as Holloway governor for fourteen years and her journal gives an account of the duties involved, from attending Divine Service and piano concerts in the chapel, to supervising the sale of handicrafts and meeting prison visitors, including three policemen from Kenya. The tone, however, is officious, except for occasional moments of enthusiasm: 'E Wing Drama class gave three short plays; enjoyed very much by all.' But despite the new governor's faith in self-discipline, there were an awful lot of punishments meted out in Holloway in the years after the war, and the padded cell was in regular use. Crimes included whispering during a chapel service, insolence to an officer, writing and receiving unauthorized letters, refusing to obey an order, idling in the laundry, defacing a library book, making toast on an iron in the laundry, and passing a cigarette to a man in a working party from Pentonville Prison.

While Holloway's new governor believed that the main requirements of a prison wardress were 'a kind heart and good feet', these were not enough to withstand the pressures of the job and there were soon staff resignations, largely attributed to the behaviour of Borstal girls. 'Conditions at Holloway are appalling,' reported one newspaper a few months after Charity Taylor took over, 'the place is like a Bedlam.' Four wardresses had 'handed their keys to the governor' after refusing to appear before a disciplinary committee.

While it's not clear what charges they faced, judging from a report by the Mass Observation it's not surprising that they'd been charged with breaking the rules, or that they'd wanted to resign.

Mass Observation, a social research organization founded in 1937, recruited observers and volunteer writers to study the lives of ordinary Britons. A team of investigators went into a variety of public situations, such as sporting and religious events, but they also went into places the public had little access to, like Holloway Prison. In the autumn of 1944 an unnamed woman from the Mass Observation started work as a temporary officer, leaving shortly before Charity Taylor arrived. She had no experience or qualifications, but found that 'as long as the candidate looks fit, is of average height and has had no convictions, she can start working at once.' The medical examination was as brief as that given to prisoners: her legs were inspected for varicose veins, which could be exacerbated by a job that involved being on her feet all day, and she was pronounced ready for duty. Her uniform had a military design, with a 'butcher blue' linen dress, a navy service overcoat similar to an air-raid warden and a Land Army-style hat with a brim. There was also a leather belt, with a three-foot-long chain for the keys, to be strictly worn under the dress. 'No weapons were issued,' and although every officer was supposed to have a whistle, very few did. Most of the regular officers were 'extremely dull, mentally and physically', with the same look of 'hopeless apathy' as the prisoners, slouching along with their toes turned out and their bodies bent forward. There was little comradeship; instead they were constantly looking for ways to catch each other out in some minor breach of the rules.

When it came to corruption, things were nearly as bad as they had been in early Victorian times. The large majority of officers were 'bribable', and would smuggle in cigarettes – £1 for twenty, ten times the retail cost – as well as sweets, cosmetics, toothpaste, soap, food and liquor. This partly explained the amount of jealousy and mistrust, as one staff member would report another, only to then take over her business. One day the volunteer came across a radio in an officer's flat that had been presented by the vicar and parishioners of a certain village 'for the use of the misfortunate women of Holloway'.

Not only were the staff as 'unpleasant as possible' to each other, they were even worse to the inmates, who were treated with violent contempt. The gatekeeper gave the temporary officer some advice: 'They'll lead you a 'ell of a life if you don't treat 'em like what they are – animals.' Kick the cell door, he told her, and if they don't answer threaten to report them to the governor for insolence. If anyone gave her any trouble, such as speaking without being spoken to first, again she should report them and if there were no grounds then 'make it up'. She could offer a cigarette, for example, and then report the prisoner for smoking, or say an inmate had threatened to hit her. The friendliness and understanding that had been encouraged under Mary Size in the 1930s had been replaced with suspicion and hatred. One inmate, on the morning of her release, attacked an officer and 'gave her such a hiding' that she was in hospital for a month. The prisoner got a further six weeks but said 'it was worth six months to beat that old bitch up'.

Young prisoners, who had been sentenced to Borstal but kept in Holloway because of the shortage of places at Aylesbury, were a particular problem. They were held on DX wing, and were commonly known as brownies, due to their brown prison uniform. The Prison Officers' Association had been concerned about DX wing for a while, and had wanted a principal officer put in charge 'owing to the fact that it is very often left entirely without an officer and with any number from 8 to 30 inmates inside without supervision'. One lunchtime four brownies managed to shut themselves in a cell and barricaded the door. A band of fifteen officers, along with two male members of the engineering staff, were sent to take them down to the punishment cells under D wing. The engineers turned on water hoses, removed the lock from the cell door and pushed it open. The men then left, leaving the fifteen women officers to deal with those inside. When the prisoners refused to strip and get into their nightdresses the wardresses attempted to do it by force, punching, pulling, pinching and kicking, and landing blows with shoes, keys and fists. The Borstal girls were then dragged down two flights of iron stairs by their hair and thrust into a bare cell, after which the engineers reappeared and 'played hoses on them until their screams died away into sobs'. For this, the prisoners were charged with insubordination and put in solitary confinement on a diet of bread and water.

There were also outbreaks of 'smashing up fits' reminiscent of Victorian times, which the Mass Observation volunteer attributed to the strain of being kept in solitary confinement for eighteen out of twenty-four hours. Prisoners were known to smash up every piece of furniture in the cell, tear blankets and clothes to shreds and then beat on the door until 'hoses are brought and played on her through a hole that was built over 100 years ago for this specific purpose'.

The Mass Observation volunteer loathed her time in Holloway, and was shocked by the behaviour of the officers, but in the years that followed, and despite Charity Taylor's reforms, Borstal girls became further renowned for their 'unruliness'. In January 1946 a two-hour uproar could be heard by those living near the prison, and one woman living directly opposite told a reporter: 'After tea we could hear women shouting in the prison, and there was a sound of windows being smashed. I cannot remember anything like this before, and I believe it must be the Borstal girls who were recently transferred there.'

In the summer of 1949 a group of ex-Borstal girls again barricaded themselves in a cell. The women had been returning from work in the prison wireless room, a hut-like building that fulfilled contracts for 'a large electrical company', when they made a dash for a cell on the top floor and for forty-eight hours 'defied prison officers from behind a barricade of beds, tables, washstand, and three chairs'. Once again, their 'screams and shouts' were heard by people living nearby. Prison officers left the girls without food and water 'after a plan to drive them out with fire hoses had been abandoned' and when they gave in, 'they were at once given tea, the normal late afternoon prison meal. Hunger is believed to have caused their capitulation.'

The POA demanded an independent inquiry. 'Our women members in Holloway are becoming more and more resentful of difficulties which confront them in discipline, particularly from younger prisoners,' explained a spokesperson. 'They feel there is too much pampering.' A few days later the chief officer and the assistant chief officer resigned. The problem according to the POA was 'lack of fitting punishments', and it urged officers not to do 'anything rash, such as resigning and throwing in their hand'. The press implied that it was the governor's gender and age that had contributed to the general 'pampering', but there had been problems well before Charity Taylor took up her post. The POA had written to the previous governor expressing 'considerable feeling of soreness and dissatisfaction', and demanding a 'definite time' for staff to talk to the governor 'regarding incidents', especially concerning defiant juveniles.

But who were these Borstal girls who were causing so much trouble at Holloway? Many were in their late teens, they came from all over the UK, and they had usually been sentenced to two or three years' Borstal detention – a form of youth detention run by the prison service. This was originally intended for those between sixteen and twenty-one, although the maximum age had now been increased to twenty-three, and the regime was supposed to be educational rather than punitive. The majority of Holloway's Borstal girls had run away – from home or approved schools or both – sometimes as young as thirteen. They had then been put on probation, broken the conditions and ended up in Holloway. Some came from a 'good home' and had done well at school; others had lost their parents at a young age, or had been left in care. One eighteen-year-old, described as a 'Barnardo's girl', was 'out of control' and 'doesn't like institutions'.

Holloway's Borstal Allocation Book recorded the young women's backgrounds and evaluated their characters. Some had been physically assaulted by a father, partner or husband, and there were also cases of sexual abuse, although they were not described as such; instead they were included under the heading 'criminal background' as if they had been the perpetrator and not the victim. One eighteen-year-old had been put on probation as a nine-year-old 'for being assaulted by an old man' and was a 'very poor type – hysteric'. Another, aged thirteen, had been 'assaulted by soldier' and sent to a remand home. Frequently they had an 'illegitimate' child of their own, and many had had relationships with men in the armed forces. Some 'associated with coloured men', virtually regarded as a crime in itself at a time when mixed-race babies could be compulsorily put into care. The notes on one young woman read: 'black baby, brothel keeper mother'.

Many of the Borstal girls had worked in domestic service or factories, and their initial crimes were minor. One had stolen 2 shillings from her father; another had spent her employer's milk money. A sixteen-year-old had been put on probation for failing to show an ID card; a fourteen-year-old who took money for a fake Girl Guides raffle was sent to an approved school and ran away. She then spent six months in custody, where she underwent 'shock treatment', electroconvulsive therapy which was used to induce seizures in those classified as mentally disturbed.

The Borstal Allocation Book provided general comments for each young woman, and then a recommendation of where she should go: Aylesbury, Exeter, Durham or East Sutton. But the tone of the assessment was judgemental and often brutal. One girl was 'shallow, sly, more like an adult', another was 'retarded, anxious', a third was 'very stupid. Lazy. Fallen type'. Many were condemned as silly, irresponsible and selfish, or dismissed as liars who would 'do anything to gain attention'.

There were occasional positive comments: one had 'some standards in life' and 'had tried to better herself'; another was 'apparently honest and now ashamed'. A few were described as 'wants loving', and one was a 'typical weak bewildered girl to whom too much has happened too quickly'.

With young women as abused and condemned as those in Holloway it was little wonder they reacted with fury to their incarceration, and conditions inside were now described as 'torture'. During a debate on women in prison in the House of Commons in 1947, led by Barbara Ayrton-Gould, MPs were especially concerned about the effects of solitary confinement. Barbara knew about Holloway Prison first-hand: a former organizer for the Women's Social and Political Union, she had been jailed on remand after taking part in the 1912 West End window-smashing raid, part of the militant suffrage campaign. She questioned numerous aspects of the Holloway regime. Prisoners were locked up at 4.30 p.m. and remained completely isolated until they were unlocked at six o'clock the next morning. They had nothing to eat or drink during this fourteen-hour period, with the last meal at 4 p.m. – three slices of bread, a very small pat of margarine, sometimes a piece of cheese or a tiny piece of Spam, and a cup of 'quite good' cocoa.

The prison also urgently needed at least twenty-one more officers, and Barbara provided some shocking statistics. In 1946, fifty-five officers had been appointed, and forty-four had left. Holloway's population was now nearly 500, reflecting an overall rise in the prison population, which was partly due to longer sentences. Only a quarter of Holloway's inmates were able to get out of their cells in the evening, for classes or recreation. The rest stayed alone, with nothing to 'occupy themselves in any sort of way'. Barbara had recently visited Holloway, and she attempted to explain to her colleagues what life was like inside. Many inmates were 'working-class people who . . . go to prison feeling very sorry, very humiliated and utterly miserable, and perhaps with grave home troubles'. The variety of home troubles were reflected in the chaplain's letters written on behalf of prisoners. He wrote to one woman's boyfriend 'to find out why he has not been to see her', to a husband 'for a reconciliation' and to a fiancé 'to tell him where she is'. He also wrote to family members about ration books, to a nursery about a child, as well as letters concerning rent and employment, furniture and luggage.

The physical structure of the prison also came under attack during the debate in the House of Commons, with Labour MP Florence Paton describing Holloway as 'a gloomy, Victorian building . . . it impresses one with a sense of awe, and, more than that, with a sense of terrible fear.' The cells had stone floors, the windows had iron railings, and 'looking down into the prison from the upper floors is like looking down into an abyss into which one feels one might fall at any time.'

In 1948 a new Criminal Justice Act was passed, the first major reform of criminal law since late Victorian times. This abolished hard labour and prison divisions, and there were further moves towards probation as an alternative to jail. But women in Holloway were constantly experiencing 'nerve storms', a modern version of the 'hysteria' seen in Victorian times, when they smashed up their surroundings and were taken to padded cells: 'this either quiets them down or sends them completely off their heads.' One prisoner emptied her slop pail over an officer, having been 'goaded beyond endurance', and was 'dragged off by six other screws to the punishment or perhaps padded cell'.

One of Charity Taylor's jobs as governor was to visit women in the condemned cell, including Margaret Williams, a twenty-one-year-old private in the Women's Royal Army Corps who had killed her husband, Squadron Sergeant Major Montague Cyril Williams. Margaret pleaded self-defence, the judge described it as 'a sad, sorry tale' and the sentence was commuted to imprisonment for life.

Less than three weeks later, twenty-nine-year-old Nora Tierney was condemned to death for killing a three-year-old girl. Again the death sentence was commuted; Nora was certified insane and sent to Broadmoor. But the brutality that had been demonstrated at Holloway since the Second World War wasn't over yet, and for the next two occupants of the condemned cell there would be no last-minute reprieve.

16

Protest Against Evil

It's midday on Easter Sunday and the only sounds on Tanza Road in South End Green are the wind coming in across Hampstead Heath and the creak of a wooden fence as I walk up the hill. I look down at the pavement where words have been carved in a strip of cement between the paving stones: 'Casa de Bliss'. The Victorian houses in this part of north London are handsome, five storeys high and set back from the road, while the street is lined with old-fashioned street lamps and tall muscular trees pointing up to a grey sky. There is no one about; this is one of the few days in the year when London partially closes down.

Number 29 Tanza Road is on the right-hand side, near the top of the road. It looks plain compared to some of its neighbours, the white paint around the door is flaking, the plants on the outside window sill need watering. There's a street lamp nearby and I wonder how well lit the road was on the evening of Easter Sunday 1955, when Ruth Ellis arrived here with a loaded gun in her handbag. She was looking for David Blakely, a public school 'playboy' who had moved in with her, and had been living off her for nearly two years. Ten days earlier she had had a miscarriage, after David had punched her in the stomach. She had last seen him on Good Friday, when he'd promised to come home that evening. This was the house where his friends Anthony and Carole Findlater lived, and where he'd been all weekend, refusing to talk to Ruth. She had repeatedly rung him, and waited outside, and at one point the couple had called the police to have her removed. For the past three days Ruth had been drinking with another lover, Desmond Cussen, who was said to be intensely jealous of David. Desmond had given her the gun, and dropped her off at the top of Tanza

Road. But just as she arrived, David's car drove off and so she headed to the next place she thought she'd find him.

I walk up to the end of the road and left on to Parliament Hill and as it starts to rain I speed up my pace, deliberately retracing Ruth's route, passing magnolia trees in front gardens, their delicate leaves turning dull brown on the ground. A few minutes later I reach the Magdala Tavern, a pub near the bottom of the hill, covered in scaffolding and its upper floors wrapped in sheets of plastic. Beside it are a small row of shops, an estate agent and a hair salon. This was where Ruth waited in a doorway, after seeing David's car parked outside. I stop to shelter from the rain; the wall of the Magdala Tavern is to my right, curving round the corner of the road. If anyone came in or out I would notice them immediately, they are in my direct line of sight.

I take a few steps nearer to the pub, put my face up against a window. The Victorian pub recently closed down, but I remember drinking beer and eating scotch eggs here as a student thirty years ago when everyone clearly remembered Ruth Ellis. The pub is at the intersection of two streets; Hampstead Heath overground station is just down the hill, then the busy South End Road. It's a very public place to take out a gun and shoot someone.

At around 9.30 p.m. on 10 April, David Blakely came out of the Magdala Tavern and passed Ruth waiting on the pavement. She said, 'Hello, David,' and when he ignored her, shouted, 'David!' Then she took out the revolver and fired two shots; the second hit him and he collapsed on the pavement. Ruth stood over him and fired three more bullets. She was arrested immediately by an off-duty policeman. 'I am guilty,' she said. 'I'm a little confused.'

Ruth Ellis was the last woman to be executed in the UK and, like Edith Thompson before her, her trial and death were widely covered in the press and there have been numerous books, plays and films inspired by her case. But just a few yards from here there lived another woman, who eight months earlier was also convicted of murder and hanged at Holloway Prison. The story of Styllou Pantopiou Christofi remains virtually unknown.

★

In the three decades since Edith Thompson had been executed at Holloway, there had been twenty-five women in the prison's condemned cell and none had been hanged. Now two women would be executed in the space of seven months. But modern-day reports, the few that exist, don't even agree on the date Styllou Christofi was executed, nor her age or in which room the crime took place. Now, as then, she tends to be described as an archetypal mother-in-law, dominating and bossy, a Cypriot matriarch opposed to the 'British way of life'.

The house where Styllou Christofi lived, along with her son Stavros, his wife Hella and their three children, is only a couple of minutes' walk from the Magdala Tavern. Number 11 South Hill Park is another large Victorian house, with two bay windows on the lower floors. The blinds on the first floor are drawn and I can't tell what anyone walking past would have seen on the night of 28 July 1954. I turn to look back down the hill; it's raining again and water trickles along the road, while the sheeting on the pub's scaffolding snaps like thunder. Did three men really break in here, kill Hella and burn her body, or was it her mother-in-law Styllou? According to the prosecutor, 'This was a stupid murder by a stupid woman of the illiterate peasant type.' But was Styllou 'stupid' or was she insane?

Styllou Christofi was born in a village in Cyprus, then a British colony, in 1900. She was married at the age of fourteen, and had three – or possibly four – children. Her son Stavros moved to London in 1941 and worked as a wine waiter at Café de Paris, a fashionable West End nightclub. He was married to Hella Bleicher, a German-born 'fashion model', and the couple had three children.

In 1953 Styllou came to stay but there were tensions between her and this 'modern London couple' and on three occasions she'd moved out and lived elsewhere in London. Now Hella was about to take the children on holiday to Germany, and when they came back her mother-in-law was supposed to have gone. But two weeks before Hella was due to leave, after Stavros had left for work and the children were in bed, Styllou murdered her daughter-in-law. 'The two women had quarrelled,' explained one newspaper, 'and the elder feared her son . . . would send her back to her native island.'

According to some modern reports, the murder happened in the kitchen, where Hella was knocked unconscious with an ash pan, then strangled before being burned. But reports of the time say Hella had been in the bath, and was set on fire in the back yard, where a neighbour saw Styllou burning what he thought was a tailor's dummy. When the fire got out of control, Styllou ran outside and stopped a couple by the train station, saying, 'Please come, fire burning, children sleeping.' They accompanied her home, later saying that Styllou 'did not seem to be disturbed' by the sight of her dead daughter-in-law, and 'did not shed a tear'. The fire brigade called the police, and she was arrested for murder. There were bloodstains on the kitchen floor, as well as on Styllou's shoes. The police found Hella's wedding ring in a box in her mother-in-law's bedroom, and there were no signs of anyone having broken in.

In her first interview with the police, her son acted as translator, although later a professional interpreter was hired. Styllou said she had been asleep and had woken to hear male voices downstairs. When she saw a man in the yard and a body on fire, she went to fetch water to douse the flames. 'I wake up, smell burning, go downstairs. Hella burning. Throw water, touch her face. Not move. Run out, get help.'

Styllou appeared before the Hampstead magistrates and was said to be 'absolutely bewildered by the proceedings'. She was sent to Holloway Prison, where she dictated a short note: 'Lady of Greek Church please come and see me and speak to me. Please I want some biscuits.' The letter was written by an officer and Styllou, who was illiterate, signed it with a shaky cross.

Dr Thomas Christie, Holloway's principal medical officer, observed Styllou for several months and decided she was suffering from a 'delusional mental disorder' that led her to 'fear that her grandchildren would not be brought up properly'. At the time of the murder she was 'incapable of knowing that what she did was wrong'. She was still, however, 'medically fit to plead and to stand trial'. Dr Christie had been called on many times to decide on an accused's mental state, often as a witness for the defence. In March 1953 he had decided a woman charged with murdering her three young sons was mentally deranged and unfit to plead. The judge agreed that 'under English law it would be mere cruelty and farce to try the accused'. Another woman, charged with trying to drown her two children, was declared unfit to plead, suffering from delusion and persecution mania. But Dr Christie's report on Styllou Christofi wasn't presented at the four-day trial, because she refused to plead insanity.

She gave her evidence in Greek, and press reports constantly emphasized her nationality. Prosecutor Christmas Humphreys described her as 'a stupid woman', who had really believed 'that after washing the floor she could eliminate bloodstains'. The motivation for the murder appeared to be jealousy and resentment. 'On the one hand,' explained a reporter, 'there was the young German girl, well dressed, working in a fashion house, out all day with her friends, and on the other the older peasant woman, staying in the house and looking after the children.'

On 28 October Styllou was found guilty of murder, with no recommendation to mercy. Asked if she had anything to add, she replied that she wanted to go into the witness box and 'say something to the court', but the request was denied. What would she have said? Judging by reports of her behaviour in Holloway, it would have been to refute the charges, accuse three unidentified men of murder and blame her son for the fact she was standing trial. That afternoon Holloway's governor Charity Taylor sent a telegram to her counterpart at Manchester Prison: 'One woman officer required for C.C. duty.' There seemed to be no reason why the execution wouldn't go ahead and staff were needed for the condemned cell. It was now that an earlier case was made public. In 1925 Styllou and two other women, including a sister-in-law, had been arrested and charged with murdering Styllou's mother-in-law in Cyprus by putting a burning piece of wood down her throat. All three had been acquitted. It appeared that Styllou Christofi had a history of cold-blooded murder.

The date of the execution was fixed for 17 November and Albert Pierrepoint was appointed executioner. He belonged to a family of executioners: his father Henry had assisted at the execution of the two baby farmers in 1903, pinioning Amelia Sach by the arms and leading her to the gallows, and his Uncle Thomas was also a former executioner. By the end of his career Albert, who believed he was 'chosen by a higher power for the task', had executed over 400 people, using the 'most humane and the most dignified method of meting out death to a delinquent'.

Two days after Styllou Christofi was sentenced to death, the Hampstead police phoned Holloway's governor to say that Stavros 'has refused to visit his mother'. In the meantime, communication was a problem inside Holloway. The six officers on 'special duty' were required to make regular reports, and though the interpreter was present each day, the staff often wrote down Styllou's words verbatim in English.

Charity Taylor visited Styllou on a daily basis, but she misspelled the Cypriot woman's name in her journal and made no comment on the prisoner's condition. The governor wrote to Stavros, urging him to visit his mother, which he eventually did, reporting that she had been 'unpleasant' and had accused him of not supporting her at the trial.

According to modern reports, there was no move to reprieve Styllou Christofi, yet in the next few weeks at least two petitions were sent from Cyprus: 'We have heard with great sorrow the sentence to death of Styliana P. Christofi, of Famagusta now in England. We have known her for the past 30 years . . . she never gave any cause for complaint and has always been honest and in very good terms with her neighbours.' Styllou insisted she had fresh evidence and that two girls passing the house had witnessed her daughter-in-law being murdered by the three men. Her Holloway file includes pages and pages of applications to the governor, to appeal, to write letters, to send a visiting order – often two or three a day.

But on 30 November Styllou was told her appeal had been dismissed and a new execution date was set. Stavros apparently visited his mother again, 'at the urging of a priest' in the week before the execution. He told the press: 'As usual she would not reason at all. She just shouted "Innocent, innocent" . . . for twenty minutes I had to listen while she poured out a stream of blame and reproach to me whose wife she did not spare.' Her statements written inside Holloway were also getting even more rambling.

The Secretary of State appointed three doctors to examine Styllou's mental health, as required by law, but the psychiatrists all found her sane; there were no grounds for a reprieve. It was only then that Holloway's medical officer's earlier report, declaring her insane, was made public. The night before her execution a group of Labour MPs, led by Sir Leslie Plummer, tried to persuade the Home Secretary to commute her sentence and attempted to hand him the medical report.

The next morning 100 people gathered outside Holloway to 'witness the last act in the drama' of the first woman to be executed in London in three decades. The prison's gallows were now in E wing, having been moved after Edith Thompson's death when the authorities had decided, along with other 'hanging prisons', to have the execution chamber next to the condemned cells. A 'suite' had been created on the first floor, consisting of five cells, which meant a condemned prisoner no longer had to be walked outside to a shed. As a result of what had happened at Edith's execution, when her 'insides' had reportedly fallen out, Styllou was made to wear padded underwear, sometimes described as 'rubberised canvas pants'. There were other changes as well, particularly the role of the prison chaplain. Legally he had to be present, but he could attend in 'such a manner as he may think best'. A prison circular explained that he was under no obligation 'to walk before the prisoner or to take up any particular position at the place of execution'. The reading was up to him, as were the prayers, but suggestions included the Lord's Prayer or 'some suitable verse of a well-known hymn'.

At 9 a.m. on 15 December 1954 Styllou Christofi was hanged at Holloway Prison. One of the last things she saw was a Greek Orthodox Cross, which she had asked to be put on the wall of the execution chamber. She was the oldest woman to be hanged at the jail in the twentieth century, as well as the only non-British prisoner.

Within half an hour of Styllou's death Sir Leslie Plummer told a reporter that if the original medical report had been put to the court, she would never have been hanged. That night he tabled a Commons motion expressing 'profound disquiet' that 'a woman who may have been insane, and had in fact been declared insane by the prison doctor, has been executed'. He urged the government to 'declare its policy on the whole question of capital punishment', and to comment on the findings of the Royal Commission on Capital Punishment which had 'declared the existing law unsatisfactory'. The commission had been set up in 1949; its inquiry had lasted nearly four years and had included lengthy testimony on Edith Thompson's execution at Holloway.

There had been little press interest in the execution of Styllou Christofi – she was, noted Albert Pierrepoint in his autobiography, 'a grey haired and bewildered grandmother who spoke no English, only the language of the tears that were on her cheek when I came to see her'. But when it came to the next woman executed at Holloway Prison, her trial, imprisonment and death received enormous coverage.

Ruth Ellis's case involved all the ingredients beloved by the British media – sex, infidelity, alleged social climbing, glamour and murder. Even the defence called it a 'sordid story', and readers avidly followed the tale of the 'blonde model and the racing car driver', with reports inevitably accompanied by a photograph of Ruth in a nightclub drinking champagne.

Ruth Neilson was born in Rhyl, Wales, in 1926. She became a mother at the age of seventeen after an affair with a Canadian soldier, worked briefly as a nude model and then as a nightclub hostess at the Court Club in Mayfair, where the women were also required to work as prostitutes. In 1950 she married George Ellis, a violent alcoholic, and they separated before the birth of her second child. Ruth then returned to the nightclub world, as manager of the Little Club in Knightsbridge, where one of her customers was David Blakely. 'Their life together alternated between love and beating, and he did the beating,' said her friend Jacqueline Dyer, who described the 'terrible strain of her life with Blakely, a strain which I am sure on the fatal night turned into a temporary state of insanity because he would not speak to her'. But the police took the opposite view: Ruth Ellis was a woman spurned and her 'action was coldly premeditated', according to Detective Chief Inspector Leslie Davies. 'On meeting Blakely and realising that his class was very much above her own, and finding he was sufficiently interested in her to live with her, it seems she was prepared to go to any lengths to keep him. Finding this impossible, she appears to have decided to wreak her vengeance on him.'

After she shot David outside the Magdala Tavern on Easter Sunday 1955, Ruth was taken to Hampstead police station, just like Styllou Christofi before her. She had no solicitor during her interrogation or while giving her statement, and after appearing at the magistrates' court the next day she was taken to Holloway Prison where she was given prisoner number 9656 and her occupation was recorded as 'model'.

The trial began on 20 June with the same prosecutor who had helped send Styllou Christofi to the gallows, Christmas Humphreys. Ruth was carefully and fashionably dressed, all in black with astrakhan fur on her lapels, and newly peroxided hair. She gave a matter-of-fact account of the night of the murder, and appeared to show no remorse. Her demeanour in the witness box, aside from sobbing when shown a picture of David, was described as calm and composed. Much was made of her 'simultaneous love affairs with two men', and she was asked how many times a week David had slept at her flat. But nothing was said about his affairs, or the fact he had been engaged to be married. There was evidence that Ruth had been beaten several times, and after one attack Desmond Cussen had taken her to hospital. But despite the fact she was pleading provocation, the defence failed to follow up on this, nor did it investigate where she had got the murder weapon, which was not examined for fingerprints. Desmond had given Ruth the gun and driven her to Tanza Road, but he was not regarded as an accomplice. Three decades earlier when it was a woman – Edith Thompson – who had been regarded as an accomplice, she was put on trial and executed.

'You are not here in the least concerned with adultery or any sexual misconduct,' the prosecutor told the jury. 'You are not trying this woman for immorality, but for murder.' But Ruth Ellis was being tried for immorality, just like Edith Thompson. She was an example of everything that was 'wrong' with 1950s Britain: women like Ruth lacked sexual 'morals' and were a threat to family life.

Even today this sexualized portrait of Ruth Ellis remains, and no newspaper or TV coverage of her case is complete without an image of her 'reclining on a bed' or posed half naked fixing a suspender belt.

Ruth had clearly been provoked; David was both violent and promiscuous and over the Easter weekend he had gone out of his way to taunt her. But the judge, Justice Havers, said provocation depended on loss of self-control, and Ruth appeared to be the epitome of self-control. When asked what she had intended to do when she fired the gun, her reply sealed her fate: 'It's obvious when I shot him I intended to kill him.' Her statement echoed the words of Kitty Byron, sentenced to death and held at Holloway in 1902 for stabbing her lover Arthur in the street. The twenty-four-year-old milliner's assistant had also appeared calm and collected, and had told the court, 'I killed him willingly, and he deserved it.' But Kitty was said to be in such a 'state of mental distress' that she was 'almost incapable of knowing what she did'. And while the jury found her guilty, they urged for the 'strongest possible recommendation to mercy' and she was reprieved.

Attitudes appeared to have radically changed since Edwardian times, when the press had found it impossible to believe Kitty Byron could deliberately kill a man and had justified the act as a fit of passion. Now women were seen as more dangerous, and some were perfectly capable of murder. Ruth Ellis was condemned for her alleged immorality, and the emotional impact on her mental state of repeated violence and a miscarriage was of little interest to the court or the media.

It didn't take long for the jury of ten men and two women to pronounce Ruth Ellis guilty of murder. She entered the dock with a nurse from Holloway Prison carrying a first-aid box, and the 'platinum blonde mother of two children appeared to reel slightly . . . when the verdict was given Mrs Ellis moistened her lips with her tongue.' Ruth did not appeal against her sentence and two days later the governor wrote: 'Ellis informed that her execution is fixed for July 18th at 9 a.m.' There is precious little else on Ruth's incarceration or execution in the prison archives, as her file was reportedly stolen in the 1960s. However, one of those on special duty was Evelyn Galilee, who later described Ruth's arrival in the condemned cell: 'In came this frail girl, a Dresden doll . . . They had taken away her false nails, eyelashes and glamorous clothes and put her in baggy prison issue clothes. But they could not strip her of her dignity. Not once did she break down, scream or cry. Ruth had this acceptance of what she'd done and felt the punishment fitted the crime.'

Ruth Ellis apparently had no complaints about her treatment in Holloway, aside from the overhead bulb, which was never turned off in the condemned cell. Evelyn and another officer made a cardboard lampshade to shield her from the glare, while Ruth spent her time reading, writing letters, doing jigsaws and making dolls. But she kept asking officer Evelyn Galilee about the six-foot-high screen that ran along one of the cell's walls. 'I think she knew what it was, but she kept badgering me to have a look.'

Another woman on special duty came from Maryport in Cumbria and according to her friend Margaret Poland, a local author, 'She sat with Ruth Ellis and tried to stop her being morbid. She was a born talker and by the end Ruth knew every street in Maryport and all about the history of the town. Ruth Ellis didn't think she would hang, and she was determined to come to Maryport because she said it sounded like a nice quiet place and she would come here and spend the rest of her days.'

In marked contrast to Styllou's sentence of death, and however much she had been portrayed as an immoral woman, much of public opinion was now firmly behind Ruth. A petition to reduce the charge to manslaughter was signed by 100,000 people, and there were several other petitions for a reprieve. But on 11 July the governor informed Ruth there were 'no grounds to interfere with the due cause of the law'. The day before the execution she gave her lawyer a new statement: she had been drinking and was 'in a terribly distressed state', Desmond had given her the gun and driven her to Tanza Road. But the Home Office decided 'this uncorroborated statement by the prisoner does not add anything material to the information before the Secretary of State when he decided not to interfere'.

On 13 July, just as governor Charity Taylor was leaving her office

The Holloway House of Correction was modelled on a medieval castle and opened in 1852 as 'a terror to evil-doers'.

Holloway was based on the radial design, which allowed inmates to be observed at all times. E Wing, shown here, originally held male juveniles.

May Caroline, the Dowager Duchess of Sutherland, was found guilty of contempt of court and sent to Holloway in April 1893. The press revelled in her downfall.

By 1905, Holloway had the largest crèche in the prison service, but while the babies were 'better off than the free-born', their blankets were branded with arrows, the 'mark of criminality'.

Victorian prisoners were expected to work a ten-hour day; here female inmates undertake needlework and knitting in the sewing room.

Amelia Sach (left) and Annie Walters were accused of murdering babies for profit. On 3 February 1903, they became the first women to be executed at Holloway Prison.

In 1907, Alice Hawkins, a shoe machinist from Leicester, took part in a march on Parliament. She was imprisoned in Holloway for disorderly conduct, and by the time she came out she was a militant suffragette.

A group of suffragettes walking in Holloway's exercise yard in 1912, unaware that a Mr Barrett is hiding in a van taking undercover surveillance photos.

THE SUFFRAGETTE
Flouts His Worship.

Suffragettes repeatedly refused to 'recognise laws in the making of which woman had no voice'. Postcards like these were produced to mock the suffrage campaign.

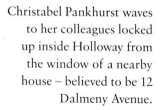

Christabel Pankhurst waves to her colleagues locked up inside Holloway from the window of a nearby house – believed to be 12 Dalmeny Avenue.

Alice Wheeldon (far right), sitting with her daughters Winnie and Hettie and a wardress at Derby Police Station in January 1917. The family were waiting trial for conspiracy to murder the Prime Minister, after falling victim to a government plot to discredit the anti-war movement.

Edith Thompson (right) and her sister Avis. Edith was hanged at Holloway Prison on 9 January 1923, for a crime she did not commit.

Colonel Victor Barker, 'an extremely handsome, well-groomed gentleman', was jailed at Holloway in 1929. His release caused a sensation, with mounted police holding back the crowds.

'There is a frightening look about the metal door of a prison cell.' Diana Mosley spent three years at Holloway during World War Two, where she was joined by her husband Oswald.

Ruth Ellis (right) with racing driver David Blakely, whom she shot on Easter Sunday 1955. She became the last woman to be executed in the UK.

'I deliberately wore my hat naughtily on the back of my head.' Judy Gibbons reported for duty at Holloway Prison in September 1958.

Zoe Progl, Britain's top female burglar, made a daring escape in July 1960, when she climbed over the perimeter wall in her prison-issue bloomers.

In the 1970s women were encouraged to join the modern prison service if they enjoyed helping others and had 'an unshakeable liking for, and belief in, people'.

A woman is arrested at Greenham Common peace camp in the winter of 1983. Hundreds of campaigners were jailed for protesting against nuclear weapons and most were sent to Holloway.

In May 2017, Sisters Uncut occupied Holloway's visitors' centre. They climbed on the roof and let off coloured smoke in protest against government cuts to domestic violence services.

to attend the execution, and with less than fifteen minutes to go, the telephone rang. A woman introduced herself as the Home Secretary's private secretary; Ruth Ellis was about to be reprieved. The governor said she would need to ring the Home Office back to confirm, but when she did no one was able to verify the call, and so she decided the execution would go ahead. Just as with Edith Thompson, the hanging appeared to have been halted at the eleventh hour and, once again, it was a hoax.

The night before Ruth was to be hanged, a crowd of 500 gathered outside Holloway's gates, led by anti-hanging campaigner Violet Van der Elst who had a 'scuffle' with the police when she was asked to move. 'This is my protest,' she told the press, 'against evil.' Holloway's governor was forced to call for police reinforcements; the crowd began singing and chanting 'Evans – Bentley – Ellis', in reference to two recent cases: Timothy Evans who had been executed at Pentonville Prison in 1950, wrongly accused of murdering his wife and daughter, and Derek Bentley, said to have 'the mental age of a child', who was executed at Wandsworth in 1953 after his sixteen-year-old friend shot a policeman during a break-in. Both men were hanged, and would be posthumously pardoned.

Inside Holloway, Evelyn Galilee accompanied Ruth to her death. She gave the officer one last glance: 'It was a look of pity – she felt sorry for me. She looked at me and mouthed, "Thank you", and she went out.' Eighteen minutes after the execution, the death notice was posted outside the prison and the crowd surged forward, blocking the road and stopping traffic. Executioner Albert Pierrepoint later recalled in his autobiography that he was 'almost besieged by a storming mob' and needed police protection to get through the crowds. At Euston station, journalists were waiting and one young reporter jogged alongside him and asked, 'How did it feel to hang a woman, Mr Pierrepoint?' He didn't answer. 'But I could have asked: "Why weren't you waiting to ask me that question last year, sonny? Wasn't Mrs Christofi a woman, too?"'

The next day a statement was issued on behalf of a group of local teachers:

Today Ruth Ellis was hanged. Not only myself but many of my colleagues were faced with the effect of this upon the boys and girls we teach. The school was in a ferment. There were some children who had waited outside the prison gates. Some claimed to have seen the execution from their windows . . . if there is any argument which weighs above all others for the abolition of capital punishment then it is this dreadful influence it has had. For not only was Ruth Ellis hanged today, hundreds of children were a little corrupted.

Officer Evelyn Galilee later avoided the area where Ruth was buried, but the chief officer 'made me go down there'. No grass was said to grow on the ground where Amelia Sach, Annie Walters and Edith Thompson had been laid to rest, but Evelyn was surprised to see, at the head of Ruth's grave, a small flowering violet. 'She'd had these big violet eyes, they were beautiful. I started to cry. I liked her officer to woman. She was helpful. She wasn't a bother and didn't throw a wobbler. Ruth Ellis was first class.'

A few weeks after the execution, the National Campaign for the Abolition of Capital Punishment was launched, but a bill to abolish the death penalty was rejected by the House of Lords. Then in 1957 the Homicide Act further restricted the use of the death penalty and added a new defence in cases of murder: diminished responsibility. The following year Mary Wilson became the last woman to be sentenced to death in the UK. Known as the Merry Widow of Windy Nook, she was found guilty of killing two of her three husbands, but five days before the execution she was reprieved and transferred from Durham to Holloway, where she died a few years later. The last execution in the UK was in 1964, although capital punishment was not finally abolished until 1998.

Albert Pierrepoint resigned the year after hanging Ruth Ellis, 'for reasons which the Home Office has asked me not to reveal fully'. While he insisted this had nothing to do with the execution, Ruth's death had led to 'the last great sentimental protest against capital punishment in Great Britain'. He concluded that executions 'solve nothing' and that the reason for a reprieve 'was always fundamentally political . . . the trouble with the death sentence has always been that nobody wanted it for everybody, but everybody differed about who should get off.' In modern times, Ruth's family have campaigned to replace the murder conviction with a verdict of manslaughter, arguing that she was a victim of battered woman syndrome, but in 2003 the Court of Appeal decided Ruth had been properly convicted of murder according to the laws of the time.

No one who worked at Holloway Prison at the time of Ruth Ellis's death would forget it, and nor would the staff who arrived soon afterwards. But never again would a prisoner be hanged at Holloway, and as the jail entered the 1960s a new regime was on the way. The idea that *all* female prisoners suffered from 'disordered minds' was gathering pace; criminal women were not bad but mad and what they needed was therapy and anti-psychotic drugs.

PART SIX

The New Holloway

17

A Worthwhile Job

The decade following Ruth Ellis's execution saw significant changes in the treatment of women in prison. The national female population was around 850, of whom two-thirds were held at Holloway, and various explanations were offered as to why the figure had stayed roughly the same over the past thirty years while the male population had tripled. Courts were said to be more reluctant to send women to prison, and women were regarded as less dangerous and aggressive. They were 'a nuisance rather than a menace', according to one official report, and instead of punishment the prison service needed to offer treatment. It also needed to recruit and train a new type of officer.

'Women Officers required for Prison Service,' ran a notice in the press. 'This essential and interesting social work involves the supervision and instruction in Prisons and Borstal Institutions of women and girls whose main chance of rehabilitation lies in the character and example of their officers.' As in Victorian times, female officers were to serve as role models, but there had been considerable changes in working conditions, with free quarters or a rent allowance, and increased pay. Many new entrants were attracted by the idea of helping prisoners, rather than simply locking them up, and they were encouraged to take a personal interest in the lives and problems of the inmates. For those like Judy Gibbons, one of the youngest women ever to sign up, the prison service had now become a vocation.

I'm meeting Judy at Didcot station in Oxfordshire, where she's told me I'll be able to identify her as she'll be holding a copy of the *Telegraph* under one arm. I come out of the ticket barrier, bewildered by all the people milling about until I see a smartly dressed figure in green tartan trousers standing to one side. I feel I'm on a secret mission, as she holds up her newspaper and steps forward to introduce herself. Despite having just had her third hip operation, Judy is a bundle of energy, while the neatness of her blue shirt collar underneath her jumper has the air of a uniform about it.

She drives us to a seventeenth-century pub in a nearby village, where we sit at a quiet table in the corner. I've brought along a photograph from the 1950s showing Holloway officers proudly displaying their new hats, after the Prison Officers' Association requested a new design that would suit all ages, stay put in the strongest wind, and did 'not resemble a permanent wave after a shower'. Judy knows nearly all the women in the picture, but as she was a junior officer she only ever referred to them as 'Miss'. Despite the formality, she remembers one Christmas they all changed into prisoners' clothes and 'everyone thought it was a hoot'. She shows me a photo of her in uniform, a long black skirt and tightly belted black jacket. 'I thought I was the best thing since sliced bread,' she says, her shoulders shaking with laughter. 'I deliberately wore my hat naughtily on the back of my head, rather than the front.'

I ask why she joined the prison service. 'I'm naturally bossy,' she says. 'I was the eldest of four, with both parents working, so I learned to organize my siblings and to take on responsibilities that perhaps others of my age did not.' Judy was born and brought up in Oxford, where she attended Notre Dame High School for Girls and was 'encouraged to develop an aura of social conscience'. Her uncle was a police officer and lived above a police station in Devon and her aunt used to 'feed the prisoners, making piles of sandwiches and scones, and I had to help. I never thought twice about it, there was never any trouble, I was never hit or anything.'

After leaving school Judy worked in a bank, which she didn't like at all, and by the time she was twenty she was wondering what to do. Then one day she saw a prison service advertisement with a photo of staff playing netball. 'I thought, Well, I could do that. It sounded very physical and I was physical. It also said you could help women and girls and I thought, I know about girls and institutions. I was brought up a Catholic and I had attended a convent school; institutions have rules and I had learned how to work with them.'

Judy was interviewed at Aylesbury Prison where she did an intelligence test, putting numbers in a sequence and shapes into boxes. 'Then I had an interview' – she chuckles at the memory – 'and I had to do a dictation test to see if I could spell!' Judy passed and she was told to report to Holloway Prison on 1 September 1958 after a six-week course at the newly opened prison training college in Wakefield, West Yorkshire. Candidates, both women and men, had to complete academic tests such as writing essays, and physical tests which included crawling through a coalmine wearing coalminers' clothing. 'It was part of the civil defence training which was part of the job in those days,' she explains. 'We had to be able to evacuate a prison and know what to do to protect ourselves and our prisoners in case of fire and a nuclear attack. They wanted people who showed grit, they didn't want wimps.'

Judy knew nothing about Holloway, except for Ruth Ellis's execution three years earlier. She shows me a photo of her sitting on the roof of the staff quarters, wearing a pretty summer dress, a view of the castle-like battlements behind her, as if she's a lady of leisure in a stately home rather than a newly fledged prison officer.

The focus of her job, however, was to 'keep prisoners within the walls. Once you have set that up you can do things. It's no good being lovey-dovey, to me that was the job, to set boundaries. After that you would do whatever you could to improve their lot. At the end of the day society would judge me on whether I could keep the prisoners under proper supervision or if I let them out.' But there was also another side to the job. Officers were now expected to offer counselling and 'to listen to the prisoners, and the older staff felt threatened, they were not trained for it'. Judy found herself in the middle, between the old 'humanely authoritarian' regime and a new way of doing things.

Judy Gibbons continued to work as an officer at Holloway for three years, and later returned as an assistant governor, and says it was 'very very rare' that she ever thought a prisoner shouldn't be there, but one particular woman has stayed in her mind.

One Christmas I had to take a statement from a woman who had killed her husband. She had put the turkey in the oven, and they had gone for a couple of drinks at the pub on Christmas Day, as people did. Then they went home. She opened the oven door and she had a knife in her hand and she said to her husband, 'Look, it's doing nicely.' He was worrying about whether he'd locked up his place of work properly and if he should go back and check. She'd had a lifetime of her husband worrying and she turned round and said, 'Shut up, stop worrying.' She had the knife in her hand and that was it. She said she didn't know how it had happened. I thought, You, my dear, shouldn't be sitting here.

We both stop speaking as the pub food arrives, and I wait while Judy surveys her ploughman's lunch. What does she think is the point of prison? 'There are lots of answers to that.' She pauses and begins to butter her bread. 'I do believe society thinks it has to have sanctions. So the point is retribution, there is an element of that, that enough is enough.' She puts down her knife.

But the main thing as an officer is to be fair. I remember being off duty one day and lying ill in bed, and a prisoner made me tea and said, 'Shall I hoover around your bed?' When I asked why she was here, which I wouldn't normally do, she said, 'I murdered my auntie.' And I said, 'Oh, did you?' I thought, Isn't this extraordinary? She has done something so horrible yet she is showing me, her incarcerator, extreme kindness.

As we leave the pub Judy gives me a copy of the *Ark*, the magazine of Catholic Concern for Animals, of which she is chair. She is also chair of Oxfordshire's Island Farm Donkey Sanctuary. 'Do you know,' she says, 'prison is full of eccentric people.' I ask if she means the prisoners and she laughs. 'No, I mean the staff.'

Many of Judy's fellow officers also joined the prison service after coming across an advert, and applicants could now apply directly for the post of assistant governor, rather than working their way up, while for some it was the abolition of the death penalty that made them change career. 'If hanging had still been an issue I would not have joined the prison service,' says another assistant governor who prefers to remain anonymous. She was the only woman among twenty men on her training course at Wakefield in the early 1960s and worked on Holloway's remand wing:

> One of my first experiences was someone hammering on her cell door one early evening, shouting, 'Unless you let me out now I will take this door off its hinges.' She had a knife or a fork in the cell and it was so ridiculous that I couldn't do anything other than laugh. It was absurd. She was a very difficult woman who had bouts of violence but I was new and I didn't know that, so I had no nervousness and in fact my reaction calmed the situation down and she was as good as gold for the rest of her sentence.

One of her jobs as assistant governor was to visit the 'dirty cells', which accommodated women who came in straight from court or off the streets: 'There was always a proportion with nits and scabies. So they went into the basement cells for fumigation. It was gruesome and very smelly. I would come out thinking, I must go wash now.' But being a prison officer was 'one of those jobs you liked or loathed and I enjoyed it, I found it endlessly fascinating, the women inside. I always liked going back to work if I'd been away or had a few days off, to find out what had happened; it was constant drama: has so and so been sent to court? Is so and so appealing?'

Recruitment booklets of the time were certainly enticing: women were encouraged to join the modern prison service if they enjoyed 'helping others' and had 'an unshakable liking for, and belief in, people'. New prisons and Borstals were being built, old ones were being modernized, and it was the ideal job for the woman who wanted 'to do something' with her life, offering 'good money, generous holidays and real comradeship'. Training included judo, self-defence and first aid, and women officers now received the same rates of pay as men, after the Civil Service introduced equal pay in 1961. Officers started on £14 a week, there was 'ample opportunity to study for promotion' and a chief officer earned just over £31 a week. But while recruitment illustrations showed women in positions of authority, notions of femininity were still crucial: 'All Officers are expected to set an example by their smart and attractive appearance. Though uniform is naturally worn when on duty, pleasing make-up and hair styling are encouraged.'

The public image of prison officers, however, was still poor. When Margaret Donnelly, who studied French and English at Dublin University and then trained as a teacher before moving to England, told her future husband about her career plan, he said, 'Oh my God, how can you? You're joining the forces of darkness.'

Margaret spent a month at Holloway, and as a newcomer she made several mistakes. Each morning staff had a parade 'around the centre of the castle, then we would escort the women to the kitchen to get their lunch. Once I turned a key and it broke in the lock and I had no idea what to do. The women said, "It's all right, miss, you go and get the engineer and we'll look after the key." When I got back the catering officer was there, this massive woman, and she bawled at me, "Didn't they teach you never to abandon your keys?"'

But she found her training at Wakefield fascinating, 'a bit of psychology, a bit of seeing offenders', and while she wanted to return to Holloway, she was posted to Bullwood Hall in Essex. 'The stories from these young girls were dreadful,' she recalls, 'they were cast adrift. One young woman gave a speech at a memorial service for a prisoner who had killed herself and she said, "Let's face it, we're all in here because we've been abused," and essentially it was true.' Margaret's time working in women's prisons made her realize 'how awful a lot of people's lives are. Some shouldn't have been inside, but I couldn't do much about that. I kept hearing stories about abuse, but colleagues thought I was mistaken or making a big deal about it.'

She also had to survive in a predominantly male environment, and was once told by a governor that as a married woman with children she 'lacked the commitment' of her single colleagues. It wouldn't be until the Sex Discrimination Act of 1975 that female governor grades became entitled to houses like the men, and in the meantime they had a 'suite of rooms'. But Margaret stayed on in the prison service, becoming governor of three male prisons. 'I suppose I had a social worker attitude; maybe you could do some good, not just with the women but how it was run, to make the system better. Female staff can be very compassionate, motherly and understanding.'

This was exactly the role Holloway's new governor, Joanna Kelley, had in mind. She had joined the prison service in 1947, at the age of thirty-seven, and had served as Holloway's assistant governor, then governor of Askham Grange. An economics graduate, she was known as a devoted Christian, and a former colleague described her as 'very, very clever. She would stand no nonsense from anybody.'

Joanna Kelley governed Holloway from 1959 to 1966 and encouraged friendship and understanding between staff and prisoners, just like Mary Size in the 1930s. Joanna was aware that female prisoners faced numerous domestic responsibilities, worrying about children, partners and parents, rent and bills. There were roast joints left in ovens, cats locked out, children coming home from school and finding no mother and no tea. When some prisoners were allowed to go out to work during the day, those who lived in London tried to fit in housework beforehand; one managed to leave the prison at 6.30 a.m., get home, make her husband's breakfast and get him off to work before starting her own job.

Governor Kelley introduced new prison-issue clothing: 'cotton frocks and cardigans of different colours, nylon stockings, cotton underwear and lacing shoes'. These were an improvement on the prisoners' own clothing, which typically consisted of one torn dress, a pair of damaged stockings, a pair of shoes in need of repair, one bootlace, one earring and some lipstick. But not everyone liked the clothes and some repeat offenders, sentenced for being drunk or 'wandering abroad', insisted on wearing the old grey prison cap, a few of which had been kept 'to please the old ladies'. One woman had stuck a 'very fine pigeon feather' in hers, and was annoyed to find it had disappeared between sentences. In 1968 the women in Holloway were allowed to wear their own clothes, initially introduced as a trial scheme and then applied to all women's prisons. This was an attempt to 'encourage individual choice and self-expression to reduce institutionalization'.

When Joanna Kelley took up her post, Holloway still looked much as it had in Victorian times, with the same two 'dragons' mounted above the great doorway and rows of thickly barred windows that seemed 'to emphasize how undomestic and strange the place is'. The new governor envisaged a far more homely environment, and soon a table of tulip wood in the central hub always held a vase of flowers, while the prison grounds were planted and blooming again, creating 'a mass of colour in summer, rather like an old fashioned cottage garden'. Food 'improved immensely'; stainless-steel trays replaced the old aluminium tins and the post-war diet of semolina and heavy pastry was supplemented with vegetables, fruit and eggs. Fish and chips were served once a week, and the cocoa, 'nourishing but unpopular', was replaced by extra tea.

Education provision also improved and the prison library stocked 6,000 books, with inmates favouring romances and detective novels, and there were six TV sets which had 'a stabilizing effect' on the inmates by 'turn[ing] the women's minds into normal channels'. There was a wider range of chaplains – Anglican, Roman Catholic and Methodist, as well as a visiting rabbi and an imam – and their role was to 'help a woman to accept her guilt and so her sentence'.

As in Mary Size's time, the medical care in Holloway compared 'very favourably' with that offered in the outside world, but now a much wider range of 'specialists' were drafted into prison. Senior medical officer Dr John Knox oversaw seventy-two staff members, including medical officers, pharmacists, nurses, a dentist, chiropodist, gynaecologist, venereologist and optician. There was a 'notable absence of illness arising from stress conditions' inside prison, such as ulcers and high blood pressure, and many inmates saw their health improve, especially alcoholics and the high percentage who arrived with nits, scabies, gonorrhoea and syphilis. Mental health was just as important to the new governor, and the prison had a psychologist, a psychiatric social worker and two part-time psycho-therapists.

The courts attached increasing weight to medical reports when it came to sentencing women, and over 1,100 were completed in Holloway each year. Report writing became the 'main occupation' of the four prison doctors and at any one time over half of Holloway's population were under mental observation. All women were given tests on arrival: Raven's Progressive Matrices (multiple-choice intelligence tests), vocabulary tests and the Rotter Incomplete Sentences Blank, which assessed psychological adjustment. Women who seemed 'seriously disturbed' were also given the Wechsler IQ Test. By the end of the 1960s about 15–20 per cent of all those in custody received some form of psychiatric treatment, but when it came to women it was over 50 per cent.

Holloway's prisoners were 'all, in one way or another . . . mentally disturbed and deviant from the norm', according to governor Joanna Kelley, and the cure for abnormality was drugs and therapy. In the outside world, prescriptions for sedatives, tranquillizers and stimulants soared in the 1960s, especially for women, and inside Holloway 5,000 doses of medicine were handed out every week. The 'liquid cosh' acted as a medical straitjacket and a modern form of restraint; soon the prison became a place of shuffling women, sedated on Mogadon, Valium and Largactil, whose side effects included double vision, slurred speech, rage and violence.

Group treatment also operated in four of Holloway's wings as a non-medical intervention, and B wing had the Cameron Group, an 'action group' that initiated projects to help both current and ex-prisoners. There was a Husband and Wife Group for those with 'domestic difficulties', and there was even a counselling group in the jam factory. On F wing, home to those serving longer sentences, counselling was made compulsory. But group counselling officers, with only one week's training, were often left exhausted after the sessions, and while staff were encouraged to see themselves as social workers the governor admitted that many, 'especially the older ones, do not want this burden'. Some inmates resented the regime as well, and 'old lags' could be nostalgic for the old days, 'when prisoners were not constantly interfered with by attempts to understand and reform them'.

The Borstal recalls on E wing were seen to need the most therapeutic help, and were aggressive on arrival, smashing furniture and threatening each other and staff. This was followed by 'inward aggression', and Joanna Kelley recalled 'a great deal of tattooing, self-mutilation and swallowing of needles'. While there had always been reports of women trying to kill or harm themselves, from Selina Salter in the 1860s to Dorothy O'Grady in the Second World

War, the 1960s marked the point when it became widespread and as self-harm was regarded as a 'crime' within the prison system this resulted in further punishment.

In 1966 Joanna left her post at Holloway and became assistant director for women in the prison department. The opportunity allowed her to 'spend my time getting Holloway changed'. The main problem was the building itself, which wasn't suited to a therapeutic regime, but built to punish. Like prison commissioner Lilian Barker in the 1930s, Joanna believed the time had come for a brand-new prison. If women were mad and needed treatment then shouldn't Holloway be more of a hospital? Female prisoners posed no threat in terms of security, there was no need to keep them in a fortress; instead the female officer would act as 'nanny', ruling with 'a kind, firm hand'. Yet it was in the 1960s that Holloway witnessed what few thought possible: a woman successfully escaping from the Victorian castle in the prison's most daring and famous jailbreak.

18

Escape

On the morning of 24 July 1960 Zoe Progl, the 'queen of the underworld', escaped from Holloway Prison. She was widely credited as being the first woman ever to do so, although both male and female inmates had been trying to escape, and sometimes succeeding, ever since the prison was built. But the model prison itself was seen as a difficult place to escape from, unlike Newgate where when three men broke out, the press explained that 'it need hardly be stated that no mischief of this sort could possibly have been attempted at Holloway'.

In the early years several men were able to evade their sentences by bribing other prisoners to swap identities, while in April 1885 John Oxley broke out of the prison hospital using a piece of iron shaped into a screwdriver. He scaled a wall with a rope made of bits of string, rags and the counterpane of his bed, but was tracked to a house in Haggerston, around three miles away, and captured after swimming across the filthy Regent's Canal. Sixteen years later a German man named Charles Marsh, about to stand trial for burglary, also managed to break free. No details were given, but Holloway's governor was confident there had been 'no collusion from inside the prison'. Escapes were far more likely to be made on the way to the jail, as in the summer of 1902 when Charles Griffiths, remanded on charges of burglary and theft, was taken by train to Holloway. On arrival at the station he 'politely stood back from the door of the compartment with the air of a man who says 'After you, sir.' The prison officer stepped out; Charles dashed from the other side of the train, jumped a wall and fled.

Once Holloway became a women's prison the suffragettes were said to have come up with 'many ingenious' escape plots. In the

1930s one inmate made her way into the prison grounds after dark, hid in a stokehole, and managed to reach the top of the outer wall before being caught by a warder, while another prisoner of the time, Betty, managed to assemble pieces of mailbag rope into a twenty-two-foot-long rope ladder with which she attempted to escape, only to be caught in the act by a workman.

By the 1940s reports of prisoners escaping from Holloway were becoming a regular occurrence, mainly because inmates were working outside the prison, both during and shortly after the war. But while the press described these as escapes, in prison service terms they involved a breach of trust rather than physical security and therefore the prisoner was said to have absconded. The majority of escapees were Borstal girls, many of whom had ended up in Holloway with considerable experience of running away from institutions, and the police were frequently scouring the streets of London for missing inmates. Two girls waiting to be sent to Borstal attempted to climb over the prison wall but 'their liberty was short lived' when one fell from the top and broke a leg. The other succeeded, but surrendered herself at a police station. In 1948 eleven young women awaiting allocation to Borstal overpowered a woman officer, gagged and tied her to a chair, and escaped with stolen keys. They were recaptured three hours later, after another girl raised the alarm, while the officer was described as suffering from shock.

Other prisoners escaped by the less violent means of imitating staff. One woman, sentenced to fifteen months for theft, had been taken to do housework in the women warders' quarters at Pentonville, where some of the Holloway officers lived. Her absence was discovered when staff noticed a grey prison dress lying on a staircase, and realized the prisoner had walked out wearing a warder's uniform. Another inmate, working as the matron's maid at Holloway, strolled out of the gates in the matron's fur coat, which she returned by post 'to avoid being up on a new charge'. She was recaptured fifteen months later when she visited a large London store where an ex-Holloway officer worked as a detective, and recognized her at once. Women also escaped dressed as men and in October 1954 there was 'an intense all-night search' for two prisoners who had walked out in workmen's dungarees, 'before disappearing in the labyrinth of side turnings near the gaol'.

But while some of these escapes had been successful, the most famous case came in 1960 when Zoe Progl claimed to be 'the first woman ever to escape over the 25 foot wall that surrounds the grim London prison for women'. Her autobiography, *Woman of the Underworld*, was apparently written while in her prison cell, and tells her story in the style of a tabloid journalist – with plenty of sex, crime and drugs – generously illustrated with photographs from the *News of the World*. It was dedicated to the Scotland Yard detectives 'who have been my very charming "enemies" for twenty years', and opened with Zoe settling into her mink coat on the way to Holloway Prison, her diamond-studded bracelet jangling as she lifted one hand to stifle a yawn. The queen of the underworld was en route to her 'palace', escorted by handsome detectives, including four men on motorbikes, in case she tried to break free again.

Born in Lambeth, south London, in 1928, Zoe Tyldesley had grown up in a bug-ridden basement flat in Limehouse, with a drunken, thieving father whose 'second home' was Arbour Square nick. She started stealing at the age of six, looking for food and swimming the Thames to raid barges. At some point in her childhood she was sexually abused by a cinema projectionist. After being evacuated during the war, when she discovered a 'newfound luxury' with foster parents who provided her with her own room and new clothes, she returned to London and 'vowed that the better-life would one day be mine – somehow!' At thirteen she broke into her first house, which gave her 'a strange thrill'; three years later she discovered Maxie's café in Gerrard Street, Soho, a 'sleazy joint', which was the 'rendezvous of every type of villain and thug'.

Zoe's mother threw her out of the house after she slept with a GI, and she started working as a nightclub 'come-on girl'. Here she met Billy the Cat, a lone wolf burglar, and learned the techniques that later 'led me to become the country's Number One Woman Burglar'. At the age of eighteen she married Joe Progl, a master sergeant in the US Army, but her real love was Johnny Gelley, better known as Johnny the Junkie, who was sent to

Wormwood Scrubs for four years for armed robbery with violence. When Johnny escaped, Zoe dyed his hair and gave him a disguise, then together they embarked on a life of crime.

In 1947 she appeared at Bow Street court charged with forgery and 'lacking any moral support from my lover' she felt 'intense shame and guilt', worried about what her parents would think. She was then sent to Holloway on remand and arrived, three months pregnant, feeling 'like Oliver Twist'. While locked in a reception cubicle she amused herself by reading graffiti on the walls scrawled in eyebrow pencil: 'I hate this hole' and 'All screws stink'.

Zoe was taken to D wing, where a previous occupant had written on the cell wall 'Queen Elizabeth slept here', and a neighbour started singing 'I get no kick from cocaine . . . Benzedrine hits me like Ovaltine . . .' until someone else snarled, 'Shut up, you whore!' Her first impression of the officers was stony-faced women 'all soured with life, who could not wait to leave the jail and get home because they were sick of the sight of us'. Holloway was a place where every whisper 'sounded like a shot; every cough a thunder-clap', and where women were made to scrub vast areas of grey stone floors on their knees, which Zoe considered to be 'as silly and pointless as making women scrub the streets of London . . . I wondered how . . . anyone could survive in such a heartless emporium of stone and iron.'

Zoe was sentenced to three years at Borstal, and in the meantime returned to Holloway. She was given prison clothes 'that might have come off any rag-and-bone stall in the East End', including 'a pair of white passion killers which came to the knees', a faded washed-out brown dress and a grey cardigan with patched-up holes. 'The degradation for me was complete,' she wrote. 'No longer was I a person, but more like a cabbage in a field.' Zoe was then trans-ferred to borstal at Aylesbury, where she gave birth to her son Tony. On release she worked as a maid for a prostitute called Annie, the 'best in the business', and had her second son, Paul. She was then put on probation after being caught shoplifting, using the methods she had learned at Borstal, and began doing 'Jump Ups', stealing lorries around the London docks and selling their contents, whether liquor or canned meat.

Before long Zoe was in Holloway again, sentenced to three months for robbing an American soldier and in 1953 she was back for the third time after stealing a safe, now facing fifteen months.

On release she became the mistress of a wealthy colonel, began injecting herself with speedballs – a mixture of cocaine and heroin – and visiting West End orgies. Homeless and pregnant again, she later attempted to kill herself, before becoming a maid for another prostitute. In 1958, after giving birth to her daughter Tracy, Zoe helped her friend Jumbo Parsons, known by the press as Scarface, to escape from Wormwood Scrubs, waiting outside in a car while he climbed down scaffolding on the gateman's lodge. After eighteen days, his lawyer and MP convinced him to return to prison.

Zoe continued to break into houses, targeting mansions across London. She used a variety of disguises, whether her 'little girl' look dressed in teenage clothes or her 'harmless school marm type' in a sporty tweed suit and false hair bun. She was arrested after breaking into a London flat, but was given bail and went on 'grafting', now in the lucrative territory of Brighton, until she was caught again. Fearing a substantial sentence, and knowing 'that I was bound to be sent back to Holloway Prison I decided that I must lay the foundations for an escape . . . I was determined to do something that no other woman had done before – I would go into Holloway and come out over the damned wall.'

At 2 a.m., fuelled on a night of drinking gin, she set out on a reconnaissance of the prison, accompanied by her boyfriend Barry and a little black poodle called Fifi. If anyone asked what they were doing, they would claim to be exercising the dog. Zoe took an extending metal tape measure from her handbag and measured the wall, before finding the little-used exit at the rear of the prison – previously used by Colonel Victor Barker and later the Mosleys – and a locked green door, which she paid a locksmith to make a set of keys for. On a second 'spy trip' to Holloway, Zoe managed to unlock the door, only to find a second locked door just a foot away that refused to open.

After a third visit she chose a spot in the wall that bounded the main entrance, and decided if she could drop over it and into the private road that ran along the east side of the prison she could dash across a bomb site and reach a getaway car. Having satisfied herself that she was about to make criminal history, Zoe went home to put the finishing touches to her plan.

On June 27, 1960, she was sentenced to two and a half years, and booked into the Holloway hotel once more. But in the nine years since she'd last been inside, things were very different, thanks to 'the warm-hearted kindness' of new governor Joanna Kelley. The old bare depressing cells were prettily adorned with curtains and flowers, the dining tables covered with dainty cloths. The prisoners were 'more cheerful, alert and as happy as they could be in prison', with many more hours of freedom and evening classes.

Zoe was allocated to DX wing, a stroke of luck as it was nearest to the point from where she planned to escape, and set about becoming a model prisoner. Four weeks later she was given a 'soft job cleaning offices' and one of her chores was to clean the senior medical officer's room. While polishing the desk she accidentally knocked a phone receiver from its hook and to her surprise she heard a high-pitched dialling tone, rather than the prison switch-board operator, and immediately called her boyfriend Barry. The phone calls continued, and the day of the escape was agreed, Sunday, 24 July 1960.

At 7 a.m. each day Zoe left her cell on DX wing and crossed the quadrangle to the nearby hospital wing, where a nursing sister unlocked a gate. She then served breakfast to the patients and at 7.30 a.m. the gate was unlocked for her to return to her block. She would therefore escape between 7.30 and 7.35 a.m. She now had another stroke of luck: a five-foot-high pile of coke was heaped against the seven-foot inner wall, which she would need to climb in order to reach the twenty-five-foot outer wall, just as John Oxley had done seventy-five years earlier. All she needed was for someone to throw a rope ladder from outside.

But as Zoe left the hospital wing on the morning of the 24th the nurse told her to take a pint of milk back to DX block for a pregnant inmate. So she rushed over, dumped the milk on the step, and raced back to the coke, now seven minutes behind schedule. Her ill-fitting prison-issue shoes meant she slipped three times before getting to the top of the inner wall, ripping her bloomers and 'grazing myself in a place that made sitting down painful for days' afterwards.

Breathlessly, she stood by the perimeter wall waiting for a sign that her friends were on the other side. Then she heard someone call her name, followed by a clang as an extending ladder was thrown against the wall. Barry's head appeared and a rope ladder was dropped down. She clawed her way to the top, 'then I almost wished I hadn't. The sheer drop below terrified me, and while I stupidly tried to stop my torn bloomers from trailing around my legs, I shouted, "I don't think I can make it . . ."'

But Barry urged her down the ladder, frantic because Bryanna O'Malley, a friend who had been released from Holloway the day before, was 'pinned in a phone box about 100 yards away by two hefty screws in uniform'. Bryanna's job had been to occupy the phone box so no one could use it to raise the alarm, but, unbeknown to Zoe, two of her friends had decided to come and watch the action and had parked outside the front gates of the prison in their pink Ford Zephyr with leopard-skin seat covers. This had aroused the suspicion of prison officers, who recognized Bryanna standing in the phone box and had gone to investigate.

Zoe managed to jump to the ground, and ran with Barry across the bomb site to the car. The prison officers released Bryanna, after her friend Bernard made 'menacing gestures', and they too leapt into the car. Then the gang sped away. By lunchtime the BBC had reported her escape, and the next day it was front-page news. In some reports the prison wall had now become thirty feet high. Viewers were told to be on the lookout for a woman who was five foot one, with grey eyes, a fresh complexion, oval face, brown hair dyed blonde and a scar under the left eye, dressed in a blue prison dress and a red cardigan.

For local children, the news was thrilling. Esther Doyle lived in Carleton Road at the rear of Holloway and vividly remembers the morning of Zoe Progl's escape: 'We were terrified we'd bump into her, although I'm not sure what we thought she'd do. Coming down Parkhurst Road after school, we deliberately went over to the prison wall to see if we could find evidence. And there was this red puddle. "*It's blood!*" I told Ma. "*Human blood!*" Because I wasn't a drama queen at all. With hindsight I realize it was more likely to have been a melted lolly.'

Zoe Progl hid at a friend's flat, then she collected her daughter and Barry drove them to a caravan site near Paignton in south Devon. Here she enjoyed 'an idyllic fortnight. Instead of feeling like a woman on the run from the police I was carefree and happy, and also found something that had been denied me for years – the joy of motherhood.' After two weeks, and having run out of money, the couple set off on 'a crook's tour of seaside towns'. But on 1 September the police finally caught up with them in London, and so ended her forty days of freedom.

Back in Holloway 'a great cheer went up' as Zoe was led back to her cell. 'I couldn't have received more attention or felt more flattered if I'd had a star on the door of a dressing room at the London Palladium. The screws never left my side.' Inmates made her an extra-special birthday card, showing her climbing the prison wall in her bloomers.

Zoe was then temporarily moved to Birmingham, because of fears she would try to escape on the way to court, but was back in London for the trial with 'the largest escort of cars and cops that any prisoner has surely been given'. Governor Joanna Kelley, 'a charming and human person', accompanied Zoe on all five trips to court. On her final return to prison, having been sentenced to a further eighteen months for escaping, the car bonnet flew open and she was hurried out in the pouring rain. But Zoe stood obediently on the pavement sharing the governor's umbrella, resisting the temptation to run away through 'loyalty to a gracious lady' until a police car arrived.

Zoe Progl now had four years to serve, but despite this she managed to 'find a laugh or two'. She helped Gin Mill Annie with an illicit still, stole milk and tinned salmon intended for the two prison cats, and formed Zoe Progl Cosmetics Unlimited face cream. The cream – made of shoe polish, powdered red paint stolen from the art class and a sprinkling of talcum powder – was stirred together in a bedpan and sold for five cigarettes a pot. At Christmas, Zoe helped decorate the prison with streamers and angels made from sanitary towels. Then on Christmas Day she had an unexpected visit from her children Paul and Tracy. Her daughter had saved her pocket money to buy a tiny bottle of Woolworths perfume, and while Zoe was allowed to take the gift, it was later removed. 'When are you coming out of hospital, Mummy?' asked Tracy and 'as she was gently led away, the tears streamed down my cheeks. I never felt less like a queen of the underworld.'

Zoe's book ends with an abrupt decision to turn her back on a life of crime. Her twenty-year spell as Britain's 'most notorious woman criminal' had come to an end. She concluded by paying tribute to governor Joanna Kelley, as well as a sympathetic and understanding officer called Mrs Timpson: 'The fact I am now able to go straight is entirely due to them, had it been left to the prison system, I am certain that it would have destroyed me.'

Like many of Holloway's inmates, both then and now, Zoe had a background of poverty, sexual abuse, drugs and attempted suicide. But she also appeared to enjoy every moment of her criminal career – the risks, skill and rewards – and maintains a tone of bravado throughout. Perhaps the publishers thought the best way to end the book therefore was for her to reclaim her 'true' role, not as the country's Number One Woman Burglar but as a mother.

Other escapes from Holloway would follow: in 1966 two women were discovered injured on the pavement outside the prison having climbed over the wall; and some twenty years later an inmate managed to get to Camden Town hidden in a lorry before she was caught eating tapas in her family's restaurant. In the spring of 1994 a man from the garage opposite the prison rang to say, 'We've just seen three of your women escaping over the gym roof.' The remand prisoners had broken a window to reach the roof of the swimming pool, and then climbed the perimeter wall. The police warned the public not to approach the women, one of whom had 'I love Martin' tattooed on her hand. All three were eventually recaptured. But no one would surpass Zoe Progl's dramatic escape over the wall in her bloomers.

19

Category A Prisoners

Female prisoners were not generally seen as an escape threat – aside from Zoe Progl – but the 1960s did see a new category of prisoner at Holloway: women deemed to be a high security risk. In January 1961 two convicted spies arrived at the prison, Ethel Gee and Helen Kroger. They were members of the Portland spy ring and had been found guilty of passing naval secrets to the Soviet Union. Their imprisonment came amid a Cold War struggle for power between the USSR and the United States, with the two superpowers intent on uncovering details of their enemies' nuclear development and preventing classified information from falling into the wrong hands.

Ethel Gee and her colleague Harry Houghton worked at a Royal Navy research station in Dorset and were arrested about to hand over secret material concerning Britain's first nuclear submarine to KGB agent Konon Molody. He had been acting as a go-between, passing information on to Morris Cohen and Lona Petka, two Americans who spied for the Soviets and who ran an antiquarian bookseller business under the names Peter and Helen Kroger. The couple transmitted nuclear secrets to Moscow and smuggled photographs of documents reduced to microdots inside antique books.

Much was made of the fact that Ethel Gee was a 'spinster', an unmarried woman in her forties and a 'plain, shy clerk'. Harry Houghton 'gave her affection', explained one newspaper, 'she gave him secret documents.' The five Portland spies were convicted under the Official Secrets Act, and Ethel and Helen were sent to Holloway as high-security prisoners. When in 1964 Konon Molody was exchanged for a British spy, he continued to send cryptic Christmas cards to Helen in Holloway signed 'Nikolai', which the governor

– who had been told to provide copies of all correspondence to the Home Office – immediately confiscated.

In 1969 the Krogers were also released through a prisoner exchange with the Soviets, and now only Ethel Gee remained in Holloway. Her local MP Evelyn King raised her case in the House of Commons, explaining that 'throughout history women in love have, through their emotions, been guilty of this sort of crime', and while he had no issue with the sentence, it was 'the political interference' that offended him.

Ethel was a model inmate during her time at Holloway, and was transferred to Styal Prison in Cheshire as a 'long term star class prisoner' where she was given a 'study bedroom' with a radio. But in 1966 George Blake, a former British spy who worked as a double agent for the Soviets, escaped from Wormwood Scrubs. This led to a government inquiry headed by Lord Mountbatten and four new security categories were introduced. Category A prisoners were defined as those whose escape would be 'highly dangerous to the public or the police or to the security of the state', while Category D could be trusted in open conditions. Women were excluded from these new categories, except for the very few who were assigned to Category A, usually on remand. Lord Mountbatten feared more escapes might happen in the future, however, and found 'several basic security weaknesses in Holloway', the country's most secure prison for women.

Although Ethel Gee had no connection with George Blake, his escape from Wormwood Scrubs meant all her privileges were withdrawn. She was sent back to Holloway and her radio was removed. After two years as a high-security prisoner, her MP argued she was nothing but a pawn who had been 'punished and punished and punished again' and now she should be freed. In 1970 Ethel and Harry were finally released, and the press reported 'the traitors' love for one another has endured the rigours of prison'.

The issue of high-risk prisoners also came to the fore with the arrival of Holloway's most infamous inmate, Myra Hindley. Found guilty of killing three children in 1966, and later confessing to two further murders, Myra eventually became the first British woman in modern times to serve a full-life term. It was her boyfriend Ian Brady who committed the murders, but it was the 'brassy blonde killer' who became the personification of evil. The British press would never lose its fascination with Myra Hindley, a 'hardened working class girl of the North' with 'pouting lips' and 'a look of defiance'. Like the two baby farmers executed in 1903 she was guilty of the worst crime a woman could commit – the murder of a stranger's child – and while the baby farmers' motivation had been money, there was no understandable explanation for the actions of the 'Moors Murderers'. With the death penalty now abolished, she couldn't be executed and so Holloway Prison would have to be her punishment.

Whether Myra Hindley voluntarily took part in the abductions, sexual abuse, torture, murder and burial of the children on Saddleworth Moor, or whether she was coerced is still argued about today, as is the nature of her behaviour in prison.

As a Category A prisoner, Myra was initially housed alongside convicted spies Ethel Gee and Helen Kroger in E wing. 'Myra said she felt sorry for Ethel,' writes biographer Carol Ann Lee, 'because she'd become embroiled in crime after falling for the wrong man.' But she didn't get on with the other Portland spy, and one day in the kitchen Helen Kroger 'hit her on the head with a teapot, then pummelled her to the ground, screaming, until officers ran in to intervene'.

In the eyes of some inmates and staff, Myra was soon a reformed woman. She reverted to Roman Catholicism – despite opposition from the prison's Catholic priest – took O-levels, and wrote an agony column for a prisoners' magazine using the name Betty Busybody. She was also noted for her tapestry, in particular her contribution to a 'magnificent carpet' commissioned by a 'well known American politician' through Lady Anne Tree, a prison visitor who established a tapestry room at Holloway and later launched the charity Fine Cell Work. Myra was polite and respectful, according to assistant governor Joanna Kozubska; she always contributed to wing activities 'although she preferred not to increase her profile too much'.

But to others inside Holloway, Myra Hindley was manipulative, her Catholicism was a sham, and she revelled in her celebrity status as top of the inmate hierarchy. She was 'fundamentally a very arrogant woman', noted one prison report, 'and considers herself superior to the other members of her wing'. Lady Anne Tree, who began visiting Myra at the request of the governor, described her as a monster who regarded herself as a heroine. 'I didn't want to have anything much to do with her,' remembered Clarice Hall, a nurse at Holloway. 'I was afraid of Myra Hindley. I was very careful with her, because she was devious – very, very devious. So we were warned about her. "Don't take any chance with her."' But Holloway's new governor, Dorothy Wing, did take a chance on Myra.

Dorothy had joined the prison service in 1965, having spent nearly twenty years in the auxiliary territorial service. She was a 'tough cookie', remembers Joanna Kozubska, liked by both inmates and staff. Dorothy ran Holloway for seven years, and was proud of allowing women to wear their own clothing, modernizing the laundry, and introducing men as cooks, teachers and education officers. But outside the prison she would be best known for taking the most hated woman in Britain for a walk on Hampstead Heath.

One morning in early September 1972, Joanna Kozubska accompanied Myra Hindley out of the gates of Holloway Prison to the governor's house. Six months earlier Myra's status had been downgraded to Category B, after she petitioned the Home Office, and while this had not been made public it meant that the governor could, if she chose, escort her out of the prison. This was a practice that had been going on since 1949, but discreetly enough that it had not been public knowledge. The gate officer opened the wicket gate in the main gates, they crossed the twenty-five yards over the cobbles to the governor's red brick house, Joanna delivered Myra Hindley and returned to the main part of the prison. The governor, Myra and the senior medical officer then drove to Hampstead Heath, less than three miles away, for an autumn walk. According to other reports, they were also accompanied by a male friend of the governor's, as well as her dog. A couple of hours later Joanna received a phone call asking her to come and pick up Myra, but news had travelled fast – an officer at Holloway apparently told her boyfriend who worked in a male prison, and he alerted the press. 'The evening papers led on it,' recalls Joanna, 'and the following morning, the national dailies shrieked the news. The furore was staggering . . . it went on for days. After that, we all knew Myra would never be released.' She was reclassified as a Category A prisoner.

On 4 September the governor noted in her journal that Joanna Kelley had visited Holloway in her role as assistant director for women. Nine days later the deputy governor wrote that the 'enquiry re. M.H.' had been concluded. Dorothy Wing retired shortly afterwards and Joanna Kozubska wonders whether the governor had acted 'off her own bat' or if she had received permission from her superiors. As a result of the walk on Hampstead Heath, Dorothy Wing 'left the service unsung and uncelebrated' and, unlike many of her predecessors and successors, she was not rewarded with an honour for her time as Holloway's governor. 'I believe it is highly likely that she had consulted her superiors in the Prison Department,' argues Joanna, who 'chose to distance themselves from a huge error of judgement'. Dorothy Wing was portrayed as having taken the decision alone, and the walk in the park was her downfall.

Dorothy later gave an interview to journalist Norman Luck, after a 'few glasses' of whisky, saying she had taken Myra out of Holloway more than once. In the spring of 1972 she had taken her to the Tutankhamen exhibition at the British Museum but the queue was so long they went for tea instead where Myra was recognized by a member of the public who thought she'd escaped from prison. But Joanna Kozubska dismisses the idea that the governor took Myra out of Holloway on any other occasion. While she could have used the prison's little-known back door without anyone knowing, then why hadn't she used this exit on the day of the walk on Hampstead Heath? Dorothy Wing was 'a victim of her loyalty and adherence to the Official Secrets Act', she was committed and humane and 'didn't deserve the disgrace heaped upon her at the end of her career'.

And so it was another governor, Dr Megan Bull, appointed 'doctor-governess' in 1973, who was in charge of Holloway Prison when Myra Hindley tried to escape.

Two years earlier Myra had started an affair with an officer, Pat Cairns, a former Carmelite nun, during practice for a table tennis tournament on E wing. When inmate Pat Ali was caught with a £5 note hidden inside a pen and claimed it was a reward for acting as a go-between, Myra dismissed the 'vicious and malignant' allegations which 'both horrify and shock me'. Instead, she said, officer Pat Cairns had provided her with 'considerable spiritual help' during a 'particularly painful religious struggle'. In March 1971 Pat Ali, who couldn't read or write, was put on trial within the prison and found guilty of making a false malicious allegation against a prison officer. Her report that Myra and Pat Cairns had been seen 'making love in the record room' was dismissed as 'fabricated nonsense', and as punishment she lost 180 days' remission and was put in solitary confinement for fourteen days.

The affair continued, and when Myra said she wanted to play the piano assistant governor Joanna Kozubska arranged for her to practise in the chapel. She took her there, locked her in, and returned to pick her up, unaware that Pat Cairns would 'pop in' while she was gone. Pat then pressurized inmate Maxine Croft, serving a sentence for forgery, to take photographs for Myra's passport. She also instructed Maxine to make a series of prison key impressions on plaster casts and soap. These were smuggled out in a tea packet and Pat Cairns posted them to a friend of Maxine's, who owned a garage, for safekeeping. But when a police officer called in to have his car repaired and feared the parcel was a bomb, he opened the packet and the escape plot was discovered.

On 2 November 1973 Holloway's governor noted that there had been a possible serious breach of security. A few days later, Maxine Croft gave a statement and Pat Cairns was arrested. She eventually confessed, saying it was a case of 'our impulses are too strong for our judgement, sometimes'. According to a fellow officer, she had 'loved Hindley more than anything else in the world' and believed the relationship was 'to be her destiny'. The plan had been to escape at night, scale the wall and then flee to Brazil where the couple would work as missionaries. If the keys had been made, meanwhile, then others on D wing could have escaped as well, including a member of the Angry Brigade, which had carried out a set of bomb attacks in England a couple of years earlier, and who was believed to have links with the IRA.

Inmate Maxine Croft had eighteen months added to her sentence, while officer Pat Cairns was sentenced to six years and sent to Styal, where she was reportedly 'difficult to manage'. Myra Hindley received a further twelve months and remained for a while in Holloway, where in 1976 she was hospitalized for six weeks following an attack by inmate Josie O'Dwyer, and spent her last years at Highpoint Prison in Suffolk. After the foiled escape plot came to light Pat Ali, whose allegations of an affair had been dismissed, was compensated £1,500 for her loss of six months' remission.

Myra Hindley's affair with a Holloway prison officer was one of the first times such a relationship had been openly reported in the press. The *Express* described 'soft whispers through the cell wall from Myra, the killer with a "crush"', while former governor Dorothy Wing insisted that Holloway Prison was not 'a glorified haven of Lesbians'. She explained that it wasn't possible to stop prisoners 'looking lovingly at each other as they meet in the exercise yard', nor could the authorities prevent the passing of love notes, 'but we can control the physical side' by moving women to different wings. She insisted that the affair between Myra Hindley and Pat Cairns had been emotional and never physical, and objected to 'innuendos' about the reason she had previously taken Myra for a walk on Hampstead Heath. But it was now that lesbian affairs became a staple way of describing life in every women's prison, and especially the Victorian castle of Holloway.

20

Sex and Love

Affairs between inmates had always occurred at Holloway Prison and ever since 1903, when hundreds and sometimes thousands of women had been locked up together, love, sex and romance had been an inevitable part of day-to-day life. But while many former prisoners talked openly about discovering friendship inside, whether the suffragettes in Edwardian times or enemy aliens during the Second World War, sexual relationships were seldom referred to. Prison officials traditionally preferred to ignore lesbian affairs, rather than call attention to what was seen as 'abnormal'. Sexual relations between women had never been criminalized in the UK, although some imprisoned for 'lewdness' or 'indecency' may have been arrested in connection with their sexuality. The Criminal Law Amendment Act of 1921 had attempted to make 'acts of gross indecency' between women illegal, but this was rejected by the House of Lords because, explained Lord Desart, it was better not to 'tell the whole world that there is such an offence' and thereby bring it to the notice of 'women who have never heard of it, never thought of it, never dreamt of it'. Officially sexual relations in prison were against the rules – as they are today – and had to be kept largely secret. Margot Pottlitzer, a Jewish refugee jailed at Holloway in 1940, remembers a warder discovering her with another woman who had sought shelter in her cell during an air raid. The warder was 'absolutely furious, I mean goodness knows what she suspected us of, in our case quite wrongly'.

By the early 1950s lesbian relationships had become 'the biggest problem in women's prisons', according to playwright and former debutante Joan Henry who was jailed for twelve months for passing a fraudulent cheque. In male prisons, on the other hand, the biggest issue was corruption.

Psychologists and criminologists were intrigued by homosexuality in women's jails. Some believed they were a 'temporary substitute' for heterosexual relationships, while others feared that women could become 'addicted' and prison authorities were encouraged to provide activities as a form of 'distraction'. According to 'experts' of the time, lesbianism was also connected to criminal behaviour and mental illness and as Holloway was the UK's largest prison for women it became the focus of several theories on prisoners' sexuality. Joan Henry suggested that some women had affairs because they were 'deprived of stimulation in their surroundings', others were 'more homosexually inclined than most people would imagine, or even than they have ever imagined themselves. They are ripe for the advances of the long-term prisoner.' Then there were those who, after a few months in Holloway, would 'sell their souls, bodies, or wedding rings' for cigarettes, sweets or cosmetics.

Lesbian relationships presented 'great management problems' to governor Joanna Kelley in the 1960s, when they were 'frowned upon as unhealthy and unnatural'. But while a great deal of talk about sex went on inside Holloway and there was 'quite often lesbianism amongst the recidivists', most 'appear to confine themselves to kissing, cuddling and holding hands'. This led to 'endless jealousies and scenes', as well as complaints from 'normal women, many of whom had never come across such behaviour before in their lives'. Drawing on homophobic theories of the time, the governor identified three main types of lesbian. The first had 'abnormal physical features', became antisocial and drifted into delinquency, with the 'boy type of lesbian' taking to housebreaking 'to show their masculinity'. Then there were the 'psychological reasons', which the governor applied mainly to prostitutes: 'perhaps they were raped as children' or had a difficult relationship with their mother. According to Holloway's governor, many wanted to be 'normal' and often 'beg for help', so a voluntary group for lesbians was formed on F wing run by a psychiatrist. The third type of lesbian 'become homosexual only in special circumstances' – such as prison. This was more of an 'experiment' through boredom, curiosity and the need for excitement and 'their minds can be diverted fairly easily by keeping them occupied and offering them alternative activities'. When actress Sarah Churchill, daughter of former Prime Minister Winston Churchill, was sent to Holloway on remand for being drunk and disorderly a girl popped into her cell and said, 'Are you a lesbian?' When Sarah said no, the woman replied, 'Well you will be if you stay here long enough.'

In the 1970s lesbianism was still being explained as an emotional attraction that occurred only in unusual circumstances. 'Many an otherwise normal woman discovers, in prison, a latent lesbianism,' wrote Holloway historian John Camp, 'which can be a source of worry, though it usually disappears once she is released.' While British newspapers were reporting that lesbianism was 'rife' in women's prisons, he insisted these relations were not 'of a very physical or sexual nature'. Women developed crushes, tried to sit next to each other in chapel or association, held hands and passed 'endearing notes known in prison as "kites"'. Like governor Joanna Kelley, he described affairs as an emotional response to prison that caused disciplinary problems: 'some of the inmates may be disturbed and revolted by this, and trouble results.'

Zoe Progl, the famous escapee, was indeed 'revolted' when she was first approached by a prisoner looking for 'a nice girl as a partner'. But then she met Millie, 'a slim girl with short, dark hair and pretty in a boyish sort of way', who comforted her when she was sobbing in her cell. Millie brought dog-ends salvaged from prison officers' fireplaces and they became 'firm friends'. Then one day Zoe received a love letter written on toilet paper asking her to 'be her girl'. She was 'tremendously amused' and decided to play along 'just to see what happened', but was embarrassed when Millie kissed her. Nine years later and now serving a longer sentence at Holloway, Zoe came to see lesbian affairs more as 'a natural outlet for sexual frustration'. One day she entered a cell in DX wing, known as 'Sex De-exy' or 'Married Quarters', to find two women passionately embracing 'in the top row of cells, which was the hot bed of Lesbianism in Holloway' because 'it took the screws longer to reach that section than any other'. After months of 'mental stagnation and enforced frigidity' lesbianism began to 'lose its horror' and Zoe 'found that I became susceptible'. She started an affair with 'the most popular of the dozen or so lesbians inside Holloway' although after a few weeks it became 'so ridiculously intense' that she broke it off before 'I too succumbed to the attractions of this strange way of life and lost interest for ever in men'. As a result, her girlfriend ended up in the prison hospital after suffering a nervous breakdown.

But many other inmates had long, loving relationships and Joanna Kozubska remembers several who were an 'item' in the early 1970s, in particular Gabriella and Billy whose relationship was 'a real prison romance'. They lived in a cell on D wing, where there were a number of double cells, and Joanna saw 'no reason under Prison Rules to deny their request to share'. While there were 'no overt displays of affection . . . we all knew that they were "together". They told us so and were proud of their relationship.'

When it came to affairs between inmates and staff, Joan Henry met women who were 'madly in love with women officers and vice versa'. Some had 'fallen in love for the first time in their lives in prison' and it was a relationship that often became permanent when the sentence finished. But in other cases, issues of power and abuse came into play. Some officers demanded sex in exchange for preferential treatment, and would bully, intimidate and assault. One inmate verbally attacked an officer, a 'dirty old bitch' who had made 'passes' at her girl friend. She called 'the screw a f-----g old cow to her face' and ended up in the punishment cells, along with three days' remission.

Consensual relationships between female officers could also cause problems and when one ended 'it was like a stack of dominoes', explains a former assistant governor; 'they wouldn't carry out certain duties, they didn't want to be on a wing with so and so . . .' She attributes the 'high lesbian contingent' among staff to an article published in *Nova* magazine: 'It said lesbianism was encouraged at Holloway and so a whole raft of them went in; they thought, That's the place to be! I refused to attend the staff club unless it was an official event because things did go on; some staff were preyed on by others. They would try to "turn" new officers, and we warned one about this. One officer was told: "If you sleep with me you'll get a good report."'

It also wasn't unusual for women to have crushes on staff members. 'I had my fair share of problems in this area,' remembers Joanna Kozubska. One woman, Babs, tattooed herself with a big heart, a huge arrow and 'Babs loves Miss K' on her arm. An inmate called 'Bashful' wrote to the agony column in the inmate magazine *Behind the Times*: 'I have fallen in love with the A.G. Is this natural under the circumstances? Do you think you could feel the same way?' The agony aunt replied: 'Dear Bashful, I think it's natural under *any* circumstances. She is rather dishy.'

In 1974 when a new prison drama was launched, the ITV series *Within These Walls*, it based several story lines on sexual relationships between staff and inmates, drawing directly on the experiences of those inside Holloway, although inmates couldn't watch it as it started half an hour after lock-up. In series one, inmate Joan Harrison is about to be transferred to an open prison but is loath to leave assistant governor Miss Parrish. 'I'll never know,' she tells her, 'if you fancy me.' The story line is then hastily resolved when Joan throws herself off a roof, before dying of her injuries.

A novel written by one former Holloway prisoner told a more celebratory story of love inside jail. Born in 1930 and educated at Cheltenham Ladies' College and the University of Cambridge, Pat Arrowsmith was a renowned political activist and an organizer of the 1958 Aldermaston March against hydrogen bomb tests. She was a co-founder of the Campaign for Nuclear Disarmament, whose members were jailed at Holloway, as were women from the anti-war group, Committee of 100. Pat was also regarded as a lesbian icon, and in 1977 would list the Gateways Club in Chelsea in her entry for *Who's Who*. This was said to be the longest surviving lesbian club in the world, and Pat described it as the centre of lesbian London where 'you could be sure to see [Holloway] screws . . . or former prisoners'.

Pat Arrowsmith was jailed eleven times as a political activist, beginning in 1958, and serving most of her terms in Holloway. In 1969, the year before her novel *Somewhere Like This* was published, she was sentenced to six months for refusing to keep the peace.

Somewhere Like This tells a story of love and longing, intrigue and lust, set against a backdrop of butches and fems, backstabbing and gossip, where inmates are drugged on arrival and lesbian prisoners are sent to be reformed. The drama takes place in the fictional prison of Collingwood although it was clearly based on Holloway with its 'grim, mock castle walls'. The novel opens with Lorry, sentenced for housebreaking and burglary, lying in her cell feeling both rage and relief. She had been taken from court to Wormwood Scrubs and made to stand naked in front of male officers before being sent to Collingwood. Now locked up in a women's prison she feels both 'caged and safe', and wonders if she will fancy anyone on her wing.

Lorry is one of the most sought-after inmates, 'a nice, healthy tom-boy – not like the other butches in at the moment, who greased and smarmed their hair' and 'cultivated pseudo-sideboards'. For Lorry, life inside is in many ways better than outside. At gay clubs there was competition, but in prison 'butches were relatively scarce' and sought after. In Collingwood 'lesbianism was not queer: it was taken for granted – even by most of the officers.'

The publishers seemed unsure how to market the book. One version of the cover showed a woman in a prisoner's uniform, two love heart tattoos on her arm, apparently dreaming about another woman whose picture hangs on her cell wall. But another cover showed an anonymous, headless and mostly naked woman sitting on a bed, with the enticing strapline, 'In an all-woman world, there's only one kind of love'. At the time the novel was published, discrimination against lesbians was still widespread: women were persecuted, ridiculed and isolated, while teachers, childcare officers and social workers lost their jobs. The prison portrayed in Pat Arrowsmith's novel offered a form of freedom, a place where women could openly have affairs and fall in love. *Somewhere Like This* provided a more honest, and more accepting, image of sex behind bars, although again the ending is far from a happy one.

Allegations of sexual harassment by Holloway staff meanwhile continued. In the 1980s one psychiatrist described 'a very negative gay subculture', while former Holloway teacher Daisy Solomons remembers being told about a mock street sign, 'Lesbiavingyou' on a corridor not far from where she worked in the education department.

'A lot of officers were ex-army,' she says, 'and if they were on the cusp of being "found out" they resigned and went into the prison service.' In 2002 things would finally come to a head after a five-month inquiry into reports that a 'hard core' of lesbian officers, known as the Magnificent Seven, sexually harassed new women recruits. The staff social club, used as the officers' 'power base', was finally closed down. Nine women officers were transferred from Holloway, as were five managers, and a new governor appointed, Ed Willetts. There was, however, no police investigation.

Aside from affairs between women, Holloway inmates also occasionally had sex with men, usually prisoners on working parties from male jails. Zoe Progl describes men filing in to carry out repairs and women giving 'low she-wolf whistles' to attract the one she fancied. Love notes written on toilet paper would be left on top of a lavatory cistern or on a high ledge in the boiler house. Three of the flirtations during Zoe's time ended in marriage.

Hilary Beauchamp, who started teaching art at Holloway in the 1980s, recalls hearing 'the female hormones jump up' when three male inmates from Pentonville arrived. Hilary ended up standing in the corridor with a male officer, sucking on boiled sweets and listening to 'the noises of frolicking and giggling . . . testosterone had collided with oestrogen and peaked in some disused shower room in the largest female prison in Europe.' She also found another prisoner 'entertaining a young man' in her cell, a prison officer 'not long in his job' who had 'taken to socializing and light coupling'.

But while female officers would eventually be sanctioned for sexual exploitation, abuse by male officers tended to be hushed up. One male governor would say, 'Well, she led him on,' recalls a probation officer from the 1990s. 'Inmates told us about a staff member known as fifty fags a shag. I gave evidence against him, but he was allowed to remain in the jail, with keys, at night.' In a more recent case, a prisoner who reported a male officer was dismissed as having mental health problems.

In Pat Arrowsmith's novel, lesbian affairs were taken for granted at Holloway and inmates rejected the authorities' attempts to 'reform' them through therapy. At the group counselling sessions prisoners passed on gossip about who was 'going with a butch on another wing', refusing to display the 'least shame or disquiet'. But therapy – and drugs – remained the main form of treatment for prisoners at Holloway who were 'all, in one way or another . . . deviant from the norm'. And now Joanna Kelley in her role as assistant director for women wanted to extend this still further. Ever since 1966 her dream had been to replace Holloway with a new building better suited to a therapeutic regime, and now at last the old Victorian castle would begin to be torn down and in its place there would be a hospital.

PART SEVEN

Holloway Hospital

21

A Place of Healing

When Ken Neale, assistant secretary for the new prison division (P4) that would oversee the rebuild, visited Holloway in 1967 he found it 'an affront to civilization'. It was 'utterly unacceptable to put women and children' in this 'Fagin's kitchen . . . a devilish hole, derelict, rundown, dirty and over-crowded'. The Victorian prison had been built to intimidate and punish, to hold its inmates in segregation and silence, to impose hard labour and flogging. It was a deliberately oppressive place and it should no longer be used for women.

The new prison would 'turn its predecessor upside down and inside out,' explains sociologist Paul Rock in *Reconstructing a Women's Prison*. The centre of the jail would now be an open 'village green', and instead of long straight wings with rows of cells, there would be small bands of self-sufficient units set out in a chain where women would live in 'family like' groups. The old castle would be replaced with 'basically a secure hospital to act as the hub of the female penal system,' explained Home Secretary James Callaghan, because 'most women and girls in custody require some form of medical, psychiatric or remedial treatment.' The project would begin with the construction of a central hospital and psychiatric unit, and the plan drew widespread publicity. 'Hospital instead of jail for girls who break law', ran a headline in the *Daily Mirror*. The old Holloway would be demolished bit by bit while the new prison was being built on the other half of the site. It was a hugely ambitious scheme and intended to take ten years. In the end it took nearly two decades.

Those behind the project at P4, like Joanna Kelley and Ken Neale, saw themselves as pioneers, leading the way not just in the

UK but worldwide. It was a time of hope; even the Home Office anticipated that by the end of the century 'penological progress will result in even fewer or no women at all being given prison sentences'. Most female prisoners were 'inadequate people who have made a mess of their lives and need a secure framework within which to rebuild their lives'. Holloway would once again be a model jail, only this time along the lines of a large 'treatment orientated' hospital, where even the cells would be the size of hospital rooms. 'We really had in mind a place of healing,' the former governor explained, 'not only of the body but also of the mind.' Holloway would hold 350 women in 'hospital conditions' and 150 in normal cells, prisoners would have greater freedom, and there would no longer be a punishment block. There were suggestions that the building could eventually be handed over to the NHS as a fully-fledged hospital and lose the word 'prison' for ever, while Holloway was almost renamed, with three alternatives suggested in 1970: Barnersbury, Chanctonbury, and Islington Barners.

The architects for the rebuild were RMJM & Partners; known for their 'modernist, functional style', they had designed several housing and university projects in the UK, as well as a nuclear power station and a shopping centre. Now they had to come up with a building suitable for a therapeutic approach to female prisoners, a place for group counselling and therapy, as well as electroconvulsive therapy. A trolley route, 'like a village high street', would link the facilities, with education followed by the library on one side and the chapel on the other, then a swimming pool and gym. The pool would be used for exercise and hydrotherapy and to prevent women 'releasing their energy in more destructive ways'. This was not a building intended as a 'terror to evil-doers', although there would be a special security unit for four Category A remand women, who would include the Portland spies and Myra Hindley. There would also be night patrols, alarm systems and a direct line to Scotland Yard, but no dog patrols, floodlighting or electronic surveillance.

In 1970 Judy Gibbons, who had been transferred from Holloway to Styal as deputy governor, received a phone call.

Joanna Kelley asked me to go to the Home Office with her, for two years as an adviser to the new prison. She said, 'Would you be interested?' And I said, 'Rather!' I went to meetings and looked at plans and met with people from abroad who were interested in new prison design, with smaller units and a more therapeutic approach. I was fond of the old castle but I could see that life and people's thinking about prisons had moved on and that we couldn't sit in the nineteenth century for ever.

Treatment would be modelled on the Henderson Hospital in Surrey, originally a social rehabilitation unit for soldiers and then a residential centre for adults with psychopathic disorders. Judy went to the Henderson and took part in group therapy training, which staff found 'fairly challenging; it meant they had to take an "in depth" look at themselves before they could expect the same from the women in prison.'

In October 1970 demolition of the old prison began, and the first brick to fall was presented to governor Dorothy Wing, who had it mounted on a stand in her office. The following January, work started at the back of the jail, pulling down the old staff quarters, the jam factory, part of the hospital and some of the perimeter wall. The former chaplain's house would be converted into a staff club and mess, while the final act of demolition would be the main gateway. Two press conferences were held, the Home Office offered journalists a tour of the prison just before demolition began, and again during the breach of the perimeter wall, and the end of the old Holloway was covered on both BBC and ITV news.

But before things could go any further the remains of the five women executed since 1903 needed to be moved. On the morning of 29 March 1971 selected works staff, two engineers and a group of officers began breaking up the concrete over the burial area. The next day a scaffold screen was erected, to prevent inmates from viewing the proceedings, and again work continued into the evening. At the end of the third day, after digging teams had struggled to get through heavy clay, the prison's two senior medical officers arrived, Dr R. Blyth and Dr Megan Bull. By late afternoon they reached the coffin of Ruth Ellis, and when Dr Bull found a wedding ring inside she placed it in the new coffin provided by the London Necropolis Company, in charge of the exhumations and transfer. Next the remains of Styllou Christofi were exhumed, followed by Edith Thompson at 10.15 p.m., and then finally, at nearly two in the morning, Amelia Sach and Annie Walters.

At 3 a.m., on the morning of April Fool's Day, the five new coffins left the prison and four were taken to Brookwood Cemetery in Surrey, some forty miles south-west of the prison. It had been decided that 'particularly careful and sympathetic consideration' would be given to the remains of Ruth Ellis 'due to the controversy and debate' that had surrounded her execution sixteen years earlier. Former governor Charity Taylor visited Ruth's sister Muriel to tell her about the exhumation, and Ruth's son Andrew was allowed to conduct a private burial at Amersham, Buckinghamshire. The families of the other four women were not informed at all, neither of the exhumation nor the time and place of reburial.

It's a sunny April day when I catch the train from Waterloo to Brookwood and as I get off at the cemetery all I can hear is bird-song. I head left, down a path bordered by pine trees and rhododendron, passing large, modern graves and memorials, while others are old and humble, overlooked by a single daffodil. Squirrels begin to dart to and fro under trees and a train speeds by as still I follow the path; it's muddy now, surrounded by spongy grass and fallen pine cones. I've printed out a map from the cemetery's website, but none of the paths are named and I'm not certain where I'm going.

I come to a wall at the far end, intending to keep following the path as it curves right round the boundary wall, when I see a black slab to my left; it looks nothing like the headstones near it and something pulls me off the path towards it, although surely this isn't the right grave, it looks too modern. The gravestone lies in a slight dip in the land, like a shiny granite book left on the grass. As I get closer I see gold letters on one side of the stone spelling out the beginning of a name, 'AME . . .', and the words 'Died 1903'. The remaining letters have nearly been worn away, but I know who this belongs to, Amelia Sach. The fact it says 'died' seems odd, for she was executed – quite possibly for a crime she didn't commit, hanged because Annie Walters had been found in a ladies' toilet with a dead baby whom she admitted she had drugged. Then I realize that of course the grave looks modern; while it had been unmarked for over twenty years this memorial stone was only put here in 1993. A special service was held by Reverend Barry Arscott, then Vicar of St Barnabas Church in Manor Park, where Edith Thompson's memorial service is now held each year.

There are plastic flowers at either end of the gravestone, while under a nearby bush is a plastic-covered paper label attached to a silver ribbon. I pick it up to see a picture of a small bunch of holly and a message: 'For Edith at Christmas and for your birthday 25 December 2014'. I later discover it's been left by Debra Melsom, who first came across Edith's tragic story as a child and has been visiting Brookwood for the past twelve years to lay a wreath on the communal grave.

This feels like a lonely part of the cemetery, as if the remains of the four women have quite deliberately been put at the furthest corner. It's hard to imagine, standing here with sunlight casting warm shadows on the grass, what this spot looked like in the darkness of pre-dawn forty-five years ago. I study the moss growing through a crack on the gravestone; hear the damp crunch of my boots as I walk around reading the names etched on three sides; Amelia Sach, Annie Walters, and Styllou Pantopiou Christofi. On the top of the stone, golden letters spell out Edith Jessie Thompson, with her date of birth and death, and below that 'Sleep on Beloved. Her death was a legal formality'. The wording sounds a little strange, but it's the first indication that the women here didn't die from natural causes.

On the train back to London I think about how the four individuals were so different: two Edwardian midwives who ran a lying-in home for unmarried pregnant women, a Cypriot 'peasant' woman who killed her daughter-in-law and who may have been insane, and Edith Thompson who was blamed for her lover's murder of her husband. All were portrayed as unnatural women – as was Ruth Ellis – and all had been tried, convicted and executed by men. They had been buried within the walls of Holloway Prison, then secretly removed in the dead of night, their families denied any sense of dignity right to the end.

In the spring of 1971, the demolition of the old prison and the construction of the new 'hospital' continued. This was despite opposition from the council, neighbours, penal reform groups and historical preservation societies. Islington council had condemned the idea of the rebuild from the beginning, arguing that the borough was overcrowded and the site should be used for local needs, such as housing, welfare projects and open space. But the project didn't require planning permission from the council, as it was Crown property and there wasn't going to be any change in use; it would still be a prison. The new design, including a 'curvy' or 'wiggly' wall around part of the perimeter, was supposed to break down barriers between the prison and the outside community. But many of Holloway's neighbours would have preferred the boundaries to stay in place. Campaigners Radical Alternatives to Prison (RAP) argued that Holloway should be phased out altogether and replaced with community-based alternatives and in the summer of 1972 it petitioned the Home Office to stop the rebuilding, citing both practical and moral objections. But still the rebuilding went on.

As for the old prison itself, to begin with there didn't seem to be much concern about its historical value. The London Society asked if the tower could be kept, and was told the demolition was too far advanced. The Ancient Monuments Society attempted to save the gatehouse, and the Home Office replied that it could be taken down and reassembled elsewhere, but only if someone else paid for it. It was then that some pieces of the building were, in a slightly haphazard way, removed and taken to the Museum of London, including the old cell door from 1902.

Then at the end of January 1977, 276 women and six babies were transferred from the old radial prison into the new hospital, accompanied by Joanna Kelley and governor Megan Bull who walked solemnly across the courtyard towards what they hoped was the future for women in prison.

With the old prison now empty, the demolition continued. 'I was one of the guys who tore Holloway down,' remembers Islington resident Allen Russell, 'way back before they had health and safety. I was working for a demolition company and I saw the cell where Ruth Ellis was hanged with the trapdoor. I also found a straitjacket; maybe I should have kept it and given it to the Museum of London. I remember a suffragette came to pull the lever of the crane, with the ball aimed at her old prison cell.' This was Enid Goulden Bach, Emmeline Pankhurst's niece and chair of the Suffragette Fellowship, the group formed in 1926 to remember and celebrate the suffragette spirit. In May 1977 Enid presided over the demolition of DX wing where some of her comrades had been held sixty years earlier, with the demolition ball draped in the suffragette colours. A few months later the castle-like gatehouse, through which Holloway's first twenty-seven female prisoners had passed in 1852, was pulled down.

But the project was already proving massively expensive; the Treasury questioned whether it was necessary to do away with 'slopping out', then it queried the need for extra security, and then the swimming pool. Rooms for medical provision were cut and the number of cells increased. The original estimate for the rebuild had been around £5 million, but the final cost was said to be nearer £40 million. The population inside Holloway had changed as well, which the planners had not anticipated. The general impression, explains Paul Rock, was that women offenders were becoming 'more dangerous, more criminal, and more like men in their offending behaviour', just as Holloway's chaplain Reverend William Morrison had warned would happen in Victorian times.

Despite provision for four Category A prisoners, when Leila Khaled became the first woman to hijack a plane in 1969 as a member of the Popular Front for the Liberation of Palestine, she was regarded as too dangerous for the old Holloway or the new low-security building and was held in a police station. Four years later Dolores and Marion Price, volunteers for the Provisional Irish Republican Army, were arrested after a car bombing at the Old Bailey and held on remand at Brixton male prison, then moved to a new secure wing for women in the predominantly male prison of Durham. If it hadn't been for the official inquiry into Myra Hindley's escape plot in 1973, they would have been jailed at Holloway.

Not only were women committing 'male' crimes, the female prison population had grown, and while it was still far lower than men, it was increasing at a much faster rate. When the rebuild project had begun, around 800 women were in prison nationwide; by 1980 it was nearly 1,500. This reflected a general increase in the overall prison population, which had been steadily rising since the 1940s. The proportion of women in jail peaked in 1970 and again in 1980. While there is no single explanation for the rise, is it a coincidence that when women were fighting for equal rights – whether Edwardian suffragettes or the Women's Liberation Movement in the 1970s – the female prison population increased? With the suffragettes the evidence is clear: they were jailed as a direct result of the militant campaign for the vote. When it came to the feminist movements of the 1970s and 1980s the link is less straightforward. But this was a time of protest, marches and strikes, as well as significant legal changes in the status of women, including the Equal Pay Act and the Sex Discrimination Act. So were women committing more crimes, or were they perceived as more dangerous to the status quo?

As Holloway became overcrowded once more, women were put two in a cell, as they had been during the Second World War. By the summer of 1976, recreation rooms were being used as dormitories and there were few facilities for exercise or education. Prison security wings were being phased out in the mid-1970s, but a new unit was created at Holloway for twelve sentenced women and six on remand. It was entered by a separate lift, and it had its own secure rooftop exercise yard, covered with mesh to prevent a helicopter landing. The unit was eventually used for segregation and punishment of sentenced prisoners, so Holloway ended up with a punishment block after all.

The days of rehabilitation were over, and those behind the new therapeutic prison who'd believed in 'freedom in captivity' and envisaged a building to 'care for and to help the failures of society' had moved on. By 1979 it was clear that the outcome of the project would be the opposite of what had been intended. Holloway wasn't going to be a hospital with a prison, but a prison with hospital facilities. Instead of holding 350 women in 'hospital conditions', now only 100–150 would be regarded as patients. According to prison officers there were many women who should have been in a hospital, and they were concerned by a growing number of 'disturbed' inmates, some linked with drug offences. Mental hospitals wouldn't take 'mentally disordered' offenders unless they could be treated, and referring women out of Holloway would become a major problem. According to one officer, when a prisoner arrived 'who shouldn't be there' hospital staff would come and interview her and decide 'she was too bad; they couldn't take her . . . because they hadn't anywhere to go with her. So she was a prisoner.'

Assistant governor Joanna Kozubska recalls being advised by medical officers to put one woman in a Victorian-style straitjacket after 'she had been flinging herself around her cell in the hospital wing, shrieking, tearing and scratching at herself with her nails'. A 'calming injection' hadn't worked, so the woman was put in the canvas jacket, which came down just below her waist, with long straps at the ends of the sleeves which buckled round to prevent her using her arms. 'It was a fight,' writes Joanna, and while it 'did the job', it was her 'first and last experience of this restraint. I never wanted to use one again.'

Holloway was also once again understaffed. More officers were recruited, but they were mainly young and inexperienced, while mature officers were being transferred on promotion. Staff turnover was high, with resignations, absenteeism and sickness, and then there was industrial action. In 1978 prison officers nationwide took action 114 times, and the POA warned of an imminent total breakdown in the prison system. Behaviour inside Holloway now resembled the years immediately after the Second World War, with fights, assaults and wing disturbances. Prisoners built barricades, set fire to cells, broke windows and held rooftop demonstrations. The inmates had a brand-new building, and they were smashing it up.

The rebuilt prison also had major flaws. How could officers maintain control over hundreds of women in a building that resembled a hospital? The Victorian radial design had given 'screws' maximum surveillance, explained one former inmate, 'so they were secure and that was better for the prisoners'. Now everyone felt increasingly unsafe. There was no central hub from which to have a clear view along rows of cells and up tiers of landings; instead there were short, low-ceilinged corridors with 'dog-leg' bends where it was impossible to see what – or who – was around the corner.

By October 1978 there was one act of malicious damage a week, whether graffiti on the walls, or washbasins torn from their stands. Art teacher Hilary Beauchamp described a huge window that stretched from ceiling to floor on the first floor. Prison planners had thought a good view of the world outside on Parkhurst Road would be a 'generous gesture' but it was nicknamed 'the Wind-up Window' and repeatedly smashed until eventually it was boarded up.

The *Evening Standard* reported the 'Holloway Hilton' had been vandalized; MPs had seen smashed windows, damaged walls and keyholes blocked with putty. One staff member described women hanging their arms and legs out of cell windows 'screaming at the flats and cutting . . . themselves.' Some could wriggle through the bars of the windows, which had been based on the measurements of an average man.

The governor reported 'mild hysteria' spreading from unit to unit, while officers complained about lack of discipline and problems of morale, just as they had during the war. In 1978 there were twenty recorded offences of assault and 'gross personal violence' per 100 women nationally in prison, compared to six in men's jails, and half of these happened in Holloway. Inmates' behaviour appeared to be more extreme, and focused on the destruction of the actual building, but the biggest difference was that Holloway's prisoners were far more visible.

The prison's neighbours had often heard screams and shouts, but with the cell blocks now nearer the perimeter, it was even easier to be aware of what was going on inside, women banging in their cells, yelling out of windows, or performing 'striptease sessions'. Residents of Penderyn Way heard what sounded like a 'mini riot', while Dalmeny Avenue tenants association protested about shouted conversations. At 10 p.m. one night a woman 'was heard calling out that she needed a woman and it wasn't her fault that she was a *lesbian*', to which another inmate called, 'Why don't you f-----g shut up.'

Inside Holloway, the relationship between inmates and officers was one of exposure and confrontation. Prisoners in D wing could see into officers' bedrooms in the new staff flats and those going to work in the morning were told, 'You looked quite nice in that pink nightie, miss!' The sense of claustrophobia increased. It was difficult to move large groups of women from wing to wing, down endless corridors and through numerous doors, while officers felt pressed up against the inmates, unable to keep a safe distance.

After three years in the new Holloway, and with over 100 assaults on staff annually, governor Megan Bull reported: 'Violence is a very serious problem in this prison . . . we have a lot of disturbed women, and women who have not been violent outside Holloway can be violent inside Holloway.' Just as in Victorian times, it was the act of being imprisoned that turned women violent.

Space was central to the unrest. The House of Correction had been built to isolate, now everyone was thrown together and inmates and officers battled over which area belonged to whom. And before long there would be an influx of prisoners of a new kind, the largest group of political protesters to walk through the door of Holloway Prison since the days of the suffragettes.

22

Jailed for an Ideal

Holloway Prison had always been home to people imprisoned for their political beliefs. In Victorian times this was largely when defending the right to freedom of religion, speech, thought or press, and prison was used as a way to silence political dissent and as a deterrent and example to others. But it wasn't until 1921 that a group of actual politicians were jailed en masse, and their imprisonment had the opposite of its intended effect. Instead, just as with the suffragettes, being locked up in Holloway only served to strengthen their cause.

In the 1919 local elections, Labour had won the vast majority of council seats in Poplar, one of London's poorest districts. The new council was made up of self-described 'class-conscious socialists', including railway, dock, laundry and postal workers. They brought in a minimum wage for council employees and, even more radically, women were paid the same as men. Their aim was to build housing, provide health programmes and offer free services to the unemployed. The council set a rate to fund these services, but residents also had to pay a precept to the London County Council and the Metropolitan Asylums Board towards citywide services such as drains, sewage and police. When the precept was increased, the council, led by mayor George Lansbury, the future leader of the Labour Party, refused to collect it and the councillors were taken to court. 'If we have to choose between contempt of the poor and contempt of court,' he said, 'it will be contempt of court.' The question was one of right and wrong, not whether their actions were against the law.

The councillors were sentenced to prison indefinitely; twenty-five men were taken to Brixton and five women to Holloway: Minnie

Lansbury, Nellie Cressall, Julia Scurr, Susan Lawrence and Jennie Mackay. The women 'looked forward to be sent to jail . . . with an equanimity amounting to nonchalance', remarked one journalist. 'We will just go. That's all,' said Julia Scurr. 'It will be necessary for me to make arrangements for my domestic affairs while I am in prison, and my sister will look after the home for me.' The night before the councillors were arrested, 6,000 people gathered outside the Town Hall, while the remaining councillors decided how to keep the borough running. At the end of the meeting they sang 'The Red Flag', their voices raised in passion on the final lines: 'Come dungeons dark or gallows grim, / This song shall be our parting hymn.' As the audience well knew, Holloway was still dungeon-like then and its gallows still in operational order. The arrest of the five women members of Poplar Borough Council sparked the most 'remarkable demonstration' that had 'ever been witnessed in a London borough'. They travelled to prison standing in the back of an open-top vehicle, amid a crowd so immense that at one point the vehicle came to a complete halt.

Like the suffragettes, the councillors wanted to be recognized as political prisoners. Minnie Lansbury cited the case of newspaper editor William Stead, jailed at Holloway in 1885, who had been 'allowed political treatment', and said the purpose of incarcerating the councillors was pure political spite. Conditions in Holloway were 'not so good as at Brixton', reported their colleagues, 'less freedom was permitted and . . . the food was atrocious', with fish 'in an advanced state of decomposition'. But the women were 'satisfied with their treatment' and the 'wardresses are exceedingly kind'. While they were not treated as first-division offenders, they could 'associate freely' during the evening. They were then allowed books from the Poplar Public Library and permitted to hold council meetings in prison, with the women taken to Brixton by cab.

George Lansbury relayed the words of a warder soon after he had arrived: 'Don't worry, you'll win. Every cause has to be fought for, and always prison opens up the way to reform.' In this case, he was right. George addressed crowds through the bars of his cell in Brixton, and trade unions collected funds for the councillors' families. Other boroughs were told that if they followed Poplar's example their councillors too would go to jail, but the rebellion spread and more councils voted to withhold the precept rate. Nellie Cressall, a laundry worker, pacifist and suffragette who had helped form the East London Federation of Suffragettes with Sylvia Pankhurst, was released early from Holloway because she was six months pregnant. Then after six weeks in jail all the councillors were freed. Soon afterwards, Poplar's rates were reduced, while those of Westminster and the City of London were increased, and George Lansbury and Nellie Cressall both went on to become mayor of Poplar.

Steven Warren was six years old when he first heard his family talking about his great-aunt Nellie Cressall and her friend Minnie Lansbury. 'Sometimes the subject would crop up and I would ask questions,' he tells me as we meet at a riverside inn in Vauxhall. 'They were proud of them.' But it wasn't until he was a teenager that he was told they had been held in Holloway Prison.

His grandmother Elsie May owned drapery shops in the East End and as a child she sewed suffragette banners with her sisters Rose and Maisey. 'Elsie May had a huge influence in my life,' says Steven, fixing me with his bright blue eyes. 'She made me the man that I am; she always gave me permission to think outside the box. My grandmother had a gob on her, while my grandfather was an academic and a gentleman. They were middle class, they had a big house, but the East End part of her meant if there was an issue then she was right in there.'

But it was only a couple of years ago that Steven found out more about his great-aunt Nellie Cressall. 'I was strolling on the South Bank looking at second-hand bookstalls and I saw one on the suffragettes, and I thought, Oh I'll pick that up. I knew relatives had been suffragettes, but I had no idea who would be in the book. I started reading it and at around page 20 there was Nellie and George Cressall and I thought, Oh my God, here we go.' Steven smiles and orders a cappuccino, brings out a family pack of Kit Kats and eats two in rapid succession. 'Poplar was a poor area,' he explains, 'the rates were disproportionate to income. People wouldn't have been able to pay when it was increased, some would have become homeless. They marched from Poplar to the High Courts of Justice with thousands of people declaring, "We will be heard." It must have been amazing, this march through the streets of London.'

But although the story of the women councillors was a triumphant one, it was also tragic. Minnie Lansbury, who had accused the government of political spite, served the whole six-week sentence but 'conditions were not good inside' and shortly afterwards she fell ill with pneumonia. 'My Auntie Rosie went to Holloway to pick her up,' says Steven; 'she waited outside the gates until a guard waved her over. Minnie was so sick that Rosie got her into a cab. She looked after her with great sadness, and it broke her heart that Minnie died a few weeks after she came out of Holloway Prison, and at thirty-two years of age . . .'

Since discovering more about his relatives' lives, Steven has given talks and included his family history on his website. 'My family and the councillors fought for three things,' he says, 'votes for women, which they achieved, and equal rights and equal pay, which are as alive today as they were 100 years ago.' What does he think about the fact they were imprisoned for this? 'When I was a child I didn't talk to friends about it, I was not sure of their reaction and I wanted to fit in. But as an adult I'm hugely proud, it brings a smile to my face. And it explains why I'm so eccentric!' Steven is a former clinical psychologist for the NHS; he worked in psychiatric hospitals up until the 1980s, including assessing serial killers held at Broadmoor. Today he leads seminars on life transitions, as well as offering psychic energy readings. 'My relatives' lives had an impact on my personality and career,' he explains. 'I've seen the weakness in people but I've also seen incredible toughness. I'm bloody proud actually, and now I know why my grandmother had such a gob.'

Thirty years after the Poplar councillors were jailed, another political activist, Wendy Wood, president of the Scottish Patriots Association and a founder of the National Party of Scotland, was sent to Holloway Prison. On 14 April 1951 she travelled to England to distribute leaflets for the Scottish Patriots, on the very day that Scotland beat England in the final of the British Championships in front of 98,000 people at Wembley Stadium.

The authorities were already nervous, as a few months earlier a group of Scottish students had removed the Stone of Destiny, traditionally used in the coronation of Scottish monarchs, and taken it back to Scotland. The stone had just been returned to Westminster Abbey and there were fears it would be taken again. Wendy urged anyone wearing a Scottish emblem to meet that evening at Trafalgar Square, and as supporters and football fans gathered, military jeeps were stationed around the square. Although Wendy had 'no intention of holding a meeting', the crowd urged her to speak and heaved her on to the platform of one of the lions. She was arrested and charged with using insulting words likely to cause a breach of the peace and obstructing a police officer. The court was told that her aim had been to 'stir' the 5,000-strong crowd, who would then have marched on Westminster Abbey. She was fined £5 and refused to pay, so on 2 May she was sent to Holloway for fourteen days. 'You are in for an ideal,' the prison doctor told her, 'not a crime,' and she was sent to hospital and allowed to stay in bed.

But Wendy 'wanted to work and to find out all I could of the conditions at Holloway . . . I was soon to learn that to be a murderer or a thief was commendable in contrast to being a patriot.' She was shoved along strange passages to a workshop where women were sewing and a wardress with 'the bark of a sea lion in the zoo' told her to re-foot socks for the inmates of Wormwood Scrubs. But when balls of wool started flying everywhere she was called to the governor's room, where according to Wendy she was made to stand against the wall, and each time she brought her head forward to answer a question, "thonk", it was slapped back at the wall again. As the conversation continued I gathered quite a collection of small potatoes on my head.'

Wendy received a book from Ethel Moorhead, the first suffragette to have been force-fed in Scotland, with the inscription: 'To Wendy Wood, Political prisoner in Holloway Prison. From an old Suffragette who was there in 1912. In appreciation of her brave and lonely protest in the Cause of Liberty'.

Then after one day in jail, Wendy was called to the governor's office and told that she must go. She replied that she had no money to pay the fine. 'I would have been thankful to get out, but not if they wanted it.' The next day governor Charity Taylor apparently came to her cell and 'angrily demanded that I should leave forthwith. As I still refused (collecting a few more potatoes in the doing), she said, "All right, you'll get hard labour."' Wendy demanded to see her lawyer, but that night she was taken to a strange-looking cell 'which seemed not much bigger than a coffin' and told it was the condemned cell. Then the leader of the Scottish Patriots was instructed to dress and go, friends had paid her fine and were waiting outside. Wendy was 'veritably bashed' through the prison's wicker gate, 'and would have landed on my face against the cobbles if I had not been agile'. But instead of a crowd of friends outside, 'there was nobody there!' The reason for her expulsion from prison was that Holloway's governor had reportedly received an anonymous telegram warning: 'Release Wendy Wood within thirty-six hours or there will be a bomb on Westminster.'

Wendy continued her political career, and in 1972 went on hunger strike for Home Rule. She also read Scottish stories on *Jackanory*, the BBC children's programme, under the name Auntie Gwen.

The Poplar councillors and the Scottish nationalist had been imprisoned over their political beliefs, as had the pacifists in the 1940s and anti-war demonstrators in the 1960s and 1970s. But it was the arrival of women from Greenham Common in the 1980s that marked the first large-scale incarceration of political protesters since the suffragettes.

23

The Women of Greenham Common

Rebecca Johnson arrives at the Vagabond café on Holloway Road wearing her cycling gear, puts her helmet on the table and orders coffee and cake. She's just come from a meeting in her role as director of the Acronym Institute for Disarmament Diplomacy and has missed lunch. A woman sits down next to us and appears to be busy on her laptop, but soon I wonder if she's listening in on our conversation, these stories of being a Holloway prisoner from over thirty years ago.

Rebecca was one of hundreds of women from Greenham Common peace camp jailed during a nineteen-year protest against nuclear weapons. Between 1982 and 1988 she was imprisoned around three times a year, mostly at Holloway. 'I liked being held in A5 best,' she remembers, 'because it was a high wing and you could see the lights of the Odeon, or the church spire opposite.'

The Greenham peace camp began in September 1981, after a group of Welsh activists walked 120 miles from Cardiff to an RAF military base near Newbury in Berkshire. The aim was to protest against NATO's decision, and the British government's agreement, to house ninety-six American cruise nuclear missiles at Greenham. Just like the suffragettes some seventy years earlier, the protesters would be convicted of public order offences, refuse to be bound over or pay fines, and most were sent to Holloway. And while it was the longest and best known feminist protest in recent UK history, there has been little written about their time in prison.

In the spring of 1982, 250 women staged the first Greenham blockade and thirty-four were arrested. A couple of months later, the local council moved in with bulldozers and four women who resisted the bailiffs were sent to Holloway for a week. That summer there was a sit-down protest and more women were arrested, then in late August twenty-seven-year-old Rebecca Johnson occupied a sentry box. 'There were eighteen of us,' she explains. 'We went in two batches, twelve of us got in the box, the rest sat down outside it. We were charged with breach of the peace; we said we were keeping the peace, by stopping the deployment of the new nuclear missiles.' Most of the women refused to be bound over and were sent to jail. 'It was a freezing cold night and we were stuck in riot vans – we called them hen boxes; they were little metal cages and the metal froze at night. One woman was pregnant, and we were given no food or drink in five hours. A few women were left at Reading and then Slough police stations, and then we got to Holloway after midnight.'

After being strip-searched and spending a night in the reception wing, the Greenham women were told they were being transferred to East Sutton Park. 'But then a screw suddenly pointed at me and said, "Not you," and wouldn't say why. So I stayed at Holloway and as they put me in a cell for the first time I was really scared. Oh God, I thought, I'm on my own and I'm in prison, it will be full of violent crazy women. But the opposite happened, the other women were really kind and showed me how to work the system.'

The atmosphere in the new building was fraught, with officers desperate to exert their authority in the low-security 'hospital', while overcrowding meant women were put three in a cell. There was also a new governor in charge. Megan Bull left in 1982 and her successor was Joy Kinsley, who had joined the prison service after a fifteen-year career in nursing. She believed that 'sociologically women were changing', group therapy wasn't working and her aim was to 'develop professional attitudes and standards' and 'enhance the role of the officer'.

For Greenham Common protester Rebecca Johnson, the new Holloway was an oppressive place:

I was used to living outdoors at the camp and I pressed my face against the long narrow window in the cell; it was like reinforced Perspex, you couldn't see much but I could get some air. I could see women down outside doing gardening and hear the constant slam, slam, slam of doors and the keys going rattle, rattle, rattle. I heard footsteps coming nearer and the key opening up my cell and someone coming in and I knew I had to turn around and see them. The door closed and there was a woman, about thirty-something, and she took one look at my face and said, 'Oh lovey, it's your first time, isn't it?' She told me not to worry, that it wasn't that bad. 'We'll show you around and tell you what to do.' That was my first Holloway lesson. I can't remember if she was in for forging a cheque or for prostitution, but she was kind and helping and part of building a community.

The woman found Rebecca a guitar with five strings and inmates asked her to sing. 'Country and Western mainly, though one wanted "Me and Bobby McGee". I thought it would be fine staying there, I was already making friends. I was asthmatic and my inhaler had been taken off me, but the women told me how to get it back.' Rebecca became known as the Singing Greenham Woman and would later be put 'in the strip cells for singing from the window; ridiculously it was called an offence against good order. It was a punishment cell with nothing in it, and a bolted toilet, but I had my voice.' She wrote a version of 'Summertime', 'and I still sing it out of the car window or on the bike when I pass Holloway now. As soon as I got into prison each time I sang the song.'

> Oh Holloway
> Where the living is dreary
> Food like poison
> Got no rights at all

This was one of three Holloway songs to be included in the *Greenham Song Book*, along with 'Lonely Holloway Prison', which Rebecca wrote to the tune of 'Brixton Prison', and 'Holloway Song' written by Mal Finch:

> And when you lock the door behind us
> You only fan the flames
> By giving us a number
> You don't rob us of our names

As breach of the peace was regarded as a civil rather than criminal offence, there was no remission. Instead the Greenham women were brought up in front of an assistant governor every day. 'And she would ask, "Do you agree to keep the peace for twelve months? Then you can leave." It was so seductive. She would say, "You don't need to be here, just sign." But we felt we were already keeping the peace by protesting, so we didn't sign.' Rebecca had been singled out on arrival at Holloway because while awaiting trial for occupying the sentry box she had been arrested again. But the charges in the second case were dropped and she was transferred to East Sutton Park.

A few weeks later, 35,000 Greenham women took part in Embrace the Base, linking hands to surround the nine miles of perimeter fence, and around 6,000 stayed overnight to Close the Base the next day. 'This time there was more violence,' says Rebecca. 'The police tried to break the blockade without arresting anyone, but we kept going back, singing "You can't kill the spirit" and we kept the base closed all day.'

Rebecca's second time in Holloway came not long afterwards. On New Year's Day 1983, forty-four women got into the base, scaled the fifteen-foot fence, covered the barbed wire with carpet, climbed on the silos that would store the missiles and danced on top for an hour. They refused bail, thirty-six were sent to prison and 'this time the authorities were prepared for us, they had the riot vans ready and we went straight to Holloway.' They also encouraged hostility from other inmates, using the tactic of divide and rule. 'The women inside had been told, "A bunch of stupid middle-class wankers from that Greenham Common are coming . . . and so all your friends have been transferred."' While the Greenham women who went to prison were largely middle class, 'it was a working-class woman from Glasgow who dreamed up the silos action,' says Rebecca, 'and women from the Welsh valleys who had the idea of occupying the sentry box. They inspired and excited us.'

The Greenham women got a mixed reaction from other prisoners, some of whom were made to stay up late in order to serve food to the new arrivals. But there was also unity inside. 'After the doors closed in the early evening, you were just in the cell with women, talking, singing.' While some saw themselves as political prisoners and 'pushed that idea and other women thought them arrogant, most Greenham women recognized that politics were behind every woman in prison'.

Lyn Barlow, who was jailed at Holloway as well as four other prisons, felt she 'related more to other women prisoners than to my Greenham "compatriots"'. She had spent most of her childhood in care 'and realized that, if I had trodden a different path other than Greenham, I would have probably ended up in prison anyway'. She described the peace camp women as 'often patronizing towards other women' and they were referred to as 'bed and breakfasts' because they usually served short sentences.

Meanwhile Rebecca, jailed for fourteen days for dancing on the nuclear silos, decided to fast. 'I didn't call it a hunger strike – one woman did that and she was taken straight to the medical wing. I just gave my food to someone else so the screws didn't notice.' Why did she decide not to eat? She looks at her slice of cake on the café table. 'In prison the mealtimes divide the hours. If I didn't eat the food it couldn't capture me, I could think outside the cell.'

Vigils were set up outside Holloway, as they had been for the suffragettes. In February 1983 *Thames News* filmed a group of Greenham women walking along the prison's new 'curvy' wall, accompanied by four police officers, trying to make contact with those inside. 'We felt very supported,' remembers Rebecca. 'They organized a rota of visitors; we were entitled to two a day when charged with breach of the peace. I was visited by a teacher from Henley who asked me to stand against Michael Heseltine! You never knew who your visitors were going to be.' Rebecca would stand against the defence secretary in that year's general election, announcing her candidacy the day she left Holloway.

But before this happened, and for the first time in the prison's history, women actually broke into the jail. On 25 February 1983 six women climbed the roof and unfurled a banner to protest at the incarceration of the Greenham peace campaigners. As Rebecca explains:

> There was ongoing building work and scaffolding and Greenham women were good at climbing. They got on, there was a flat bit of a roof still being used and it was in sight of part of the prison. Suddenly we heard a shout and cheers and the other women excitedly told us, 'Some of your women are in Holloway! We've never heard of anyone breaking *in*! Are they going to get you out?' There was an immediate lock-down, but those who could see the women passed on what was happening. Men came from somewhere and got them down, but the women were running and dodging.

The protesters were arrested and charged with causing a disturbance of the peace, but their lawyer argued there was no peace to breach in jail. Holloway officers were brought to court to claim the rooftop protest had caused disruption within the prison. One said, 'It would be very difficult if women sang in prison all the time,' but another, under cross-examination, was clearly sympathetic to the Greenham women who in the end were acquitted.

On 1 March Rebecca and her colleagues were released, greeted by supporters, and like the suffragettes before them immediately gave interviews to the press, their words echoing statements made in Edwardian times. 'The government is not listening to us when we've gone through the political channels,' said one. 'If it means going back to prison,' said another, 'then I'm afraid I'll have to go back to prison.' Once back at Greenham they were greeted with a 'Welcome Home' banner.

Over the next year, hundreds of women were charged with Greenham-related offences and their actions grew more militant. They cut and pulled down miles of perimeter fence, blocked and climbed on to military vehicles, and repeatedly blockaded the gates. Now they were charged with criminal damage and obstruction, and the courts began handing out fines and prison sentences.

In November 1983 the first of the American cruise missiles arrived and defence secretary Michael Heseltine told the press that those who entered guarded areas of the base could be shot. It was hard to tell the difference, he added, between 'a terrorist and a peace protester'. That same month Rebecca and twelve other women filed an injunction in New York to stop cruise missiles leaving the United States. Although the injunction failed, it raised public and political awareness, and developed legal arguments that were later taken to the International Court of Justice.

Two weeks before Christmas 50,000 women encircled the fence at Greenham in a Reflect the Base protest. Protesters pulled down miles of the fence, and hundreds were arrested. The police admitted it was impossible to secure the site; TV footage showed a thick line of swaying women opening up 'doors' to the base as police tried and failed to keep the fence up. It was an image of physical strength and determination; the women were no longer just an 'irritant'; like the suffragettes before them they were deliberately causing criminal damage, in what was supposed to be a high-security military base.

The backlash against the peace protesters intensified. The previous year, TV news had filmed the Greenham women in sodden sleeping bags surrounded with Christmas cards from well-wishers, and noting that 'they have been to prison for their beliefs'. Now they were portrayed by the media as hysterical – much like the women of Holloway Prison – aggressive, dirty lesbians and unfit mothers. Here were women, living in their own camps and refusing to be intimidated by a combined force of male authority; they could only be neutralized by being treated as mad or made the butt of misogynistic and homophobic jokes.

When Michael Heseltine was asked about base security, he 'pompously declared that though "these women" kept getting into the base, we couldn't reach any "sensitive area",' recalls Rebecca Johnson, 'so just after Christmas three of us proved him wrong'. They crawled through five rows of fencing and barbed wire and occupied the air traffic control tower for over five hours. The women waved a 'Peace on Earth' bed sheet from the top, and read classified documents for dealing with nuclear, chemical and biological weapons 'incidents'. Rebecca was arrested and convicted of criminal damage and sentenced to twelve months at Cookham Wood, but her lawyer successfully appealed and she was released after thirty days. The use of violence against the women of Greenham continued, both by British police, members of the public, and the US military, with night-time attacks and assaults. In 1983 Ann Harrower was hit by a US military vehicle and was hospitalized with a broken leg. A few months later, the US Department of Defense wrote an end-of-year letter to its employees, noting that 400 peace women had been arrested, and 'we hit one . . . with a vehicle . . . It has been a productive year. You should be proud of your accomplishments.'

At the beginning of 1984 Ginette Leach, who kept a diary during her time at Greenham, noted abuse by soldiers who masturbated in front of the women, urinated into their washing, smeared tooth-brushes with excrement and threatened gang rape. There was also surveillance, with some home phones tapped and mail opened. In January the following year Ginette was jailed after being arrested during a blockade. She wrote in her diary, recently published as *Orange Gate Journal*:

> I realise in retrospect that I have been pretty scared at the unnerving prospect of time in Holloway. I think it was mainly the feeling of having no control over my own destiny for even a short while, and also that it was the sort of situation that I'd no idea how I'd react to . . . I've seen enough documentaries on telly about prison, not to make a real fool of myself by yelling 'let me out', but all the same I'm really glad it is all over.

After refusing to pay a £25 fine she was sent to Holloway for seven days, along with two other women. On reception she was told to remove her Greenham bracelet and anklet, given 'a bag of foul soap' and instructed to wash in a 'very tide-marked bath'. Then she was 'escorted with clanking keys attached to screw to [her] cell for the night'. When other inmates asked what they were in for, 'we all said "Greenham" and we didn't have to explain further. We were accepted.' Ginette found that most of the other prisoners were in for 'fairly petty crimes', like cheque card forgery, and when a very quiet young woman who 'didn't even come up to my shoulder' said she had been sentenced for GBH 'we all fell about laughing'. Then the woman explained she had 'stuck a knife in a fellow's eye, and it had damaged it so badly he had the eye removed and now had a glass one in its place'.

Ginette's description of Holloway reflected how the new building was different from the old: the spy hole in the cell door was now a thick, three-inch-wide glass slit; each bed had a bell next to it; the women had their own 'very bright light' over their beds, which they controlled themselves; the floor was lino, rather than stone, and the wall was painted pale green. 'To a prison visitor the impression would be of a pleasant room with pleasant decor, privacy, radio, etc. etc.,' but Ginette was more conscious 'of the clanking doors, jangling keys, strident authoritative voices, petty rules which were often altered by individual screws, terrible stodgy food, tea and ever more tea . . . plastic utensils, and of course the continual feeling of being harassed and put down by those in command'.

Lock-up time was now later than in the recent past: at 8.30 p.m. tea and a biscuit were put through the hatch and at 10.30 p.m. the corridor lights were turned out and a screw called 'Goodnight, girls' to every cell. The Greenham women objected to this: 'We all hated being called girls, and when she came to our door we waited, then called out in unison, "Women," and listened. Down the rest of the corridor, she called out "Goodnight" only.'

One of Ginette's cellmates was a twenty-year-old from Holland, who had been in Holloway on remand for seven months charged with smuggling heroin, and was convinced her stepfather had set her up. Another had been charged with jumping out of a taxi without paying, and was worried about her mother who was paralysed and her sister's child whom she had been looking after and who might now be in care.

Like Rebecca Johnson, Ginette generally found sympathy and support from the other prisoners. She was told that the Greenham inmates, like the suffragettes, had helped to get better conditions because they knew who to complain to and how to get things changed. But she found the officers fearsome: 'I must say, by the look of some, I wouldn't care to get in their bad books,' and they applied or bent the rules in an arbitrary fashion 'so the inmates never really were sure if they were obeying them or not'.

★

On 11 January 1985 Ginette Leach was released, but she didn't go back to Greenham and when I ring her at her home in Brighton she explains why:

> I had just started at Sussex University the autumn before, at the age of fifty plus, to study English literature. I knew I couldn't do both. Before I went to Holloway I had to go and see some staff and say I was not going to be around for a few days and being Sussex they said, 'Wow,' and 'That's absolutely fine.' If I hadn't been at university, I would have gone back to Greenham and done the same thing again. I'm eighty-three now and I've lived a lot of lives, but Holloway was an extraordinary time. We were loved!

Why does she think so little has been written about the experiences of Greenham women in prison? 'People didn't talk about having been in Holloway a whole lot when they came back to the camp,' she says. 'In prison we were small naughty children, we were all the time being *demeaned*, and not seen as adult *women*. I didn't say a lot about it either.' But for Ginette, her brief spell in Holloway changed her life. 'I left a bad marriage and lived with a woman and we're still together now, it was a complete turning point.'

A few months after she was released, the Ministry of Defence introduced new by-laws that made entering the base a criminal offence, and there were more arrests at Greenham. That spring, 400 women took part in a mass trespass, and in a 'no name action' they refused to give their identities, just like the suffragettes. But Rebecca Johnson was too well known to remain anonymous. 'I was constantly picked up; when I refused to give my name the police knew me already. But it was unmanageable for the authorities, a big bunch of women with no names!' The protesters were taken away in riot vans and some were sentenced to seven days' 'special police custody' in Holloway.

Conditions at Greenham were now bleak, and only four of the nine gate camps that had been set up in the early 1980s remained. The women were exhausted from the cold, rain and frequent evictions and in 1987 the camp split into two acrimonious groups over issues of non-violence and accusations of racism. But the effects of the Greenham protest were international and long-lasting. That same year, Presidents Ronald Reagan and Mikhail Gorbachev signed the Intermediate-Range Nuclear Forces Treaty, agreeing to ban and eliminate all the cruise, Pershing and SS20 missiles deployed by the US and the Soviet Union in Europe. By 1991 the cruise missiles had left Greenham, but the peace camp remained for another nine years until the base was closed and the land returned to the public.

Today Rebecca Johnson is Green Party spokesperson on security, peace and defence, and vice-president of CND, and a photo of her being arrested at Greenham was recently included in a Peace Signs exhibition by photographer Ed Barber at the Imperial War Museum. As she leaves the Vagabond café on Holloway Road she takes a postcard out of her bag to show me, an image of a glorious rainbow pouring out of a prison cell window. It was sent to her by someone she didn't know, addressed to 'Rebecca Johnson, Greenham Common woman, Holloway Prison'. I can see Blu-tack on the corners of the card where I guess she's been keeping it on a wall at home for the last thirty years. It's a reminder both of her time inside and of how incarcerating the Greenham women at Holloway failed to kill the spirit at all. Instead, their experience in jail led to political change, as it had done with the Poplar councillors, and as with the suffragettes this was not just on a local level but worldwide.

24

C1: The Psychiatric Unit

The Greenham Common women learned a lot from their time in prison and helped bring attention to what was going on inside Holloway, and particularly on C1, the unit for 'highly disturbed' women.

C1 had been set up in 1977 and could house forty-six inmates in basement accommodation described by one psychiatrist as 'a dungeon'. But it was the campaigning group Women in Prison (WIP), formed by ex-prisoner Chris Tchaikovsky and criminologist Pat Carlen that really put C1 on the national agenda. This was the first radical campaigning group to come out of the country's most famous women's prison, and would provide the British public with a horrifying insight into life behind bars. While Holloway had witnessed periods of chaos before, the violence that had been building up ever since the days of the rebuild was about to explode. In the eyes of the prison authorities, the inmates were now both mad and dangerous.

Chris Tchaikovsky was born into a middle-class family in Cornwall. Repeatedly expelled from school, she ran away to London at the age of fifteen, and a later meeting with three ex-Borstal girls in Exeter started her on a criminal career when together they robbed a newsagent's. It wasn't long before Chris ended up in Holloway for psychiatric treatment, where she 'learned the foulest of lessons . . . and all of them from the screws', who 'bullied defenceless, simple girls who ran after them as if they were some kind of demon mothers'. The prisoners' crimes were mainly poverty and ignorance, 'but their ignorance was nothing compared to the ignorance of the screws; some were ex-army women, dragon closet lesbians who would put you on report for hugging another woman if the mood took them . . . I may have been difficult before entering Holloway, but I had not been vile; it was in there, on my first sentence, that I first learned that women as vile as screws existed.'

Chris also learned how to forge Post Office books at Holloway, and on release went straight back to thieving. After serving a further six months, locked up on an empty wing for twenty-three hours a day, she set up her own criminal firm cashing forged traveller's cheques:'We were known as "the happy firm" to other villains and it was true . . . it was the sixties and I was making a pile of money, running two flats and driving a finely tuned sports car.' In 1974, after two years of the high life, she was arrested again and sentenced to Holloway for two years. It was during this final sentence that inmate Patricia Cummings burned to death in her cell, reportedly because her alarm bell had been disconnected so the staff could sleep. When, a few years later, Chris heard that another woman had 'burned alive' in Holloway, she formed Women in Prison to 'unite women of all classes, ethnic background and sexual orientation' to highlight 'the injustices presently suffered by Britain's hitherto neglected women prisoners'. Taking the most hurt people out of society and 'punishing them in order to teach them how to live within society' was futile, because 'whatever else a prisoner knows, she knows everything there is to know about punishment because that is exactly what she has grown up with. Whether it is childhood sexual abuse, indifference, neglect; punishment is most familiar to her.'

WIP's manifesto listed ten demands, beginning with the need for 'improved safety conditions, particularly in Holloway Prison'. An early article in Spare Rib made it crystal clear what the group was concerned with: 'What the fuck is going on in the new Holloway? Death from burns, or death by sexism?' The new prison looked good, a cross between a modern council estate and a college, with a gym, drug unit, education and welfare department. But for all the glass and new bricks, 'NOTHING has changed . . . women in Holloway are still dying from mistreatment and neglect.' Chris cited several further deaths: Christine Scott had died in 1982 after injuries sustained from throwing herself around her cell for up to twenty-four hours. A Belgian woman died the same year, refused an asthma spray or medication for a heart condition. 'If we need an example of women's invisibility,' wrote Chris, 'we need look no further than women in prison. [They] are the least protected group in society.'

WIP wanted to open prisons up, to find out 'what went on in these secret autonomous states'. In October 1984 it picketed the Home Office to protest at the worsening situation on C1, where 'women who should be receiving treatment in a psychiatric hospital are kept in prison in degrading and barbaric circumstances'. Over the course of six weeks one woman had 'put her eye out', another had attempted 'the same a week later' and a third 'cut her breast and arms to get out of the cell for a few minutes'. Women were isolated for up to twenty-two hours a day, with little food, minimal light and limited access to exercise. They were also regularly being called to adjudication – charged with breaking prison rules. One twenty-year-old who had spent seven months in C1, where she had cut her arms, tied a ligature round her neck and swallowed 'small objects', was put on report for 'refusing to return to her room'.

The use of psychotropic drugs, meanwhile, was now higher than in any other prison in the country, and three-quarters of the women in Holloway were sedated. One prisoner explained: 'First they come round and ask you: Who needs drugs? And then they ask: Who *wants* drugs? They encourage drug-taking. If one day they stopped doing it, doling out all those sedatives, they'd have a riot in there.' The use of prescription drugs was particularly prevalent on C1, where the vast majority were on remand and therefore couldn't be transferred to hospital. The unit had 'some of the most personality-damaged and dangerous young women anywhere in the country', according to one psychiatrist; 'frankly the staff were terrified of them.' The press began to refer to the 'cuckoo's nest at Holloway' and when local MP Jeremy Corbyn visited the unit he was met by the continuous screams of a woman banging her head against the walls of her cell.

Holloway was making headlines again, and as ever for all the wrong reasons. Nick Davies wrote an article in the *Observer*, describing the 'horror wing' of C1. There had been twenty-four incidents in twenty days where women 'have tried either to kill or to mutilate themselves'. In the spring of 1986 he wrote another article, 'Welcome to the Muppet House', in which the average day began with 'a miserable cacophony of foul abuse and pitiful wails and screams, occasionally broken by the crashing of someone destroying all the cardboard furniture in her cell'. Victorian prisoners had been known for destroying bedding, clothing and furniture, and there had been growing reports of self-mutilation in the 1960s when one assistant governor described it as 'relief from the pain of being'. But now 'cutting up' was becoming endemic. Women were breaking lights and smashing chips off sinks, and would then 'saw away at themselves with the splinters'.

Prison officers had their problems too, and objected to being portrayed as 'animals in charge of animals'. The POA took national action in 1980, accusing the government of being more concerned with money than the health and safety of officers. Holloway Prison was not a posting many looked forward to. Says one assistant governor:

> It was the last place on earth I wanted to go; it did not have a good reputation. Seven assistant governors before me had resigned or demanded transfers. So I thought, I'll go and do my best; I'm not going to be the eighth. Holloway was hard; it was notorious for arson and had the second highest number of people setting fire to their cells in the country after Parkhurst. But my God I learned a lot when I was there. All prisons have a particular smell – men's smell of urine, unwashed bodies and boiled cabbage. Holloway smelled of talcum powder and women's type of things – except in the highly disturbed unit with excrement on the walls.

Nonetheless, she says, 'There was a lot of good work at Holloway that went unrecognized. There was a lot of wrong, but a hell of a lot of right and the staff were unsung heroines.'

She recalls numerous incidents of self-harm: 'One nineteen-year-old in C1 cut herself and with the blood that spurted out she drew flames on her cell wall. She was going for a parole report, but she had a compulsion to set fire. Another woman, they couldn't restrain her, her forearms were like sliced bread, they just couldn't get hold of her.' The new building meanwhile just added to the problems, especially the L-shaped corridors and the design of the cells: 'You couldn't see the toilet, but the toilet is where people try to hang themselves. With a high level of instability you needed to see the women for their own safety.'

Staff became more nervous, they wanted prisoners handcuffed on escort outside prison and began to refuse to work in areas that they felt weren't safe; they also demanded shields and helmets ready for emergencies. Ten per cent of Holloway's officers were now off sick on an average weekday, many had alcohol-related problems and there was growing awareness that some had their own histories of physical and sexual abuse. In the midst of all the media horror stories and growing industrial unrest, Joy Kinsley was transferred to Brixton, becoming the first woman to govern a men's prison in England and Wales, and for the first time in forty years a male governor was appointed to Holloway Prison.

Colin Allen was a former Borstal housemaster, who had worked at three male prisons and at the time of his appointment was governor of Maidstone in Kent. Like Charity Taylor in the 1940s, Colin took over at a difficult time, against a backdrop of lurid press headlines, staff protest and political pressure. A major part of his job was to implement the recommendations of a Project Review Committee set up by the Home Office, and its forty-eight-page report listed plenty of ways in which conditions at Holloway could be improved. The new prison had been designed 'to give inmates as much freedom as possible within a secure perimeter' but instead 'precisely the opposite effect was being achieved'. Prisoners needed proper access to work, education and association in the new facilities that were still not being used. But in his efforts to provide this, Colin ended up facing a POA strike and running a prison virtually without prison officers.

Today Colin Allen is a trustee of the Prison Reform Trust and we meet in their open-plan offices in east London, where he has just finished attending a trustees meeting. He is formally dressed, with the golden buttons on his cricket blazer giving him the air of a benevolent naval officer. He offers me tea, fetches sandwiches left over from lunch, and questions me closely before we move on to Holloway in the 1980s. Colin has been cautious about this interview: 'It is essential that people understand Holloway. I have not spoken to anyone about it because most people won't understand. The very name Holloway is so well known, it has a reputation for extremely disturbed behaviour from women prisoners, it's associated with Ruth Ellis and the suffragettes: it has a fixed reputation. Most people are just looking for reinforcement of the press headlines they have gobbled up.'

Colin never dreamed he'd be sent to Holloway, until one day a phone call came from a senior official at headquarters.

> He said, 'Are you standing up?' I said, 'Yes.' He said, 'I suggest you sit down.' So I sat down on the stairs and he said, 'We are sending you to Holloway.' There was a two-minute pause and then I said, 'Are you serious?' I'd never been near a women's prison in my life.
>
> I don't think I was scared, because I was brought up with women, I had three younger sisters, my wife, my mum, my grandmother who I lived with when I was younger. Women didn't scare me, I like women, why wouldn't you?

But there were strange things coming out of women's jails in the 1980s, especially Holloway, and Colin wasn't sure what to expect.

For the first few months as governor he felt completely lost. 'My deputy was also a man, and it was difficult to understand what was going on. I thought I was going bonkers. Then I got Ann Hair as my deputy governor and my sanity was saved.'

Ann had joined the prison service in 1971, in the early 1980s she was posted to P4, the division that oversaw the rebuild, and two years later she served as secretary to the Project Review Committee. 'Radical changes were needed in many areas,' she remembers, 'practices about the care of the women had to be challenged.'

The psychiatric unit was full of inmates who wanted to go to a special hospital, but under the law, explains Colin, 'if they were not treatable then they couldn't go'. His first adjudication in Holloway involved a woman who had attempted to kill herself 143 times. When Mark Sancto, a transsexual prisoner, was found attempting to strangle himself with his trousers no report was made, and an hour later he hanged himself with his cardigan. 'It happened at teatime, a very busy time,' remembers Colin, 'with women shouting and screaming, and amidst all this someone had died. I had to do something about it. Mark had been a victim of problems between officers and nurses. It was my worst time at Holloway. Mark had wanted help and hadn't got it. I'd been there long enough to feel responsible.'

So Colin set about changing the culture within Holloway and especially on C1, aided by the appointment of Dr Dorothy Speed as principal medical officer. She had overall responsibility for C1, a place she initially described as 'a form of torture', but soon women were locked in for sixteen hours rather than twenty-one, the unit had a new dayroom and prisoners had access to education. Outside visitors from Women in Prison and the Samaritans began to work with inmates, and those who were mentally ill were no longer submitted for adjudication. In 1993 Holloway would join the Listener scheme, founded by Kathy Baker, where prisoners are selected, trained and supported by Samaritan volunteers to become Listeners, providing confidential, emotional support to fellow prisoners who are struggling to cope.

The results of the changes within Holloway were impressive. There was a decrease in non-fatal self-injuries, and no suicides between 1987 and 1990. By the time Colin left, self-mutilations had dropped from 1,000 to 150 a year. 'The women actually started talking to us,' remembered the new senior medical officer Norman Hindson, and as they did the staff discovered that 90 per cent of those on C1 had previously suffered serious physical abuse, and 70 per cent had been subjected to sexual abuse. Before long, Norman had managed to move most of the C1 inmates out of the unit, with the majority transferred to outside hospitals.

Under Colin Allen's governorship the swimming pool and gym finally began to work properly; there was less supervision and more of a 'free flow' of prisoners during the day, and inmates were now called by their first names. Education, which had always played an uncertain role at Holloway, was vastly improved. When Colin arrived prisoners were not being taken to classes, reportedly because of staff shortages, the education department had been moved into Portakabins in the exercise yard and the previous governor had requested guard dogs to monitor women going from the wings to evening classes. Colin also used the media to help change conditions inside. Representatives from newspapers, radio and TV were invited to tour the jail, much as print journalists had been welcomed in during Victorian times and, more recently, during the demolition of the old castle prison in the 1970s. The Board of Visitors were handed their own keys and their annual reports were, for the first time, given to the press.

But one change wasn't so welcomed. In March 1986 six senior male officers were drafted in to Holloway, a move that Chris Tchaikovsky from Women in Prison described as a disastrous decision. 'Bringing men into an environment which holds an all-female, captive population causes us great concern.' Colin explains there were just four senior officers, when they had places for forty and 'it was impossible to manage Holloway without more senior officers; their job was to see that things happened as they should on the ground, and we didn't have enough. Once women were promoted they were transferred. It was a huge culture breaker and a massive step forward, not only at Holloway but throughout the prison service.' In 1988 a 'cross-sex' postings agreement between the POA and the prison service would allow women to work in men's prisons and vice versa. For the first time women could be promoted into the male estate, which was far larger than the female estate. Many of Holloway's senior female staff meanwhile approved of the introduction of men. 'Male officers brought a good influence on the behaviour of the women,' says one; another describes it as 'a jolly good thing; often these men were the first positive male role models these women had ever had.'

The POA championed the new postings agreement as a major step forward for equal opportunities, female officers 'could never achieve' as long as they could only work in female prisons, and Holloway had led the way. But relations with the union remained a major source of conflict. 'They were running the show,' says Colin.

Home Office policy in the early 1980s was to avoid conflict with the POA at all costs; they didn't want to risk an industrial relations war when many prisons were in a horrible condition. In the last part of Holloway's rebuild the POA had held the prison to ransom, saying it was god-awful for security and needed more staff. They refused to take over newly finished parts of the prison, such as the education department and part of the gym, until the Home Office provided manning levels that were unrealistic.

Colin had only been in the job for little over a year when, in April 1986, the staff took industrial action and organized a national twenty-four-hour ban on compulsory overtime. Prisoners built a barricade on B5 and smashed up two dormitories, and the POA described Holloway as a dangerous place. Two years later officers went on strike, and 235 walked out of Holloway Prison. Colin was on holiday when he got the news:

> It was a Friday, and my deputy rang to say the POA was withdrawing members from several parts of the prison. I got there that evening and the POA chair rang and said, 'We're now withdrawing officers from C1,' and I said, 'You're joking, you can't be serious,' and he said, 'Well, it's your responsibility, Governor.' As soon as the staff walked off, we went and told the prisoners. That first night I didn't go home, I slept in my office and I didn't know if I'd get through it. We had three night patrols and we needed something like twelve, but there was an experienced principal officer on duty and I asked her to go around and see what the prison was like. Less than half an hour later she came back and said, 'It's very quiet.' She had told the women to settle down and they had.

Colin told regional headquarters that he would 'call in the police if necessary, although I didn't actually have the authority to do that. But I knew the Highbury superintendent because we're both Arsenal supporters and he said he would put twelve police officers on the landings if it ever came to it. Then I was able to sleep, which shows you how quiet the prison was.' So would he now run a prison without most of its prison officers? 'From the night that Mark Sancto died we had set out to run a regime that treated prisoners with dignity, making as full use as possible of the facilities and recognizing the special needs of many of the women. When the POA acted to try and make this impossible, we simply tried to overcome each problem as it came up. So yes, we decided we'd give it a bloody good try.'

Suddenly there is a burst of applause, and I turn to see all the Prison Reform Trust staff are standing up and clapping, and it's only when they move away that I realize it's somebody's birthday and they're cutting a cake.

When the strike began, Colin gave nurses on C1 their own sets of keys, after training and background checks, and called on volunteers who had keys, such as prison visitors, while the Roman Catholic nun Sister Austin brought in a group of nuns. Soon C1 was being managed only by medical staff, and there were times when just one staff member was supervising 120 inmates. To everyone's surprise, the atmosphere inside C1 and the rest of Holloway without 90 per cent of its discipline staff improved. 'The prisoners were tickled that the POA was being challenged,' says Colin. He carried out just one adjudication in the following six weeks, when normally it could be seven in a day. Instead of being violent and disturbed, Holloway's prisoners were now behaving in a far more rational and responsible way.

'Most of those on strike were not revolutionaries,' says Colin. 'They were not nasty people, but they were influenced by the dominant culture; it was about power not malice. The staff that did stay were committed and I knew they weren't going to wind up the women.' One union activist publicly accused the POA's National Executive Committee of 'behaving like a Junta' and using 'bully tactics' over their handling of the Holloway dispute. Towards the end of August 1988 the POA voted to go back to work and so the bizarre, unplanned, six-week period of running a jail without a sufficient number of prison officers came to an end.

To sociologist Paul Rock the strike demonstrated that although the new prison was full of design problems and the hospital-like structure made people feel anxious and afraid, the building itself wasn't the primary problem: it was what was going on inside. But a few months after the strike ended Colin Allen was transferred. There was to be no inquiry and instead, according to one senior officer, he was 'made a bit of a scapegoat'. Colin left the prison service and joined the independent prison inspectorate, becoming deputy chief inspector of prisons. He also worked on prison improvement projects in Brazil, Algeria and Libya. Today he says:

> You can get addicted to prisons. They are a microcosm of what's going on but in a more intense way; a crisis is always just around the corner and always will be. If you deny people their liberty they will react and occasionally the system can't hold it down and it bursts out. Many men deal with prison by cutting off the reality and living the life inside. With women – it's a generality – but they remain themselves, with all their loads and experiences. To some men, prison is more of a game. Women are far more real.

And one thing that has always made prison more real to women is children, whether separation from their daughters and sons, giving birth in prison, or witnessing their baby grow up behind bars.

25

Childbirth

Should babies be born, and stay with their mothers, in prison? It's a question that has been argued about ever since concerns over prisoner treatment in the UK began; would babies of 'criminal women' have a better life in jail, or would they be forever tainted by the 'sins' of their mothers? To Victorian penal reformers, children were innocent and needed to be properly provided for; they were not prisoners, and yet they were. Over the next hundred years, through prison nurseries, crèches and mother and baby units, the underlying concerns were similar: should women be jailed if they were pregnant, where exactly should they give birth, how long could mothers keep their babies and did it benefit or damage an infant to grow up behind bars?

In the early 1860s when Henry Mayhew visited the convict nursery at Brixton he found babies playing with rag dolls and drinking their daily pint of breakfast milk with an 'almost angel-innocence beaming in their pretty little cherub faces'. The nursery was a place of tolerance and goodness, but it was also a pathetic environment and Henry wondered what fate awaited 'the wretched little things that have made so bad a start in the great race of life'. When he held out his hand to two-year-old Eliza, dressed in the 'convict baby clothes' of a spotted blue frock, she had so 'long been accustomed to see no man's face but that of the chaplain and the surgeon' that the nearer Henry went the more she screamed. The chaplain played a central role in infant welfare and his own children took an older child to Sunday school 'so that she might mix a little with the world'. But while there had been as many as thirty children in the Brixton nursery, the Secretary of State had recently ordered the prison not to take children from other jails. If a woman arrived with a child, explained the chaplain, then it was to be sent to a workhouse immediately.

Babies were generally removed from their imprisoned mothers once they were around a year old, either sent to a relative or put in the workhouse. But in practice, some women kept their children for longer and infants had stayed at Brixton for up to four years. At Millbank one 'had been kept so long incarcerated, that on going out of the prison it called a horse a cat'.

In the first decades of Holloway's existence, and with a very small female population, there were few reports of childbirth behind bars. The first baby born in the prison, aside from an undated stillborn, was in 1856, but many women were imprisoned along with their children or arrived pregnant. In 1892 Florence Osborne was only weeks away from giving birth when she was sent to Holloway on remand, charged with stealing two pairs of earrings. She was transferred to the infirmary, restless and hysterical, and then sent home on medical grounds. Home Office procedure, explained the press, was to release 'any woman whose continued imprisonment might seriously imperil her life or the life of a child about to be born'. Five years later Mary Hamilton was charged with concealing the birth of her child in Holloway, an event that 'created much excitement in prison circles'. Mary was confined to bed in the hospital, and the Home Secretary ordered a full investigation.

When Holloway became a women's prison in 1902 it had a dedicated crèche for babies and according to Major Arthur Griffiths, a former inspector of prisons, the prison born were now 'better off than the free born'. They were 'more cared for, more delicately nurtured' than those who had been 'dragged up in the purlieus and dark dens of the town'. Prison was a healthier environment for mothers as well: 'There are no disturbing emotions within the walls, no incentives to neglect of offspring, no drink, no masterful men, no temptation to thieve or go astray; and thus their better feelings, their purer maternal instincts, have full play. So the prison baby has, for the most part, a good time.'

Holloway's crèche was widely reported to be the first in the UK, although six years earlier one had been established at Wormwood

Scrubs. Such was the ignorance among the all-male prison board that no bibs had been provided, the first toys were large waxen dolls – so frightening the children wept – and bouncing balls as big as those used by a rugby team. However, the crèche, once improved by 'anxious feminine officials', proved such a 'triumph' in 'ethical improvement' that other jails followed suit.

But what clothing should a prison baby wear? In the early days of the Wormwood Scrubs crèche, the entire female prison population of 350 had broken the rule of silence to protest against the texture and colour of the official infant pinafore. Several prisoners had torn up their bed sheets to make their own white pinafores, while plain garments sent to the prison laundry came back with embroidered designs and the baby's name, or 'Darling' and 'Pet', written in scarlet thread. The thread was taken from the stripe that ran through the prison bed-linen, and prisoners in the laundry used it to embroider 'a motherly sentiment' on other women's baby's clothes.

When journalist Annesley Kenealy paid a visit to Holloway in 1905, it had the largest crèche in the prison service. Mothers brought their babies each morning before going to the workroom, and the child was bathed and dressed 'by more tender hands than hers'. She was allowed to visit the baby twice during the day, to feed it and 'take it for an airing' in the exercise yard. She then had the child 'to bear her company in the loneliness of her cell', with a small cot standing by her plank bed, from 5 p.m. until after breakfast the next morning.

Holloway's crèche was part of the hospital building, a bright, sunny ward, with walls enamelled in light blue. The floor was covered in lino and furnished with 'snug warm crawling-rugs', the walls were hung with 'nursery masterpieces' such as Cinderella, and the tables held vases of fresh flowers. Wicker bassinettes could be rocked to comfort the 'hapless little persons hovering on the horizon of crime'; the children had fluffy dolls, bouncing balls and a live kitten to play with. There were twelve lacquered and brass-trimmed cots, covered with checkered counterpanes with 'spotless though coarse prison linen' and white fleecy blankets. The blankets, however, had the broad arrow of prison property in one corner, and the 'mark of criminality' was also branded on the babies' white flannel petticoats and woollen undergarments.

Prison was no longer recorded on the registration of birth, but babies who reached nine months were still often sent to the parish workhouse. Not surprisingly, women frequently altered their baby's age on admission to Holloway to fit in with the length of their sentence. Some also arrived with babies who were older than the official age, such as Harry, a fourteen-month-old who was a 'living skeleton' when his mother was sentenced to two months, and was now 'quite fat and bonnie'. Harry was not the only one who needed feeding; all the nursery babies were weighed every week and some gained as much as one and a half pounds in seven days. In summer Holloway's crèche was moved outside to the 'babies' garden', bright with flowers, where a tent was pitched on the grass and they were looked after by officers 'chosen for their fondness for children'.

But the prison baby, wrote Annesley Kenealy, 'offers a very grave problem to the State', and, like Henry Mayhew forty years earlier, she wanted to know 'What comes after?' One woman had given birth to four babies in prison and her youngest were then 'hawked as beggars all over London by father and mother'. Wouldn't it be better if a 'bad woman' was no longer allowed to have care of her child? The idea of saving babies from bad mothers would become a dominant theme in the following decades, and prison would protect them from cruel, inadequate parents, while a jail sentence would eventually be seen as an opportunity for women to be taught to be 'good' mothers.

But as welcoming as Holloway's crèche appeared to be, when the suffragettes arrived they were shocked by the sight of children. Alice Hawkins wrote in her prison diary:

> One day, whilst at exercise, I saw a number of women with babies in their arms, and, on asking the warder about them, she informed me that they were allowed to have their babies under twelve months, and said that they were well looked after. But, oh, the thought that a young life just born into the world should have to spend its first months of life in prison. It was one more injustice added to our cry for the right to stop some of these horrible things being allowed.

★

It wasn't until the 1920s that childbirth in prison really attracted press attention, and the case of heavily pregnant Ivy Cusden caused considerable public indignation. In 1924 Ivy was convicted of throwing acid at her 'rival' Wallace Jones who had married the father of Ivy's child, a Mr Jones. The judge noted that Ivy had been badly treated; Mr Jones had admitted to 'walking out' with her, but said he'd never promised marriage and denied he was the father. While the assault on Wallace wasn't under doubt, and she was left with permanent damage to her eyes, such was the concern over Ivy giving birth in prison that a petition for her release was signed by 63,000 people in her hometown of Reading. The appeal was rejected, and Ivy gave birth in Holloway's infirmary. There were several offers to adopt the child and marriage proposals from 'all classes of men', some writing from as far away as Australia and Canada, where the case had been reported in the press.

By the 1930s, during Mary Size's reign, Holloway now had state registered nurses who were qualified midwives, offering medical care 'equal to that of any public hospital', as well as training in child welfare and management. Mary believed that 'prison babies are some of the finest to be seen anywhere', they received an excellent start in life and if they were then reasonably cared for 'they should grow up to be healthy, sturdy citizens'.

In the early part of the decade there was around one baptism a month at Holloway, as recorded by the chaplain in a Register of Baptisms. In February 1931 he noted that two children had been baptized, John Herbert and Jean Barbara, born in prison to Olive Kathleen Wise. No information was given for the occupation, residence or name of the father, but this was a case that had been extensively reported in the press. Olive Wise had been sentenced to death the previous Christmas for killing her nine-month-old baby in an oven. It was a case 'fraught with great sadness', said the judge, who described the thirty-seven-year-old as a devoted mother thrown into despair because of poverty. Olive was separated from her husband, and although in a relationship with Alfred Wheatley she lived alone with her four children. The jury recommended mercy, and the sentence was commuted to life imprisonment, just weeks before she was due to give birth.

At once questions were raised in Parliament – how had a pregnant woman received the death sentence in the first place? – and it was argued that she should be transferred to a private maternity home. Mary Clynes, wife of the Home Secretary, visited Olive at Holloway and reported that she was in a bright, cheerful room with six other women and was 'receiving all care and attention'. Her three other children meanwhile had been taken to Dr Barnardo's homes.

Olive gave birth to the twins in 'the greatest secrecy', and Holloway Prison was 'not mentioned on the birth certificates', explained the press; 'the name of the street in which the hospital section of the prison stands will be given.'

The case attracted so much attention that the government rushed through the Sentence of Death (Expectant Mothers) Bill. If a woman sentenced to death asked for a stay of execution because she was pregnant, a jury of twelve 'matrons' was appointed to establish if she was 'quick with child' and if she was, then the sentence was postponed. But the Lord Chancellor, during a debate in the Lords in which he cited Olive Wise, explained that this was very unlikely to then be carried out; instead the death sentence would be commuted to penal servitude for life. The result was that 'the Judge and all present have to go through the trying ordeal of formally sentencing the woman to death although everybody in Court knows that the sentence will never be carried out'. The new Act would stop pregnant women being sentenced to death in the first place, get rid of the jury of matrons, and leave the confirmation of pregnancy to a doctor. In the summer of 1932 Olive Wise was released, having served seventeen months of her life sentence at Aylesbury Prison, along with her twins who were now a year and a half old. A few months later she married Alfred Wheatley, who had visited and taken her flowers in Holloway.

But the question of where exactly prisoners should give birth continued. During the inquest into an eleven-month-old baby who died in Holloway shortly after Olive had her twins, the coroner said he 'had often wondered whether when a woman was known to be expecting a child she might not be taken out of prison so that the child should not suffer from any stigma of birth'. One magistrate who sentenced a woman to Holloway for theft commented, 'Your baby will be born in prison. It is no reflection on the baby. It is not the baby's fault.'

Yet other women preferred to give birth inside. A twenty-three-year-old servant with seven previous convictions stole clothing from her employer 'so that she could get back to prison for the birth of her baby', according to the arresting detective. She had 'inquired' at several hospitals, but each one had asked 'if she were single'. The magistrate decided to send her to Holloway 'for a sufficiently long period to enable her baby to be born and for her to regain her health and strength' and sentenced her to six months.

But while women were supposed to be moved to the prison hospital well before giving birth, this didn't always happen. Pacifist Vera Mayhew, jailed in the Second World War, recalled the emergency bell ringing for hours one evening, accompanied by a woman's pitiful cries. 'We could all hear her calling for help, and getting more exhausted. The whole landing was awake in the finish, and several other prisoners were ringing their bells and calling to draw attention to her.' In the morning, when help finally came, the woman had given birth in her cell.

Then in 1948, with the passing of the Criminal Justice Act, the era of giving birth in prison came to an end, and women could now be transferred outside to a local hospital. During the last month of pregnancy they were kept in the prison infirmary, given weekly knitting lessons and a class on the care of babies. In the centre of the ward was the reclining bronze figure of a small child, *Happy Baby*, the work of Latvian-born sculptor Dora Gordine whose art was then being regularly exhibited at the Royal Academy.

Babies who grew up in Holloway's nursery continued to be well treated, according to Pathé News which recorded a four-minute Christmas film entitled *Hope for these Women* in 1960. Women with babies could 'give them maternal care in their spare time', and while at work the children were looked after by kindly nurses in a nursery decorated with paper chains and a Christmas tree. As in Victorian times, convict women were 'taking their punishment. Their sins must not be visited upon the children.'

Holloway's small labour ward was rarely used, according to governor Joanna Kelley, and most women were rushed to a public hospital when labour started 'so that their babies' birth certificates may be issued from there'. Once infants reached nine months they were 'sent out. It is said that at about that age a baby begins to be aware of its surroundings and should therefore be removed from the sight of bars and the sounds of clanking keys.'

Babies born behind bars still wore a prison uniform, however, and mothers were instructed when to feed them. Zoe Progl, the Holloway escapee, had her first child at Aylesbury Borstal where at six every morning the night officer, keen to get off duty, stamped down the ward twisting the women's big toes and bellowing, 'Feed your baby!' Nothing was allowed to be sent in from outside and Zoe asked the visiting magistrate, 'Why can't our babies have rattles? They are not here to be punished.'

When John Camp published his history of Holloway Prison in 1974 he was anticipating a rosy future for prison babies. Once the new hospital building was finished there would be an obstetric unit to provide antenatal and postnatal care, as well as accommodation for mothers with children up to the age of five. But then, in a complete reversal of prison policy, women would no longer be taken to an outside hospital, they would have to give birth in prison again. 'To many people this is a retrograde step,' he admitted, 'but the Home Office, with a certain degree of naiveté, considers that the new Holloway will be so like a hospital that no stigma will be attached to having a child there.'

The financial costs of the rebuild soon put a stop to children under five living with their mothers. While women could keep a newborn baby until the age of two, if they were transferred from Holloway to Styal, many children living outside the prison were put in care. Yet as late as the 1980s no records were kept of the number of children in care as a result of their mother's imprisonment, nor had there been any research on the effects of prison life on pre-school children.

When principal medical officer Dr Dorothy Speed took up her post in 1986 she put mothers and babies in separate new quarters, and soon Holloway's chaplain would record 'IX Parkhurst Rd N7' as the place of birth in the baptism book. But the prison had no funds to provide anything but a cot, buggy, basic bedding and baby food because the Home Office's legal responsibility was to the prisoners, not their families. If a woman brought her child to Holloway then it was up to her to provide everything else – whether nappies or toys. Scientist Beatrice M. Burgess, a former general inspector of schools, questioned the effects of a prison environment on child development; how could a baby learn to crawl without a safe, clean place to explore? So she raised the funds to make the new mother and baby area child-friendly with early-learning play items and safe crawl pools, as well as providing baby clothing and toiletries.

But babies growing up in prison were still deprived of outside life. When a nine-month-old girl left Holloway for the first time and was taken to Styal with her mother, she screamed the whole way, scared by all the unfamiliar sounds and sights. So Beatrice Burgess and her husband, Holloway's chaplain, helped to form the charity Babies in Prison, with volunteers taking babies on trips to the outside world. A later charity, Birth Companions, was also established, by a group of London-based antenatal teachers.

Then policy changed once again: women would now give birth not in prison but at outside hospitals. Before long Holloway was at the centre of a national scandal triggered by the treatment of pregnant prisoners. Its reputation as a whole in the 1990s was one of the worst it had ever been and conditions had deteriorated sharply since Colin Allen's governorship. The jail was overcrowded, infested with rats, pigeons and rotting rubbish, and inmates were locked up for twenty-three hours at a time. Security was becoming increasingly heavy-handed, partly as a result of riots at men's prisons and particularly the twenty-five-day riot and rooftop protest at Strangeways Prison in Manchester, the longest in British penal history.

In 1995 the new chief prison inspector Sir David Ramsbotham left in disgust halfway through a week-long inspection, 'appalled that any country, let alone my own, could treat vulnerable women in the way that I saw in Holloway'. He found two fifteen-year-old girls in the antenatal unit, not because they were pregnant but because no one knew where else to put them. Then a young mother asked him whether it was right that she had been in chains while giving birth. The chief inspector of prisons questioned the governor Janet King, and was told 'it was regulations'.

The following year Channel 4 News filmed Holloway prisoner Annette Walker handcuffed at the Whittington Hospital labour ward. Her baby was born on 2 January 1996, and when the officer's shift changed a male officer came into the room while the placenta was being delivered. Within a month Annette had developed post-traumatic stress disorder.

Prisons minister Ann Widdecombe was subjected to fierce questioning in Parliament. She argued that it had never been prison service policy to keep women handcuffed during labour and childbirth. But her insistence that security was the main priority and that pregnant women were an escape risk was met with ridicule, with the Speaker repeatedly having to call for order. MP Diane Abbott described the minister's statements as repellent and said a pregnant woman in labour 'will not be running anywhere'.

As for babies living inside Holloway, there had still been very little research on the effect of prison life. Then in 1995 psychotherapist Pamela Stewart decided to use Holloway as her 'lab' in order to observe and test the impact of anxiety on a mother's relationship with her baby. Pamela was working on her Master's degree at the Tavistock Clinic, a specialist mental health clinic in north London, and had 'found that the work at the Tavistock was all about the inner world and the inner life and that annoyed me. We weren't taking the social context into account. I was driving down Holloway Road one day and I thought, Where would I find women and babies who are very anxious? I know, Holloway Prison.'

Pamela was allowed into the jail, and found herself 'listening to a woman who had to apply for a place in the mother and baby unit. There I was, just off the street, watching them interview a heavily pregnant woman who was pleading for a place, with social workers and prison officers. Can you imagine, she was *pleading* to keep her baby?' Pamela soon realized it would be difficult to work one to one, as women served such short sentences, so she decided to run a group. 'We would sit in the association room, and they just started coming and it was brilliant. The women wanted somebody to validate their experiences, to know that their relationship with their baby was important.'

But Pamela's belief that the prison would be 'a harsh place, disrespectful of the mothers' was proved wrong. 'I had made a fundamental mistake. My assumption that HMP Holloway was a terrible dungeon and the women in the mother and baby unit would be very anxious and depressed had to go; to be honest what I was experiencing was quite the reverse. The mothers and babies were doing well, until the time for release.'

Once Pamela had finished her MA and written her dissertation 'Born Inside', a study of mothers and babies in prison, she completed her training as a psychotherapist at the Philadelphia Association, a charity founded by R.D. Laing. Then she asked the prison for an honorary post. 'I began to see women weekly, and started up the group again. Women can get inside what society has failed to give them; it can be an opportunity to be a mother.'

'On the mother and baby unit, the women were freer,' remembers Maggie Hamand who worked as a breast-feeding counsellor with the National Childbirth Trust and then the Breastfeeding Network. 'Babies aren't prisoners so the doors were left ajar, but women weren't allowed to leave them. It could be very difficult if a baby was fretful at night. Women were worried they'd be seen as a bad mother, but they couldn't walk around with the baby, except in the cell. The night staff might walk the baby for you, and there were baby walkers who took the babies out, otherwise they'd grow up never having seen trees or traffic.' Maggie was shocked that women who were breastfeeding had an evening meal at 5.30 p.m. and were then locked up without food until the next day. She also witnessed children being removed from their mothers, with babies over nine months being taken away once more. 'Women wanted to do the best for their children, and it was awful when they were separated. It was like a scene from Solzhenitsyn's *The Gulag Archipelago* in which babies were torn from their mothers by the evil Soviets. This was happening at Holloway. Women would be depressed and upset, saying that next week their baby was going.' Maggie later became the first writer in residence at Holloway and helped prisoners write children's stories in the mother and baby unit, recording them on tape and sending them home.

One male officer will never forget the day a woman had her child taken from her: 'She began head-butting the wall and throwing herself against it. I tried to restrain her; we were just alone in the cell. When she came back to prison the next time she pointed at me and told her friend, "That man, he saved me." Those words will remain with me for ever.'

In 1990 Save the Children launched a project – the first of its kind – to promote the rights of children whose parents were in prison. Ann McTaggart decided to volunteer. She arranged all-day visits at Holloway for children under the age of sixteen. 'Up until then it had been an hour every two weeks. Imagine as a child, seeing your mum once every two weeks.' In the early days she experienced hostility from officers 'who didn't understand what it was about, to them it went against the grain; a woman might have kicked off and then she was allowed all day with her kids, it was seen as a soft touch. Some did take advantage, there were drugs brought in via the children, like cocaine in nappies.' The scheme could take a maximum of thirty women every Sunday, and often that would mean 100 children. They used the swimming pool, while the education department was turned into an art and reading area. Says Ann:

> We hoped it was the best thing for keeping a relationship with a mum; it gave them time to talk. Before, if a child was brought in it was with another adult and the child would sit there and draw while the adults talked. But now the child was brought in and left with their mum. The kids must have benefited, it was a lovely day. Within a year the officers were a great support, they saw the human side of it. But oh my God, it was very hard at the end of Sunday when the children had to leave.

Teenage boys in particular were 'really emotional; for some reason the girls seemed to hold it together. One boy aged around fifteen fell against the wall and cried his eyes out at the end of the visit.'

Towards the end of the 1990s, statistics on mothers in prison were finally being gathered. David Ramsbotham published a wide-ranging report, a direct result of his earlier inspection of Holloway, which found that nearly two-thirds of female prisoners were mothers, on average with nearly three children and at least one under the age of sixteen. Only a quarter were being cared for by their biological father or their mother's current partner, whereas in male prisons 90 per cent of inmates' children were being looked after by the mother or partner.

While officially no pregnant woman would be subjected to man-acles during labour again, the issue of childbirth in prison would not go away and the position of babies behind bars has never been resolved. In June 1999 a new prison drama began on ITV, *Bad Girls*, the story of inmates in the fictional HMP Larkhall. The prison appeared to be based in south London, and exterior shots were initially of HMP Oxford, but the series adviser was ex-Holloway inmate Chris Tchaikovsky and some of the story lines were based on what she had witnessed inside. Episode one opened with a pregnant woman screaming in her cell, calling for the doctor and being dismissed by the staff as 'attention-seeking'. By the time she was unlocked in the morning she had miscarried, and was lying unconscious and covered in blood.

The miscarriage scene in *Bad Girls* was brutal, as was much of the TV series. The popular image of women's prisons had certainly changed since *Within These Walls* in the 1970s. HMP Larkhall was a place of uproar, the inmates were aggressive, jeering and heckling the governor. 'You can't run this prison,' one warns, 'unless we help you.' And as for Holloway itself, it was time for a radical rethink of the purpose and nature of prison.

PART EIGHT

Holloway in the Twenty-First Century

26

Holloway Rebranded

The twenty-first century began with a series of damning inspection reports for Holloway Prison. In 2002 chief prison inspector Anne Owers found 'serious deficiencies'; children's visiting days had been stopped, inmates were using sanitary towels to cover filthy toilet seats and plug gaps under doors to keep out mice, and there were still high levels of self-harm and attempted suicide. But, as had happened several times in Holloway's history, all this would change with the arrival of a new, visionary governor.

Tony Hassall came from a working-class background in the Midlands and after leaving school he'd worked in his local Sainsbury's. 'After six years I was looking for something different,' he explains. 'I had moved to the capital to manage a new hypermarket in south-west London, but I wanted to do something with my life where I was helping people instead of working in a purely commercial environment.' Tony took a sociology degree through the Open University, and then one day he saw a recruitment advert for the prison service. 'It said: "Must have a sense of humour" – which is certainly true.' First he worked as a prison officer and then governor grade at several male prisons, before becoming governor of the women's prison Bullwood Hall. When he was appointed to Holloway in June 2004, it was overrun with rats, pigeons and rubbish, and women were locked up for eighteen hours a day.

Staff were 'cutting down up to five women a day from nooses', reported the *Guardian*, and one inmate had recently been saved six times in a single night. Women made up just 6 per cent of the prison population, but they now accounted for 20 per cent of all suicides. 'Staff at Holloway were fantastic when dealing with this,' says Tony. 'I have seen prison officers sitting on beds crying with women and holding them like small children. No training prepares you for that. A death is devastating. I remember them all. There was a death one Friday evening, self-inflicted. I had known the woman well and was shocked when they called me. I went into the prison and the duty governor was in tears as were some of the staff.' The following week he drove to Birmingham with a prison officer.

> My job was to return her belongings to her parents. I drove to a very nice area of Birmingham and felt guilty, as I had made some assumptions about what her family were like. I could not have been more wrong. As I walked up the drive my heart was pounding, even though I had done this a few times in my career. But her mother was a tower of strength. She said her daughter had mental health problems and for twenty years had been trying to get help. Months later at the inquest she was so dignified and considered, not angry as I expected. I really did feel the system had let her daughter down.

The transfer of Prison Health Services to the NHS meant that Tony was soon able to improve mental health services. He also increased provision for education and training and like some of his most successful predecessors he was keen for the outside world to know about improvements at Holloway. At the beginning of 2005 he invited guests in to celebrate the opening of a new mother and baby unit, a 'state-of-the-art facility' that could accommodate twenty-three babies. It had been 'completely refurbished', the bathrooms and laundry refitted, and there was a 'fully equipped crèche staffed by childcare professionals'. Soon after the unit opened, Holloway's governor was pictured in the *Islington Gazette* having a blow-dry at the prison's new hair salon, Hairy Poppins. Tony brought in a former salon owner to run it, inmates could work towards an NVQ qualification, and he was quick to point out that it was funded through profits made from the prison shop. A few months later, he was again pictured in the local paper, this time standing beaming outside the prison after Holloway had been rated in the top ten jails in the country. 'Tony is a visionary,' said the chair of the prison's monitoring board, 'and treats the women as human beings.'

The following week, however, another report in the *Islington Gazette* was less congratulatory, with the headline 'Plush rooms help ease women into life inside'. Just as in Victorian times, there were concerns that prison was becoming too cushy. Prisoners were 'kept in comfort and style in new "hotel" facilities', with a 'brightly decorated' First Night Centre, which had a 'bistro-style dining room', a TV room with DVD and video player, 'comfy bedrooms' and showers. The article didn't discuss the purpose of the First Night Centre, where staff helped with issues the majority of women faced, such as saving rented accommodation and setting up care arrangements for children, or the fact that the risk of self-harm fell if 'entry level distress' was minimized.

An anonymous critic was incensed: 'Years ago prison used to mean prison. It was one of the most feared things. Now they live the life of Riley . . . all the lefties and do-gooders need a good kick up the arse.' Governor Tony Hassall explained that it was not his job to punish people: 'If I lock people in here and do nothing with them they'll go out and re-offend but if you treat people with respect that will help them be good citizens.' Most of the women in Holloway didn't have a GP, over half had been excluded from school and 'we're the end of the line. If they can't get help and care here where can they get it?'

The following summer the prison produced a booklet, '200 Years of History and Progress Continue . . .', with a picture of the Victorian House of Correction on its cover. The jail was now 'standing at the forefront of development of modern prison standards', just as it had done in 1852. Rehabilitation had come to the fore again, Holloway was being rebranded.

For Tony Hassall, his biggest achievement was winning the Most Improved Prison Award in 2006. Today he is deputy commissioner in the Department of Corrective Services in Western Australia, and I ask whether the advert he saw all those years ago was right, that a governor needs a good sense of humour. 'You need to be able to get on with people,' he says. 'Prisons are all about relationships. Humour at the right time can be very powerful. Prisons are a reflection of society. Society is complex and therefore the issues prisons deal with are complex. Locking people up without trying to change them is a waste of money. The purpose of prison is to rehabilitate and protect the public – they are not there to dish out punishment, that's the courts' job.'

But while life inside Holloway improved significantly during Tony Hassall's time, the female estate in general was in crisis and the number of women in prison had nearly trebled in a decade. In 2007 Baroness Corston published a 110-page report on women with vulnerabilities in the criminal justice system; written in a forthright and often angry tone, it provided a blueprint for the future of women in prison and made an urgent call for alternative community solutions.

Jean Corston had been asked to conduct the review following the deaths of six women at Styal Prison, but it was Holloway that she cited in her foreword: 'My interest in women in the criminal justice system goes back many years, to the first time I visited Holloway prison. I was shocked at the reality of prison life, at the life stories of some of the women in prison and, above all, will never forget my first sight of a baby in prison . . . I have concluded that the nature of women's custody in many of our prisons needs to be radically rethought.' 'Radical' was a key term in the report, although she acknowledged that many of the recommendations had been made before, and indeed sections echoed the words of penal reformers going back eighty years as well as previous Holloway governors. 'We must find better ways,' wrote Baroness Corston, 'to keep out of prison those women who pose no threat to society and to improve the prison experience for those who do.' Instead of being subjected to heavy-handed security, women required the sort of place envisaged by Mary Size in the 1930s and Joanna Kelley in the 1960s: 'they need help and caring, therapeutic environments to assist them rebuild their lives.' But the Corston Report did have radical implications, for if 'community solutions for non-violent women offenders should be the norm', then that would mean the end of most women in prison.

The report had a dual focus: internal changes were needed in the criminal justice system, but prevention was just as important and better 'gender sensitive services' were needed in the community in order to stop so many women ending up in jail in the first place. Baroness Corston praised women's community centres like Asha in Worcestershire, set up by Jenny Roberts, a chief probation officer, and Calderdale in Halifax, which helped women stop re-offending 'in a way in which prison has manifestly failed to do'.

In 2007 the UK's prisons were full of women awaiting trial, over half of whom were not then given a jail sentence. Prison had become a place to send those who were addicted, abused, mentally ill and already excluded from society, and the practice of sending a woman to prison 'for her own good' had to stop. Jail should not be 'expected to solve social problems', argued Baroness Corston, and yet Holloway's history, ever since Selina Salter had been repeatedly sentenced in the 1860s, showed that this had always been the case.

Conditions for prison officers meanwhile were increasingly violent, prisons were overcrowded and the POA had been weakened as a result of privatization, beginning in 1992 when G4S were given the first private contract to manage Wolds Prison in Yorkshire. Within a decade, Britain had the most privatized criminal justice system in Europe, and the POA was not recognized within privately run jails. The union reported increased problems with drugs and gang culture, officers were being sidelined as civilians took over rehabilitation and resettlement roles, and the creation of NOMS, the National Offender Management Service, in 2004 was regarded as 'a new and ominous entity'. The year the Corston Report was published, union officials threatened further industrial action following a national one-day strike, the first in the prison service's history. A major concern was officers' health and safety, and at Holloway there was an average of one attack a week on staff.

But the POA praised Holloway's latest governor, Sue Saunders, for working well with the union. She had joined the prison service in 1989, because 'I knew it would be a people job, which is what appealed to me,' and had recently served as governor of Bullingdon. In 2009 she would allow ITV cameras into Holloway to film 'a new fly-on-the-wall TV series', telling the press that many inmates did not belong inside:

I always feel that there but for the grace of God go I. I was lucky enough to be brought up in a caring family. I didn't live in poverty. I didn't have a man who beat and abused me. The women in Holloway have unbearably difficult backgrounds. I'd never excuse their crimes, but even with twenty years in the prison service I'm still appalled by their stories. That's why I don't think jailing women is always the best solution.

She spoke of the 'vulnerability, sadness and loneliness a lot of these girls live with' and praised staff for being 'compassionate, forgiving and generous with their time . . . I was talking to a prisoner the other day who is on a long sentence. She says Holloway has saved her life. The mess she was in on the outside meant she may well have been dead by now.'

But the life of the vast majority of female prisoners was of little interest to the press. While the Corston Report had demonstrated that few were a threat to society, the media continued to focus on the handful who were, and now they would go to increasing lengths for inside stories.

27

The Monsters Ball

In the autumn of 1995 Rose West went on trial for ten murders; all but one were believed to have been committed with her husband Fred West, who killed himself in prison before the trial. The couple had sexually assaulted and killed nine young women, many at their home in Gloucester, and Rose West was also convicted of killing her eight-year-old stepdaughter. The forty-two-year-old became the first woman since Myra Hindley to be given a full life term and she was portrayed by the press both as a 'celebrity' inmate who lorded it over others and as someone who was likely to be attacked at any moment. Rose West came to personify every stereotype about women's prisons, a 'black widow' who preyed on terrified new inmates and 'enjoy[ed] lesbian romps'.

In 2006 the *Sun* published a photograph of a 'Monsters Ball' in which women serving life sentences dressed up as devils and Draculas for a Halloween party at Holloway Prison. The women 'anointed themselves with fake blood as they enjoyed the party', according to the *Telegraph*, 'which saw them dance the night away to songs such as Michael Jackson's "Thriller" and the "Monster Mash"'. Tales of 'evil women' enjoying life inside Holloway gathered pace. In 2009 Tracey Connelly, her boyfriend Steven Barker and his brother Jason Owen, were convicted of 'causing or allowing' the death of her seventeen-month-old son 'Baby P'. The *Telegraph* reported that 'prison was a comfort' to Baby P's mother; she had 'piled on the weight, eating chocolate, watching television and taking part in the odd pottery class'. When nursery worker Vanessa George was convicted of sexually abusing children the *Mirror* quoted from letters she sent from Holloway explaining she enjoyed watching *Top Gear* and sunbathing in an association room: 'the trick is to move with the sun so we don't get bar stripes.'

In 2013 teaching assistant Maxine Carr was sentenced to three and a half years for giving a false alibi after her boyfriend Ian Huntley murdered schoolgirls Holly Wells and Jessica Chapman. The *Sunday Mirror* told its readers that she lived in 'room two on the medical wing', and began her cleaning job at 8 a.m. 'dressed in a white prison issue pinafore'. After a 'buffet' dinner she was locked in at 8 p.m., changed 'into a white knee-length prison nightie and cream dressing gown' and spent hours 'stretched out on her bed writing letters to her admirers'. A photo showing her 'strolling happily around Holloway Prison, smiling, laughing and pointing in fun as she stops for a chat along the way' only served to cement the image that Holloway was no longer a terror to evil-doers but more of a holiday camp.

The public image of Holloway was firmly entrenched; ever since the 1980s it had been known for housing violently disturbed women. And yet many first-time prisoners discovered a reality that was far different from what they had been led to believe in the pages of the press.

'Can you hear me God?' wrote Rosie Johnston in the opening lines of her book *Inside Out.* 'Do you know where I am? This is a single cell in Holloway prison.' In December 1986 she had been sentenced to nine months for possessing and supplying drugs after her best friend and fellow Oxford student Olivia Channon died while celebrating the end of her exams. To the media this was no ordinary heroin story. Olivia, whose father was a Tory cabinet minister, was a 'child of privilege', while Rosie's co-defendant was Sebastian Guinness from the wealthy brewing family, and the media couldn't wait to see what she would experience inside Holloway Prison.

Rosie Johnston's *Inside Out* would be the first of several modern publications written by women who wanted to tell the truth about Holloway Prison. Like other middle- and upper-class inmates who had never imagined seeing the inside of a jail cell, she discovered a dehumanizing regime that drove her to petition for change.

First-division prisoners like Sylvia Pankhurst had wanted to 'secure prison reforms, not for ourselves' but for the ordinary third-class prisoners. Pacifists in the Second World War had brought attention to poor medical care and lack of hygiene, while the women of Greenham Common had alerted the press to conditions on the notorious unit C1. Now Rosie Johnston described Holloway as 'a social dumping ground: a way of removing women from society to which they were little actual danger, and by doing so achieving nothing'. And despite her crime being drug-related, Rosie soon discovered that illegal drugs were easily obtainable inside and 'some of the screws' were 'known to pass cannabis between inmates during a bang-up. Smoking kept the level of tension down.'

Rosie spent a few weeks in Holloway before being transferred to Bullwood Hall, with the media camped outside looking for stories from released prisoners and running headlines such as 'Lesbian torment for prison girl Rosie'. But she came to realize that the women inside posed no danger to her or anyone else, and her experience 'opened my eyes to aspects of society which I would never have come across otherwise . . . [it] made me sceptical and shook my confidence in my country'.

For Sheila Bowler, imprisoned six years after Rosie Johnston's release, her time in Holloway caused her to lose faith in the entire justice system. One evening in May 1992 Sheila, who had been recently widowed, picked up her late-husband's aunt, eighty-nine-year-old Florence Jackson, from her residential care home in order to spend the weekend with her in Rye, East Sussex. When the car had a puncture, she left Florence alone to get help and when she returned her aunt had gone. The next day her body was found in the River Brede, around 500 metres from the car. Like many of the nurses at the care home, Sheila believed that Florence, who had dementia, wasn't able to walk. But she was portrayed by the police and the press as a 'cool, calculating killer' who – fatally for a woman – didn't show enough emotion in court, and she was sentenced to life imprisonment.

Sheila was put on Holloway's C1 unit, regarded as a suicide risk. The room was filthy, with cockroaches coming in the window, and the inmates behaved 'like animals in a cage'. When Sheila was asked if she had come to accept her situation, the doctor seemed surprised when she said no. Holloway was 'the saddest place I'd ever come across – so many youngsters, really only children . . . most of them are between seventeen and twenty-three – most on drugs and many with several children. I have never seen such a dejected group of human beings.' The majority were in for minor offences such as non-payment of poll tax or TV licence: 'no way should they be locked up . . . it only magnifies their deep sense of guilt and inadequacy.' Sheila Bowler's supporters launched a campaign and her conviction was finally quashed in 1997, when new medical evidence proved her aunt could have walked to the river alone. She returned to Rye, having spent four years of her life in prison for a crime she hadn't committed.

For charity director Ruth Wyner, who was wrongfully committed along with her colleague John Brock for allowing heroin to be sold in the courtyard of a day centre for the homeless run by a Cambridge charity Wintercomfort, it was the environment and the attitude of the officers that proved to be the real threat. Within three days Ruth had developed a prison persona, 'hands in pockets, a slow uncaring walk, shoulders hunched, scowling and grumpy; a woman of few words but always a curse at the ready'. The irony of being locked up for allegedly allowing drug deals and then put in a place where drugs were rife didn't escape her. Ruth wrote to then Home Secretary Jack Straw to make him aware of the supply of class A and B drugs: 'after all, I do not want to see you doing a five-year stretch as I am.' Three weeks later she received a reply from 'a minion in the government's Drug Strategy Unit', asking her to 'grass on my fellow inmates' or to ring Crimestoppers. Prison, she wrote in her memoir, was a 'form of institutional abuse' that made people feel even more alienated and it was based on vengeance, not rehabilitation.

But the press, politicians and a large section of the public did want vengeance. In order for prison to 'work', it needed to serve the same role as the ducking stool, stocks and gallows in the past. It must humiliate, degrade and punish as publicly as possible. So it was no wonder that when economist Vicky Pryce was sent to Holloway she was warned to expect the worst.

When I arrive at Vicky's south London home it's impossible not to note my surroundings and to imagine, as the tabloids repeatedly did, what it would have been like going from this genteel Victorian crescent to Holloway Prison. Vicky lets me in; she's busy helping one of her daughters who is on crutches after a netball injury and needs transport to a doctor's appointment. We sit in the kitchen and as Vicky makes coffee, she briefly sets out her terms: she won't say anything about the reasons she was in Holloway, and she won't mention her ex-husband. But I can't help asking if she felt she was made an example of during the trial. 'The press interest in me,' she says, 'was because I was prominent, and because of their expectations of what my time in prison would be like. They were proved very wrong. They said I would be badly treated, I would be different from everyone else and I would be victimized.' And did she herself think this would happen? She gives a dismissive shrug. 'I wasn't reading any of it. But as a woman going through this you have to look okay, or otherwise you can look like a victim. You have to carry on.' It's this matter-of-fact attitude that characterizes her book *Prisonomics*, published in 2013, the year that Vicky and her ex-husband, then a cabinet minister, were sentenced to eight months for perverting the course of justice. She had accepted his penalty speeding points on her driving licence some ten years earlier, and after his arrest he resigned.

Vicky kept a diary during her time in Holloway, making notes on the injustices within the prison system and drawing on her long career as an economist. The *Daily Mail*, which had published photographs of her huddled in the prison van on the way to Holloway, ran extracts of the book under the headline, 'Diary of a middle-class jailbird: Bitching, biting and snogging in the library', and promised to reveal 'the grim reality of life inside Britain's most notorious women's prison'. But *Prisonomics* was in fact a considered appraisal of the social and economic costs of incarcerating women.

While Vicky found the prison system frequently cruel in terms of the length of time women spent locked up in their cells, the environment was much better than she had expected. Even entering Holloway was 'more civilized' than she'd been told, there was no strip search and prisoners were processed as if they were in an airport. 'Many people,' she wrote, 'think that prison must be a terrifying place with lots of violent women locked up behind bars. It isn't.' The reception process was 'smooth, humane and expertly carried out. Quick fingerprinting and BOSS chair (Body Orifice Security Scanner, essentially a metal detector).'

She was met by a welcoming group of prisoners, a procedure introduced by former governor Tony Hassall, and once in her cell she was amazed by the 'solidarity of the women' as they rushed around finding her extra blankets, fruit, sandwiches and toilet roll. Vicky spent just four days at Holloway, before being transferred to East Sutton Park, but in general she found a supportive environment:

> There are things that bind the women, like children or elderly parents. Some had their community turn against them. They said the worst part was the trial, when they felt singled out by the judge and the press for being a 'bad' female. There was lots of chatting. When I went out for a walk for the first time people said, 'We thought you wouldn't want to mix with us.' But they were there to help me and it restored my faith in people.

To Vicky, prison acted as a social leveller. She had been led to believe that as a middle-class professional she would be targeted by other prisoners, but instead she discovered a prison full of working-class women who had been victimized by the justice system.

I ask if her use of the term 'guards' in her book, rather than officers, was deliberate. 'They were guards,' she says. 'I've had security guards in all my offices and all the firms I've worked in, we always had guards. They guarded the place; it's what prison officers do.' But while prisoners 'made demands for all sorts of things, I never saw rudeness or "I can't be bothered" attitude. That's not what you hear generally about prison staff. There was no "us and you" attitude.'

Vicky has not been back to Holloway since her release, aside from a recent TV interview outside the prison, although she has visited many other jails and when the media need the view of an ex-prisoner she is often first on their list. She explains that she agrees to interviews, talks and events because of her interest in penal reform and as patron of the charity Working Chance. But her brief time as a prisoner is also 'part of me. I could have ignored it and never talked about it again . . .' But you haven't? I ask. She nods. I put my notebook away; she has an appointment in the City and needs to leave, and as I do she says that what she learned overall – both from her experience and from listening to the stories of others – was how a life can change so suddenly and completely. However, unlike the majority of women in prison, Vicky was well aware that she had a safe home to go to on release, and that her children would still be there.

28

Life After Prison

The problems facing ex-prisoners have barely changed since Victorian times, and the same questions have been asked for over a century: what should women learn to enable them to return to the outside world, and what help should be available on release? In 1852, Alderman Wire had hoped that Holloway's prisoners would become honourable and useful members of society, which would be achieved through 'the judicious and humane treatment' they received inside, along with 'moral and Scriptural instruction'. Governor John Weatherhead was said to have questioned every prisoner 'as to his means of subsistence, or what he or she intends to do for the future'. But the large majority of Holloway's inmates returned over and over again. One woman was imprisoned twenty-four times for drunkenness; another 'decently dressed elderly woman' repeatedly broke courtroom windows 'when work [was] slack' in order to be sent back to jail. She had been in and out of Holloway for twelve years, and on receiving yet another sentence of twenty-one days 'appeared perfectly satisfied'.

Repeat offenders continued to be an issue in the early twentieth century. Prison was supposed 'to fit the women on leaving to earn their own living', according to the press, through lessons in laundry work and cooking, as well as lectures by lady visitors on 'hygienic subjects'. But 70 per cent of women were repeat offenders, compared to half of men. Female prisoners were generally seen as easier to reform, so why were so many ending up back inside?

In 1922 the Holloway Discharged Prisoners Aid Society was formed, a voluntary organization whose aim was to 'see that those who were friendless, without visible means of subsistence, and without a chance of employment, should meet not only with sympathy and advice, but should receive means of obtaining an honest livelihood and, where necessary, financial assistance'. It opened a hostel on Dalmeny Avenue to provide accommodation for women trying to find work. 'I can never tell you what the sanctity and peace of the place meant to me that dreadful morning of my release,' recalled one resident, 'for I really felt I had got to the end of the road – the very *end*.' The Holloway society reflected the idea that the public had a responsibility towards ex-prisoners and in 1928 it helped around 80 per cent of inmates, most of whom were said to be 'doing well or fairly well'. As a result, the number of women locked up for 'street offences' fell by over half in just one year. The society promised that 'no woman or girl leaves Holloway without an offer of assistance and the hope of making good', and it wanted to 'turn out fine citizens, not crushed women'.

In the 1930s deputy governor Mary Size was determined to 'send the women back into the world in every way improved'. Within the prison, lady visitors were assigned to look after eight to ten women, and released offenders were given clothes, attaché cases and toilet accessories, as well as hostel accommodation. The idea was to 're-establish' a former prisoner 'as a useful citizen' and to try and 'destroy any feeling of resentment which she might feel'. But despite these intentions some came straight back to prison, where they were dubbed 'the haristocracy of Holloway', and one frequent visitor would call out, 'Home, John,' when she entered the prison van.

Holloway's governor of the 1960s, Joanna Kelley, found that many women dreaded their impending date of discharge: 'It is often said that the worst part of a prisoner's punishment begins on the day of release.' They were given a 'liberty kit', after their measurements had been sent 'to a large London store' which provided 'carefully chosen and charming trousseaux'. This included a coat and dress, or a suit and blouse, shoes, stockings, a hat, two handkerchiefs and underwear. It was easy to get a job on release, according to Joanna, although few inmates were qualified to be 'anything other than factory workers or cleaners'.

In 1965 the Holloway Discharged Prisoners Aid Society was

replaced by the Griffins Society, and it offered a wide range of services to ex-inmates. Its introductory newsletter explained that it had been 'thought best to select a name with no obvious link with ex-prisoners', although few would have failed to link the image of a griffin with Holloway Prison. The Griffins bought a house in Camden and converted it into a six-bedroom hostel named Stockdale House. A Holloway psychotherapist ran weekly sessions; women could get free legal advice on maintenance, hire purchase agents, evictions and rent problems, and 'classes in citizenship'. The newsletter ended with a list of much needed items, such as fireside chairs, an eight-pint kettle and an egg poacher. In the following thirty years the society set up five hostels for women offenders in north London, with the backing of Lord Mayor Sir Edmund Stockdale, after whom the first hostel was named, and who was chair of the prison visitors at Holloway. He 'used to give ten shillings . . . to the women who were going [out] and say, "Don't you come back again,"' recalled one Griffins member. 'There they were, all homeless, absolutely. It used to really worry him stiff.' The Griffins established a bail hostel, as well as a hostel for homeless women who had finished their sentence and could get their children out of care if they had somewhere to live. But then Home Office funding became less generous, there was a shift in penal care and housing policies, and the hostels began to close.

In 2007 the Corston Report identified accommodation as the single biggest problem facing women released from prison. It also cited lack of education, learning, training and skills inside prison, and recommended that women be taught 'emotional literacy' and 'life skills' – a modern form of the Victorian good citizen model – including 'how to live as a family or group, how to contribute to the greater good, how to cook a healthy meal'. Support should also be offered to any woman who had been abused, raped or experienced domestic violence, or had been involved in prostitution. 'When women came out they could be vulnerable,' says one former member of Holloway's Independent Monitoring Board, 'there might be no one to pick them up, and there were men hanging around outside waiting for them.' Those who had been in prison for more than seven days were given £47: 'Some used the money to go straight to the off-licence, or they went back on the street; what option do they have? They have lost their children; their family didn't want to know them.'

Many also returned to prison for breaching probation. The UK's probation service has its roots in Victorian times when temperance missionaries were attached to London police courts to 'reclaim' those convicted of drunkenness. In 1907 they became known as probation officers, and were appointed and employed by the courts, and the Home Office later took control of the probation service. While the Criminal Justice Act of 1948 introduced punitive measures, such as attendance centres, the main role of a probation officer remained the same, to 'advise, assist and befriend'. In the 1970s probation 'worked on the assumption that most people are not evil, but that their life was a mess', explains Liz Hogarth, who headed the probation team at Holloway for eight years. 'The role was about welfare; perhaps a woman had arrived at prison and her suitcase was missing, or she had left a dog at home that needed to be fed.' Liz would take women out on day release, alone in her clapped-out old Mini, but some didn't want to be released at all. One day she was called to reception because a woman had taken off her clothes and was 'screaming, refusing to leave. She said she was safe and looked after at Holloway; like a lot of women she didn't want to go.'

In the 1990s the job of the probation officer changed again when the Labour government started 'pushing the punitive approach'. If a woman failed to attend a probation appointment, then after two warnings it was back to jail. 'The fact that she might need to pick her children up, or have to avoid a violent ex-partner,' says Liz, 'wasn't taken into consideration.' Parts of the probation service have now been privatized and handed over to rehabilitation companies, and today one of the main roles of a probation officer is to make sure people adhere to court orders. There has been a sharp increase in women being sent back to prison accused of breaching their licence, especially those on short sentences.

'One woman released from Holloway went to a hostel in Southend-on-Sea,' explains the Independent Monitoring Board member, 'but she had to report to her probation officer forty miles away in Harlow. Half the time women don't get the letters about appointments; they might be sent to the wrong address, or sent to their mother's and not caught up with them yet. Then they get sent back in again; it has done nothing to help.'

For prisoners released from Holloway in the twenty-first century, there was still limited access to social housing and, explained an inspection report, some 'were released without an address', just as in Victorian times. This is what happened to Mary (not her real name), a lawyer who was convicted of conspiracy to commit fraud and who was sentenced shortly after an operation for cancer. We meet in a central London coffee shop. Christmas is just a few weeks away, the café is crowded and we both keep our voices down. Mary is in her late fifties, confident and self-possessed, but this is not an easy subject to talk about. 'It was the loss of liberty that was key for me,' she says, 'apart from missing my three children, which was the worst thing for most of the women.' She felt different from the other inmates, she was a professional and much older than the average prisoner and she saw women being re-committed soon after release, one having deliberately stolen meat from a supermarket in order to go back to prison. Mary trained as a Listener with the Samaritans: 'The women's stories could be just horrifying. People were distraught and afraid. But it took my mind off what was happening to me, it gave me some authority and responsibility. I realized we're all the same in prison. It is an experience that enriches you, in a funny way.'

After serving thirteen months, Mary was released on tag for a further year and allowed to be out during the day between 8 a.m. and 6 p.m. The Samaritans supported her, and she is now a support volunteer, but she had lost her home while in Holloway and although the charity Housing for Women helped her get re-housed, this still left the problem of work. She automatically lost her licence to practise as a lawyer as a result of her conviction and she struggled to get work through an employment agency. 'I'd like to see a more meaningful sentencing system,' she says. 'I could have served the community, I could have painted a building, taught children, cleaned floors . . . prison doesn't serve any purpose. I lost my licence, I lost my reputation. And people throw it at you; I live in fear of someone coming across my name. I've well and truly served my time and paid the price, now I should be given a chance.'

For another ex-prisoner, her experiences in Holloway led her to launch a project reminiscent of the Griffins Society in the 1960s. Mandy Ogunmokun lives in Islington, not far from the prison, and she speaks with the intensity of someone who has recovered from twenty years of heroin and crack addiction and who spent most of her adult life in and out of jail. 'Holloway saved my life,' she says. 'Sadly, there were times when I wanted to go back because inside I was safe, more safe than I was outside. My parents were paedophiles, my grandmother was a prostitute, and so was my mother. My grandmother sold me to a client when I was four years old.'

As a child Mandy went shoplifting with her mother, who suffered from depression, addiction and self-harm: 'She would call us children round her as she slit her wrists. As a child I would fetch the razors, it was a ritual. Then she would ask us to send for help.' Mandy started drinking alcohol at the age of eleven, and by the time she was twenty she was in Holloway for theft:

> It was more militant in the 1980s, you had to answer to your number, you were not allowed to sit on your bed in the daytime. It was very clear that you were a prisoner. But I was a kid from the streets and I knew I'd be looked after. It was like going from home to home. Holloway was a rest period, a place to get well. I was let out, then I came back in again. What's the point of prison if there is not enough rehabilitation? People need to relearn how to live. If you commit an offence you should be punished, you can't just get away with it. But there is no point if you don't rehabilitate people. There is something wrong underneath that needs to be addressed. A lot of women in Holloway have suffered sexual, emotional and physical abuse. And the majority are inside because of drugs and alcohol, so why is there no rehab in prison? It should be mandatory.

Mandy has now been drug-free for sixteen years, and attributes this to the support she received from a Christian church organization.

She became a volunteer at Holloway, set up a church group on the detox landing, and then applied for a job as a trainee CARAT worker, part of a prison drug treatment programme. At the age of forty-five, it was her first paid job, supporting some of the very same women she had taken drugs and stolen with. In 2011 – frustrated by stories of women with no housing on the outside – Mandy set up Treasures Foundation, which provides safe long-term accommodation for ex-prisoners and help with addiction.

For Mandy, like many others, her time in Holloway changed the course of her life. 'A lot of good work goes on there; the structure of the building is rubbish, but the people, they put their heart into it . . . Holloway for me was a concrete parent.'

Whatever its flaws, the prison could be a place of security, and rehabilitation and resettlement were working better than in the recent past. In October 2013 the chief inspector of prisons Nick Hardwick reported that Holloway had become a safer prison and most women were treated decently. The level of self-harm had fallen from 143 incidents a month to 63, and there had not been a self-inflicted death in nearly seven years. Staff were sensitive, interacting with women who needed continuous monitoring 'rather than the bleak, passive observation through the bars of a gated cell which we saw too often in the past'. The chief inspector stressed the advantages of Holloway's location, which enabled women to stay in contact with family, friends and community, while 'an exceptionally wide range of community agencies' provided good support. Women in Prison and Hibiscus, a charity based on the Holloway Road that works with foreign national, black and minority ethnic women, were on hand to respond to urgent calls, particularly if women were released late in the day. Another locally based charity, the theatre workshop and touring company Clean Break, set up in 1977 by two prisoners, ran highly successful theatre residencies in Holloway. Only 5 per cent of women who complete a Clean Break course then go on to re-offend.

There was still work to do; the prison retained a 'fearsome reputation' with a layout that made it hard to supervise. There was bullying and intimidation, and not enough access to activities or family support work. But it seemed that Holloway was finally overcoming its architectural problems, and once again it had become one of the most improved prisons in the country. So when in 2015 the government announced plans to close down 'ageing and ineffective Victorian prisons', Holloway's future appeared secure. Prison inspectors were singing its praises, self-harm was down, its staff were caring and hard-working. And, after all, the new Holloway was not a nineteenth-century castle, it was barely even thirty years old.

29

The End of an Era

On 25 November 2015, as Chancellor George Osborne was standing up in the House of Commons to announce his annual spending review, senior staff were called into Holloway's boardroom where a Ministry of Justice representative informed them the prison was closing. Shortly afterwards, psychotherapist Pamela Stewart was walking along a corridor to the psychotherapy room when an officer asked if she was coming to a full staff meeting. 'I said, I'm not staff, I'm NHS, and she said, "I think you should come." It sounds awful but I thought, Oh God, another death in custody. Then I went to the chapel, heard the news and saw big burly officers burst into tears. No one inside knew about it, no one was consulted; no one thought it was a good idea. It was like the announcement of a pit closure.'

George Osborne began by explaining that 'old Victorian prisons in our cities that are not suitable for rehabilitating prisoners will be sold.' This would bring long-term savings and allow nine new prisons to be built, and 'today the transformation gets under way' with the closure of Holloway. This was met with a muted response from his fellow parliamentarians, but when he added that 'in the future women prisoners will serve their sentences in more humane conditions better designed to keep them away from crime', Prime Minister David Cameron, sitting behind him, nodded enthusiastically and there were cries of 'Hear, hear.' Yet what were these 'more humane' conditions, had prison ever kept women away from crime, and what would happen now to the prisoners and staff?

There had been calls to close Holloway ever since the 1930s when trade unionist Margaret Bondfield said it should be blown up and replaced with a new alternative. If war had not broken out in 1939, inmates would have been moved to smaller units in the countryside, as envisaged by prison commissioner Lilian Barker. In the 1970s Radical Alternatives to Prison had campaigned against the new hospital building, arguing that money was being spent on the wrong things and there was 'no need for a massive women's prison at all'. The suggestions had all been ignored, so why now, after all these years, was the prison finally going to close?

The Prison Officers' Association issued a press release expressing serious concerns: 'Holloway has turned around the lives of many offenders and this decision will do nothing to address offending behaviour and rehabilitation.' Instead, the closure would destabilize the lives of staff and prisoners, further demoralize prison officers and was 'another example of a government that will stop at nothing to save money'. The Holloway branch of the POA put a motion to conference to condemn the decision, which was carried unanimously. But according to Justice Secretary Michael Gove, the government was embarking 'on a radical reform of our prisons to rehabilitate offenders, cut crime and enhance public safety' and, just as in Victorian times, his solution was to build more jails.

In the language of the prison service, the women at Holloway would now be 'decanted'. Those on remand would be held at HMP Bronzefield in Middlesex, while the rest would go to HMP Downview in Surrey. What was going to happen to the site wasn't made clear, but Juliet Lyon from the Prison Reform Trust wrote to Michael Gove with a 'challenging proposition'. Closing Holloway offered the opportunity to put in its place an alternative to women's imprisonment. Part of the ten-acre site could be used to establish a women's centre, providing access to mental healthcare, drug and alcohol treatment, debt advice, skills training and parenting support. Instead of throwing women into prison, women's centres – championed by the Corston Report nine years earlier – could help repair lives.

'Why close a prison built thirty years ago and put women in another prison built thirty years ago?' asked Frances Crook, chief executive of the Howard League for Penal Reform:

I'm pleased to close a prison; it's great, if it's to get women out and create social housing. But if women's best interests are at heart then they should have consulted the Minister for Women and Equalities and they didn't. It's a sleight of hand and it's dangerous. There will be more sentencing of women, because of propaganda that women will be better treated inside. Magistrates will believe this, and faced with a chaotic woman they will send her to prison.

For mental health workers at Holloway, their immediate concern was how to continue providing treatment and support. Not long after the closure announcement, they held their own meeting in the prison chapel where Pamela Stewart asked her colleagues to 'honour the years of therapeutic work done within these walls, which will soon fall down'.

Life inside those walls had, of course, changed enormously since the birth of the model prison in the 1850s when inmates were silent and segregated and expected to work ten hours a day. The purpose of Holloway had also changed, reflecting shifting views on the nature of women, crime and punishment. The House of Correction had been built to inspire terror in bad women; the new hospital was erected to provide treatment for mad women.

Over 164 years, as penal policy evolved, cells had become rooms, turnkeys had become officers and social workers, capital and corporal punishment were abolished. Inmates could now talk to each other, wear their own clothes, take classes in computer studies or hair-dressing. But the hardships of being imprisoned remained similar, especially the separation from children. And Holloway's modern inmate population was in many ways similar to that of Victorian times. Heroin addiction might have overtaken alcoholism, benefit fraud had replaced the theft of coal, but most of its prisoners were still poor, often homeless, vulnerable and abused, convicted of petty crimes and serving short sentences.

Female prisoners still reacted to incarceration in similar ways as well. In Victorian times Selina Salter had destroyed the furniture in thirteen cells, ripped up six prison gowns and all her clothing, before trying to kill herself. In the 1940s Borstal girls had 'smashing up fits' and barricaded themselves in wings; a decade later Holloway's inmates were constantly experiencing 'nerve storms' and were put in padded cells. During the 1980s, in the new hospital building, prisoners tore washbasins from their stands and set fire to their rooms, and there were record numbers of self-harm and attempted suicide. Throughout Holloway's history women had taken out their fury and distress on their environment and themselves. In response, they had been further punished, isolated, forcibly fed, accused of attention-seeking, deemed abnormal and drugged.

The idea that women react differently from men to prison had been raised as early as the 1860s. The medical officer at Brixton Female Convict Prison found that 'females as a *body* do not bear imprisonment so well' and that a prison sentence to a woman 'seemed more severe'. Female prisoners were always seen as difficult to manage, partly because there are different expectations for the behaviour of women. Those who tore up their clothing were classified as hysterical in the nineteenth century, in the 1950s female prisoners were far more likely to be referred for a mental report, while in the following decades they were classified as insane, given therapy and sedated with drugs.

Former Holloway governor Colin Allen believes men deal with prison by cutting off the reality, an option that isn't so available to women who still have the demands and responsibilities of family and the community. 'Men in prison differ from women in several ways,' says Frances Crook, who has worked in penal reform for thirty years. 'Men have women to look after them, to bring in clothes and money, while women don't.' A second major difference is children: 'Very few women give birth in prison, but there are a huge number of women with small children and they have to apply to have them. By then they might have been separated for two months. If you are arrested for shoplifting and sent to Holloway on remand and asked if you have kids would you tell them?' asks Frances. 'I wouldn't. Social services will be involved.'

Punishment levels for women are also much higher than for men:

A woman telling an officer to fuck off isn't tolerated. If you punish women for expressing their anguish then they have no way to express that. If you are distressed and want to lash out, to scream and shout, then you lose your privileges and are put in solitary confinement. So how do you express that anguish? You punish yourself. A higher level of punishment means a higher level of self-harm. The walls shrink as you're put in segregation until there is nothing left to smash but yourself.

The closure of Holloway Prison means that over a century of incarcerating women in London will come to an end. But this isn't the end of the prison system that Holloway has always represented. Now women will simply be imprisoned elsewhere, in one of fourteen other female jails in the UK. The practice of sending vulnerable women to prison, even when they are yet to be sentenced, will continue. Imprisoning women has always led to self-harm and suicide, because the prison system was designed to punish, not to help.

30

Hope Dies Last

On 11 January 2016 Sarah Reed became the last woman to die in Holloway Prison. According to the Ministry of Justice, she was 'found unresponsive' in her cell at 8 a.m.; prison staff 'attempted CPR, but she was pronounced dead shortly after'. The thirty-two-year-old mixed-race woman had suffered severe mental health problems ever since the death of her baby in 2003, including grief, depression, schizophrenia and bulimia. Four years before her own death, Sarah had been brutally assaulted by white police officer James Kiddie on the floor of a shop in Regent Street, accused of shoplifting. The assault was caught on CCTV cameras; the police officer's punishment was a community order.

In 2015 Sarah had been sectioned at a mental health unit, where she was charged with an alleged assault on another patient. She told her family she had been defending herself from attempted rape. Sarah was sent on remand to Holloway for psychiatric reports, where she was classed as at low risk of self-harm. She was placed in segregation, and then moved to C1, the psychiatric unit that had become notorious in the 1980s. When her mother Marylin visited, she found her daughter looking unwell and acting strangely; it appeared she wasn't being given her anti-psychotic medication. One of her last letters home read: 'Mum, this is just to say Merry Xmas . . . PS. Get me out of jail.'

Sarah Reed's death quickly became linked to the Black Lives Matter movement, which had started in the United States and which highlighted deaths of black women and men in custody. Lee Jasper, who coordinated a justice campaign, wrote that: 'This is a horrific tale of institutional racism, sexual violence, corruption and brutal incompetence/negligence that defies belief.'

On the night of 8 February, the day of Sarah's funeral, hundreds gathered for a vigil outside Holloway Prison. Her name was marked out in candles on the pavement, and the crowd chanted, 'Say her name: Sarah Reed. Black Lives Matter.'

Racism within the prison service had only been officially recognized in the year 2000, but there had been reports of racist treatment inside Holloway since at least the 1980s. Few records exist on the experiences of women from black, Asian and minority ethnic groups prior to this, and in the first 100 years of Holloway's existence the vast majority of inmates were white. In Victorian times it was rare for a prisoner's ethnicity to be recorded, whether in official documents or press coverage. By the 1940s, reference to ethnicity was still unusual, except for the occasional newspaper report of a 'coloured' inmate, such as Theresa Mackenzie, a 'cabaret dancer' imprisoned at Holloway in 1948. A 'habitual criminal' who had absconded with her employer's jewels while working as a maid, she was sentenced to three years, but was allowed to bring in 'a mandolin with her own money', received gramophone records from her agent and a room at the prison was 'placed at her disposal for practice'.

Theresa had apparently received preferential treatment, but novelist Jean Rhys, who spent a week on remand in Holloway in 1949 after assaulting a neighbour, wrote about a different side to the prison in her short story 'Let Them Call It Jazz'. Her narrator Selina Davis is a mixed-race woman from Martinique. Jobless and homeless, after her savings have been stolen and her abusive landlord has thrown her out, she's picked up by a Mr Sims, who offers her a flat. Selina spends the days drinking and singing, her racist white neighbours complain and she's arrested and fined £5. When the neighbours then accuse her of being a prostitute, she picks up a stone and hurls it through their window. Unable to pay her fine, Selina is sent to Holloway as a 'nuisance'.

When she arrives at prison, a white girl hands in her belongings, and the officer on reception returns them with a smile. But when it comes to Selina, her compact, comb and handkerchief are thrown at her 'like everything in my bag is dirty'. The prison system is as racist as the world outside, 'so I think, "Here too, here too." But I tell myself, "Girl, what you expect, eh? They all like that. All."'

Selina is put in the prison hospital, told that she is 'sick', and when she's unable to eat her porridge the officer asks sarcastically if she's hunger striking. Then she hears a woman singing from a high-up barred window – 'a smoky kind of voice . . . as if those old dark walls theyselves are complaining, because they see too much misery'. Another inmate tells her, 'That's the Holloway song. Don't you know it yet? She was singing from the punishment cells, and she tell the girls cheerio and never say die.'

It's a song of pain but also defiance, sung out of the punishment block where one of the few things a woman has left is her voice, able to 'jump the gates of the jail . . . and nobody could stop it'. The next morning Selina's appetite returns; she is released and soon finds a new job and home. One evening a musician overhears her whistling the Holloway song, jazzes it up and sells it for cash. But to Selina he plays it wrong, it's not the tune she heard at Holloway, the one that sang of a woman's determination to 'never say die' and which inspired her to fight on despite being victimized by society, police and the courts.

Forty years after Jean Rhys was jailed, an estimated 30 per cent of Holloway's prisoners were black. As in the United States, the number of black prisoners was increasing at a faster rate than any other ethnic group. Black women were more likely to be arrested and given custodial sentences than white women, especially for drug offences, and less likely to be given bail. Like Jean Rhys's narrator, they experienced discrimination right the way through a criminal justice system that was dominated – then as now – by white male police, judges and QCs. Within prison, meanwhile, black women received harsher treatment – denied medical attention, excessively punished, and verbally and physically assaulted by both staff and other prisoners.

Adaku, jailed at Holloway in the 1980s, described being sent to the punishment block for two days after a fight with a white inmate: 'She called me a black bitch . . . then she hit me and I had to hit her back.' Black women were refused baths, their visitors were more thoroughly searched and watched, and hair, skin and cosmetic products handed out on reception were only for white women. Aduku was also refused access to her inhaler for asthma, told she only wanted it to 'make myself high'.

Another inmate, Abbena, spent the first five months of a twenty-month sentence at Holloway in solitary confinement because the prison authorities wouldn't recognize her Rastafarianism or its dietary beliefs. 'They kept coming each mealtime, each week, with a pork sausage. This one officer kept calling me all these names like gollywog and nig-nog . . . One day I was having a wash and she was standing at the door calling me a black bastard and I threw the soap at her.' Prisoners were refused black magazines like *West Indian World*, as well as Marcus Garvey books, and staff tried to keep black women separated from each other: 'They'll put one black girl in among thirty white girls. It's common practice.' There were no senior officers who were black, and no black doctors, while 'one racist doctor . . . used to prescribe Depixol for non-white prisoners. About two-thirds of the black women prisoners are drugged.'

Between 1994 and 2003 the number of black females imprisoned in the UK rose by nearly 200 per cent, higher than all other ethnicities. Angela Devlin, author of *Invisible Women*, identified two main stereotypes when it came to staff attitudes to black female prisoners: 'poor mules' and 'strong fighters'. Poor mules were women serving long sentences for importing drugs from abroad, often West Africa, and they were regarded with some sympathy. British black women on the other hand were seen as physically strong, aggressive and potentially violent and were treated very differently from white women on admission, despite being charged with similar offences. 'White women, especially if they were young, attractive and well dressed, were patted on the head and told to run away and behave better in future,' writes Angela Devlin, while black women's crimes were regarded more judgementally and 'any attempt at assertiveness was quashed immediately.' Black prisoners were more likely to be disciplined, and heavily supervised, and male officers described them as 'loud', 'mouthy' and 'gobby'.

The rate of foreign national women in prison was also beginning to rise in the 1980s and many were young black women, 'poor mules' charged with drug-related offences. Some had been forced to import drugs at gunpoint and made to swallow lethal amounts of heroin or cocaine in 'fingers' of rubber gloves. But instead of focusing on the traffickers, punishment fell on the victims and they were sent to Holloway. Foreign national women were also charged under immigration laws – often initially arrested for a minor crime and then incarcerated at Holloway. By the beginning of the twenty-first century up to a third of its 500 prisoners were foreign nationals, and the prison was also a designated detention centre for alleged illegal immigrants. One woman, 'Ms K', had come to the UK from Nigeria as a victim of torture. She took part in a five-week hunger strike over conditions and treatment at Yarl's Wood immigration removal centre in Bedfordshire, and in 2010 she was transferred to Holloway where she was told, 'You are from the jungle, you should go back.' Denise McNeil, a black woman from Jamaica who had left to escape domestic abuse, was labelled a 'ringleader' at Yarl's Wood and held at Holloway for a year – without being charged. As with the fictional Selina Davis, prison was being used to control and punish 'loud' behaviour, and being black was almost an offence in itself.

There was also a disproportionate rise in the number of black and ethnic minority female prisoners dying, following the use of force or as a result of medical neglect in prison. In 1987 a woman from Pakistan died in Holloway while awaiting trial for allegedly smuggling heroin. She had a heart condition and had complained of chest pains, yet was put in the punishment block a week before she died and her medical state was not seen as an emergency. Criminologist Ruth Chigwada-Bailey notes a 'disturbing pattern of deaths in custody' since the early 1990s, and those responsible were rarely if ever prosecuted. In 2000 Cheryl Hartman, a twenty-year-old black woman with a history of self-harm and psychiatric admissions, was put in a dormitory at Holloway despite asking to be moved to the psychiatric wing. After being assaulted by two prisoners, and pleading to see a doctor, she took her own life. Her mother was informed by phone, while other family members found out when they heard the news on the radio.

That same year the Commission for Racial Equality announced

it would investigate the prison service after a nineteen-year-old Asian man, Zahid Mubarek, was killed by his openly racist white cellmate at Feltham Young Offenders Institution in west London. Shortly afterwards the National Association for the Care and Resettlement of Offenders published a report on racism at Brixton Prison. One in ten prisoners from ethnic minorities had been the victims of a racially motivated physical attack, while three in ten black prisoners, and nearly half of Asian inmates, had been verbally abused. Both reports focused only on male prisons.

Prison staff were victims of racism too. The prison service, union and Independent Monitoring Boards all remained predominantly white, and only around 4 per cent of staff were black, Asian or minority. In 2001 two white prison officers were arrested after police found neo-fascist literature and Ku Klux Klan memorabilia in their Holloway Prison quarters, following complaints by black staff of intimidation and racist jokes. That same year Martin Narey, director-general of the prison service, acknowledged that the service was 'an institutionally racist organisation' with 'pockets of blatant and malicious racism . . . It is time to face up to these things.' In response, he received hate mail from within the prison service.

But now, at least to some extent, racism within UK prisons was being acknowledged. In 2005 the chief inspector of prisons' thematic review of race – in both male and female prisons – found that black inmates were more likely to be in a segregation unit 'for reasons for Good Order or Discipline', and more likely to have force used against them. They had less access to outside exercise, were stopped from touching family members during visits and staff took longer to respond to their cell bells. Prisoners would be treated well, said one woman, 'if your face fits, your hair flicks and you have blue eyes'.

At the time of Holloway's closure, nearly 40 per cent of inmates were black and minority ethnic women, and reports of racism were rare. 'There are a lot of black women inside; people wouldn't try it on with us,' says one recently released prisoner, 'and there are a lot of black officers.'

But Sarah Reed's death brought attention back to racism in the prison service, and public fury was directed at prison officers, who were assaulted in a local pub. According to Lee Jasper, the family reported being 'treated shoddily' by prison staff who were hostile and aggressive and Sarah's mother was not allowed to see her daughter's body until three days after she had died. But prison was only one part of a system – which included the crown prosecution service, the courts and mental health services – that had played a role in her death. When Samaritans volunteer Louise Warner went to Holloway the night Sarah died, she found it 'a sad place to be; the staff were very distressed and affected, some of them knew her well. I'd never felt such sadness there.'

The last woman to die in Holloway Prison was working class, mixed race and highly vulnerable, and like thousands of women before her she had been repeatedly failed by the system that sent her to jail. There were eleven other self-inflicted deaths in female prisons that year, more than double the year before and the highest since 2004.

'Sarah Reed was one of twenty-two women who died in women's prisons in 2016,' says Deborah Coles, director of INQUEST, 'three of whom were women of colour. The fundamental question in this case, like so many more before it is: Why was Sarah ever sent to prison in the first place?'

A couple of weeks after the vigil for Sarah Reed, mental health workers gathered at the Saturday Forensic Forum to discuss Holloway's closure. The forum was set up by Pamela Stewart for therapists to share information about complex patients in difficult settings, and when I arrive at the meeting room at the Philadelphia Association, off a cobbled mews in Hampstead, north London, people are helping themselves to tea and shortbread; the air is full of chat. But once the meeting gets under way, the mood among the forty participants switches to one of despair, anger and hopelessness.

Maureen Mansfield, mental health services manager at Women in Prison, stands up to speak. 'Women in Prison is abolitionist,' she explains, 'it wants the closure of prisons, and so do I. But when I heard the news I was devastated. It showed a total lack of understanding.'

'What is the social purpose of prison?' asks Pamela Stewart, who first entered Holloway twenty years ago when chief inspector Lord Ramsbotham was walking out in disgust. 'People don't want to think about it and the trauma of the women inside – it's more of a case of out of sight, out of mind. But the treatment of women in prison is better than what it was.'

Holloway's last ever inspection report, based on an inspection carried out in October 2015 but not published until two months after the closure announcement, confirmed that mental health provision had improved. Relationships between officers and prisoners were mainly decent and respectful, some staff were 'exceptional', psychosocial services were 'very impressive' and mental health support 'excellent'. But Her Majesty's inspectors had no idea they were writing a report, as well as an action plan, for a jail that was about to close.

A few days after the Forensic Forum meeting, I'm at a Caribbean restaurant in Camden Town. I've come to see Jo Thompson, a former Holloway teacher, who has something she wants to show me. She takes what looks like a heavy green blanket out of a shopping trolley and lays it on the floor. I stand back as she unrolls it; on and on it seems to go as we move chairs and tables out of the way in order to view this colourful quilt made by Holloway prisoners in 2012. Jo explains that along with her colleagues Ella Simpson and Dinah Mulholland she formed a charity around arts, literacy and self-esteem and they decided on a project as an extra activity and a way to get funding. 'It took a lot of conversations with the prison before it happened. We ran workshops, but as scissors weren't allowed it was difficult. But it was the time of the Olympics and the Queen's Jubilee, things were happening in the world and we wanted to record the experiences of women in prison, both good and bad.'

Each woman designed a square on paper and then a lifer embroidered it. 'The most heartbreaking was a girl who didn't speak English, but another woman could communicate with her, and started writing down what she said. The last three words were *Hope dies last.*' The final quilt was made up of around 100 squares, and was displayed during a festival commemorating suffragette Emily Wilding Davison, who was imprisoned at Holloway. The quilt has a thick black border, then a layer of multicoloured blocks, while in the centre is a mass of squares grouped like windowpanes, designed to resemble the suffragettes' Holloway brooch.

The prisoners were asked what they wanted that they didn't have, and their answers are embroidered around the edge: Family, Love, Sex, Cake. At the top are the words Bird Word, the name of the charity and, explains Jo, 'because it was made by birds doing bird – serving time in prison. Here,' she says, pointing to the black border, 'this was made out of officers' trousers, and we used their shirts for the squares; some still have buttons. And those' – she points at the coloured cloth – 'represent bricks; they were made from prison curtains and bed sheets.' At first the squares look like blocks of neat graffiti, as if a young girl has written on a wall, decorated with the occasional angel or fairy. Then I read the words: *I deserve respect, Innocent until proven guilty, I wish for a better life.* Most are written in black, but one square has a bright pink imprint of a baby's foot. When governor Julia Killick was asked which one was her favourite, she chose *Contained but never controlled.* I stand up and walk slowly around the quilt, reading out square after square: *I wish to feel and touch my children after 8 years in prison; Prison is a nightmare and it will pass.* I return to where I started, and see the final square embroidered in purple: *Hope dies last.*

I ask Jo what she thought when she heard about Holloway's closure and she sits down on the floor and gently starts rolling up the quilt:

> It was a complex set of emotions. On the one hand I'm thrilled. The building is oppressive, it's the wrong design, it is exactly like a hospital, even down to the pastel colours on the walls. But I'm sorry for my colleagues who work there and what will happen to the women inside, especially family contact. Closing Holloway could be a moment for reform, but I don't think in my heart it will be. If we had community sentences and if our drug and rehabilitation systems were better, if we were dealing with domestic violence and eradicating poverty, and if our mental health service was working then . . . that would be reform.

Jo tells me she once taught a class on the history of Holloway, but for one young woman who was on methadone 'all the talking about baby farmers and everything freaked her out, I think it brought back bad memories. So I cleaned up the history a bit and sanitized it; the stories of Holloway Prison were just too overwhelming.' Jo is right, the history of women in Holloway is a bleak one and stories of triumph are few and far between. It's impossible not to feel depressed at a century and a half of women betrayed and coerced, condemned and mistreated, wrongly imprisoned, punished and executed. But this is why its story has to be told, because women have for too long been kept out of sight and out of mind behind the walls of Holloway. Their lives have rarely been documented, and now that the prison is about to close down it's more important than ever that they are.

31

The Ghosts of Holloway

On 1 March 2016, the last day any woman will ever be admitted to Holloway as a prisoner, I have finally been given permission to view the prison's archives. I pass the visitors' centre, see a glimpse of children's toys and colourful furniture inside, and then I enter a gloomy reception area where a mat on the floor bears a handsome City of London griffin and the words 'Welcome to Holloway Prison'. The last time I came here was in 1990, when everything had been newly built and now the place feels tired. Three stern-faced men sit behind the glass on my right; one looks like a bouncer. I show my ID and hand in my phone, then two glass doors slide open and I'm let into the authorized personnel area.

The officer I've come to meet, Dean Barrow, arrives, much younger than I'd been expecting. Dean knows more about Holloway than anyone here: he has written a short history for the prison library and single-handedly rescued the archives. 'We're taking the trolley route,' he says, leading me back down through the building and opening a door covered with blue painted bars. This was the route designed to resemble a village high street, linking all the modern facilities in the 1980s. We go past the gym, along hallways painted custard yellow and which are so short I can't see if anyone is around the corner. We reach the library, and then suddenly we're outside. 'Remember this?' asks Dean and I stand quite still, because I do. This is the courtyard to the education centre, much smaller than I remembered, with a couple of benches, a patch of grass and a clump of daffodils. Opposite is the window of the classroom where I taught twenty-six years ago, and now it doesn't seem intimidating at all.

We go on through yet more doors – 'Please lock me', says the sign on one – past the swimming pool with a large tiled griffin on the floor. Then we're outside again; there are flowerbeds and rows of plastic-covered tunnels. 'This is where Oswald Mosley was kept,' says Dean, 'and this is where the van would drive in to drop the ladies.' Then he points ahead: on the ground beneath A block are the two stone griffins that once stood above the Victorian prison entrance. The contrast between old and new is bizarre, as if someone has put an ancient statue, a symbol of nineteenth-century terror, under a modern block of flats. Up close the griffins look furious, with roaring faces, sharp teeth and huge talons, and I can imagine them looking majestically down from their pillars as hundreds of suffragettes arrived singing 'Glory, glory, hallelujah / And the cause goes marching on'. But the griffins are in a bad state now, half covered in green moss and with broken claws, and today this area is one of the prison's two designated smoking spots.

Dean takes me to the main chapel, where the Roman Catholic and Church of England ministers share an altar. There is also a separate prayer room for Muslims; almost 30 per cent of prisoners in London are Muslim, and at Holloway the percentage has almost doubled in five years to 12 per cent. Staff meetings are held in the main chapel, such as the one in November 2015 when staff were told the prison was closing.

'It's very quiet and peaceful,' I say, almost whispering.

'Not when you have to search it at night,' says Dean.

I think of Louisa Henson, the warder who worked at Holloway in 1872, urging prisoners to keep themselves out of trouble for the sake of their religion and themselves. I ask Dean if there are any ghost stories around here. One night, he says, as he was walking through the unit where the Victorian treadmill used to be, all the lights went out, even the emergency ones, and as he was looking for his torch and feeling his way along the wall with his hand, he felt something or someone go past and all the hairs on his arms stood up. Years ago another officer set off the alarm after she saw a woman wearing an old Victorian gown and boots and holding a cross. This was not, Dean stresses, the sort of officer who would easily panic or ever believe in ghosts.

I ask how he first got into the prison service, and he explains he liked history and crime books as a child. 'I always wondered about Holloway, I thought it was a castle. Obviously when I arrived, I found it was not.' Dean tells me we're going to the lifer wing and we get into a red lift; all four walls and the floor are painted deep red and it's like being inside a metal heart. There are no windows, nothing on the walls, and I'm fighting a sense of complete claustrophobia when the lift stops. We come out into a corridor, built in an L shape, and it's only now that I really understand the poor design; prison officers can't see the women they're supposed to be supervising, and neither they nor the inmates can see what might be happening around the corner.

The lifer unit, which can hold forty-five women, is empty. Things are moving quickly; in three months women have already been moved out. Dean shows me a small kitchen, with a metal stove and sink, and then the dining room, like a deserted schoolroom, except for the flat-screen TV on the wall. The place feels spooky; where have all the women gone? It's as if the rooms were suddenly abandoned during a disaster, and no one had time to clean up.

I look into a cell with an empty metal bed frame and a toilet behind a wall in one corner. The window has two metal ventilation strips; the view outside is a blank wall. Dean's trying to move me on but I want to nose around. The floor is covered in a blue patterned carpet with lots of stains and I can't tell if the most recent-looking is food or drink, sick or blood. 'Women in this wing were usually in for murder,' says Dean, as we step into another cell with two separate beds. I examine the door, thinking of the cell door I saw in the Museum of London's Hackney warehouse from 1902. This modern door doesn't have a peephole; instead it has a thin strip. Dean explains women could cover this up from the inside, in which case officers would look through a bigger panel in the door. But because of the way the new cells were designed in the 1980s, they wouldn't necessarily be able to see the woman at all.

'What's this for?' I ask, putting my hand on a round covered hole under the slit.

'It's where we put the hose,' he says, 'if a lady sets her cell on fire.'

The life of an officer is beginning to sound fraught, unable to see round corners, check on women in cells, or open a door if there's a fire.

We pass another cell with handprints in pink paint on the wall and then a room with a row of small wooden-framed mirrors, just waiting for women to sit down and look at themselves. It's a mess in here, with pieces of jigsaw puzzles spilling on to the floor, books thrown here, there and everywhere. There are also half a dozen brand-new orange metal lockers all wrapped up in plastic. New furniture has arrived, but the women have gone. We go into a dormitory cell with five beds; on the window sill is a small plastic air freshener but the room still smells of stale urine. Some women like to be in rooms together, says Dean, there is a sense of cama-raderie. I read the graffiti on the wall: 'miss ya' and a woman's name, and 'I ♥ my girls'. Was the woman writing about her children, or about the other women in the cell? But there's no point asking, the inmates have been 'decanted', leaving sad signs behind.

Now we're going down to the segregation unit, which hasn't been used in years. 'It's a bit of a dungeon,' says Dean, 'be careful.' The basement adjudication room feels like a squat, as if its inhab-itants have ripped things up on their way out. This is where women were brought for a mini trial when they were accused of breaking a rule and asked if they were guilty or not. 'Watch out for that,' says Dean, guiding me away from exposed nails and a gash in the floor. Then he points outside, through the bars on the door: 'This was the cage.' The cage? I remember the first day I came to Holloway, being taken around by the education officer and seeing a metal cage on the top of a slight incline, the exercise yard for segregated prisoners who were held in solitary confinement. I ask if we can take a look. Dean unlocks the door and we step outside. The perimeters of the cage can still be seen, faint lines marked out on the ground. We take six steps and we've reached the end of the exercise yard. 'We would put the ladies' dinner through a hole in the bottom of the door in this wing,' says Dean. 'That was horrible.'

Outside again we walk past the Village Green, with bushes and bulrushes and a couple of thin palm trees, then Dean points to a red door in the distance, the same colour as the lift. This is C1, the psychiatric unit, the infamous 'Muppet House' of the 1980s. Dean worked in C1 for five years and loved it. 'The ladies think so differently in there. We're looking for beds for them now.'

He takes me round the perimeter of the prison, shows me where the jam factory was, famous in the 1950s and 1960s for its quality jam, and then the spot where Edith Thompson was executed in 1923. We start to follow a massive metal inner fence, so tall it's like we're in a zoo, while on our other side is an even taller brick wall, the famous curvy wall that was intended to break down the boundary between prison and the outside community. Where is everyone? I ask. Dean says all the women are at work or education. I'm surprised; I thought there weren't enough staff to get inmates to anything. It's strange to think there are still some 300 women locked up in here and I've hardly seen a soul. 'This is Pizza Hut,' says Dean, where the inmates on C1 eat, and I don't have to ask him what he means because the layout looks exactly like a mini Pizza Hut. We reach the exercise yard for the enhanced security and segregation units and Dean points up to the top floor: 'That was where the IRA were kept,' the yard covered so an escape helicopter couldn't land. He shows me the area where the suffragettes were once held, in what was the Victorian castle's D wing, and then we're inside again, passing the hair salon opened by governor Tony Hassall that used to be known as Hairy Poppins.

Then finally it's time to see the archives. I've been told by the Ministry of Justice that the collection is small, but when we enter a conference room there are dozens upon dozens of boxes and journals piled on the floor and laid out on the table and chairs. It's warm in here, the windows are covered in vertical blinds and Dean moves around opening latches, letting in a breeze. He explains that one day he found the death warrants for Edith Thompson and Styllou Christofi in a black bin liner, ready to be thrown out: 'There was no nostalgia then, they were seen as worthless.'

He hands me Edith's file, and the first document is the exhumation report written in 1971 when the remains of the five women executed at Holloway were dug up in the dead of night and removed. I read a list of the things Edith left at Holloway after she died: one fur coat, one hat and forty-five letters. Together we read the official correspondence surrounding her execution, the required details of weight and height, the length of the strap. 'They were nervous,' says Dean, 'they were doing everything by the book. Did you know,' he asks, 'it was raining that day?' He hands me the death notice that was stuck on the door to the prison, and I flinch as the blinds in the conference room start smacking together in the wind. Edith's name has smudged, but only slightly, as if someone has flicked a wet paintbrush over the letters, or bent over the notice in tears.

While Ruth Ellis's records were stolen from Holloway in the 1960s, there is a report on her exhumation here as well. But there are too many archives in this room to even begin to look through in my allotted two hours. This is a collection of 164 years of crime and punishment, records of women convicted of 'crimes' that no longer exist, like attempted suicide and abortion, and records of those whose actions or beliefs were such a threat to morality, law and order that they were locked up in Holloway Prison.

I pick up a folder labelled Cynthia Payne, the 'luncheon voucher Madam' who spent four months here in 1980, and then a folder labelled Carole Richardson, the seventeen-year-old falsely convicted of an IRA bombing in 1975 and sentenced to be held indefinitely 'at Her Majesty's pleasure'. Dean passes me photos of officers in their new uniforms from the 1970s – the women look like flight attendants and the men like pilots – then of inmates in flowery dresses and cardigans, after prisoner uniform came to an end in the 1960s.

I sit down at the table, aware that each document or photograph he hands me tells a slice of Holloway's history, every rescued archive taking us further back in time. And here I am at last, in the place where these stories actually happened. We look at a register of deaths, servant girls in wartime Britain dying of syphilis, babies dead just two hours after they were born. We flick through a commissioner and inspector's minute book that begins in the summer of 1909: 'The two suffragettes Paul and Brown were forcefully fed this morning . . . the prison is in good order.' Olive Wharry, declared insane by the prison's medical officer, has complained about the ventilation in her cell. Mary Leigh, the first suffragette to endure forcible feeding, has objected about the condition of the exercise yard and the method of serving potatoes. Emmeline Pankhurst wants a copy of her warrant, and reports that the dustbins are unhealthy and offensive. Then we turn to the register of prisoners committed for want of sureties in the 1850s and carefully I open this ancient ledger that smells of dust and damp. One woman was sentenced to three months for assault. 'Wait,' says Dean, 'she was charged with a man, they'd both assaulted the same person. He got six months. But he was bailed and she wasn't.' Dean laughs. 'Oh the poor sod. At least she got out first.'

Finally my time is up and I'm escorted out of the conference room and back through the prison. 'You asked me earlier why I became a prison officer,' says Dean as we stand in the authorized personnel area. 'It's because I love what I do. I want to make a difference. The government says it's closing Holloway to treat women more humanely. But things had changed. Didn't we treat them humanely?' He looks at me as if he couldn't think of a bigger insult. Yet prison is a closed world to most people, we don't hear of what goes on unless there is a death or a riot, and very little has ever been written on the lives of prison staff, either in the past or now. Officers work largely out of public sight, generally viewed with fear or ridicule, and are still described as warders in the press. Until Stewart McLaughlin took me round Wandsworth, I'd never knowingly met a prison officer and, aside from Colin Allen, I'd never met a prison governor in my life. What has it been like to run the most famous jail for women that is now in the process of being closed down?

32

What is the Point of Prison?

When I arrive for my interview with Holloway's governor on 10 March, a 'state of alert' sign in reception says 'heightened' and I overhear a man in front of me saying he has come for a security meeting. Emily Thomas has been in her post for less than three months, and our meeting takes place in an area of the prison known as the Ivory Tower, in an overheated office with yellow walls and a purple carpet. 'You wouldn't believe,' she says, resting her hands on the table, 'how hard it is to move women out of Holloway Prison.' Emily is struggling to find secure hospital beds, for while a prison psychiatrist might recommend that a woman needs a bed, people at risk within the community might be allocated it first.

An efficient-looking woman in her early forties, she is a former Cambridge student who read history at Girton College. This was followed by a career in PR, including account officer for Head and Shoulders, the anti-dandruff shampoo, until one day she saw an advert for a prison graduate programme in the *Guardian*. In 1999 Emily spent a year as an officer at Pentonville, and then a year in Holloway, which she loved, although there were severe staff shortages. 'As a good feminist, I certainly knew about Holloway. I knew that the suffragettes had been held and force-fed here, and that Diana Mitford had . . . how should we say it, "lodged" here. And of course, Myra Hindley. Holloway is iconic and has a longer history than many other prisons.'

What is the point, I ask, of prison? She looks a little surprised, and as she lifts a hand to her throat I see the number 366 written in pen on her palm. 'My opinion,' she says, 'is that the point of prison is to rehabilitate people so they can go back to the community and live successful lives.'

When she heard that her predecessor Julia Killick was retiring Emily applied to be Holloway's governor, and shortly before the closure announcement she got a call. 'We have something to tell you,' she was informed, 'you'll be leading a closure.' Emily came in on the day the closure was publicly announced 'because I wanted to; I knew it would be emotional. The staff have been amazing, they were *so* upset.' Why were they so upset? She takes a deep breath: 'Because there is a sense of community, people love the place. There is something about Holloway Prison, it's what you feel when you're at the front line and you've got to take what is thrown at you and that makes people become a close team.'

Emily is the former governor of Cookham Wood in Kent, a male young offenders institution, and she says society has a mixed view of women in prison:

> They have complex problems and there is more sympathy in general for women in prison and their plights. But if people are in prison because they've been dealt a bad hand in life, growing up in poverty, being in care, excluded from school, witnessing domestic violence and substance abuse, then this applies to men too. It's quite a difficult idea that women shouldn't be in prison and that we have to make a different case for them. If victims become offenders, then that's the same with men.

I say that the vast majority of women inside are not a threat to public safety. 'Neither are men,' she says, 'just go and ask them at Wandsworth. If we're talking about prisoners in terms of harm people pose to others then the same is true of men and women.'

There were around 500 inmates here when the closure was announced; this morning the population is 366, which explains the number written on her hand. On 1 May women began to be 'decanted' to Downview; thirty left every week and the prison emptied fast.

Holloway's last ever governor picks up her coffee mug, emblazoned with the text 'promoting positive change and valuing lives at HMP Holloway', and then to my surprise she asks if I'd like to come back to witness the prison closing down.

★

A couple of weeks later I return to meet Simon Peters, branch chair of the Prison Officers' Association. There is a woman in reception today with a boy aged around seven who looks very smartly dressed, as if ready for something special. But he appears anxious by the surroundings, shivering and pressing himself up against the radiator by the desk. Simon Peters has been at Holloway for twelve years, following six years at Feltham Young Offenders Institution and he's waiting for me in the authorized personnel area. We walk along corridors that are starting to feel familiar, and into a tiny claustrophobic lift where I can't ignore the fact that I'm standing in close proximity to a man who is six foot seven. We stop at the staff mess, which is set out like a French bistro, with half a dozen tables covered in checkered tablecloths, each with a vase of fake flowers. Then Simon takes me down to his office, where the floor is covered in old blue lino, a filthy metal sink has a broken tap, and there are tiny flies floating in the air. On the walls are family photos and a poster: 'No to fascists and fascism in the workplace'.

I ask how he got into the prison service. 'It's quite a long story,' says Simon, who describes himself as a boy who just wanted to leave school. At seventeen he was a manager at a video shop, followed by outdoor security work, a one-year stint in the Israeli army and then a degree in business management. Worried that he would end up deskbound, at the age of twenty-two he got a job transporting prisoners between jails for the G4 Group, the security services company. 'I loved it, I absolutely loved it. I got into every single prison from Durham to the Isle of Wight. I was completely naïve about prison; I could sit there and read all about the prisoners, all their history, all the reports, and it was fascinating, plus the person was actually there in front of me to talk to.'

He explains that every jail has a different culture and atmosphere, and when he started at Feltham there were

few staff and a lot were ex-soldiers and they had a certain way of doing things. They were very disciplinarian and keen to resort to physical intervention. I challenged and reported things; staff were provoking prisoners so they could assault them. I ostracized myself because of my views. The fact people would see me and say, 'Jesus Christ, you're massive,' helped. But I'm soft-spoken; people say I have a soothing voice. I'm very calm, I don't shout and scream. Though I swear quite a lot.

Simon then decided to apply for a transfer to Holloway. 'I knew the place because my young offenders had mothers here, but on my first visit I was gobsmacked. There was no staff at all. The place was deserted. The women were just locked in and the mental healthcare was appalling. You had to walk down the centre of a landing because women had cleaning equipment in their rooms' – he points to a broom, bucket and mop in the corner of his office – 'and if they saw staff they didn't like they would push the broom handle through the hatch to hit you on the head.' But worst of all was the noise: 'Oh the wailing and the keening, women calling "sir . . . sir . . ." and "officer . . . officer . . ." It echoed everywhere. There were some very unwell women.'

He says what female prisoners need is vastly different from men: 'They have been victims of assault, domestic violence, gang rape, drug dealer rape; it was an eye-opener coming to Holloway and traumatic.' When he started there was no mentoring for staff:

> You were expected to grow a thick skin and carry on. The trick is to be empathetic but to not absorb, because that would be deadly. I have cried over these women, the violence, their problems. One woman begged me for a razor, saying she was hairy and needed to shave her legs and I asked a member of staff and they said yes. She was a huge woman and she snapped off the end of that razor and cut her arm all the way across.

He grasps his own arm to demonstrate, miming dragging a blade from his armpit all the way over his arm and round to his chest. 'She did it in front of us, her skin just flapped forward. And then I sat in a governor's office sobbing because it was my fault and I'd only tried to help.'

I ask my usual question: what is the point of prison? Simon makes a face, a slow grimace, and attempts to swat away the flies in the air. 'Prison is awful. Holloway is an amazing place with a great health service. What spoils it is there are not nice people.

What prison does is to contain them in order to change their behaviour but these women have been failed, by teachers, their GPs, social workers, police, courts, and then they are given to us and we're told, right, fix them.' So does prison work? 'For some. But there are dangerous, prolifically dangerous women. They make weapons in their cells: one woman made a garrotte out of two pencils and wire taken from a radio; she was going to use it on a member of staff; another made a whole hand, like a glove, out of radiator parts left over from smashing up her cell.' I ask him in what ways Holloway has changed since he's been here, apart from the fact he's now older and wiser. He nods. 'I'm still fat and bald though. What's changed is the way we deal with confrontation.' When Simon started there were 350 staff, now there are just 140. This is due to cuts, not because it's closing down, and the numbers have been dropping steadily over the past decade.

He has many personal stories to tell, such as the ex-prisoner who sends him a Christmas card every year, another who named her baby after him. But he tends not to tell people he's a prison officer, 'because of the adverse reaction; but secondary to that is they want to know everything and it's fucking annoying. So at parties, not that I go to parties, I end up being questioned all night. Some do put a uniform on and became fascist bastards who want to boss people about, and I enjoy weeding them out. But the others are passionate people and want to help.' He talks about the buzz and the adrenalin of the job, but also the trauma when someone dies in custody: 'We're committed, it's not just a job, it goes beyond that.'

As we get up to leave I see a shield in the corner of the room; it looks like something from a riot scene on TV and I ask if he ever uses it. 'All the time,' he says, explaining that officers use the shield to create a box around themselves for protection. Then he picks up a smaller one, shows me how it's used to cover the door hatch on a cell. I ask what the noise is as we step into the corridor where there is an ominous rumbling sound. 'It's the food trolleys,' says Simon, striding ahead. He says he has Obsessive Compulsive Disorder, that all staff have some element of OCD: 'You have to, we work to a very rigid routine but there is also the unexpected.

I'm OCD about when I get up, when I eat, everything is regimented. I have everything timed, down to my bowels.' I hurry behind him trying to catch up, glancing through doorways into rooms in the process of being emptied, piles of chairs and boxes of books, a hallway blocked with mattresses, fans and cupboards. 'What a waste,' says Simon. 'A waste of money, of resources . . . it's just a waste of everything. Most of this will just be chucked into skips. Pigeons are getting in' – he stops to unlock a door – 'and there have been rats in education.' I follow him outside; it's 11 a.m. and exercise time is about to begin.

By early May over two-thirds of the women have gone and I'm back at the prison with Chris Impey, managing editor of National Prison Radio. He's making a programme on Holloway's history and has asked me to share some of my research with the prisoners. I follow him into one of the classrooms and it's only when I get inside that I realize this is the very same room where I briefly taught twenty-six years ago. It's quite bare inside, a single blue pottery bowl on a window sill, a group of Formica tables set out as if for a conference. There are seven women waiting and it's as if I've gone back in time, their arms wrapped resentfully around their chests. I wonder what was said that made them decide to come to the education unit, and whether they are regretting it now. Most are young and black or mixed race; three look and speak just like my sixteen-year-old daughter.

I start unpacking my archives, spreading them out on the table, wondering if I've brought the right things and if anyone will be interested. 'Wow,' says one woman, picking up a large black and white photo of Holloway when it was a castle, 'was it really like this? It looks scary. I wouldn't want to go there. I couldn't have coped with that.' She turns to a picture of the Victorian staff. 'See how all the women are sitting on the ground? You can see the men are in charge.' Then she points at a picture of John Weatherhead, the governor from the 1860s who designed his own straitjacket: 'Ooh he's the man. He thinks he's the man. He has a beard just like Abraham Lincoln.' Another woman spots the griffins in one of the pictures and shouts, 'Look, they're out there!' and points out of the window to A block, while a third rushes to the library to get the history booklet written by officer Dean Barrow. The awkwardness of a few moments ago has gone.

We take turns reading out convictions from the 1850s. 'He got six months' hard labour for trying to kill his wife,' comments one woman, 'and this one got three months' hard labour for stealing a *handkerchief*.' She shakes her head. 'What sort of madness is this?' But what they really want to ask is: Women were executed here, weren't they? Where was it done, was it really from the tree outside in the courtyard? Where were they buried, are they still here? I talk about the two Edwardian baby farmers, hanged in 1903, and explain that Annie Walters gave a baby chlorodyne and was probably addicted to it herself. 'Is that the same as chloral?' asks a woman, referring to the sedative first used in Victorian times. 'They give that to us now.'

We read a letter from Edith Thompson to her friend Bessie, written two weeks before her death in 1923 after she lost her appeal, when her hopes for mercy and justice had been crushed and she realized 'how very difficult it is to fight prejudice'. The prisoner who has chosen to read the letter stumbles over the words. English is not her first language but it's the content that makes her voice crack. 'Edith Thompson was right,' she says, 'because when it's prejudice there's nothing you can do.'

The second thing they want to talk about is the suffragettes, and we read letters and diary extracts by Sylvia Pankhurst, Elsie Duval and Mary Richardson from when they were locked up in Holloway and forcibly fed. One woman says she can't believe what she's just heard and I think she has tears in her eyes. The others react with horror. Why would wardresses hold them down? It was orders, wasn't it? But why would women do that to other women? 'The suffragettes did it for us,' says one, 'they did all that so we can have the vote. I have a lot of admiration for them going through that for the sake of all of us.' I tell them about the suffragettes who bombed Holloway in the winter of 1913, detonating the explosives near the flats they can see from the exercise yard, and they laugh and cheer. They cheer even more when they hear about the suffragettes who attacked the medical officer with whips.

Holloway's last prisoners identify immediately with the women from the past. But they say nothing about their life in prison, or what injustice might have brought them here.

I ask what they think of the closure, and one woman says she is being moved to Bronzefield: 'Holloway is okay; there's good and bad. I'm anxious about moving, my family are in London. I don't want to leave but I don't have a choice.' Another says that when they were first told the news, 'we all said, yeah, whatever,' but now as the landings close down 'it's really unsettling, we have a hard time in here but it's still sad to leave.'

In the world outside Holloway there have been growing concerns over what will happen to the site, with public meetings and protests. The Reclaim Justice Network, which includes Women in Prison and Kill the Housing Bill, wants the land signed over for social housing and no new prisons built. A week after my visit with National Prison Radio the newly formed campaign group Reclaim Holloway! holds a demonstration to demand 50 per cent affordable council housing and community services on the prison site. They have organized a petition, set up a website and urged people to write to their MP. The demonstrators started outside London Metropolitan University, and when I get to the prison they haven't yet arrived but an elderly woman is waiting. 'Where is everyone?' she asks furiously. 'Does nobody *care*?' Then there is a low roar from Parkhurst Road and the marchers arrive. They hold placards and banners: Kill the Housing Bill, Build Homes Not Prisons.

The demonstrators know exactly what should happen here, because once Holloway is pulled down, millions of pounds could be put into housing and a women's centre, and small units could be built for the very few women who pose a threat to society. But the way the prison system has been run in the UK over the past century and a half shows we rarely learn from our mistakes. There has never been agreement on the purpose of prison, and it has rarely been able to rehabilitate. Holloway has been used to lock away the most powerless in society, and to remove those who threaten the status quo. Prison has been a way for successive governments to demonstrate they are 'tough on crime', yet it has had no impact on the level of crime and now Britain locks up more people than anywhere else in Europe but for Turkey. Conservative Home Secretary Michael Howard once declared that 'prison works', but the only way it works is to punish, control and contain. It doesn't lower crime or lead to reform, and in most cases it doesn't make society any safer.

On Friday, 17 June 2016 the last prisoner ever to be released from Holloway will walk out of the gates, after spending over a year and a half inside. I meet her a few days earlier, on the roof top exercise yard where she sits with a prison officer 'Loads of officers have told me I'll be the last woman to leave,' says Holly (not her real name).

> It's the end of an institution, isn't it? And it's just about money. They will build it into flats and rich people will live here and they say there will be affordable housing but there won't be. It's disgusting that they didn't tell the officers they were closing it down. I'm a prisoner and I'm saying that! Most girls prefer Holloway to other prisons; it's a community. People have been coming in and out of here for thirty years and we worry about them now.

Holly tells me she's a Listener, having been trained by the Samaritans.

> I volunteered because they have helped me in the past. You hear heavy shit, paedophiles, murder, rape . . . I'll volunteer for the Samaritans when I get out. I got four years; it's a long time to be out of society. I'm looking forward to just being able to walk where I want to walk without keys jangling behind me. I'm coming out on licence and if I muck up once I could be back for two years. They let people out and they have nowhere to live, but they expect us to start life again.

★

A week before Holloway's official closure, day care centre manager Carrie Fitzgerald invites me to see an exhibition she has put together for the commemorative barbecue on 16 July. There will be tea and squash but no alcohol; the prison's flag will be taken down. Inside the day centre there is a massive poster, 'Goodbye Holloway', on which prisoners and staff have written comments: *This is social cleansing at its worst*; *You'll never recreate this sanctuary anywhere else.* Some have written apologies for things they have done; one woman has scribbled, 'Oh my God where will I end up?' Carrie shows me into a room where every single inch of the wall is covered with drawings and paintings of children. Above me, hanging from the ceiling, are dozens and dozens of children made from cloth and wool. They were made by a woman who was addicted to kat and who had her four children taken away. 'Every day she drew them,' explains Carrie, 'in every way she could.'

I walk back through Holloway for the last time, past a pile of plastic dolls from the mother and baby unit and the chapel's wooden cross lying in a corridor. The doors are all unlocked now. Holloway is a decommissioned prison. Outside bright red poppies are growing among the weeds; massive skips are full of broken furniture. I come to the yard at the back, see a metal trolley with four words graffitied on the side: 'Bad Girls is D3'. The prisoners have gone and so have most of the staff; the terror to evil-doers to some and the concrete parent to others is finally being demolished. What will happen to the place now?

Conclusion

Reclaim Holloway

On a muggy Saturday afternoon in May 2017 eight women climbed undetected through an open window at Holloway Prison's deserted visitors' centre, occupied the building and claimed squatters' rights. Outside around 150 demonstrators had gathered to demand that the prison land be given back to the community. Some had already climbed on to the roof of the visitors' centre, the spot where the chaplain's grand house once stood in Victorian times, unfurled banners calling for affordable housing and let off coloured smoke. Then they stood, their hands raised in triumph against the sky.

The press wrongly reported that Sisters Uncut, a feminist direct action group, had occupied the prison itself, but their action was symbolic enough. They had taken control of a building that was part of one of the most famous women's prisons in the world.

'We are protesting cuts to domestic violence services,' explains Gabe, a Sisters Uncut member, when I arrive the next day. 'The Tories want an industrial prison complex; it's the same thing the government wanted when Holloway was built.' She says that 46 per cent of women in prison are survivors of domestic violence, and if they had received the necessary support then many wouldn't have ended up in jail. I ask how long they had been planning the occupation. Gabe smiles. 'For a while. We wanted to reclaim a site of violence and use the space for the public good.'

Around seventy police officers arrived on the scene, along with four vans and a fire engine. 'They over-exaggerated,' says Gabe, 'it was a waste of resources. They cornered us down that alley there, it was intimidating. They said this was a crime scene, and then they cordoned it off.'

★

Holloway Prison has always been a crime scene, a site of state-sanctioned crimes against women committed in the name of justice and security. It has been a place of violence for 164 years; women have been driven to prison through violence, and often met with violence within. Holloway was always designed to hold the most vulnerable people in society – which is why at the time of its closure so many of those inside had backgrounds of abuse, addiction, mental health problems and poverty.

Victorian prisons were specifically built to hold the working classes. Holloway's Edwardian governor Richard Quinton pointed out that prison wasn't meant for 'educated convicts', and when more privileged prisoners fell foul of the law Holloway designed new divisions for them. Its purpose was to discipline the poorer segments of the population and it became a tool used by the state to exert control in terms of class, and then gender and race. Holloway punished women and girls who violated laws that defined accept-able feminine behaviour, whether a love affair or prostitution, 'masquerading' as a man, or ringing the Prime Minister's doorbell. It removed and controlled women who were seen as difficult, and who refused, or were unable, to fit in.

Holloway's car park is empty today; the prison signs have gone, as have the hanging baskets of geraniums. For the past year there have been two security guards based in the visitors' centre, although it's not clear where they were at the time of the Sisters Uncut occu-pation. The door to reception is padlocked and little remains of the prison inside but for the Victorian griffins that once adorned the entrance pillars. They are waiting to be taken to their new home in the Museum of London, along with the Holloway Quilt from 2012, made by 'birds doing bird'.

Inside the visitors' centre, however, the place has come alive again. The lights are on, a pink banner reads 'This is a political occupation', there is the sound of music and the smell of cooking and incense. A woman stands in the canteen, behind piles of fresh bread, bananas and oranges, while a stew simmers on the hob. The eight members of Sisters Uncut, as well as some of their colleagues, will be staying here all week. They are running a community festival, with workshops on women's well-being, self-defence and legal rights, and it starts in just over an hour. A whiteboard maps out today's events, beginning with '8 a.m. breakfast' and then '11 a.m. propaganda'.

The Reclaim Holloway Network has now proposed a Women's Building on this site, which will generate income through a café and lecture theatres as well as providing 'a living legacy' for the prison's historic connection with suffragettes and the women's movement. Today the window seats in the visitors' centre have been covered with cushions, embroidered with the old suffragette slogan, 'Deeds not Words'. Sisters Uncut see themselves as the modern link in the chain going right the way back to the militant campaigns of the early 1900s, and one of their aims is to highlight why women end up in jail.

Half of women in prison today have mental health problems – anxiety and depression are made far worse by the trauma of being locked up in prison – and nearly a third have had a previous psychiatric admission, compared to 10 per cent of men. Almost 50 per cent of women in prison have tried to kill themselves at some point in their life – twice the rate of men in prison and seven times higher than in the general population. Sending a woman to prison does nothing to address the problems that may have driven her there in the first place, whether abuse, racism, grief or illness.

A year after Holloway closed the inquest into Sarah Reed's death was finally held. The jury found that unacceptable delays in psychiatric assessment, the removal of her anti-psychotic medicine, and failures in care contributed to her death. She had been on remand for over three months, waiting for two psychiatric reports to confirm whether she was fit to stand trial for the alleged assault in the mental health unit. The first report, completed a few weeks before she died, stated that she was not.

Yet Sarah remained at Holloway, where she spent her last days chanting, screaming and banging, or in a trance-like state. Prison notes described her as 'completely psychotic', but the twice-hourly suicide checks were reduced to one an hour. Four officers were required to be present before her cell was unlocked, as she was deemed too dangerous.

Visits from her family and lawyer were cancelled, and in the last five days of her life her cell wasn't cleaned. She wasn't allowed a shower and was kept in virtual isolation. The jury were not convinced that she had intended to take her own life. 'Sarah Reed was a woman in torment,' says Deborah Coles, Director of INQUEST, 'she needed specialist care not prison.' Her mental health was treated as a discipline problem and the 'inhumane and degrading treatment she was subjected to must result in an end to the use of prison for women'.

Very few female prisoners have ever posed a threat to society; instead most have been victims of circumstance and, in one way or another, victims of men. Eighty-four per cent of women sentenced to prison have committed a non-violent offence, often theft in order to support their families. Men are responsible for 88 per cent of crimes against the person, 90 per cent of murders and 98 per cent of sex offences.

Frances Crook, from the Howard League for Penal Reform, believes that if other agencies offered sufficient help with debt, mental health, drug and alcohol abuse, then there would be twenty to fifty women left in England and Wales who require a custodial sentence. 'Prison is not a safe place for women to be,' she tells me, 'and closing Holloway and shipping them off doesn't solve it.'

But the number of women being sent to jail is on the rise again; there are just over 4,000 female prisoners in England and Wales, the highest in five years.

And once again the government is set on a 'prison-building revolution', just as in the nineteenth century. In the 1970s, when the old castle jail started to be demolished, Radical Alternatives to Prison argued for a rethink of the nature and purpose of prison. But campaigners weren't listened to then, when the female prison population was a fifth of what it is now, so will those arguing along very similar lines be listened to now, nearly fifty years later?

I leave the visitors' centre and set off to walk around the prison perimeter, past chained metal gates and a faded sign banning mobile phones. I come to the old officers' block of flats, which rises directly over the prison, near enough to call out a message. It was these flats that caused such conflict in the 1980s, when staff and prisoners could look directly through each other's bedroom windows.

When I started this book I assumed prison officers enjoyed locking people up and having a power they might not have in the outside world. But instead they talk repeatedly about wanting to help those who have 'fallen through the cracks', they feel fulfilled and say prison is like a 'family'.

Prison staff have – right the way through Holloway's history – consistently challenged the system in which they work and tried to make it more humane, from Victorian wardress Louisa Henson who cried over the prisoners, to the warder who was fined for bringing a boy plum pudding and Reverend William Morrison who lost his job for calling the English prison system a disastrous failure.

Prison staff, especially women, have always been encouraged to have a closer relationship with female prisoners than with men. Despite their reputation for colluding in forcible feeding, women officers have been known for their sympathy and understanding. Constance Lytton was held by a wardress while she sobbed in her cell; the Poplar councillors found the officers 'exceedingly kind'; the family of Edith Thompson wrote to thank the governor and all his staff for their consideration before she was executed. Holloway's modern officers meanwhile were shocked at the news that the prison was closing, because they worried about who would look after the women then.

In 2017 the government launched a new prison service recruitment campaign, with the question, 'Is it in you to be a prison officer?' It's a far cry from prison officer recruitment campaigns of the past; there is no mention of the social worker aspect of the job that attracted women like Judy Gibbons in the 1950s. 'If you care for people and mind what happens to them, why not consider a career as a Prison Officer?' asked a Home Office recruitment booklet from 1977. The modern-day advert warns, 'Like anything worth doing, this job isn't easy.'

It's a massive understatement: the UK's prisons are overcrowded and understaffed once again, and, just as in 1990 when I first went into Holloway as a trainee teacher, prisons are rarely out of the news. In November 2016 around 10,000 prison officers staged a twenty-four-hour protest over a 'surge in violence' in jails, and the following month several hundred prisoners were involved in a twelve-hour riot at HMP Birmingham. The inquiry into Sarah Reed's death confirmed the popular belief that prison officers don't care for those in their charge. But Holloway's history also shows that many do and that it is the penal system itself that is flawed, not necessarily the people who live and work in it.

I return to Parkhurst Road, see a glossy sign advertising a new block of flats, and then a side gate near the prison's curvy wall, splattered with stains like white moss. Litter is piled in front of the gate, a scattering of fox shit and burger cartons. I look through the wire mesh: there's a long green piece of cloth hanging over the wall; it trails right the way down and along the ground as if someone has just escaped and left their rope behind.

The use, value and ownership of this land on which the prison sits is key to the future, just as it was in Victorian times. In the first six months after Holloway's closure the Ministry of Justice spent nearly £140,000 on utility bills alone, which suggests it expects a large return on its investment. One of the most valuable sites in the women's estate will be sold off, not to improve conditions for female prisoners but to fund new prisons for men. When Holloway first opened, residents objected to the proximity of a penal institution and feared local property prices would go down. Now, with the closure, the opposite is happening.

On Dalmeny Avenue a former Edwardian hostel for low-waged working women has been turned into an empty building site. There's an 'illustrative view' on the wall showing how the finished project will look, a group of city slickers walking along a pristine pavement towards their shiny new homes.

This was the road where the suffragettes bombed the prison from the back garden in 1913, where the Discharged Prisoners Aid Society established a hostel in the 1920s, and where penal reformer Margery Fry could see the great prison building from her bedroom window before visiting Edith Thompson in the condemned cell.

This is where I stood in November 2015 after the closure was announced, when a woman let me into the flats and I tried to peer over the wall, wanting to know about the women inside.

The story of Holloway Prison is the story of how women have been treated in our justice system, what crimes — real or imagined — they committed, who found them guilty and why. It is a tale both of victimization and resistance. Women have been punished, tortured and executed here; its inmates have been demonized as dangerous, unnatural women. But newcomers have often found a place of friendship, support and solidarity, and while jail has been a shocking revelation for some, it has been a place of safety for others.

Ever since Holloway opened, the press has played a large part in shaping public opinion about female prisoners. Who was guilty and how could we tell? Was it the hat they wore at court or the fact they showed no emotion? Women have been held up to different expectations and standards: were they obedient wives and mothers, did they know their place? It was the press, as much as the courts, that put women on trial and decided if their punishment was suitable.

So will women be treated more humanely now that Holloway has closed, or will they continue to be sentenced like Selina Salter in the 1860s, 'not in the expectation that the punishment would do her any good' but because the authorities could not think what else to do with her? As yet the government has not suggested anything better to put in its place; instead women have again been disappeared, this time outside London.

The House of Correction was always intended to hold women who 'can't be helped', and to incarcerate those who refused to be 'good girls'. Now the flag has been lowered, the women have been decanted, the officers transferred. Will there be a Women's Building here, a living legacy to the prison's inmates, or will the inhabitants of luxury flats sleep peacefully in their new apartments, undisturbed by the spirits of Holloway's past?

Acknowledgements

How do you condense 164 years of prison history into a single book? When I first started *Bad Girls* I was amazed that only one book on Holloway's history had ever been published, John Camp's 1974 *Holloway Prison: The Place and the People*. At just 155 pages long, it was written with the support of the Home Office to coincide with the prison's rebuild, and what was left out was almost as interesting as what was left in.

I wanted to write a fuller story of the prison and the women inside, but I was soon overwhelmed. The first draft of *Bad Girls* was nearly three times the length of this finished book and with each draft I had to cut stories out – whether Lady Ida Sitwell, who in 1915 clutched the dock with a bottle of smelling salts in her hand, Helen Duncan, a spiritualist medium from Perthshire imprisoned in World War Two under the Witchcraft Act, or Christine Keeler and Mandy Rice-Davies jailed during the Profumo Affair of the 1960s. I wanted to try and focus on less well-known women, but this was hard when they tended not to be interviewed or to write about their experiences. When it came to prison staff – especially officers – then it was just as difficult. They were not supposed to speak about their job, let alone publicly.

Several people started me off or kept me going along the way and I'm very grateful for their support, help and trust. In particular Jean Winchester (who writes under the name Molly Cutpurse) who freely shared her knowledge and answered endless emails; Holloway officer Dean Barrow who rescued the priceless archives from the prison and without whom this could never have been written; Stewart McLaughlin, curator of the Wandsworth Prison Museum, who knows everything there is to know about prison history; and Dr Helen Johnston from the University of Hull and Professor Yvonne Jewkes from the University of Brighton who previously researched the history of Holloway from 1902 to 1945 and who immediately offered tips and enthusiasm.

I'm indebted to all interviewees for reading and correcting drafts, and to those who provided invaluable documents and photographs, in particular Judy Gibbons and Ann Hair, who patiently responded to dozens of panicked emails, as well as Colin Allen, Liz Hogarth, Bill Hetherington and Ruth Clarke.

Thank you to Muriel Allen, Jennifer Adams Young, , Nicola Avery at the London Metropolitan Archives, Beverley Cook at the Museum of London, Howard Falksohn, archivist at the Wiener Library, Laura Walker at the British Library, Margaret Butler who is writing a biography of Joan Henry, Ros Hutchinson, James Yorke, Jane Hickman, and to interviewees who prefered to remain anonymous.

Thanks also to Dr Tom Clark from the University of Sheffield, who is researching Myra Hindley, and Danish author Kirstine Kloster Andersen, who is researching Vera Erikson, for providing me with insight into their own work as well as copies of documents from the National Archives. I'm grateful to the support of my agent Robert Kirby, the first agent to wholeheartedly agree that this was not a 'niche' book but an important story that deserved to be told, and to my editor Kate Craigie for seriously knocking things into shape.

A final thank you to the prisoners and staff who agreed to speak to me, Governor Emily Thomas for letting me into Holloway, Alice Booth, senior press officer for women at the Ministry of Justice, and the Retired Prison Governors Association.

Illustration Credits

The author and the publishers would like to thank those interviewed in the book who have generously granted permission for their own personal photographs to be reproduced.

The location and date of the picture of Edith Thompson and her sister Avis are uncertain. If anyone does recognize the location please contact r.weis@ucl.ac.uk.

Picture Research by Jane Smith

Bridgeman/Holloway Prison: Willis Collection, 1895 (b/w photo), English Photographer, (19th century) / London Metropolitan Archives, City of London. E Wing: courtesy of Wandsworth Prison Museum. May Caroline, Dowager Duchess of Sutherland: courtesy of Dr Bruno Bubna-Kasteliz. Holloway nursery and prison sewing room: courtesy of Howard League for Penal Reform archive at the Modern Records Centre, University of Warwick. Annie Walters and Amelia Sach: courtesy of the Mayor's Office of Policing and Crime. Alice Hawkins: courtesy of Peter Barratt and the Hawkins family. Suffragettes exercising in the yard: Getty Images/ Heritage Images / Museum of London. Suffragette postcard: courtesy of Hunter Davies. Christabel Pankhurst: Alamy/Heritage Image Partnership Ltd. Wheeldon family: Topfoto.co.uk. Edith Thompson: copyright © Rene Weis. Colonel Victor Barker: Mirrorpix. Diana Mosley: Getty Images/ ullstein bild Dtl. Ruth Ellis: Alamy/Trinity Mirror/ Mirrorpix. Judy Gibbons: courtesy of Judy Gibbons. Zoe Progl: Alamy/Keystone Pictures USA. 1970s recruitment booklet: courtesy of Ann Hair, ex-Assistant Governor at H.M.P. Holloway. Greenham Common: Alamy/Trinity Mirror/ Mirrorpix. Sisters Uncut: Alamy/ Matthew Chattle.

Notes and Sources

Bad Girls draws on a wide array of sources and many important documents relating to Holloway Prison, its inmates and staff, can be found at the following archives:

The London Metropolitan Archives, City of London, is home to the HM Prison Holloway collection, CLA/003. Some documents are available for public inspection; others can only be viewed with prior permission.

The Museum of London holds the archive of the Suffragette Fellowship, donated in 1950, a vast collection of papers and personal memorabilia relating to the militant Suffragette campaign.

Wandsworth Prison Museum is situated in the prison's North Gate Car Park and run by a volunteer Hon.Curator, Stewart McLaughlin. It covers Wandsworth Prison's 166-year history, and also contains a small selection of documents relating to Holloway.

The Women's Library, London University: London School of Economics, holds a collection of printed material, archives and 3D objects relating to campaigns for women's rights and equality, including the suffrage movement and the Greenham Common peace movement.

The Imperial War Museum's Sound Archive is the largest oral history collection of its type in the world and contains oral interviews with many women who were incarcerated in Holloway, particularly during World War Two.

The National Archives holds papers relating to several of Holloway's former inmates, including suffragette Olive Wharry, wartime spy Vera Erickson and Myra Hindley.

Chapter 1: The Model Prison

Impey, Chris, 'A Brief History of HMP Brixton, London's Oldest Prison', http://www.brixtonbuzz.com, 2014

Jackson, Lee, 'The Dictionary of Victorian London', http://www.victorianlondon.org/

Lea, John, 'The Development of the Modern Prison in England', http://www.bunker8.pwp.blueyonder.co.uk/history/36808.htm, 2004

London Metropolitan Archives, CLA/003/PR/06/001 Register of prisoners committed for want of sureties at City New Prison Holloway, 1852–1868

McLaughlin, Stewart, *Wandworth Prison: A History*, Wandsworth Prison Museum, 2001

Zedner, Lucia, *Women, Crime and Custody in Victorian England*, Oxford University Press, 1991

Chapter 2: The Duchess of Holloway Jail

Aylmer, Alfred, 'Detective Day at Holloway Prison', *The Windsor Magazine*, 1897

Bell, Gilbert T., *A Prospect of Sutherland: The Building of a Castle and the Making of a Duchess*, Birlinn Ltd, 1995

McKenna, Neil, *The Secret Life Of Oscar Wilde*, Arrow, 2004

Mitchell, Ian, 'Duchess Mary Caroline Michell', http://www.devon-mitchells.co.uk/getperson.php?personID=I9&tree=Bruton

Proceedings of the Old Bailey, 'The Trial of Annie Frost (aka Mrs Gordon Baillie)', 22 October 1888, https://www.oldbaileyonline.org/browse.jsp?div=t18881022-938

Stead, W. T., 'My First Imprisonment', E. Marlborough & Co, 1886, http://www.attackingthedevil.co.uk/steadworks/imprisonment.php

Thompson, Brian, *A Monkey Among Crocodiles: The Life, Loves and Lawsuits of Mrs Georgina Weldon – a disastrous Victorian*, HarperCollins, 2000

Yorke, James, *Lancaster House: London's Greatest Town House*, Merrell Publishers, 2001

Chapter 3: The Baby Farmers

Banks, Stephen, *The British Execution*, Shire Publications, 2013

Fielding, Steve, *Pierrepoint: A Family of Executioners*, John Blake, 2006

Grey, Daniel J. R., 'Discourses of Infanticide in England, 1880–1922', unpublished PhD thesis, Roehampton University, http://roehampton. openrepository.com/roehampton/handle/10142/47339

Homrighaus, Ruth Ellen, 'Baby Farming: The Care of Illegitimate Children in England, 1860–1943', unpublished PhD thesis, University of North Carolina

Chapter 4: Turnkeys and Colonels

'A Short History of Prison Visiting', http://www.naopv.com/A_Short_ History.htm

Glen, W. Cunningham, *Prison Act, 1865: with Other Statutes and Parts of Statutes in Force Relating to Gaols and Prisons and an Extensive Index to the Whole*, Shaw and Sons, 1865

Henson, Louisa, Diary, 1872, courtesy of HM Prison Holloway officer Dean Barrow

Johnston, Helen, 'Gendered Prison Work: Female Prison Officers in the Local Prison System, 1877–1939', *Howard Journal of Criminal Justice*, Vol. 53, Issue 2, May 2014

Lombroso, Prof. Caesar, and Ferrero, William, *The Female Offender*, D. Appleton and Company, 1895

North London News, 'The City Prison, Holloway,' 27 September, 4, 11, 18 and 25 October 1862

Robin, Gerald D., 'Pioneers in Criminology: William Douglas Morrison (1852–1943)', *Journal of Criminal Law and Criminology*, Vol. 55, Issue 1, March 1964

Thomas, J. E., *English Prison Officer Since 1850: A Study in Conflict*, Routledge & Kegan Paul Books, 1972

'Victorian Crime and Punishment', http://vcp.e2bn.org/teachers/11466-timeline.html

Chapter 5: The Hollowayettes

'Alice Hawkins Suffragette – a Sister of Freedom', http://www.alicesuffragette.co.uk/

Crawford, Elizabeth, 'Woman and her Sphere', https://womanandhersphere.com

Holloway Jingles, Museum of London, Suffragette Fellowship Collection, 1912, reference 50.82/317

Lytton, Constance, and Warton, Jane, *Prisons and Prisoners: Some Personal Experiences*, William Heinemann, 1914

Pankhurst, Emmeline, *My Own Story*, Eveleigh Nash, 1914

Pankhurst, Sylvia, *The Suffragette Movement: An Intimate Account of Persons and Ideals*, Longmans, Green and Co., 1931

Purvis, June, 'The Prison Experiences of the Suffragettes in Edwardian Britain', *Women's History Review*, Vol. 4, 1995

Quinton, Richard Frith, *Crime and Criminals, 1876-1910*, Longmans, Green & Co., 1910

Suffragettes 'In and Out of Prison' game and puzzle, The Women's Library, TWL/2004/1089

Chapter 6: Forcible Feeding

Elsie Duval's prison diary: 1913, The Women's Library, reference /D/33

Holloway Prison's Nominal Register: 1912, Wandsworth Prison Museum

Letter from Constance Craig to OW Specks, 4 March 1912, The Women's Library, reference 10/54/124

Macpherson, Deirdre, *The Suffragette's Daughter, Betty Archdale: Her Life of Feminism, Cricket, War and Education*, Rosenberg, 2002

Miller, Ian, '"A Prostitution of the Profession?" Forcible Feeding, Prison Doctors, Suffrage and the British State, 1909–1914', *Social History of Medicine* Vol. 26, Issue 2, January 2013

Papers of Katie Gliddon: 1900-1965, The Women's Library, 7KGG

Papers of Mary Ann Rawle: 1906-c1974, The Women's Library, 7MAR/04

Chapter 7: The Fight is Won

Hopkinson, Miriam, 'Suffragettes at Kew', http://www.kew.org/blogs/library-art-and-archives/suffragettes-kew

McGowan, Joe, 'Constance Georgina de Markievicz', http://www.sligo-heritage.com/archMark.htm

Markievicz, Countess Constance, *Prison Letters of Countess Markievicz*, Virago, 1987

Old Bailey Proceedings, 'Olive Wharry, Damage to Property, Arson, 4 March 1913', https://www.oldbaileyonline.org/browse.jsp?id=t19130304-69&div=t19130304-69&terms=olive_wharry#highlight

Olive Wharry's medical report: National Archives, http://www.national-archives.gov.uk/education/resources/cats-and-mice/olive-wharry-medical-report/

Olive Wharry's scrapbook 1911–1928: The British Library, Manuscript Collection, MS 49976

Whitmore, Dr Richard, *Alice Hawkins and the Suffragette Movement in Edwardian Leicester*, Breedon Books, 2007

Chapter 8: The First World War

'A Miscarriage of Justice', http://www.alicewheeldon.org/about/

Chandler, F.W., *Political Spies and Provocative Agents*, Sheffield, 1936

Hetherington, Bill, 'The Wheeldon Case', *Housmans Peace Diary 2017*, Housmans Bookshop

Hiley, Nicholas, 'Internal Security in Wartime: The Rise and Fall of PMS2, 1915–1917', *Intelligence and National Security*, Vol. 1, Issue 3, 1986, pp. 395–415

Jackson, John, 'Losing the Plot: The Trial of Alice Wheeldon', *History Today*, Vol. 57, May 2007

Melikan, R.A., ed., *Domestic and International Trials, 1700–2000: The Trial in History, Volume II*, Manchester University Press, 2003

Rippon, Nicola, *The Plot to Kill Lloyd George: The Story of Alice Wheeldon and the Peartree Conspiracy*, Wharncliffe Books, 2009

Rowbotham, Sheila, 'Alice Wheeldon: a False Accusation, and Why the Case Still Matters', *Independent*, 16 April 2015

Rowbotham, Sheila, *Friends of Alice Wheeldon: The Anti-War Activist Accused of Plotting to Kill Lloyd George*, Pluto Press, 2015

Simkin, John, 'Alice Wheeldon', Spartacus, 1997, http://spartacus-educational.com/CRIwheeldonA.htm

'The World is My Country', http://theworldismycountry.info/posters/poster-3-alice-wheeldon-was-a-prophet/

Thomson, Basil, *Odd People: Hunting Spies in the First World War*, Biteback Publishing, 2015

Thomson, Basil, *The Story of Scotland Yard*, Grayson & Grayson, 1935

West, Nigel, *Historical Dictionary of World War I Intelligence*, Rowman & Littlefield, 2014

Chapter 9: 'The Messalina of Ilford'

Hodgkinson, Peter, *The International Library of Essays on Capital Punishment*, Volume 3, Routledge, 2016

London Metropolitan Archives, City of London CLA/003/PR/04/002 Correspondence and papers relating to Edith Thompson, 1922–2012

Obituaries of Dr John Morton, *British Journal of Psychiatry* (July 1935) and *British Medical Journal* (June 1935)

Weis, René, *Criminal Justice: The True Story of Edith Thompson*, Hamish Hamilton, 1988

Chapter 10: Reform

Bennett, Rachel, 'Debates over the Appointment of Female Governors and Medical Officers in Women's Prisons', March 2017, https://histprisonhealth.com/2017/03/15/appointment-of-women-to-senior-roles-in-womens-prisons/

Gore, Elizabeth, *The Better Fight: The Story of Dame Lilian Barker*, Geoffrey Bles, 1965

Chapter 11: Celebrity Prisoners

Collis, Rose, *Colonel Barker's Monstrous Regiment*, Virago, 2002

Harskamp, Jaap, and Dijstelberge, Paul, 'Bliss and Blitz', April 2012, https://abeautifulbook.wordpress.com/2012/04/21/1369/

Chapter 12: Enemy Aliens

Borchard, Ruth, *We Are Strangers Here: An 'Enemy Alien' in Prison in 1940*, Vallentine Mitchell, 2008

Brinson, Charmian, 'In the Exile of Internment: German-Speaking Women Interned by the British During the Second World War', *Politics and Culture in Twentieth-century Germany*, ed. William Niven and James Jordan, Camden House, 2003, pp. 63–88

Brinson, Charmian, '"Please Tell the Bishop of Chichester": George Bell and the Internment Crisis of 1940', *Contemporary Church History,*

Vandenhoeck & Ruprecht (GmbH & Co. KG), 2008, pp. 287–299

Imperial War Museum, Margot Pottlitzer, 1978, catalogue number 3816.

Imperial War Museum, Suzanne Schwarzenberger, 1980, catalogue number 4591.

Kershaw, Roger, 'Collar the lot! Britain's Policy of Internment During the Second World War', National Archives blog, 2015, http://blog.nationalarchives.gov.uk/blog/collar-lot-britains-policy-internment-second-world-war/

Linton (Liebermann) family papers, The Wiener Library for the Study of the Holocaust and Genocide, WL1851. The collection includes correspondence relating to the family's internment (1851/2), and a transcript of Susanna's diary written during her stay at Holloway prison in 1940 (1851/3)

London Metropolitan Archives, City of London CLA/003/PR/02/025 Convict nominal register, Jan–Oct 1939, not available for general access

Chapter 13: Fascists and Spies

Goldman, Aaron L., 'Defence Regulation 18B: Emergency Internment of Aliens and Political Dissenters in Great Britain During World War II', *Journal of British Studies*, Vol. 12, No. 2, Cambridge University Press, May 1973,

Gottlieb, Julie V., *Feminine Fascism: Women in Britain's Fascist Movement, 1923–45*, I.B. Tauris, 2003

London Metropolitan Archives, City of London CLA/003/PR/02/026 Convict nominal register, May 1941– June 1942, not available for public access

Mass Observation, File Report number 2198, January 1945. Quoted with permission of Curtis Brown, London, on behalf of The Trustees of the Mass Observation Archive, University of Sussex

Mitford, Diana, *A Life of Contrasts*, Gibson Square, 2009

National Archives, Vera Erickson, The Security Service: Personal (PF Series) Files, Reference KV 2

Searle, Adrian, *The Spy Beside the Sea: The Extraordinary Wartime Story of Dorothy O'Grady*, The History Press, 2012

Simpson, Alfred William Brian, *In the Highest Degree Odious: Detention Without Trial in Wartime Britain*, Clarendon Press, 1992

Chapter 14: Pacifists

Bales, Mitzi, 'They said "No" to War: British Women Conscientious Objectors in World War II', *Women and Conscientious Objection – An Anthology*, ed. Ellen Elster and Majken Jul Sørensen, War Resisters' International, 2010, http://www.wri-irg.org/es/node/11902

'Bulletin of the Central Board for Conscientious Objectors', March 1944, provided by the Peace Pledge Union

Childs, Peter, 'Woman of Substance', *Chemistry World,* January 2003 http://www.rsc.org/chemistryworld/issues/2003/january/substance.asp

Hetherington, Bill, 'British Pacifism in World War Two', Peace Pledge Union, http://www.ppu.org.uk/pacifism/pacww2.html

Imperial War Museum, Stella St John interview, 1971, catalogue number 4997. Copyright IWM and used with permission.

'Jailed for their Beliefs, BBC News Online (19 October 2000), http://news.bbc.co.uk/1/hi/uk/978638.stm

Kramer, Ann, *Conscientious Objectors of the Second World War: Refusing to Fight*, Pen & Sword Books, 2013

London Metropolitan Archives, CLA/003/ST/03/003 Wartime requests to prison governor, includes POA meetings, 1947–1957

Lonsdale, Kathleen & Others, *Some Account of Life in Holloway Prison for Women*, Prison Medical Reform Council, 1943

POA History in Prisons, http://www.poauk.org.uk/index.php?poa-history-in-prisons

St John, Stella, *A Prisoner's Log,* The Howard League for Penal Reform, 1944 http://blogs.lse.ac.uk/library/2014/04/28/a-prisoners-log-part-1/

Chapter 15: The Lady Governor and the Borstal Girls

'Holloway Prison (Conditions)', House of Commons Debate, *Hansard,* Vol. 433, 14 February 1947

Jacobson, Sydney, 'Inside Holloway Prison', *Picture Post*, September 1947

London Metropolitan Archives, CLA/003/AD/01/001 Governor's Journal, Lady Charity Taylor, September 1949–November 1955, not available for general access

London Metropolitan Archives, CLA/003/AD/01/002 Governor's Journal, Lady Charity Taylor and J.E. Kelley, December 1955–

October 1962, not available for general access

London Metropolitan Archives, CLA/003/HB/02/001 Borstal Allocation Book, – not available for general access

Perera, Kathryn, 'For what we have done and for what we have failed to do: Barbara Ayrton Gould', History of Labour Women, LabourList, 2011, http://labourlist.org/2011/01/for-what-we-have-done-and-for-what-we-have-failed-to-do-barbara-ayrton-gould/

Yates, Daniel, 'Obituary: Lady Taylor', *Independent*, 7 January 1998

Chapter 16: Protest Against Evil

Ballinger, Anette, *Dead Woman Walking: Executed Women in England & Wales, 1900–1955*, University of Sheffield, 1997

Christou, Jean, '"Middle aged, unattractive and foreign": the Cypriot murderess', *Cyprus Mail*, January 2016

'Haunted by Her Memories', *Northumberland Gazette*, August 2005 http://www.northumberlandgazette.co.uk/news/local-news/haunted-by-her-memories-1-1361971

Lee, Carol Ann, *A Fine Day for a Hanging*, Mainstream Publishing, 2013

London Metropolitan Archives, City of London CLA/003/PR/04/003 Correspondence and papers relating to Styllou Christofi, Oct–Dec 1954

Rowland, David, 'Evil Female Murderers', The Old Police Cells Museum, http://www.oldpolicecellsmuseum.org.uk/page/evil_female_murderers_part_2

Chapter 17: A Worthwhile Job

Kelley, Joanna, 'The New Holloway', *Prison Service Journal*, Vol. X, No. 37, October 1970

Prison Recruitment Booklet, Home Office, undated, circa late 1960s

Chapter 18: Escape

Progl, Zoe, *Woman of the Underworld*, Arthur Barker Limited, 1964

Chapter 19: Category A Prisoners

Burrell, Ian, 'A Life Behind Bars: How the Moors Murderess Paid for Crimes that were "Evil Beyond Belief"', *Independent*, 16 November 2002

Clark, T, 'Why was Myra Hindley Evil?', paper presented to the York Deviancy Conference: *Critical Perspectives on Crime, Deviance, Disorder and Social Harm*, July 2011

Gee, Ethel, House of Commons Debate, *Hansard*, Vol. 792 cc1838–50, December 1969

Hall, Clarice, 'They Deal with Everybody as an Individual', *People with Dementia Speak Out*, ed. Lucy Whitman, Jessica Kingsley Publishers, 2016

Harrison, Fred, *Brady and Hindley: Genesis of the Moors Murders*, Grafton, 1987

Lee, Carol Ann, *One of Your Own: The Life and Death of Myra Hindley*, Mainstream Publishing, 2011

London Metropolitan Archives, City of London, CLA/003/PR/04/001 Correspondence and papers relating to Helen Kroger, 1967–9

'Myra Hindley: Women Prisoners' Exercise Facilities', House of Lords Debate, *Hansard*, Vol. 335, September 1972

National Archives, Myra Hindley's records http://discovery.nationalarchives.gov.uk/details/r/C11267489

Chapter 20: Sex and Love

Arrowsmith, Pat, Interview for 'After Hiroshima Project', Katie Nairne and Ruth Dewa, 2015, http://www.londonbubble.org.uk/uploads/Pat%20Arrowsmith%20Transcript.pdf

Arrowsmith, Pat, *Somewhere Like This*, W.H Allen, 1970

Freedman, Estelle B., 'The Prison Lesbian: Race, Class, and the Construction of the Aggressive Female Homosexual, 1915–1965', *Feminist Studies* Vol. 22, No. 2, Summer 1996

Imperial War Museum, Pat Arrowsmith interview, 1995, catalogue number 12525. Copyright IWM and used with permission.

Chapter 21: A Place of Healing

'Holloway Redevelopment: New Bulletin Number 3', Home Office, December 1971

Jakubati, Muriel, with Monica Weller, *Ruth Ellis: My Sister's Secret Life*, Robinson, 2005

'Treatment of Women and Girls in Custody', Home Office Prison Department, 1970

van Wingerden, Sophia A., *The Women's Suffrage Movement in Britain, 1866–1928*, Palgrave Macmillan, 1999

'Women in Today's Prison Service', Home Office recruitment booklet, 1977

Chapter 22: Jailed for an Ideal

Rosenberg, David, *Rebel Footprints: A Guide to Uncovering London's Radical History*, Pluto Press, 2015

Warren, Steven, 'The Power of Caring', http://www.stevenwarren.co.uk/a1-auntie-nelllie-suffragette-the-power-of-caring.htm

Wood, Wendy, *Yours Sincerely for Scotland: The Autobiography of a Patriot*, Arthur Baker, 1970

Chapter 23: The Women of Greenham Common

Barlow, Lyn, *How I Met Chris, Ready Steady Go*, undated, http://www.womeninprison.org.uk/perch/resources/lyn-barlow-84-87.pdf

Fairhall, David, *Common Ground: The Story of Greenham*, I.B. Taurus, 2006

Greenham Common Song Book, http://www.aldermaston.net/sites/default/files/Greenham%20Songbook1.pdf. Permission to quote from 'The Holloway Song' granted by Rebecca Johnson

Johnson, Rebecca, 'The Women Who Refused To Give Up', *Morning Star*, 14 November 2013

Leach, Ginette, *Orange Gate Journal: A Personal View of the Greenham Common Women's Peace Camp*, http://www.orangegatejournal.co.uk/

Liddington, Jill, *The Road to Greenham Common: Feminism and Anti-militarism in Britain Since 1820*, Syracuse University Press, 1989

Omonira-Oyekanmi, Rebecca, 'Memories of a Protest', *Lacuna Magazine*, February 2014 https://lacuna.org.uk/protest/memories-of-a-protest/

Stead, Jean, 'The Greenham Common Peace Camp and its Legacy', *Guardian*, 5 September 2006

Chapter 24: C1: The Psychiatric Unit

Benn, Melissa, 'Women in prison . . . breaking the silence . . .', *Spare Rib*, Issue 137, December 1983

Davies, Nick, 'Violence of Jail Women', *Observer*, 25 November 1984

Davies, Nick, 'Welcome to the Muppet House', *Observer*, 23 March 1986

Radical Alternatives to Prison (RAP), 'Rapping on Holloway', *Spare Rib*, June 1972

'Report of the Holloway Project Committee', Home Office, 1985

Ryan, Mick, *Lobbying From Below*, Routledge, 1997

Tchaikovsky, Chris, 'Looking for Trouble', in *Criminal Women*, ed. Pat Carlen, Polity Press, 1985, pp. 14–58

Tchaikovsky, Chris, 'Who Guards The Guards?', *Spare Rib*, 1983

Chapter 25: Childbirth

'Babies in Prison', Annual Report 2007, http://babiesinprison.co.uk/wp-content/uploads/2007-report.pdf

'Holloway Prison', House of Commons Debate, *Hansard*, Vol. 269, 9 January 1996

Griffiths, Major Arthur, 'In Wormwood Scrubs Prison', *Living London*, ed. George R. Sims, 1902 http://www.victorianlondon.org/prisons/wormwood.htm

Kenealy, Annesley, 'A Crèche for Prison Babies', *The Lady's Realm*, 1905

'Mystery of Dora Gordine's Bronze Baby Solved', Kingston University London, http://www.kingston.ac.uk/news/article/351/12-may-2011-mystery-of-dora-gordines-bronze-baby-solved/

Ramsbotham, Sir David, HM Chief Inspector of Prisons, 'Women in Prison: A Thematic Review', Home Office, 1997, https://www.justiceinspectorates.gov.uk/hmiprisons/wp-content/uploads/sites/4/2014/07/WOMEN-IN-PRISON-1996.pdf

Wynn Davies, Patricia, 'Pregnant Prisoner Tells of her Ordeal in Chains', *Independent*, 19 May 1997

Chapter 26: Holloway Rebranded

Briggs, Gemma, 'First Night in Prison? It's Just Like a Hotel, Say the Inmates,' *Islington Gazette*, 29 September 2015

Carlen, Pat, *Women's Imprisonment at the Millennium*, Nuffield Foundation, 1997

'Holloway Jail Chief Argues Prison is Not Always the Answer for Women with Troubled Histories', *Mirror*, 17 March 2009

'The Corston Report', Home Office, 2007

Chapter 27: The Monsters Ball

Cooke, Rachel, 'The Innocent', *Guardian*, 4 October 2001

Devlin, Angela and Tim, *Anybody's Nightmare: The Sheila Bowler Story*, Taverner Publications, 1998

Johnston, Rosie, *Inside Out*, Michael Joseph, 1989

Langdon-Down, Grania, 'If I had been sent back to prison, I would have died', *Independent*, 6 February 1998

Pryce, Vicky, *Prisonomics: Behind Bars in Britain's Failing Prisons*, Biteback Publishing, 2013

Wyner, Ruth, *From the Inside*, Aurum Press, 2003

Chapter 28: Life After Prison

Aumord, Danielle, 'How to Stop Women Leaving Prison for the Streets', *Inside Housing*, 7 June 2016

Clean Break, http://www.cleanbreak.org.uk/

Griffins Society Newsletter, March 1965, http://www.thegriffinssociety. org/system/files/attachments/griffins_society_-_newsletter_1965.pdf, http://www.thegriffinssociety.org/about-us/history

Guiney, Thomas, 'Total Recall: Why More Women Are Being Returned to Prison than Ever Before', The Justice Gap, http://thejusticegap. com/2016/11/total-recall-women-returned-prison-ever/

Hibiscus, http://hibiscusinitiatives.org.uk/

Hogarth, Liz, 'Trapped in the Justice Loop? Past, Present and Future of the Woman-Centred Services at the Heart of the Systems-Change Called for in the Corston Report', Centre for Crime and Justice Studies, 2017

Rumgay, Judith, *Ladies of Lost Causes: Rehabilitation, Women Offenders and the Voluntary Sector*, Willan Publishing, 2007

Treasures Foundation, http://treasuresfoundation.org.uk/

Chapter 29: The End of an Era

'Closure of HMP Holloway: A Proposal for the Establishment of a Women's Centre on the Site of the Existing Visitors Centre', Prison Reform Trust, 1 December 2015, http://www.prisonreformtrust.org.uk/

Saner, Emine, 'A woman's place? Why the closure of Holloway could bring a prison revolution closer', *Guardian,* 28 November 2015

Chapter 30: Hope Dies Last

Bright, Martin, 'Failure to Sack "Racist" Prison Staff Condemned', *Guardian,* 26 September 2004

Casale, Silvia, *Women Inside: The Experience of Women Remand Prisoners in Holloway,* The Civil Liberties Trust, 1989

Cheliotis, Leonidas K., and Liebling, Alison, 'Race Matters in British Prisons Towards a Research Agenda', *British Journal of Criminology,* 2005, Issue 45, 1 March 2006, pp. 1–32

Chigwada-Bailey, Ruth, *Black Women's Experiences of Criminal Justice,* Waterside Press, 2003

Devlin, Angela, *Invisible Women,* Waterside Press, 1998

Gayle, Damien, 'Sarah Reed Told Family of Alleged Sexual Assault in Hospital', *Guardian,* 4 February 2016

'Hunger Striker Released from Holloway', April 2010, Women Against Rape and Black Women's Rape Action Project, http://www.womenagainstrape.net/content/press-release-hunger-striker-released-holloway

Jasper, Lee, 'Sarah Reed: A Black Woman Victim of Vicious Police Assault Found Dead in Her Cell', http://leejasper.blogspot.co.uk/2016/02/sarah-reid-black-woman-victim-of.html

'Nature and Extent of Young Black People's Overrepresentation', Select Committee on Home Affairs Second Report, 2007 https://www.publications.parliament.uk/pa/cm200607/cmselect/cmhaff/181/18105.htm

Padel, Una, and Stevenson, Prue, *Insiders: Women's Experience of Prison,* Virago, 1988

'Parallel Worlds a Thematic Review of Race Relations in Prisons', HM Inspectorate of Prisons, December 2005

'Preventing the Deaths of Women in Prison: the Need for an Alternative Approach', Inquest, January 2014 http://inquest.org.uk/pdf/briefings/

Jan2014_updated_INQUEST_Preventing_deaths_of_women_in_prison.
pdf

'Race in Prisons', *Prison Service Journal*, September 2010, No 191

Rhys, Jean, *Let Them Call It Jazz and Other Stories,* Penguin Books, 1995

'Twenty-Five Years of Saving Lives', *Inside Time*, 30 August 2016

'Yarl's Wood Hunger Striker Released After a Year!', January 2011, Women
Against Rape and Black Women's Rape Action Project, http://www.
womenagainstrape.net/inthemedia/yarls-wood-hunger-striker-released-
after-year

Chapter 31: The Ghosts of Holloway

London Metropolitan Archives, City of London, CLA/003/PR/06/001
Register of prisoners committed for want of sureties at City New
Prison Holloway, 1852–1868

London Metropolitan Archives, City of London, CLA/003/AD/03/003
Commissioners and inspector' minute book June 1909-June 1935

Conclusion: Reclaim Holloway

Centre for Crime and Justice Studies, 'How much does it cost to keep
an old prison empty?', https://www.crimeandjustice.org.uk/news/
how-much-does-it-cost-keep-old-prison-empty

Empty Cages Collective, 'What is the Prison Industrial Complex?', http://
www.prisonabolition.org/what-is-the-prison-industrial-complex/

Reclaim Holloway, http://reclaimholloway.strikingly.com/#home

Roberts, Rebecca, Alternatives to Holloway, https://www.crimeandjustice.
org.uk/news/alternatives-holloway

Ryan, Mick, and Ward, Tony, 'Prison Abolition in the UK: They Dare Not
Speak Its Name?', *Social Justice Journal*, Vol. 41, No. 3

Select Bibliography

Barrow, Dean, *A Brief History of H.M. Prison Holloway*, Holloway Prison

Beauchamp, Hilary, *Holloway Prison: An Inside Story*, Waterside Press, 2010

Brodie, Allan, Jane Croom and James O. Davies, *English Prisons: An Architectural History*, English Heritage, 2002

Camp, John, *Holloway Prison: The Place and the People*, David & Charles, 1974

Evans, David, with Sheila Cohen, *The Everlasting Staircase: A History of the Prison Officers, Association 1939–2009*, Pluto Press, 2009

Henry, Joan, *Women in Prison* (also published as *Who Lie in Gaol*), White Lion Publishers, 1952

Home Office, *People in Prison, England and Wales*, Her Majesty's Stationary Office, November 1969

Jewkes, Yvonne and Helen Johnston, *Holloway Prison for Women, 1902–1945*, www.cityoflondon.gov.uk

Kelley, Joanna, *When the Gates Shut*, Longmans, 1967

Kozubska, Joanna, with foreword by David Ramsbotham, *Cries For Help: Women Without a Voice, Women's Prisons in the 1970s, Myra Hindley and Her Contemporaries*, Waterside Press, 2014

Liddington, Jill, *Rebel Girls: Their Fight for the Vote*, Virago, 2006

May, Trevor, *Victorian and Edwardian Prisons*, Shire Publications, 2006

Mayhew, Henry and John Binny, *The Criminal Prisons of London*, Griffin, Bohn and Company, 1862

Oliver, J.L.C, 'The History and Development of Holloway Prison from AD 1849 to AD 1990', report prepared for The Governor by The Head of Works Services, December 1990, Wandsworth Prison Museum

Pierrepoint, Albert, *Executioner Pierrepoint*, Coronet Books, 1974

Radical Alternatives to Prison (RAP), *Alternatives to Holloway*, 1972

Radzinowicz, Leon, and Roger Hood, 'The Status of Political Prisoner in England: The Struggle for Recognition', *Virginia Law Review*, Vol. 65, No. 8, 1979

Rock, Paul, *Reconstructing a Women's Prison: The Holloway Redevelopment Project, 1968–88*, Clarendon Press, 1996

Sims, George, *Living London*, Cassell, 1902

Size, Mary, *Prisons I Have Known*, George Allen & Unwin, 1957

Stern, Walter, 'Holloway Prison as the City of London's House of Correction, 1852-1877', *Studies in London History Presented to Philip Edmund Jones*, Hodder & Stoughton, 1969

Useful Websites

The British Newspaper Archive: https://www.britishnewspaperarchive.co.uk/

Capital Punishment UK: http://www.capitalpunishmentuk.org

Holloway inspection reports: https://www.justiceinspectorates.gov.uk/hmiprisons/inspections/

John Simkin, *Women's History Index*, Spartacus Educational: http://spartacus-educational.com

Women in Prison: http://www.womeninprison.org.uk/

Index

Abbena (prisoner), 310
Abbott, Diane, 275
Aboagye, Justice (Botswana), 6
Acronym Institute for Disarmament
    Diplomacy, 244
Aduku (prisoner), 309–10
Ainsworth, Laura, 79
Aitken, Bessie, 112–13
Ali, Pat, 215–16
Aliens Tribunals (World War II), 137,
    143–4
Allen, Colin, 259–64, 274, 305, 323
Anderson, John, 138
Anderson, Louisa Garrett, 78
Angry Brigade, 215
Ansell, Gertrude, 79
Anti-Suffrage League, 71
Archdale, Betty, 78
Archdale, Helen, 78
Arrowsmith, Pat, 221; *Somewhere Like
    This*, 221–3
Arscott, Revd Barry, 231
Asha, Worcestershire, 285
Asher, Penninah, 42–3
Asquith, Herbert Henry, 27, 57, 59, 69,
    75
Austin, Sister, 264
Aylesbury prison, 104, 118, 141
Ayrton-Gould, Barbara, 171–2

Babies in Prison (charity), 274
baby farmers, 39, 41–3
'Baby P', 287
Bach, Enid Goulden, 233
Bad Girls (TV series), 278
Baker, Arthur Reginald, 37
Baker, Kathy, 261
Bankhead, Tallulah, 129

Barber, Ed, 254
Barker, Lilian, 119–20, 122, 133, 141,
    160, 200, 303
Barker, Steven, 287
Barker, Colonel Victor (born Lillias
    Irma Valerie Barker), 125–9, 205
Barlow, Lyn, 248
Barney, Elvira, 130–2
Barratt, Peter, 92–5
Barrett, Mr (photographer), 63
Barrow, Dean, 317–23, 330
Barry (Zoe Progl's boyfriend), 205–7
Battered Woman Syndrome, 6
Beauchamp, Hilary, 223, 236
Behind the Times (inmate magazine),
    221
Bell, Annie, 85
Bell, George, Bishop of Chichester, 138
Bell, Gilbert, 25, 27
Bell, Mary Jane, 49
Bentham, Jeremy, 11
Bentley, Derek, 185
Berners, Gerald Tyrwhitt-Wilson, 14th
    Baron, 149
Billington, William, 40
Billington(-Greig), Teresa, 57–9, 61, 65,
    68, 166
Binny, John, 13, 16
Birmingham prison: riot, 339
Birth Companions (charity), 274
Black Lives Matter movement, 307
Blake, George, 211
Blakely, David, 174–5, 181–3
Blyth, Dr R., 229
Bolam, Connie, 158
Bondfield, Margaret, 123, 302
Booth, Herbert, 102, 104
Borchard, Kurt, 137

Borchard, Ruth, 137–8, 141–2; *We Are Strangers* (unfinished novel), 138–9, 142–3
Borstal, 120; girls in Holloway, 168–71
BOSS (Body Orifice Security Scanner), 291
Botswana, 5–6
Bournonville, Eva de, 99–101, 113
Bowler, Sheila, 289–90
Bradley, Dr Charles Lawrence, 53
Brady, Ian, 212
Brighton Museum and History Centre, 129
Brinson, Charmian, 138
British Union of Fascists: detained in World War II, 142, 147, 150; Mosley forms, 148
Brixton, south London: female convict prison, 13–15, 266, 305; (male) prison, 34
Brock, John, 290
Bronzefield prison, Middlesex, 303
Brookwood Cemetery, Surrey, 230–1
Bubna-Kasteliz, Dr Bruno, 28
Bull, Dr Megan, 214, 229, 232, 237, 245
Bullwood Hall women's prison, Essex, 196, 281, 285, 289
Bunning, James, 15
Burgess, Beatrice M., 274
Burns, Lucy, 75
Byron, Kitty, 37–8, 183
Bywaters, Freddy, 108–12, 114, 116–17

Cairns, Pat, 215–16
Calderdale, Halifax, 285
Callaghan, James, 227
Cameron, David, 302
Camp, John, 110, 119, 141, 219, 273
Campaign for Nuclear Disarmament, 221
Campion, Inspector, 131
capital punishment, 108; abolition campaign, 115, 181; ended, 186, 212
CARAT (drug treatment programme), 300
Carden, Sir Robert, 16
Carlen, Pat, 255
Carr, Maxine, 287–8
Channon, Olivia, 288
chaplains, 51–3
Chapman, Jessica, 288

Chartists, 60
Chigwada-Bailey, Ruth, 311
children: and mothers in prisons, 266–78
Christie, Dr Thomas, 177–8
Christofi, Hella (*née* Bleicher), 176–7
Christofi, Stavros, 176–7, 179
Christofi, Styllou Pantopiou: executed, 175–80, 184–5, 230–1, 321
Churchill, Clementine, 148, 154
Churchill, Sarah, 219
Churchill, Winston, 76
City Lunatic Asylum, Kent, 20–1
Clarke, John S., 105
Clarke, Kathleen, 91–2
Claymore House, north London, 38
Clean Break (theatre company), 300
Clifford, Lady *see* de Clifford, Lady
Clynes, Mary, 271
Cohen, Leonora, 83
Cohen, Morris, 210
Coldbath Fields Prison, London, 44
Coles, Deborah, 313, 337
Commission for Racial Equality, 311
Conference of Women's Organizations, 166
Connelly, Tracey, 287
conscientious objectors: in Great War, 102; in World War II, 158
convicts *see* prisoners
Cook, Beverley, 64
Cookham Wood prison, Kent, 325
Corbyn, Jeremy, 257
Corston, Jean, Baroness: report on women in the criminal justice system, 284–6, 296, 303
Court of Aldermen (City of London): and appointment of prison governor, 49–50
Craig, Constance, 77
Craig, Dr Maurice, 84
Craiginches Prison, Aberdeen, 86
Cressall, George, 240
Cressall, Nellie, 239–40
crime: numbers fall, 119
Criminal Justice Bill (1938), 133
Criminal Justice Bill and Act (1948), 172, 272, 297
Criminal Law Amendment Act (1921), 217
Croft, Maxine, 215–16

Cronin, Elizabeth, 114, 116, 118
Crook, Frances, 303, 305, 337
Cummings, Patricia: burnt to death, 256
Cusden, Ivy, 270
Cussen, Desmond, 174, 182, 184

Daily Mail: coins word 'suffragette', 57; reader pays Teresa Billington's fine, 58; reports on Vicky Pryce, 291
Daily Mirror, 165, 287
Daily Sketch, 112
Daily Telegraph, 132, 287
Darling, Justice Charles John, 39, 100, 113
Davies, Detective Chief Inspector Leslie, 181
Davies, Nick, 257
Davison, Emily Wilding, 86–7, 94, 315
de Clifford, Dorothy Evelyn, Lady, 130
Defence of the Realm Act (DORA), 99–100
Defence Regulation 14b, 101
Defence Regulation 18B, 141, 146, 147, 150, 154, 162
de Laessoe, Major Harold, 153
Derby People's History Group, 105
Desart, Hamilton John Agmondesham Cuffe, 8th Earl of, 217
Devis, Jacky, 23
Devlin, Angela: *Invisible Women*, 310
Dilnot, Frank, 99
Discharged Prisoners Aid Society, 339
Domvile, Alexandrina, Lady, 152
Domvile, Admiral Sir Barry, 152
Douglas, Lord Alfred, 31
Downview prison, Surrey, 303
Doyle, Esther, 207
drugs: testing for, 131; in prisons, 290
Drummond, Flora, 68
Duke, Sir James, 15
Dundee Courier, 61
Dungey, Cicely, Lilian and Rachel, 159
Duval, Elsie, 78, 330
Dyer, Amelia, 39
Dyer, Jacqueline, 181

East London Federation of Suffragettes, 240
Easter Rising (Ireland, 1916), 91
Ellis, George, 181

Ellis, John, 113, 115–16
Ellis, Ruth (*née* Neilson): tried and executed for murder, 174–5, 181–7, 231; remains exhumed and moved, 229–30, 322; prison records stolen, 322
Emerson, Kathleen, 63, 72
enemy aliens (World War II), 137–46
Erickson, Vera *see* Schalburg, Vera
Evans, Timothy, 185
Evening Standard, 236
executions: end in UK, 186

Fabian Society, 62
Fatima (prison officer), 88
Fawcett, Millicent Garrett, 60
Feltham Young Offenders Institution, 312, 326
Fenians, 60
Field, Barry, 157
Fields, Gracie, 122
Finan, Miss (prison officer), 88
Findlater, Anthony and Carol, 174
Fine Cell Work (charity), 212
First World War (1914–18) *see* Great War
Fitzgerald, Carrie, 332
43 Club, Soho, 129–30
Forward, Dr Francis E., 85–6, 89–90
Fox, Norah Dacre, 154
Fox, Dr Selina, 118
Frances, Justinia, 49
Friedmann, Susanna Maria (*later* Susan Linton), 141–5
Frost, Robert, 30
Fry, Elizabeth, 45–6
Fry, Margery, 116, 339
Fry, Roger, 116

G4S (company), 285
Gabe (Sisters Uncut member), 334
Gabriella and Billy (lesbian couple), 220
Galilee, Evelyn, 184–6
Galley, Ada, 38, 43
Gandhi, Mohandas Karamchand (Mahatma), 161
Gateways Club, Chelsea, 221
Gavron, Sarah, 64
Gee, Ethel, 210–11
Gelley, Johnny ('Johnnie the Junkie'), 203–4

George, Vanessa, 287
Gibbons, Judy, 191–4, 228, 338
Gin Mill Annie, 208
Gladstone, Herbert, 58
Gliddon, Katie, 79–80
Goddard, Police Sergeant George, 130
Goebbels, Josef, 148
Gonne, Maud, 91
Gorbachev, Mikhail, 254
Gordine, Dora: *Happy Baby* (bronze sculpture), 272
Gordon, Alex *see* Rickard, William
Gordon, Dr Mary, 110–11
Gore, Elizabeth, 120
Gore-Booth, Constance (Countess Markievicz), 91–2
Gore-Booth, Eva, 91
Gounod, Charles, 30
Gove, Michael, 303
Graydon, Avis (Edith Thompson's sister), 112–13, 115–16
Graydon, Ethel (Edith Thompson's mother), 112–13, 116
Graydon, Newenham (Edith Thompson's brother), 114
Great War (1914–18): outbreak, 90, 99; conscription introduced (1916), 102
Greenham Common: women imprisoned, 4, 243, 244–9, 251–3; protests and violence, 247, 249–50; backlash against protestors, 250–1; mass trespass, 253; effects, 254
Greenham Song Book, 246
Griffins Society, 296, 299
Griffiths, Major Arthur, 267
Griffiths, Charles, 201
Guinness, Bryan, 148
Guinness, Sebastian, 288

Hair, Ann, 260
Hall, Clarice, 213
Hall, Inspector Francis, 110
Hallgarten, Katherine, 137–9, 143
Hamand, Maggie, 276–7
Hamilton, Mary, 267
Hammerer's (suffragette magazine), 88
hangings (public): end (1868), 34
Hardwick, Nick, 300
Harris, Captain Vernon, 43
Harrower, Ann, 251
Hartman, Cheryl, 311

Hassall, Tony, 281–3, 292, 321
Hastings, Sir Patrick, 131–2
Havers, Michael, 183
Haward, Elfrida, 125, 127
Hawkins, Alice, 65–7, 70, 92–5, 269
Heath, Lady Mary, 132
Henderson, Arthur, 103–4
Henderson Hospital, Surrey, 229
Henry, Joan, 217–18
Henson, Louisa: keeps diary as prison officer, 46–8; moral influence, 53, 318, 338
Heseltine, Michael, 248–50
Hetherington, Bill, 159
Hibiscus (charity), 300
Highpoint prison, Suffolk, 216
Hiley, Nicholas, 105
Hill, PC George, 81
Hindley, Myra: imprisoned, 7, 211–16, 228, 287, 324; escape plan, 214–16, 233
Hindson, Dr Norman, 261
Hitler, Adolf, 148
Hoare, Samuel, 133
Hogarth, Liz, 297
Holloway Discharged Prisoners Aid Society, 294–5
Holloway prison, London: bombed by suffragettes, 1–2, 90, 330; author visits and teaches in, 3–5, 317; character, 3–5; Greenham Common women in, 4, 244–9, 251–4; closure announced (November 2015), 6–8, 302–4, 306, 313–15, 325; history, 7; built (as City House of Correction), 15–16; early routines and life in, 17, 20; cells and furnishings, 19; early dress, 19; Duchess of Sutherland's accommodation in, 27; privileged classes and conditions in, 29–32; as male prison, 31; declining conditions, 32; nature of inmates' crimes, 32; executions at, 33, 40–2, 108, 114–16, 176, 180, 330; becomes all-female jail (1902), 34–5; old prison remnants preserved, 34–5; accommodation numbers, 36; misbehaviour and violence in, 36, 43, 48–9, 235–7, 255, 304–5; holds women under death sentence, 37–8, 43; role and conditions of prison

officers, 44–7; matrons, 48–9; male governor, 49–51; chaplains, 51–3; medical officers, 53; suffragettes imprisoned in, 57–73, 78–80, 82–4, 86–7, 95; political prisoners, 60, 76, 238–43; suffragettes' dress, 61; brooch (suffragettes'), 63; routines, 65–6; relations between staff and prisoners, 71, 78–9; wardresses' attitude to votes for women, 71–2; force-feeding of prisoners, 74, 78–9, 82, 105; privileges withheld, 76; suffragettes' behaviour recorded, 77; Great War prisoners (1914–18), 99, 101, 103; population and conditions, 110, 120, 123–4, 191; Mary Size appointed deputy governor, 118, 120–1; reforms and activities, 120–2; handicrafts, 122; drug use, 131, 290, 304; proposed demolition and move to rural site, 133–4; houses enemy aliens in World War II, 137–46; evacuated in World War II, 140–1; Fascists detained in World War II, 147–50, 154; near-bombing in war, 151; prison language and terms, 151; conscientious objectors in, 158–9; wartime conditions, 159–61; first woman governor (Charity Taylor), 162; punishments, 166; staff unrest, 166, 235; Mass Observation reports on staff, 167–8; Borstal girls and young prisoners ('brownies'), 168–72, 199, 202; officers' violent and tyrannical behaviour, 168–9, 255–6; Borstal Allocation Book, 170–1; debated in House of Commons, 171–2; turnover rate of officers, 172, 235; prisoners' 'nerve-storms', 173, 305; Ruth Ellis last prisoner executed, 187; officers' uniforms, 192, 322; officers' commitment and routines, 195, 328–9; improvements under Joanna Kelley, 197–8; medical and psychiatric care, 198–9; women given tests on arrival, 198–9; self-harm and suicides in, 199–200, 257–61, 281–2, 306, 336–7; escapes and attempted escapes, 200–2, 205–9; convicted spies in, 210; Category A prisoners in, 211–12; lesbianism and love affairs, 216–23; heterosexual flirtations, 223; demolition and rebuilding (1970–), 227–9, 232; executed women's remains moved, 229–30; campaign to phase out, 232; overcrowding (1970s), 234; unrest in new building, 236–7; Labour councillors imprisoned, 238–9; improved conditions, 252; C1 Unit (for 'highly disturbed' women), 255, 257–8, 261, 264, 320–1; prisoners burnt to death, 256; prisoners' deaths by violence and neglect, 256–7; psychotropic drugs administered, 257; troubles and difficulties (1980s), 258–60; new male governor appointed (Colin Allen), 259; reputation, 260, 274; self-mutilations and suicides decline, 261; Board of Visitors, 262; senior male officers drafted in, 262; officers' strike, 263–4; childbirth and babies in, 267–77, 305; crèche, 268–9; writers in residence, 277; bad inspection reports (2002), 281; mother and baby unit, 282; reforms under Tony Hassall, 282–3; First Night Centre, 283; 'Monsters Ball' (2006), 287; press reports on indulgence in, 287–8; modern demands for reforms, 289; public demand for punitive policy, 290, 297; conditions and treatment of discharged prisoners, 294–8; Independent Monitoring Board, 296; recent improvements, 300–1; black prisoners, 309–10, 312; foreign national prisoners, 310–11; deaths in custody, 311; prisoner-made quilt, 314–15, 335; archives, 317, 321–2, 329–30; interior layout, 317–21; ghosts, 318; staff numbers reduced, 328; closing down, 329–33; post-closure reclaim campaign, 331, 335–6; squatters occupy, 334; working-class inmates, 335; value of site, 339; function and achievements, 340

Holmes, Eva, 144–5
Homicide Act (1957), 186
homosexuality: in prisons, 217–18

Hope for these Women (Pathé film), 272
Houghton, Harry, 210–11
House of Commons: debates Holloway, 171–2
Housing for Women (charity), 298
Howard, John: *The State of Prisons* (1777), 13
Howard League for Penal Reform, 119, 303, 337
Howard, Michael, 332
Huddersfield by-election (1906), 62
Humphreys, Christmas, 178, 182
Huntley, Ian, 288

Impey, Chris, 329
infanticide, 43
INQUEST (organization), 313
Intermediate-Range Nuclear Forces Treaty (1987), 254
Isle of Man: internment camps (1939–45), 137, 139, 143–4, 150, 162
Islington Gazette, 39, 282–3

Jackson, Florence, 289
Jasper, Lee, 307, 313
Jeune, Sir Francis, 24
Johnson, Rebecca, 244–9, 253–4
Johnston, Helen, 45
Johnston, Rosie: *Inside Out*, 288–9
Jones, Ellen: reprieved, 113
Jones, Wallace, 270

Kelley, Joanna: reforms and humanisation, 197–200, 206, 284; leaves Holloway, 200; accompanies Zoe Progl to court, 208; Zoe Progl praises, 209; visits Holloway as assistant director for women, 214; and lesbian relationships among prisoners, 218–19; plans replacing Holloway with new building, 224, 227, 229, 232; on birth of babies to prisoners, 273; and discharged prisoners, 295
Kenealy, Annesley, 268–9
Kennedy, Eleanor, 49
Kenney, Annie, 59, 65
Kew Gardens: damaged by suffragettes, 81–3
Khaled, Leila, 233
Kiddie, James, 307

Kieboom, Charles Albert van den, 156
Kill the Housing Bill (organization), 331
Killick, Julia, 315, 325
King, Evelyn, 211
King, Janet, 275
Kinnoull, Mary Ethel Isobel, Countess of (*née* Meyrick), 130
Kinsley, Joy, 245, 259
Knight, Adelaide, 59
Knox, Dr John, 198
Kozubska, Joanna, 212–15, 220–1, 235
Kroger, Helen, 210–12
Kroger, Peter, 210–11

Ladies Association for the Improvement of Female Prisoners in Newgate, 46
Laessoe, Major Harold de *see* de Laessoe, Major Harold
Laing, R.D., 276
Lancashire Evening Post, 58
Lancaster House, London (*formerly* Stafford House), 22–3
Lansbury, George, 238–40
Lansbury, Minnie, 238–41
Lawrence, Susan, 239
Layton, Dr Catherine, 29
Leach, Ginette: imprisoned in Holloway, 251–3; *Orange Gate Journal*, 251
Lee, Carol Ann, 212
Leigh, Mary, 75, 322
Lenton, Lilian, 81–4
lesbianism, 217–23
Liddell, Guy, 156
Liddington, Jill: *Rebel Girls*, 62, 92
Liebermann, Ludwig (*later* Louis Linton), 144–5
Listener scheme, 261, 298, 332
Lloyd George, David, 92, 94, 102, 104
London, Bishop of (Arthur Foley Winnington-Ingram), 79
Lonsdale, Hugh Cecil Lowther, 5th Earl of, 31
Lonsdale, Kathleen, 159–61
Luck, Norman, 214
Lyon, Juliet, 303
Lytton, Lady Constance: imprisoned as suffragette in Holloway, 58, 69–73, 76–7; comforted by prison officer, 338; *Prisons and Prisoners*, 69

McCarthy, Peter, 153
MacDonald, Ramsay, 66
Mackay, Jennie, 239
Mackenzie, Theresa, 308
McLaughlin, Stewart, 11–12, 323
McNeil, Denise, 311
McTaggart, Ann, 277
Magdala Tavern, Hampstead, 175
Mandela, Nelson, 4
Mansfield, Maureen, 313
Maria (violent prisoner), 47
Marion, Kitty, 78
Markievicz, Countess see Gore-Booth, Constance
Marsh, Charles, 201
Martin, Emma, 14, 118
Mary (pseudonym), 298
Mason, Alfred, 102–3, 105
Mason, Chloe and Deirdre, 105–6
Mass Observation (organization), 17
Matheson, Dr John, 124, 152
Maxie's café, Soho, 203
May, Elsie, 240
May, Rose and Maisey, 240–1
Mayhew, Henry: visits prisons, 13–17, 50, 52, 266, 269
Mayhew, Vera, 272
Melson, Debra, 231
Meyrick, Kate, 129–30
midwifery: professionalized, 40
Midwives Act (1902), 40
Military Service Act (1916), 102
Millbank prison: built (1816), 13; women transferred to, 47; children in, 267
Miller, Sarah, 51
Milman, Lieutenant-Colonel E.S., 51, 58
Mitford, Diana see Mosley, Diana, Lady
Mitford, Tom, 152
Mitford, Unity, 148
Molody, Konon, 210
Moorhead Ethel, 242
Moors Murderers, 212
Morning Advertiser, 39
Morrison, Herbert, 152
Morrison, Sybil, 161
Morrison, Revd William, 52–3, 233, 338; Crime and Its Causes, 52; Juvenile Offenders, 52
Morton, Dr John Hall, 112, 114, 118, 121, 124

Mosley, Diana, Lady (née Mitford): imprisoned in Holloway, 147–52; shares accommodation with husband, 153; leaves Holloway and placed under house arrest, 154; freed at war's end, 162
Mosley, Sir Oswald, 148, 150, 152, 154, 162
Mountbatten, Louis, 1st Earl, 211
Moxon, Dr Frank, 76
Mubarek, Zahid, 312
Mulholland, Dinah, 314
Mullens, Sir John and Lady, 131
Mulligan, Carey, 64
Murray, Revd Granville, 115–16
Museum of London: Social and Working History store, 34, 319; suffragette campaign collection, 64
Myer, Clara, 126

Narey, Martin, 312
National Association for the Care and Resettlement of Offenders, 312
National Campaign for the Abolition of Capital Punishment, 186
National Health Service: takes over Prison Health Services, 282
National Offender Management Service (NOMS), 285
National Prison Radio, 329, 331
National Union of Women's Suffrage Societies, 57, 60
Neale, Ken, 227
Nesbitt, Mary, 70
New, Edith, 75
Newgate prison, 34, 46
No-Conscription Fellowship, 102
North London News, 50
North, Phyllis see Wharry, Olive, 84
Nova magazine, 220

O'Dwyer, Josie, 216
O'Grady, Dorothy (Pamela Arland), 155–7, 199
O'Grady, Vincent, 155
Ogunmokun, Mandy, 299–300
O'Malley, Bryanna, 207
Osborne, Florence, 267
Osborne, George, 6, 302
Owen, Jason, 287
Owers, Anne, 281
Oxley, John, 201, 206

Page, Nora, 159–60
Pankhurst, Adela, 62–3
Pankhurst, Christabel, 59, 69, 77
Pankhurst, Emmeline: imprisoned in Holloway, 1; social background, 58; leadership challenged, 68; attacks treatment in Holloway, 69; and suffragettes' hunger strikes, 75; in Holloway Nominal Register, 78; announces end of militancy on outbreak of Great War, 90; prison records, 323, 330
Pankhurst, Helen, 94
Pankhurst, Sylvia, 59, 61, 63, 240, 289
Parker, Fanny, 79
Parsons, Jumbo ('Scarface'), 205
Paterson, Alexander, 119
Paton, Florence, 172
Payne, Cynthia, 322
Peace Pledge Union (PPU), 158
Pearce-Crouch, Ernest, 125
penal reform: in 1920s and '30s, 119–20
Pentonville prison, London, 34, 133
Perfect Home and How to Keep It, A, 73
Peters, Simon, 326–9
Pethick-Lawrence, Emmeline, 70, 78
Petka, Lona, 210
Philadelphia Association (charity), 276, 313
Pierrepoint, Albert, 178–9, 181, 185–6
Pierrepoint, Henry, 40–1
Pierrepoint, Thomas, 17
'Plantagenet, Hon. Frank and Reggy', 31
Plummer, Sir Leslie, 180
PMSD2 (intelligence unit of Ministry of Munitions), 102
Poland, Margaret, 184
Poplar: Labour councillors imprisoned (1919), 238–40, 243
Popowitch, Marie Edvige de, 101–2
Popular Front for the Liberation of Palestine, 233
Porridge (TV sitcom), 36
Portland spy ring, 210, 228
Pottlitzer, Margot, 217
Prain, Sir David, 81
Press Association: invited into Holloway, 133
Prince, Dolores and Marion, 233
Prison Health Services: transferred to NHS, 282

Prison Medical Reform Council, 161
prison officers: character, role and conditions, 44–7, 161–2, 285; female, 45–7; pay scales and allowances, 48, 195; recruitment and training, 191–6; lesbian practices, 220, 222–3; cross-sex postings, 262; racism, 308–13; low ethnic minority numbers, 312; concern for helping inmates, 338; protest at violence in jails, 339
Prison Officers' Association (POA): founded, 161; warns of violence in Holloway, 168–70, 235; attacks government policy, 258; and cross-sex postings, 262; industrial action, 263–4; not recognized in privately run jails, 285; on Holloway closure, 303
Prison Reform Trust, 259, 264, 303
prisoners: first and second divisions, 26, 60; political, 60, 76, 238–43; rehabilitation, 191; Categories A–D, 211
prisons: taken over by government (as 'Her Majesty's prisons'), 48; reforms, 118–19; role and purpose, 194, 324–5, 327–8, 331–2; escapes, 201, 211; industrial action in, 263; overcrowded and understaffed, 338; see also rehabilitation
Prisons Bill (1840), 26
probation service, 297
Progl, Joe (Zoe's husband), 203
Progl, Paul (Zoe's son), 204, 208
Progl, Tracy (Zoe's daughter), 209
Progl, Zoe (née Tyldesley): criminal background, 201, 203–5, 209; escape from Holloway, 205–8; captured and returned to Holloway, 208; and lesbian approaches, 219; witnesses heterosexual flirtations, 223; gives birth at Aylesbury Borstal, 273; Woman of the Underworld, 203
Project Review Committee, 259–60
Provisional Irish Republican Army, 233
Pryce, Vicky, 291–3; Prisonomics, 291
Pullen, Mary, 16

Quinton, Richard Firth, 58, 71, 76, 335; Crime and Criminals, 58

racism: in prison service, 308–13
Radical Alternatives to Prison (RAP), 232, 303, 337
Ramsay, Archibald, 147–8
Ramsay, Revd James, 107–8
Ramsbotham, Sir David (*later* Baron), 274, 314
Reagan, Ronald, 254
Reclaim Holloway! (organization), 331, 336
Reclaim Justice Network, 331
Reed, Sarah: death in Holloway, 307–8, 312, 336–7, 339
rehabilitation: as policy, 16, 21, 120, 123, 191, 229, 233, 283–5, 290, 299–300, 302–3, 324, 331
Representation of the People Act (1918), 91
Rhys, Jean: 'Let Them Call It Jazz' (story), 308
Richard (prison supervisor), 3, 5
Richardson, Carole, 322
Richardson, Mary, 79, 89, 330
Rickard, William ('Alex Gordon'), 102–5
Right Club, 147
Rivière, Jules, 29
RMJM & Partners (architects), 228
Roads, Barbara, 158
Roberts, Jenny, 285
Rock, Paul, 264; *Reconstructing a Women's Prison*, 227, 233
Rollit, Sir Albert, 29
Rowbotham, Sheila, 105
Royal Commission on Capital Punishment (1953), 181
Russell, Allen, 233

Sach, Amelia, 38–43, 100, 115, 178, 186, 230–1
Sach, Eunice, 42–3
Sach, Jeffrey, 39, 42
St Barnabas Church, Manor Park, Upper Holloway, 107–9, 116
St John, Stella, 161
Salter, Selina: behaviour, 17–21, 29, 46, 155, 199, 285, 304, 340
Samaritans (organization), 261, 298
Sancto, Mark, 260–1, 263
Sass, Dr Wilfred, 105
Saturday Forensic Forum, 313–14

Saunders, Sue, 285
Save the Children (charity), 277
Scarborough, Jane, 59
Schalburg, Vera (Vera Erickson), 154–5
Schwarzenberger, Rolf, 143–4
Schwarzenberger, Suzanne, 143
Scott, Christine: death in prison, 256–7
Scott, Dr James, 53–4, 77, 79
Scottish Patriots Association, 241
Scurr, Julia, 239
Sentence of Death (Expectant Mothers) Bill (1931), 271
Sex Discrimination Act (1975), 196
Shearman, Sir Montague (Mr Justice), 111–13
Sheffield Evening Telegraph, 57
Sheppard, Jack, 35
Simpson, Ella, 314
Sims, George, 26, 36, 48
Sisters Uncut (action group), 334–6
Size, Mary: appointed deputy governor, 118, 120, 124; reforms, 122–3, 132–3, 160, 168, 197, 284; and celebrity prisoners, 125; and Victor Barker, 125–7; on heroin smuggling, 131; on release of short-term prisoners in World War II, 141; retires, 157; and welfare of children in prison, 270; and discharged prisoners' conditions, 295; *Prisons I Have Known*, 120
Smith, Harold Arkell, 125
Smyth, Dame Ethel, 63, 78
Solomons, Daisy, 222
Spare Rib (magazine), 256
Sparkes, Vyki, 34
Speed, Dr Dorothy, 261, 274
spies, 210
Spillane, Mary, 37–8
Stead, William Thomas, 32, 60, 154, 239
Stephen, Michael, 131
Stewart, Pamela, 275–6, 302, 304, 313–14
Stockdale, Sir Edmund, 296
Stockdale House, Camden, 296
Stone of Destiny (Scottish), 242
straitjackets, 50, 235
Strange, Mrs (Kew Gardens lessee), 83
Strangeways prison, Manchester, 4, 274
Straw, Jack, 290
Styal Prison, 211, 216, 228, 273–4, 284

Suffragette Fellowship, 90, 233
Suffragette (film), 64, 94
suffragettes: bomb Holloway prison,
   1–2; imprisoned in Holloway,
   57–73, 78–80, 82, 84, 86–7, 95;
   behaviour in prison, 58, 74–5, 77,
   82, 88–9; protests and activities,
   58–9, 68–9, 75, 77, 83, 89–90;
   numbers arrested and imprisoned,
   62, 64; board game, 71; hunger
   strikes and force feeding, 74–8, 82,
   86, 330; granted first-division prisoner status, 76; damage Kew
   Gardens, 81; prisoners released at
   outbreak of Great War, 90; subsequent lives and legacy, 92–4; escape
   plots, 201–2; shocked at babies in
   prison, 269
Sun (newspaper), 287
Sunday Express (newspaper), 156
Sutherland, Anne, Duchess of (formerly
   Countess of Cromartie), 24, 28
Sutherland, Cromartie Leveson-Gower,
   4th Duke of, 24
Sutherland, George Granville William
   Leveson-Gower, 3rd Duke of, 23,
   28
Sutherland, Mary Ann, 30
Sutherland, May Caroline, Dowager
   Duchess of Sutherland: sentenced
   and imprisoned, 22–7, 76, 150;
   settlement and death, 28; reputation
   and behaviour, 29
Swan, Thomas, 153

Taylor, Dr Charity: appointed governor
   of Holloway, 162; administration
   and reforms, 165–6, 170; back-
   ground and career, 165; visits
   condemned cell, 173; and Styllou
   Christofi case, 178–9; at execution
   of Ruth Ellis, 184–5; visits Ruth
   Ellis's sister to explain exhumation,
   230; demands Wendy Wood leave,
   243
Taylour, Fay, 132, 154
Tchaikovsky, Chris, 255–6, 262, 278
Thewlis, Dora, 67, 92
Thewlis, Eliza, 67
Thomas, Emily, 324–5
Thompson, Edith (née Graydon):

executed, 107–8, 114–15, 175, 180–2,
   321; memorial services, 107–8;
   marriage, 108; affair with Freddy
   Bywaters, 109; and husband's
   murder, 109–10; in Holloway,
   110–11; trial and sentenced to death,
   111–13; hoax pardon message, 114;
   inquest and suspicions over manner
   of death, 115–16; aftermath, 116;
   grave, 186; remains moved, 230;
   records on, 321–2; letter, 330;
   thanks prison staff, 338; visited by
   Margery Fry, 339
Thompson, Jo, 314–16
Thompson, Percy, 108–10
Thomson, Basil, 100–2, 106
Tierney, Nora, 173
Times, The, 103
Timpson, Mrs (prison officer), 209
Toye & Co. (badge-makers), 94
transgender roles cases, 125–9
treadwheel, 51
Tree, Lady Anne, 212–13
'200 Years of History and Progress
   Continue . . .' (booklet), 283

Van der Elst, Violet, 185

Wakefield: prison training college, 193,
   195–6
Walker, Annette, 275
Walker, Dr Dora, 113
Wallace-Dunlop, Marion, 74
Walters, Annie, 38–42, 100, 115, 186,
   230–1, 330
Wandsworth prison, London: architec-
   ture and design, 11; executions, 12;
   history, 12–13
Warner, Louise, 313
Warren, Steven, 240–1
Waters, Margaret, 39
Watson, Ivy, 160
Waugh, Evelyn: A Handful of Dust, 129
Weatherhead, John, 50–1, 121, 294, 329
Webster, Kate, 12
Weis, Professor René, 108, 116
Weldon, Georgina, 29–30, 32
Wells, Holly, 288
Wentworth, Vera, 68, 78, 86
West, Fred, 287
West, Rose, 7, 287

Wharry, Olive: suffragette activities, 81–5; scrapbook, 86–9

Wheatley, Alfred, 270–1

Wheeldon, Alice (*née* Marshall), 102–6

Wheeldon, Hettie, 102–4

Wheeldon, Winnie, 103–5

Whitworth, Edith, 68

Widdecombe, Ann, 275

Wilde, Oscar, 31

Willetts, Ed, 223

Williams, Margaret, 173

Williams, Squadron Sergeant Major Montague Cyril, 173

Wilson, Mary ('The Merry Widow of Windy Nook'), 186

Winchester, Jean ('Molly Cutpurse'), 107, 116–17

Wing, Dorothy, 213–14, 216, 229

Winson Green prison, Birmingham, 86, 88

Wire, Alderman, 16, 294

Wise, Olive Kathleen, 270–1

Within These Walls (TV series), 220, 278

Wolds prison, Yorkshire, 285

women: reaction to imprisonment, 13–15, 265, 305, 327; misbehaviour, 36, 43, 48–9; 'lady visitors', 45, 47; as prison officers, 45–8; rehabilitation, 45; demand improved prison conditions, 61; first elected to Parliament, 91; win right to vote (1918), 91–2, 95; spies in Great War, 99–101; post Great War position, 106; appointed to senior prison and administrative positions, 118–19; and sexual identity, 126–9; conscripted in World War II, 158; wartime conscientious objectors, 158; change in treatment, 187, 191; entitlements as prison officers, 196; policy to reduce number of prison sentences for, 228; criminal behaviour worsens, 233–4; prison population grows, 234, 284–5, 337; separation from children, 265; and children of prisoners, 266–9, 305; Corston Report on, 284; prisoners with mental health problems, 336; non-violent offences, 337; treatment, 340

Women in Prison (WIP; campaigning group), 255–6, 261, 300, 313, 331

Women's Freedom League (WFL), 68, 118

Women's Social and Political Union (WSPU), 57, 60–2, 64, 67–9, 77, 79–80, 86

Wood, Wendy, 241–3

World (newspaper), 31

World War II (1939–45): outbreak, 134; enemy aliens interned, 137–9; executions of spies, 156; ends, 162

Wormwood Scrubs prison, London, 34, 267–8

Wright, Daisy: sentenced to death and reprieved, 113

Wright, Captain George, 49

Wyner, Ruth, 290

Yates, Edmund, 31

From Byron, Austen and Darwin

to some of the most acclaimed and original contemporary writing, John Murray takes pride in bringing you powerful, prizewinning, absorbing and provocative books that will entertain you today and become the classics of tomorrow.

We put a lot of time and passion into what we publish and how we publish it, and we'd like to hear what you think.

Be part of John Murray – share your views with us at:

www.johnmurray.co.uk

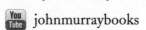 johnmurraybooks

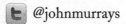 @johnmurrays

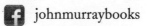 johnmurraybooks